CW01659962

ABSTRACT VIDEO

ABSTRACT VIDEO

The Moving Image in Contemporary Art

EDITED BY
Gabrielle Jennings

Foreword by Kate Mondloch

UNIVERSITY OF CALIFORNIA PRESS

University of California Press, one of the most distinguished university presses in the United States, enriches lives around the world by advancing scholarship in the humanities, social sciences, and natural sciences. Its activities are supported by the UC Press Foundation and by philanthropic contributions from individuals and institutions. For more information, visit www.ucpress.edu.

University of California Press
Oakland, California

Chapter 2 originally appeared as "Film Image/Electronic Image: The Construction of Abstraction, 1960–1990," by John G. Hanhardt, in *Visible Language* 29.2 (May 1995): 138–59, and is reprinted here with permission.

The volume editor, chapter authors, and publisher wish to express their appreciation for the artwork that appears in this book to the individuals and institutions named in the figure captions.

Library of Congress Cataloging-in-Publication Data

Abstract video : the moving image in contemporary art / edited by Gabrielle Jennings, foreword by Kate Mondloch.
pages cm.
Includes bibliographical references and index.
ISBN 978-0-520-28247-6 (cloth : alk. paper)
ISBN 978-0-520-28248-3 (pbk. : alk. paper)
ISBN 978-0-520-95813-5 (ebook)
1. Video art. 2. Art, Abstract. I. Jennings, Gabrielle, 1966– editor.
N6494.V53A246 2015
777—dc23 2015009739

Printed in China

24 23 22 21 20 19 18 17 16 15
10 9 8 7 6 5 4 3 2 1

The paper used in this publication meets the minimum requirements of ANSI/NISO Z39.48–1992 (R 2002) (*Permanence of Paper*).

CONTENTS

ACKNOWLEDGMENTS

This book exists only because of my wonderful and varied contributors; I want to thank them for entrusting me with their writing. Several helped to shape my ideas for this anthology; several I have yet to meet; and several I've worked with over the years. It has been quite an odyssey communicating with many of the writers almost exclusively via e-mail: sensing who they are; getting to know them through the written word; trusting; negotiating deadlines, words, images, ideas—all without ever having been in the same room. Marvelous and at the same time a little mysterious. I hope to meet all of them one day. Maria-Christina Villaseñor generously spent snatched hours chatting and conspiring to make this book a reality; though it got deeper and wider, her essay was one of the first topics decided upon. Jeremy Gilbert-Rolfe has been a supportive mentor, colleague, and friend since graduate school, and I thank him for his early support of the project and for writing an essay for this volume. John C. Welchman entertained me in his dining room filled with antique Schramberg pottery, listening intently to my first inklings of what the book should be, while his twins toddled about upstairs. Philip Brophy, whom I met during a residency in Melbourne a lifetime ago, was immediately receptive and a pleasure to work with. Cindy Keefer was also gracious with her time and first meandered through ideas with me over Vietnamese noodles. Katja Kwastek committed to write early on and was the very first to submit her fine essay on interactive works. Both Gregory Zinman and Siona Wilson were immediately intrigued by the subject matter and brought their own research to bear in exciting and relevant ways. Christine Ross and Lumi Tan were asked to produce in record time and came through with flying colors. Seeing the three conversation pieces unfolding was a pleasure. Two were produced by dynamic duos, one consisting of Trinie Dalton (with whom I've had the pleasure of teaching) and Stanya Kahn, and the other, the fortuitous team of Johanna Gosse (thanks for sticking with it) and Michael Connor (thanks for coming on board and producing on a very tight schedule). The third was a discussion between the fantastic four: Tilman Baumgärtel, Sarah Cook, Charlotte Frost, and Caitlin Jones, who each brought a depth of knowledge to the virtual table. My pure admiration and respect goes to one of my video-scholar idols, John G. Hanhardt, who supported the project from the beginning, generously offering advice and granting permission to reprint his essay "Film Image/Electronic Image: The Construction of Abstraction, 1960–1990." And last but certainly not least, I want to thank art historian Kate Mondloch who had the distance to write a foreword that lends the book currency and context. I thank each of you for accepting the challenge and thinking deeply about a sometimes obscure topic.

Early and almost-daily strategizing with friends and colleagues was fruitful. I'm grateful for the encouragement and generosity of spirit of my best friend, Melissa Hertz, and of my mom, Penny Jennings. Thank you for listening. Thanks also to Rachel Berney for countless conversations about the writing process. I was also the beneficiary of early, enlightening conversations on writing books and video art with Rosetta Brooks, Mark Calkins, Bruce Hainley, Hilja Keading, Carole Ann Klonarides, Jane McFadden, Terry Myers, Catherine Taft, Jan Tumlir, Holly Willis, and Penny Florence, who wisely advised me to drop the last essay—"That belongs in the next book, not this one." You were right, Penny. Both Mark and Jane also generously gave first reads of the Introduction, helping to hone it and to make it stronger; Patti Podesta, Christine Robinson, Maria-Christina Villaseñor, and Ethan Johnson were equally helpful readers of that sometimes unwieldy text.

Thank you, Mark Breitenberg for your expert, line-by-line proofing of the book proposal and too many dinners to count. The tedium of tailoring early book submissions was bearable only under the attentive eye of my graduate teaching assistant, Alexandra Noel. I owe Yael Nov a huge debt of gratitude; her grad TA duties ranged from author communications, image permissions, transcribing a conversation, and keeping track of an ever-expanding bibliography and mediography to being keeper of forms—all with a sweet and cheerful demeanor.

To my colleagues in the Graduate Art Department at the Art Center College of Design—Lita Albuquerque, Walead Beshty, Stan Douglas, Jeremy Gilbert-Rolfe, Taft Green, Bruce Hainley, Timothy Martin, Patti Podesta, Jason E. Smith, Diana Thater, and Annette Weisser—I learn from you every Wednesday. Art Center's Samsung Faculty Enrichment Grant has generously funded honorariums to the writers and also contributed to image permissions fees.

I am also grateful to all those individuals and institutions who kindly granted permissions associated with the reproduction of the images that illustrate each essay. Additional funding for image permissions fees and indexing was raised through the generosity of contributors to an Indiegogo campaign for which Sasha Freedman gave his time and skills to shoot and edit the crowdfunding video.

I'd also like to thank the anonymous peer reviewer whom Yoram Allon, the editor at Wallflower Press, enlisted to read my first proposal. The tough criticism led me to a much more expansive and discursive approach. Allon expressed early and sustained interest in the book, and for that I am thankful. I am also grateful to the peer reviewers at University of California Press for their time and thoughtful responses to the manuscript.

Ultimately, this book would not exist if it weren't for all the good people at University of California Press, especially Kari Dahlgren, my initial editor, who immediately expressed enthusiasm for the project and was an absolute pleasure to work with from the start, offering a calm, even-keeled approach to my sometimes harried and amateur questions. Since Dahlgren departed to SFMOMA, I have had the privilege to work with the Cinema and Media Studies editor, Mary Francis, a real listener, astute advisor, and inspired finder of solutions. Karen Levine, Dahlgren's successor, has proven to be attentive and responsive, and I'm sure her career at UC Press will be long and successful. And my thanks and utmost respect to editorial assistant Jack Young, whose patience in explaining the minutiae of formatting and publishing etiquette was always reassuring. The unsung heroes of publishing deserve credit here as well—Barbara Armentrout, copyeditor (eagle-eyed wordsmith); Rachel Berchten, principal editor; Amy Boyer, e-book coordinator; Chalon Emmons, production editor (keeper of a tight ship); Aimée Goggins, marketing manager; Claudia Smelser, designer (what a cover!); Alexander Trotter, indexer; Janet Villanueva, production coordinator—thank you all for your incredible devotion to this project.

And last, but never least, heartfelt thanks to my partner, Ethan Johnson, and our daughter, Phoebe (who, at age eleven has proven to be an adept research assistant), for your love and devotion; this book is for you.

FOREWORD

Kate Mondloch

Gabrielle Jennings's preface to this book issues a playful challenge. Ever notice how sparse the literature on abstract video is? Google it, she suggests.

I took the bait. "Abstract video" [enter]. She's right—the top results offer links to a disordered avalanche of moving images. I refined my search. "Abstract video art" [enter]. This changed things up a bit. Jennings's larger point still stands; there is indeed, a surprisingly meager scholarly corpus of literature on video and abstraction (an absence that this present volume expediently fills). But my second, more aesthetically inclined search query engendered an especially intriguing top result—one that handily demonstrates the historically resonant concerns at the heart of Jennings's *Abstract Video* collection. The search result proclaimed, in a rain shower of caps: "*Abstract Currents:* An Interactive Video Event / CALL FOR SUBMISSIONS! SEE ABSTRACT VIDEO ART AT MoMA." One more click brought me to a comprehensive, action-packed description on the Museum of Modern Art's website, MoMA.org:

> In conjunction with the exhibitions *Inventing Abstraction, 1910–1925* and *Abstract Generation: Now in Print,* PopRally invites you to channel your own ideas of the abstract through video! Create a one-minute video exploring abstract forms of any kind, then follow the directions below to upload it to our dedicated Vimeo group. Use a camera, use your phone, or use an app. The videos will be played on various screens and projections in MoMA's lobby and on the Marron Atrium walls during a special party. . . . Dream Pop queen Tamaryn will DJ the event, providing a hypnotic soundtrack to the collectively built abstract videoscape.

You might reasonably wonder how dream pop, Vimeo, and DIY abstract art ended up side by side in this energetic press release—even more peculiar given its issuance from New York's traditionally stodgy Museum of Modern Art (MoMA). An attempt to develop more edgy, youth-oriented art programming, MoMA's PopRally initiative began in 2006; *Abstract Currents* numbers among the myriad festive celebrations of visual art and pop culture hosted at MoMA over the past decade, albeit the only one that involved screening audience-generated abstract video onto the museum's illustrious white walls. Although video art fell outside the early-twentieth-century scope of the two abstract art shows this event complemented, the institution (or at least the institution's marketing department) nonetheless found a way to incorporate it. It appeared, however, not as a peer art form but as a twenty-first-century crossbreed: part arty abstraction, part social media caprice.

What I find striking is that the PopRally event deliberately muddied the boundaries between two conceptions of video: it appears here both as a MoMA-worthy art object and as an instrument of social media. In doing so, this curious event—still promoted in the recesses of Google like a fraying event poster on a campus bulletin board—perfectly illustrates the long and intimate relationship between video art and the mass media public sphere, from broadcast news to clip culture. However unintentionally, PopRally's inventive *Abstract Currents* programming posed a series of trenchant questions: When does video become art? What is the role of the institution in assigning it an art status? What role does abstraction play in this process?

Fortunately for us, these intractable and ever-timely issues are among the topics thoroughly explored in Jennings's *Abstract Video*. Written by an impressive international lineup of artists, educators, curators, and scholars, the essays collected in this book are in orbit around three overlapping questions left unexamined by PopRally's otherwise provocative *Abstract Currents* project: What is abstraction? What is video? And, ultimately, what is video art? Gabrielle Jennings, a distinguished video artist in her own right with nearly two decades of teaching experience at the Art Center College of Design in California, is the ideal companion to guide us through these heady inquiries. Jennings's extensive practical experience with video art, especially in its transition from analog videotapes to digital files, makes the self-described digital immigrant especially attuned to identifying historical transformations in video production, distribution, and reception. In Jennings's words, *Abstract Video* examines abstraction in "video art after 2000—moving-image artworks that were made just after analog video went nearly extinct and the world of bytes and pixels became dominant." *Abstract Video* delivers even more than Jennings suggests, however. It's not just about video and isn't limited just to the post-2000 period. (How could it be otherwise, considering video art's continual intermixing with other media, and given the extensive history of abstraction?)

The book is divided loosely into three sections: the first focuses on theoretical analyses of abstraction, the second explores video art's reach into its many ancillary art forms (experimental film, painting, music, software, and so on), and the third concentrates on specific video artists and methods of abstract video production. Taken collectively, the book's essays evaluate how the concept of abstraction transforms in different historical contexts and according to medium. But this is not your grandmother's abstraction: this is abstraction beyond the merely formal and nonrepresentational. Reflecting the heterogeneity of video art itself, the authors engage abstraction in relation to a range of formal, economic, and sociocultural concerns that expand and exceed the modernist canon to encompass contemporary culture at large.

Abstract Video spans the history of video art since the 1950s as it relates to other artistic media but also to electronic moving images in general. Secretly, I think the latter issue motivates the entire collection. The question is not a minor one. How *do* we define video art in our era of nearly ceaseless video production and distribution, a time when *all* electronic moving images are commonly referred to as video, irrespective of their initial material support (film, videotape, digital file, etc.)? Indeed, and on the issue of support, the compiled conversations about video art and abstraction ironically also here inspire renewed attention to the insistent *thingness* of video art. *Abstract Video*'s essayists rightly affirm the physicality of video art in both its analog and digital variants: from videotapes to glitches, to exhibition architectures themselves. Abstract, yes, but also concrete.

One of *Abstract Video*'s greatest contributions is the broad range of artists and lesser-known works it discusses and generously illustrates. Even better, every media artwork, performance, and music piece mentioned in the volume is thoroughly documented in the book's substantial mediography. This is a gift to the practitioner and the fan, as well as to the teacher and the student. Issues of access, preservation, and copyright restrictions make video art notoriously challenging to teach and research. Like me, you might use this mediography as a jumping-off point to track down a moving-image piece that sparks the imagination. In the process, you might discover that MoMA's PopRally's was on to something in celebrating the potentials of social media for video art, but with a twist. Videos uploaded to sites such as Vimeo are among the best resources for viewing these hard-to-find moving-image works. I don't mean just artists' videos screened online; I'm talking about user-generated social media video documentation of users' site-specific experiences with all manner of abstract video art, including its installation variants. Go ahead, Google it.

What the future of experimentation at the intersection of abstraction and electronic moving images will bring is anybody's guess, but one thing is certain: the next time you search for "abstract video," the results will be infinitely richer.

1

INTRODUCTION

On the Horizon

Gabrielle Jennings

> Abstract art is propelled by . . . hope and hunger. It reflects the urge to push toward the limit, to colonize the borderland around the openings onto nothingness, where the land has not been settled, where the new can emerge.
>
> KIRK VARNEDOE, *PICTURES OF NOTHING: ABSTRACT ART SINCE POLLOCK*

Video art has rarely been analyzed through the lens of abstraction; it is often amorphous, ungovernable, and disembodied with spaces that confound Renaissance perspective and encourage contemplation. As the late art historian Kirk Varnedoe put it, "pictures of nothing."[1] And of everything. In light of scholarship on abstraction in other mediums, it is useful to consider this history because video has transformed from an essentially narrative analog form (TV) to a pervasive digital art medium. This collection examines abstraction in video art after 2000—moving image artworks that were made just after analog video nearly went extinct and bytes and pixels became dominant.

Video Art has had film and television, the twin hounds of narrative, nipping at its heels for decades now, referencing these forms while distinguishing itself through various means—reflexivity, nonlinear narrative, and medium specificity, to name just a few. The title for this volume, *Abstract Video: The Moving Image in Contemporary Art,* illustrates its own problematic: it carries a history of video art proper that points towards both its predecessor (film) and its offspring (new media art). Like the horizon, abstract video is visible but unattainable, an idea as much as an image, looking left and right, an interrupted and a continuous line, movement and stillness embodied.

This volume examines the term *abstract* in traditional ways that modernism embraced but also in the ways that film historians discuss Structuralist and experimental film, according to perception and duration, and in ways media historians use the term in referring to the digital. It looks at how we think through abstraction and tracks changes as the medium itself continues to evolve. Though video emerged with the advent of videotape, the term *video* now encompasses all moving image media.

The closest Varnedoe comes to discussing moving image works in *Pictures of Nothing* is his consideration of James Turrell's light installations, *Afrum-Proto* (1966), and *Wedgework* (1974).[2] These works exemplify important formal qualities of abstract art: they don't exist in the natural world, and like architecture and film, they reference things outside themselves. These phenomenological events are a useful place to begin a consideration of abstraction in video art because, like video, they are made of light and are best experienced through prolonged viewing. Crucially, *movement* over time is not a quality of either piece, but it is an essential aspect of this book.

The only mention of the moving image in *Pictures of Nothing* is in the discussion of two feature films: Stanley Kubrick's *2001: A Space Odyssey* (1968) and Ridley Scott's *Blade Runner* (1982). It seems no coincidence that these masterpieces of modern cinema contain the peculiar sense of the abstract often found in science fiction: the unknowable colliding with the familiar. Varnedoe reminds readers of the "great, grey, forbidding slab that first appears to a group of apes at the beginning of *[2001]* and later reappears on the moon, sending out a piercing signal in the direction of Mars" and connects modernist sculptor John McCracken's "planks" to the monolith.[3] The sculptures are very much about presence and in this context pose an important question in regard to the moving image: can an image—which is not a thing, which may be fleeting, and is always moving—have the same kind of gravity and presence as an actual object? Varnedoe refers to *Blade Runner* in the context of an android's expiration, thereby illustrating his inability to be comprehensive in the span of six lectures and hinting at the heartache of his terminal illness. It is tempting to think that, had Varnedoe had more time, more lectures ahead of him, that he would have wanted to consider new forms of abstraction—experimental film, video, and new media practices among them.

Aesthetic dialogues used to occur in parallel worlds—painting, sculpture, and film each on fairly separate tracks. This has changed. Previously concurrent discussions now intersect regularly, requiring greater elasticity and new definitions. For this book, I asked a diverse set of writers and practitioners to attend to the abstract in the contemporary moving image, to contextualize, and to guide the reader through the countless streams of light.

· · ·

Ecstatic Resistance is an inquiry into the temporality of change. Time, the time of transformation, the duration and physicality of the experience of change. And drama—the arc of history. The temporality of the ecstatic opens a non-linear experience in which connections are made at breakneck pace and a moment later time appears to stop us in the dynamism of one challenging thought.

—EMILY ROYSDON, *ECSTATIC RESISTANCE*

With a fair bit of excitement, I opened *Abstraction* (2013), the latest anthology in the Whitechapel: Documents in Contemporary Art series.[4] The collection runs the gamut from social and political utopias to a more Greenbergian "focus on medium-specificity and self-reflexiveness" and opens up the field in expansive ways though not specifically in terms of moving image practices.[5] Similarly, most of the essays in *Abstract Video* shrug off the enticing conveniences of formal abstraction in favor of examining the topic by looking through the lens of film and video art itself—imagery that literally moves over time; "the medium is the message" and "the medium is the medium."[6] Nevertheless, it still seems appropriate to begin again, with a look at the differences between the abstract, the nonrepresentational, the nonfigurative, the nonobjective, and the slightly different but useful term *abstracted.* To be abstract is, according to Webster's dictionary, to be "disassociated from any specific instance [or] . . . having only intrinsic form with little or no attempt at pictorial representation or narrative content." To be nonrepresentational or nonobjective means "representing . . . no natural or actual object, figure, or scene." It is my hope that *Abstract Video* will widen these definitions since, as we will see, abstract video works include much more than nonrepresentation. Abstraction in the moving image is, and has always been, an artistic strategy (or result) used in a myriad of ways towards infinite ends.

Hans Richter's classic avant-garde film from 1921, *Rhythmus 21,* is an early experiment in moving image abstraction. The piece, which evolved from the artist's painting and graphic design practice, is derived from geometric abstraction and has been called an "absolute film." Squares and rectangles of black, white, and gray appear and disappear in various configurations, expanding, contracting, mutating. In the first issue of *G: Material zur elementaren Gestaltung* (1923), a magazine Richter edited, he wrote this of *Rhythmus 21:* "An attempt has been made to organize the film such that the individual parts stand in active tension to one another and to the whole, such that the whole remains intellectually *[geistig]* mobile within itself."[7] Even here, in the context of a nascent film practice, the filmmaker exhorts an active reading of the piece. We will see, in *Abstract Video,* that the writers have engaged the subject with this same kind of *"geistige Mobilität."*

Since we are well into the cybernetic, digital age—what Michael Sanchez calls our "liminal media-historical moment"—where the moving image is already an abstraction (as opposed to celluloid and electronic tape, which have a physical reality), the abstract is all around us.[8] Abstract painting is, for the most part, handmade, whereas film and video—unless you are a Structural or experimental practitioner like Len Lye, Stan Brakhage, or Jennifer West—are not.[9] And in the case of the moving image, a one-to-one, physical relationship with the medium never existed. Film and video already contain the idea of abstraction in their very ability to hold images that are not immediately visible or tangible: Film is a photographic medium and therefore has to be developed, and video can be seen as it is being recorded. However, unless it is closed circuit or webcam, video requires replay and, in the case of the digital, cannot ever be literally grasped: the data that make up the digital image are, as Boris Groys writes, "invisible."[10] Here we can start to talk about the differences between being in the presence of a painting or a sculpture, where we can physically identify with a gesture, and being in the presence of electronic light and movement, where there is an extreme acceleration—usually the still frames that constitute a moving image are moving so fast that we can't see them individually (works like Douglas Gordon's *24 Hour Psycho* being the exception).

Video then is not about a bodily relationship with a thing, but instead about the *speed of thinking*. This of course becomes more complex with video installations, where often the most critical thing is the viewer's body in relation to the work. A body moving in space perceiving is very different from a body sitting and *watching:* a sense of the overwhelming sublime, for instance, is achieved very differently in video than in an abstract painting like a Rothko. There is a perceptual difference between looking *at* a surface and *into* an electronic moving image. The space of a painting requires a leap of imagination, a sensorial looking that is felt differently than when virtual movement is in play. Movement is understood on different levels depending on the medium: In painting, we can sense movement as gestural, narrative, or a compositional pointing from one place to another through such factors as color, form and location. In the moving image, movement can be understood both inside and outside the frame, through the actual speed of recording or playback, through montage and editing, as well as through the narrative unfolding. Time functions differently in a painting than in the moving image, primarily because in one it is imagined, and in the other, temporal-spatial relations are brought to the fore and put into question. These are but a few ways in which we might begin to discuss abstraction from painting through to moving image artworks.

Abstraction is unruly. As a culture, we have become savvy image consumers. We are fluent in the language of the moving image; we take for granted conventional filmic techniques that create a sense of continuity as well as the "mixed-up" narrative—most notably in the films of Mike Figgis, David Lynch, and Tom Tykwer. In the medium formerly known as video art, there are so many differing strategies today in regard to narrative that it is impossible to list the artists representing them all—Eija-Liisa Ahtila, Stan Douglas, Cao Fei, Mark Lewis, Pipilotti Rist, and Mark Tribe are only a small start. Elliptical storytelling à la early Pierre Huyghe and the essayistic or narrative montage have also become commonplace in wider cultural production. The Structural, the pseudo-documentary, the performative, the rhetorical, the activist, the abject, and the textual/linguistic—these approaches, which almost constitute a catalogue of the history of video art, make their appearance in this collection. There have also been many important advances in thinking about time as material in film and video.[11] Related and important ideas that are not explicitly discussed in this volume are (1) presence—as in Simon Payne's color field videos,[12] where the viewer is immersed in pure color and form (much like the early Turrells) but with the added perception of movement over time—and (2) the abstract as enabling the representation of memory (or its incomprehensibility)—as in a piece like Stan Douglas's *Win, Place or Show* (1998). Abstraction alone is all but absent from the video art canon. Even now, after a century of nonrepresentation in painting, entering the world of abstraction in video is like venturing out of the house alone for the first time, at once thrilling and frightening, the sublime might be met along the way.

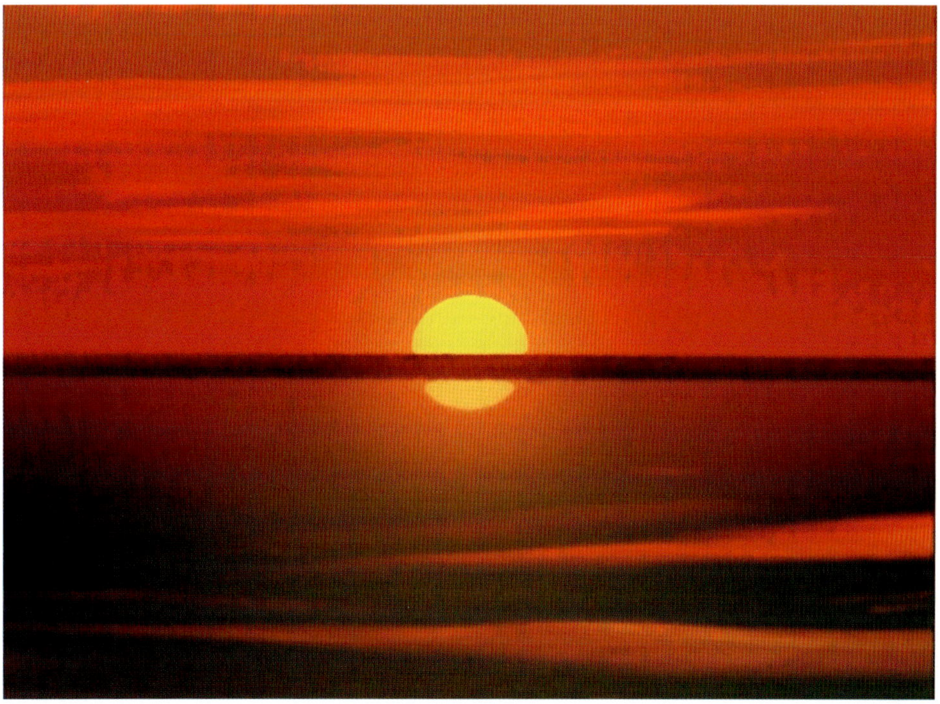

FIGURE 1.1
Paul Pfeiffer, *Morning after the Deluge,* 2003. 8mm film transferred to digital video loop; projection dimensions: 144 × 192 inches; 20 minutes. Courtesy of the artist and Thomas Dane Gallery, London.

Reverse zoom out through the evolution from the photographic to the electronic, from film through video to the digital, from analog to digital and linear to rhizomatic, to this moment where an abbreviated history of the horizon and the spiral in the moving image proves useful. A line is an abstract form, while the spiral is a line made figurative. First consider the horizon: a line that stretches as far as the eye can see in both directions, separating sea or land from sky. It has been made to mean any number of things: limitlessness, stability, flatness, the edge of the world, a place from which sailors plunged to their demise. How we see comes into play here—the perception of something that is at once there and not there. The horizon, like the abstract, is the representation of an unreachable place. The horizon has always signaled a certain kind of looking beyond, a looking towards and away at once. *Morning after the Deluge* by Paul Pfeiffer (fig. 1.1) is a video projection of a wavering horizon. The piece merges two film images of the sky over the ocean on Cape Cod, one of sunrise, the other sunset, one inverted so that the two half suns become one, with the horizon line joining the two. The effect is a certain kind of timelessness, at once a literalization and an abstraction of what we know to be scientifically true.[13] Pfeiffer has said that around the time he made this piece, he began working in Manila, and one can begin to see this doppelganger sunrise/sunset as a looking both towards and away from the artist's homeland.[14] The artist's newer works tend to be collaborative and sculptural, and embedded in them is a sense of a cultural past and present colliding. This notion of the eternal, or the infinite, is essential to the digital in a way that analog, a linear form, was not. Video can be thought of as moving horizontally, whereas film is a vertical medium, having, until recently, moved downwards, snaking through the film projector, propelled by parallel sprocket holes. In the digital age, the two have combined to form an ever-present-now wherein there is neither up nor down, left nor right, here nor there—an abstraction to be sure.

Enter the spiral: a line made representational and a symbol for the sun, the hypnotic, dizziness, and a movement from the inner to the outer and back again. A spiral has an implied depth or perspective and indicates a movement from one place to another. This undulating target, pulsating vortex, swirling sign for the unconscious, comes to visit the filmic avant-garde early on in Oskar Fischinger's and Marcel Duchamp's works from the 1920s, in Jean Cocteau's *The Blood of a Poet* (1930), and in Richter's *Dreams That Money Can Buy* (1947), for which Duchamp and John Cage collaborated to make the famed *Discs* sequence—one of seven surreal dream sequences inserted into a more traditional narrative and crafted by a who's who of avant-garde artists. Alongside these corkscrews are appearances of the spiral in mainstream Hollywood films such as *The Wizard of Oz* (1939) and *Vertigo* (1958). In the art realm, there is, of course, the legendary film *Spiral Jetty* (1970), written and directed by Robert Smithson and shot by Smithson and Nancy Holt. Besides documenting the building of the jetty, the film stands as a record of Smithson's philosophical ideas as well as providing what the artist called a "cosmic rupture"—a state of disorientation that frees the viewer from the dialectic of history.[15]

It is not insignificant that two female artists, Jennifer West and Elaine Sturtevant, have remade (one more literally than the other) works by two of the most celebrated and mythic male artists of the last century—as Siona Wilson posits in chapter 4, theirs is "repetition with difference." In 2013, Jennifer West made her own Spiral Jetty films: *Spiral of Time Documentary Film* (fig. 1.2) and *Salt Crystals Spiral Jetty Dead Sea Five Year Film*. The films circle back, revisiting the now-fabled place while literally, textually, and conceptually layering upon it, history and materiality with a sight line towards and away from the temporal. Sturtevant remade Duchamp's *Discs* and titled it *Dreams Money Can Buy* (1967). A digital projection, this piece follows Sturtevant's practice of remakes and has been shown in installations along with other Duchamp look-alikes. The master copier remaking a piece by the original ready-maker, "Sturtevant repeats works for the necessity of a catalytic recognizability," says art critic Bruce Hainley, "sparking an investigation of what allows 'art' to be, so that the entirety of the structure of art is reconsidered horizontally not linearly."[16] Writing about Sturtevant's work, Hainley configures and reconfigures her practice and teases out a call to view art anew—as part of the whirlpool of images, not a chronology but something more akin to a helix, moving in and out of history, around the central axis called Time.

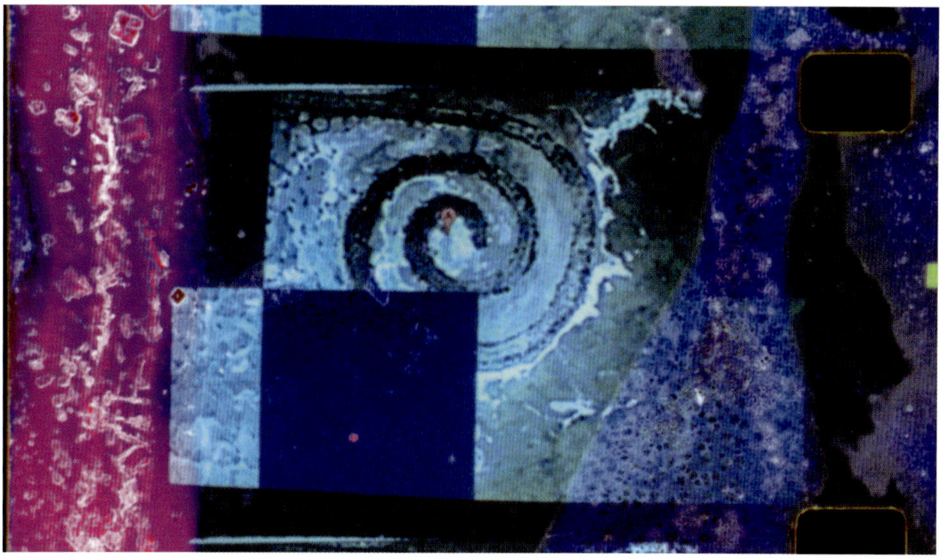

FIGURE 1.2
Jennifer West, *Spiral of Time Documentary Film (16mm negative strobe-light double and triple exposed - painted with brine shrimp - dripped, splattered and sprayed with salted liquids: balsamic and red wine vinegar, lemon and lime juice, temporary fluorescent hair dyes - photos from friends Mark Titchner, Karen Russo, Aaron Moulton and Ignacio Uriarte and some google maps- texts by Jwest and Chris Markers' Sans Soleil script -shot by Peter West, strobed by Jwest, hands by Ariel West, telecine by Tom Sartori)*, 2013. 16mm film negative transferred to high-definition; 9 minutes, 1 second. Courtesy of the artist; Marc Foxx Gallery, Los Angeles; and Vilma Gold, London.

Nonrepresentation then, is where this book begins: the "Transmission" section discusses moving image artwork that descends on the one hand from abstraction in experimental film and on the other from television and early video art. The second section, "Interference," ranges between video, media art and "net art" and shows how these genres, from virtually all angles, have embraced the abstract from the beginning. The essays in "Interference" make possible those in the third section, "Reception," which discusses the abstract in video art from the inside out—those strategies that are not formally descendent from earlier traditions—disembodied digital plays with movement, time, space, sound and narrative, and color as metaphor.

TRANSMISSION

In one sense, this collection is an experiment, to see what happens when a significant variability of opinions on a topic are brought together. The volume intends to acknowledge the history of abstraction in painting, sculpture, and experimental film without remaining there. Instead, its purpose is to pick up where studies of abstraction plateau—

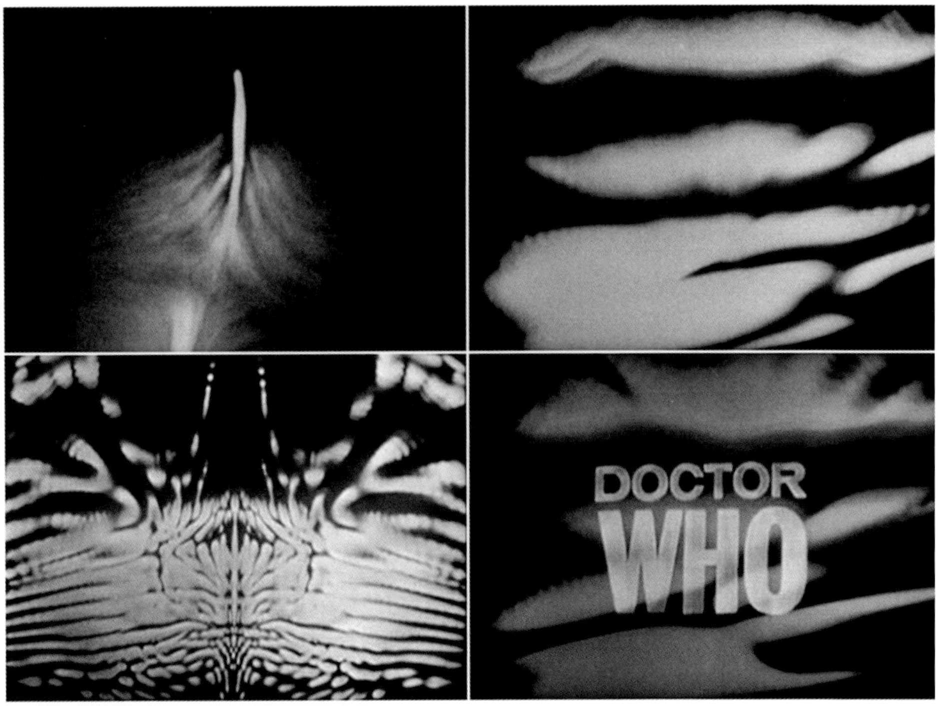

FIGURE 1.3
Bernard Lodge, Ben Palmer, Hugh Sheppard, and Norman Taylor, stills from the original title sequence of *Dr. Who*, 1963. Music written by Ron Grainer and performed by the BBC Radiophonic Workshop. Courtesy of BBC Worldwide Learning.

in film, where P. Adams Sitney began; in video, where John Hanhardt left off; and in new media studies, where the exhibition *Abstraction Now* and media scholars like Lev Manovich continue—and to examine not only where we've been but where we are now.[17]

Fifty years have passed since the death of John F. Kennedy was captured on 8mm Kodachrome film, on November 22, 1963, and later transmitted around the world. Fifty years have also passed since *Dr. Who* first aired on the BBC. (Legend has it that the first episode was delayed by ten minutes due to extended coverage of Kennedy's assassination the previous day; in fact, the show aired only eighty seconds late.)[18] The opening title sequence appears as if out of the tailpipe of a rocket, smoke dissolving into clouds that disperse into fog (fig. 1.3). The accompanying soundtrack can only be characterized as space-cowboy, and the mood as interstellar psychedelic, even in black and white. The video feedback "howl-around" technique was created by BBC electronics engineers Ben Palmer or Norman Taylor, and the titles created by graphic designer Bernard Lodge.[19] I was told by the artist and film historian Lutz Becker that he collaborated with Palmer to develop visual effects that would later appear in Becker's *Horizon* (1967), titled after it was broadcast as part of the BBC documentary series *Horizon: Will Art Last?* (1967).

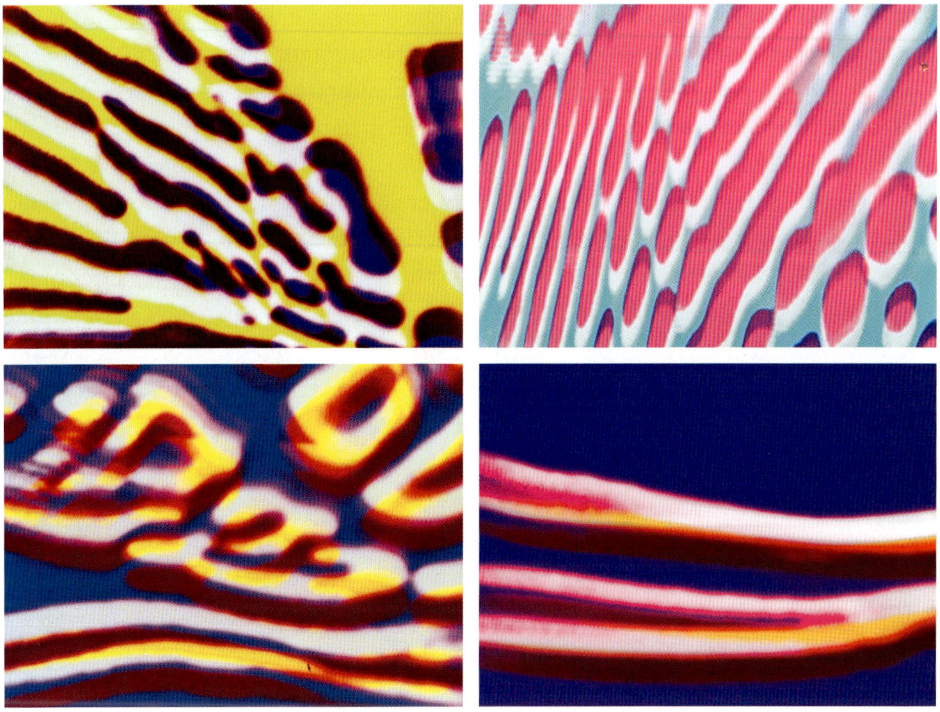

FIGURE 1.4
Lutz Becker, *Horizon,* 1967. 16mm film, color, sound; 3 minutes. Copyright Lutz Becker.

Lutz and Palmer shot the images produced by a feedback loop between a television camera and a monitor on black-and-white 35mm film. The film was later colorized with an optical printer, edited and output to 16mm film for inclusion in the BBC *Horizon* show, which had just recently begun broadcasting in color. The result is an ecstatic, oozing, microcosmic array of bright white and yellow organic shapes outlined with fuchsia on a background of deliciously vivid grape (fig. 1.4). The images look like neon and are clearly not of this world—meaning electronically generated, wholly nonrepresentational. Becker recalls, "The music, only used in the broadcast, was played and composed as a solo piece by cellist Joy Hall. It was quite experimental containing fragments of harmonies and a mixture of noise effects she created on the cello. Otherwise the film was projected silent, like 'music for the eye.'"[20] Becker has said that his "ambition was to be able to create some kind of visual equivalent to electronic music."[21]

In addition to being an example of Visual Music, Becker's *Horizon* is also a link between then and now: a television camera transmitting images to a monitor while simultaneously being recorded (an electronic proto-selfie).[22] The piece is an early example of a generation of experimental works made in conjunction with technicians working in the bowels of television studios. Engineers like Palmer, Shuya Abe, and David Jones, made groundbreaking innovations in video possible through the development of early video-processing tools—namely, synthesizers, sequencers, keyers, and colorizers.

Technical developments in video have gone hand in hand with what artists have made and how it has looked. The 2009 exhibition *Abstract Cinema and Technology* at MOCA North Miami, curated by then–executive director and chief curator Bonnie Clearwater, elucidated the relationship between technological developments and artistic innovation from early film by artists associated with the Visual Music field (such as Fischinger, James Whitney, Jordan Belson, and Len Lye) to early video pioneers (such as Nam June Paik) and more recent practitioners (such as Cory Arcangel, Jeremy Blake, and Jennifer Steinkamp). The exhibition traced a technological evolution from film to video and then the digital, and although these distinctions are useful, the aesthetics of such varied media, the *what* and *how* they say, have, until this volume, been left largely unexamined.

This is where this volume begins. The writers in the "Transmission" section take on the hard questions: What does it mean when notions of the abstract change over time? And what does the abstract say when it appears as an embedded system and not necessarily as a visual sign?

John G. Hanhardt's 1995 essay "Film Image / Electronic Image: The Construction of Abstraction, 1960–1990" begins this exploration. The essay (chapter 2) details the interrelation between video art and the history of avant-garde cinema during the twentieth century and proposes "that a specific body of film and video works has explored the issue of abstraction as a means to define their respective media." This has been done, Hanhardt points out, "by choosing the basic temporality of the moving image and the material basis of the image itself as sites for an epistemological inquiry into the viewing experience, thus exploring the perceptual transaction between spectator and text." Hanhardt shows some of the fundamental interconnections between video art and the history of avant-garde abstractionism, for example, as reflected in the work of experimental filmmakers like Stan Brakhage.

Two years after Becker's *Horizon* aired on the BBC, artist Joseph Kosuth mounted an exhibition titled *Joseph Kosuth—October 1969* at the Douglas Gallery in Vancouver. The piece involved a media intervention appearing as unexplained text from Roget's thesaurus on Canadian television. In chapter 3, "Joseph Kosuth's *The Second Investigation* in Vancouver (1969): Art on TV," art historian John C. Welchman argues that Kosuth's piece was part of one of the most significant projects of early Conceptual Art. Germane to this volume, the Douglas Gallery show raises a number of key questions about the relation of art and media, as well as new ideas about color, abstraction, and public encounters with art at the end of the 1960s.

Siona Wilson's contribution, "Abstract Transmissions: Other Trajectories for Feminist Video" (chapter 4), associates video art with habits of television viewing and the idea of transmission as a way to recontextualize early feminist video art, and then moves into the contemporary space to see how this reframing informs recent video made by women. She asks, "What kind of a feminist politics emerges, both then and now, when we shift the lens towards the abstract?"

Jeremy Gilbert-Rolfe's essay, "Abstract Video" (chapter 5), contemplates video as a sensation, the electronic as a medium that produces abstraction in the absence of the kind of physicality that is the basis for a medium like painting (or writing, for that matter). This piece explores the relationship of the abstract to the photographic and then proceeds to consider what the properties of an abstract video might be, using the examples of two works that deal with the formless in different ways—one, an LCD-light–based work by James Turrell and the other, a video work by Diana Thater. Just as Varnedoe says of Smithson's *Spiral Jetty,* "the overhead view of things unintelligible from the earth speaks to enigma and to mystery,"[23] Gilbert-Rolfe describes a looking up and out, beyond our own vision.

INTERFERENCE

Early in her seminal essay "Video: The Aesthetics of Narcissism," Rosalind Krauss noted that artists' video, like Pop Art, "is largely involved in parodying the critical terms of abstraction."[24] Among these strategies, she identifies a "pointing towards the center" typified by Vito Acconci's work *Centers* (1971), in which he literally points at his own video image for the duration of the twenty-minute tape—the length of a ¾" field tape. The theorizing of video as the medium of narcissism is born.[25] Rewind back to our electronic selfie, *Horizon.* An example of this kind of video feedback loop (the mirroring of the filmed subject in between camera and monitor being the thing that was missing from Becker's *Horizon*) is Nancy Holt and Richard Serra's video *Boomerang* from 1974. The piece sets up an audio feedback loop wherein Holt hears her own reactions, both voiced in the present and almost simultaneously played back through her own headphones. This leads to a feeling of "self encapsulation" resulting in an exaggerated presentness.[26]

The essays in the "Interference" section consider artworks characterized by a pulsing mandala; tearing, scratching, screeching visual noise; chance encounters; a breaking apart of the image; and code, hacking, hypertext, and interactivity. Two essays in this section consider glitch art, an early example of which is Joan Jonas's *Vertical Roll* (1972), which deconstructed both the televisual medium and the performing subject through the use of a persistent interference mechanism—the vertical roll—an aesthetic annoyance that most of us who grew up with cathode-ray-tube television had the luck to behold, but that has now gone the way of the dodo bird and been replaced by the glitch.[27] This section opens with "Visual Music's Influence on Contemporary Abstraction" (chapter 6), by Cindy Keefer, director of the Center for Visual Music. Keefer curates and restores works of such experimental-film luminaries as Oskar Fischinger and Jordan Belson, whose works serve as precursors for contemporary Visual Music practices. One of the earliest genres of abstraction in film, Visual Music explores the myriad relations between image and sound. Keefer's essay discusses classics of Visual Music in order to introduce contemporary works associated with the genre.

Gregory Zinman's essay, "Chance and Glitch in Contemporary Video Art" (chapter 7), delves into the work of three artists—Lynn Marie Kirby, Takeshi Murata, and Jennifer West—who use the fabric of film and video to lay bare inherent limits, sensitivities, and random properties. Here different sorts of "messy" material manipulation produce remarkable (and arguably, "handmade") abstract imagery that often includes shredding the figurative image.

"Delirious Architectures: Notes on Jeremy Blake, *Liquid Crystal Palace,* and Digital Materialism" (chapter 8) is an interview with curator Michael Connor by art historian Johanna Gosse. The conversation centers on topics inherent in *Liquid Crystal Palace,* an exhibition that Connor curated with Nate Hitchcock in 2014. The exhibition takes as precedent Blake's feverish *Liquid Villa* (2000), placing it alongside pieces by a new generation of artists working in moving image abstraction, or what Connor calls "digital materialism." From there, they get to the differences between the material and "philosophical abstract." The discussion moves nimbly between "fantasy architecture" and abstraction as a visual style and concludes with the sublime, the psychedelic, and the decorative.

Chapter 9, "Abstract Video: Net Art2," is a virtual roundtable, bringing together a diverse group of media scholars invested in Internet art: Tilman Baumgärtel, Sarah Cook, Charlotte Frost, and Caitlin Jones. The discussion is wide ranging, moving between ASCII works, webcam cinema, online glitch, and animated GIFs. The writers astutely identify the means, complications, and sign systems at work in online moving image art practices through four examples that embody the ever-unfolding nature of artistic techno-strategy at play on the Internet, giving interpretation, disconnection, interruption and dissociation particular agency.

In chapter 10, "Interactive Abstractions—Between Embodied Exploration and Instrumental Control 'Underneath Your Fingertips,'" art historian Katja Kwastek discusses abstract moving images generated or shaped by means of real-time audience interaction. The essay outlines the development of interactive works from their analog beginnings in the 1960s, via their diverse directions in the form of screen-based interactions, environments for bodily experience, and audiovisual instruments/apps for mobile devices. Kwastek argues that such "interactive abstractions" often make visible the processes of interaction, involving what we may think of as "virtual reality," and encourage viewers to create their own abstract animations. She finds that though such interactive abstractions are often neither narrative nor figurative, they may well be referentially representational.

RECEPTION

The Kitchen, a New York artist collective founded in 1971 by video artists Woody and Steina Vasulka, supported many early video artists and continues to operate today as a space for experimental multimedia works. Lumi Tan, associate curator at this institution, has contributed *Real Time, Screen Time* (chapter 11), an investigation into how the "presence of the apparatuses of production [in the exhibition space] shift the viewer's perception of time." Tan examines the live-mixing, production-based work of Mika Tajima, New Humans, and Charles Atlas before turning to the performative video work of Alix Pearlstein. Through this exploration, abstraction can be found in the spaces left when conventional viewing habits are uprooted and time becomes slippery.

The very properties of video (light, sound, movement) can produce not only a wavering and questionable sense of time but also, as Christine Ross argues in "The Spreadability of Video" (chapter 12), a permeability that allows for an unfolding, malleable multiplicity. This becomes fully apparent through her close reading of *Pierre Huyghe* (2013), the artist's mid-career retrospective at the Centre Pompidou in which discrete works—including video, performance, and participatory works—were exhibited in close proximity, thereby producing an organic, radically alive environment.

Maria-Christina Villaseñor's essay "Spectral Projections: Color, Race & Abstraction in the Moving Image" (chapter 13) looks through Paul Pfeiffer's *Home Movie / Four Locations for a Home Movie* (2012), Cory Arcangel's *Colors* (2006), Rico Gatson's *The Promise of Light* (2013), and Ariel Jackson's *Here's Hoping (AKA The Blues;* 2013) to form a theory of electronic color that illustrates the complex ways that media artists are using color as an abstract sign.

The Abstract, like the Beautiful and the Sublime, appears from out of nowhere, as if from a dream, formless and evasive, surprising and obscure. And yet we know it when we see it—sometimes geometric, other times symmetrical, and again, fluid, oozing. "Go With the (Unregulated) Flow: Fluidity, Abjection, and Abstraction" (chapter 14) is a conversation between writer Trinie Dalton and video artist Stanya Kahn. The piece is a lively, meandering discussion that leaves us with the notion that the abject is its own sort of abstraction and that fluidity has everything to do with narrativity.

The spiral, like the labyrinth, allows a retracing of past steps, a return from whence we came. Audiophile and artist Philip Brophy's "Sine Qua Son: Considering the Sine Wave in Video Art" (chapter 15) doubles back to listen closely to the sine wave tone—the tone by which millions of televisions in a bygone era bid generations good night. The "sign-off" often consisted of a high-pitched tone accompanied by video static or snow (the electronic abstract). The piece is a thoughtful meditation on a sound that is at once recognizable and abstract, a floating, dislocated signifier.

· · ·

The word *abstract* gets conjured up in regard to the word *idea,* as something existing in the ether—up there in the clouds, outside the airplane window; more and more, the invisible is expressed everywhere: networks and cloud computing, Facebook and Twitter, modes of communication made visible (which, these days, means "real") on screen. To examine the multivalent aesthetics of abstraction in contemporary video art is to study artists' interpretations of the always, already digital now: the embodiment of systems—the visual representation of ideas. Why is it important to look at these images, these ideas? If, at this moment, we fail to thoroughly inspect the "abstract" in moving image artworks, we risk being swept away by the dumb stream of images that surrounds us. This collection establishes a critical dialogue regarding the complexity and richness of abstraction in video art and, at the same time, extends scholarship on abstract art.

The essays in *Abstract Video: The Moving Image in Contemporary Art* fill a gap, bring us up to speed, help us awake from the post–post-historical twilight of modernism to come fully into the brightness of the *video now,* to wade into the river of pixels with our eyes wide open, to see where abstraction can be found clinging to the banks, the roots on the shore, or letting go, diving in, understanding there is where we've been, this is where we are, attentive to where we are going. Abstraction defines our age, and the moving image artworks that capture instances, point them out, isolate them for a moment are essential to the thinking of this period; they say, "Look, I can be this, and this, and this. I am incessantly moving, changing, morphing. I am a shapeshifter, a seer, and I can escape the forest of signs."

NOTES

Epigraph: Kirk Varnedoe, *Pictures of Nothing: Abstract Art since Pollock* (Princeton, NJ: Princeton University Press, 2006), 43.

1. Varnedoe, *Pictures,* 1. "The main title of this year's [2003] Mellon Lectures, 'Pictures of Nothing,' is from an essay by William Hazlitt about one of his contemporaries, the early-nineteenth-century English painter J. M. W. Turner."

2. *Afrum-Proto* (1966) is a tungsten projection that forms the illusion of a cube of light in a corner, and *Wedgework* (1974) is a glowing rectangle of red light that, at first glance, resembles a projection but, upon further inspection, is revealed to be a rectangular hole in the wall with fluorescent tubes mounted inside.

3. Varnedoe, *Pictures,* 93. See also Frances Colpitt, "Between Two Worlds: John McCracken," *Art in America* 86, no. 4 (April 1998): 91.

4. Emily Roysdon, *"Ecstatic Resistance,"* in *Abstraction,* ed. Maria Lind, Documents of Contemporary Art (London: Whitechapel and Cambridge, MA: MIT Press, 2013), 222. Text from *Ecstatic Resistance,* typographic poster work (2009) reprinted in *Microhistorias y macromundos,* vol. 3, *Abstract Possible,* ed. Maria Lind (Mexico City: Instituto Nacional de Bellas Artes y Literatura, 2011), 178–84, www.tenstakonsthall.se/uploads/65-MicrohistoriasYMacromundos3MariaLinded.pdf.

5. Maria Lind, "Introduction," in *Abstraction,* 10.

6. Marshall McLuhan, *Understanding Media: The Extensions of Man* (New York: McGraw-Hill, 1964), 7. Riffing off McLuhan's famous statement, in 1969, WGBH television invited six artists to work with television technicians for the creation of "The Medium is the Medium," one of the earliest examples of collaboration between public television and the emerging field of video art in the United States. The film is available from Electronic Arts Intermix, www.eai.org/title.htm?id = 1443.

7. Jannon Stein, "Abstract Films from the 1920s: Making Rhythm Visible," *The Getty Iris* (2011), http://blogs.getty.edu/iris/abstract-films-from-the-1920s-making-rhythm-visible/.

8. Michael Sanchez, "Painting and Screen Otherwise," *Whitney Biennial Catalogue,* (New York: Whitney Museum of American Art, 2014), 114. Sanchez was writing about Ken Okiishi's recorded paintings on flat screens.

9. For more, see Gregory Zinman's essay in this volume (chapter 7) as well as his excellent website *Handmade Cinema* (www.handmadecinema.com/), "a guide to the people, practices, and themes of artisanal moving image production."

10. Boris Groys, *Art Power* (Cambridge, MA: MIT Press, 2008), 83.

11. See Amy Cappellazzo, Adriano Pedrosa, and Peter Wollen, *Making Time: Considering Time as a Material in Contemporary Video and Film.* (Lake Worth, FL: Palm Beach Institute of Contemporary Art, 2000); Sean Cubitt, "Vector, Space, and Time," in *Resolutions 3: Global Networks of Video,* ed. Ming-Yuen S. Ma and Erika Suderburg (Minneapolis: University of Minnesota Press, 2012), 297; and Los Angeles Filmforum at MOCA screening *Time as Material* (Los Angeles, CA: Museum of Contemporary Art, 2013).

12. Though the works of artist Simon Payne are not covered in this volume, it is worth mentioning the extraordinary screening series he curated for the Tate Britain: *Assembly: A Survey of Recent Artists' Film and Video in Britain 2008–2013,* November 23, 2013–March 15, 2014, www.tate.org.uk/whats-on/tate-britain/eventseries/assembly-survey-recent-artists-film-and-video-britain-2008–2013. See also the artist's website: www.simonrpayne.co.uk/.

13. Gabriel Coxhead, "Berlin: Carlier Gebauer: Paul Pfeiffer: *The Morning after the Deluge,*" *Contemporary* 60 (2003), www.contemporary-magazines.com/reviews60_3.htm.

14. Paul Pfeiffer, artist lecture (Graduate Seminar Lecture Series, Art Center College of Design, Pasadena, CA, March 11, 2014).

15. Robert Smithson, "The Spiral Jetty, 1970," *Robert Smithson: The Collected Writings,* ed. Nancy Holt, (New York: New York University Press, 1979), 109–13. Virginia Dawn and Douglas Chrismas funded the film *Spiral Jetty.* Chrismas's gallery was also responsible for the Kosuth piece discussed by John C. Welchman in chapter 3 of this volume.

16. Bruce Hainley, "Erase and Rewind, Elaine Sturtevant," *frieze* 53 (June–August 2000): 84.

17. P. Adams Sitney. *Visionary Film: The American Avant-Garde 1943–1978.* (New York: Oxford University Press, 1974); John G. Hanhardt, "Film Image/Electronic Image: The Construction of Abstraction, 1960–1990," *Visible Language* 29.2 (May 1995): 138–59 (reprinted as chapter 2 in this volume); Sandro Droschl and Norbert Pfaffenbichler, eds., *Abstraction Now* (Graz: Edition Camera Austria, 2004); and numerous essays by Lev Manovich at http://manovich.net/, including "Abstraction and Complexity" (2004), http://manovich.net/index.php/projects/abstraction-and-complexity, and "Data Visualization as New Abstraction and Anti-Sublime" (2002), http://manovich.net/index.php/projects/data-visualisation-as-new-abstraction-and-anti-sublime.

18. *"Dr. Who," Wikipedia,* http://en.wikipedia.org/wiki/Doctor_Who, which cites David J. Howe, Mark Stammers, and Stephen James Walker, *The Television Companion: The Unofficial and Unauthorised Guide to Doctor Who,* 2nd ed. (Tolworth, Surrey: Telos, 2003).

19. *"Dr. Who:* Evolution of a Title Sequence," h2g2: *The Hitchhiker's Guide to the Galaxy:* Earth Edition, created December 27, 2002, updated September 13, 2010, http://h2g2

.com/approved_entry/A907544. There is some controversy about who "discovered" the remarkable video effect, but it seems to be agreed that even though Bernard Lodge received the accolades for the *Dr. Who* title sequence, it was one of the engineers, Ben Palmer or Norman Taylor, who originally thought to point the television camera at the monitor, with Hugh Sheppard working the camera. Lutz Becker, e-mail message to author, November 22, 2013; Anthony Hayward, "Norman Taylor: Creator of the 'Howl-Around' Visual in the Original *Dr. Who* Title Sequence," Obituaries, *Independent*, March 10, 2011, www.independent.co.uk/news/obituaries/norman-taylor-creator-of-the-howlaround-visual-in-the-original-dr-who-title-sequence-2237431.html; and "Norman Taylor's Story of *Dr. Who*," A Tech-Op's History, posted November 28, 2010, http://tech-ops.co.uk/next/2010/11/norman-taylors-story-of-dr-who/.

20. Lutz Becker, e-mail message to author, November 27, 2013.

21. Lutz Becker, "Lutz Becker: Electronically Generated Moving Pictures 1966 to 1969," unpublished manuscript, November 22, 2013.

22. The term *selfie* was Oxford Dictionaries Word of the Year in 2013. "Oxford Dictionaries Word of the Year 2013" (press release), Oxford Dictionaries, November 19, 2013, http://blog.oxforddictionaries.com/press-releases/oxford-dictionaries-word-of-the-year-2013/.

23. Varnedoe, *Pictures of Nothing*, 160.

24. Rosalind Krauss, "Video: The Aesthetics of Narcissism," *October* 1 (1976): 50–64.

25. Krauss, "Aesthetics of Narcissism," 50.

26. Krauss, "Aesthetics of Narcissism," 53.

27. For more on Joan Jonas's *Vertical Roll*, see Siona Wilson's contribution to this volume (chapter 4).

PART ONE

TRANSMISSION

2

FILM IMAGE / ELECTRONIC IMAGE

The Construction of Abstraction, 1960–1990

John G. Hanhardt

The past three decades have witnessed remarkable changes in our thinking about film and video as art forms. The avant-garde cinema enjoyed critical acclaim during the 1960s and 1970s, one of the greatest periods in the history of independent film in America. In the 1980s, filmmakers, critics, and historians, who viewed the artists of the previous two decades as creators of the canon of works defining avant-garde film, increasingly began to question definitions of contemporary avant-garde film practice. At the same time that avant-garde film was undergoing this self-analysis and self-critique, the new electronic medium and aesthetic discourse of video art, which began in the 1960s, had firmly established itself as an art form. Today, the dialogue between film and video artists has increased as the electronic medium has become more pervasive and artists have begun to work in both fields, while at the same time acknowledging the unique properties and differences that distinguish these media.

The questions facing the writing of the histories of both art forms are background to the examination of the issue of abstraction in film and video over the past thirty years. In both art forms there are a variety of genres and styles which would constitute any history of American film and video art; these include the models of abstract expressionism and other lineages within art history (minimalism, conceptual and fluxus art) as well as genres such as character and abstract animation, image processing, and techniques such as hand-painted film and colorizing in video. Such a catalogue of techniques and image making philosophies is certainly required as the basis for any history of this period and for any codifying summary of abstraction.

I have chosen to examine the issue of abstract image making in film and video in a transitional period during which video's rise to prominence stimulated efforts to redefine both this new medium and film as art forms. My thesis is that a specific body of film and video works has explored the issue of abstraction as a means to define their respective media. This has been done by choosing the basic temporality of the moving image and the material basis of the image itself as sites for an epistemological inquiry into the viewing experience, thus exploring the perceptual transaction between spectator and text. A historical subtext to this argument is the fact that the American, avant-garde cinema had for a variety of reasons become, like surrealism and fluxus art, an art-historical movement defined by a period and body of work.

Therefore, even though one continues to see new avant-garde films and fluxus works by the same artists or by artists working in a similar vein, these genres are no longer functioning as the "avant-garde." A further part of this argument is that there has been a reexamination of the original avant-garde impulse within the emerging discourse of video art; throughout the 1970s and 1980s the arguments of avant-garde film have been carried out and renewed within the differing practices and possibilities of this electronic medium. It is within the issue of abstraction that this argument bears particular interest and rewards. Through a reexamination of specific film and video projects, including installations, we can identify specific strategies and practices which reveal a poetics of abstraction emerging out of the artist's effort to redefine these media as aesthetic discourse.

I want to begin my reexamination by going back to 1958 and a work by Stan Brakhage entitled *Anticipation of the Night*. With that film and in related writings, Brakhage proclaimed a new kind of filmmaking guided by a camera liberated from the constraining logic of bourgeois cinema. *Anticipation of the Night* rejects drama and the notion of a narrative representing a coherent and stable point of view. Instead, cascading, fragmentary images of color and light filter through scenes from the artist's life; the editing and camera movement, through a new and radical appropriation of filmic space, form a constant inquiry into liberating the film from the narrative constraints of shot-to-shot continuity and a single vantage point. Brakhage urges the liberation of the camera from the linear language of narrative to an intense, personal space of evolving forms created from light and color and mediated by "metaphors on vision," the title of his manifesto published in 1963 by the journal *Film Culture*. The camera lens refines and distorts reality, collapsing perspective into an abstract two-dimensional plane and then opening it up into an illusionistic space; the film frame becomes a single space as foreground and background are joined into a continually shifting field of action. Variations in camera speed, from eight, to sixteen, to twenty-four frames per second, and the use of different film stocks create subtle changes and modulations in the image.

The aesthetic stance in *Anticipation of the Night* prefigures many later developments in independent film. In his interplay of camera movements from editing, even scratching directly on the film surface, Brakhage manipulated the tensions between the recognizable photographic image and the abstraction of the film frame. He strove to erase the surface and boundaries of illusion and create a new language of filmmaking.

Anticipation of the Night provides a convenient overview of various aesthetic strategies which sought to break through the logic of a cinema constructed as illusionistic space and dramatic narrative. Brakhage articulated that quest directly in *Mothlight* (1963) where the bits and pieces of moths, creatures attracted to the beam of the projector's light in a darkened theater, are literally captured on the strip of celluloid. Like Brakhage's hand-painted films—*The Dante Quartet* (1987) and *The Glaze of Cathexis* (1990)—which acknowledge the materiality of the image in the strokes of the paintbrush across the frames of film, *Mothlight* ignores the boundaries of the film frame through the chance assemblage of the fragmented moth wings directly applied to the film. In *Mothlight,* Brakhage rejected the film and camera as the basis of the film image, as what we see appears by the chance application of material to the continuous surface of celluloid.

Brakhage, as is the case with all filmmakers, does not see his films until the laboratory processing and printing of the film negative is completed or, in the case of film which is painted, scratched, or collaged, until the film is projected onto the screen.

Through the radical exploration of film in the terrain of the abstract image, Brakhage revels in the imaginings of the artist exploring and exposing the apparatus of cinema as celluloid and projector. For Brakhage, film does not exist as a still image but as movement, and so the final ingredient in his films is the viewer whose eyes complete the film experience. *Anticipation of the Night* is emblematic of strategies which create abstract images from the recorded image, the moving camera, and through editing of single and multiple frame sequences; the disruption of the film frame in *Mothlight* represents the use of the strip of celluloid as a means to make new forms of abstract image. In both of these works, Brakhage is manipulating time and acknowledging the passage of film through the camera and the projector.

The articulation of the single frame has been a conceptual and compositional element in work by Stan Brakhage, Robert Breer, Tony Conrad, Paul Sharits, and many others. It is animation, the filming of single frames of hand-drawn images, that perhaps best represents this strategy. The work of Robert Breer is exemplary in its carrying forward of an aesthetic of abstraction through manipulating the speed of alternating images. In *69* (1969), Breer constructs a visual tension as he moves between hard-edged geometrical forms and freely evolving line drawings. What I want to focus on here is Breer's exploration of depth illusion and his exposure of the mechanisms of creation. Objects appear to gyrate in and out of frame, images alternate with sequences of color frames, graphic and object animation alternates with live action shots, a variety of techniques all coalescing around the distention of filmic space and the breakdown of illusion. Our perception of a three-dimensional off-screen space is suddenly broken as Breer acknowledges the boundaries of the frame. Sound adds another dimension as visual associations and perceptual cues are played with on the audio track. As Breer himself notes, *69* was a synthetic film: "I mean frame by frame synthesis . . . I was analyzing the construction of the film. That's part of my idea about concreteness and exposing the materials of the film itself."[1]

My selection of artists and artworks in this investigation of abstract image making in film focuses on those works which do not treat abstraction as the illusion of something else (the interior of the mind, the mystical pathway to a new consciousness) or as a way to illustrate a narrative. Rather, the focus of my presentation is on "process" or conceptual works which anticipated and then in the 1970s became identified as the "structural film." I would define these films as having as their primary goal the anti-illusionistic treatment of film. Unlike Brakhage's mythic, poetic ideology of the self of the artist, which grew out of the paradigm of abstract expressionism, or Breer's affiliation with neo-plasticism and his painterly concern with the limits of the canvas (frame) of the screen's surface, other artists in the 1970s and 1980s turned to the material of celluloid—of its meaning and imagery projected onto the screen. This is a concrete cinema of abstraction, an abstraction which negates the cognates of language in a cinema of the unsayable. As [Ernie] Gehr writes, "Most films teach film to be an image, a representing. But film is a real thing and as a real thing it is not an imitation. . . . Film is a variable intensity of light, an internal balance of time, a movement within a given space."[2]

The totally abstract image, tearing away the recorded image and treating the beam of light as the means to expose the grain as the basis of the recorded image, exposes at the same time the apparatus of the cinema, showing the projector and the screen not as neutral elements but as active ingredients in the hermeneutics of film reception and composition. Paul Sharits's installations are an extension of his single-frame films *T,O,U,C,H,I,N,G* (1968) and *Color Sound Frames* (1974) into the exhibition space. In *Episodic Generation* (1979), four aligned loop projectors present a continuous sequence of moving images on the gallery wall. The images of rephotographed strips of celluloid, each frame colored and rephotographed, compose alternating panels of color and movement. The images were projected on their sides with their sprocket holes visible on the top and bottom of the image. Sharits scratched the surface of the celluloid so the solid colors appeared to be torn and stretched as the fields of color rhythmically play off each other. Accompanying the installation of projectors/films was a display of the actual strips of film, called "frozen film frames," which showed the compositional material of the projected images and how the artist worked with the celluloid.

Sharits further explored the destruction of the film celluloid and the scale of the image within the gallery space in his installation *Third Degree* (1982). Here the three projectors were each placed at a different distance from the wall, creating projected images of different scale in relation to each other. He synchronized the movement of the three films through the projectors in order to develop visual relationships between the projected images. Because the two larger images are successive refilmings of the first, layers of time are created, disrupting and expanding the temporal dimension of the original footage. In *Third Degree* Sharits confronts the material basis of the film medium by burning the individual frames. The exploding, overheated film alters the material medium, the recorded image is torn apart to expose raw colors and textures through the abstract layers of burning celluloid. The chemical properties of the celluloid and the light of the projector remove film from its traditional setting and transform it into a plastic, abstract field. Within the space of the gallery, the viewer is able to move about in front of the beams of light from the projectors, touch the screen surface, and become engulfed in the abstract play of light and color.

The engagement of the viewer becomes total in Stan VanDerBeek's *Steam Screens* (1979) which he created with Joan Brighan. In this project he sought to break down the two-dimensional surface of the filmic screen and further explore his animated and computer generated abstract imagery. Presented in the Whitney Museum of American Art's Sculpture Garden in the dark of an autumn evening, it was an installation which encouraged the active participation of the viewer. A grid of piping was laid out on the garden floor; compressed steam from a truck was pumped into the piping and released through tiny holes to create sheets of steam which filled the space. VanDerBeek's films were then projected into the sheets of steam from half a dozen projectors. Moving three-dimensional abstract images suddenly appeared to float within the immaterial, fluid, and constantly changing "steam screen." Viewers caught the images on different parts of their body as they moved within and through the filmic space and three-dimensional fields of VanDerBeek's abstract patterns and constantly changing imagery.

I have chosen to highlight those artists and approaches in film which create their abstract imagery directly from the properties of the medium—whether it is by exploring camera movement (Stan Brakhage's *Anticipation of the Night*), applying materials directly onto celluloid (Brakhage's *Mothlight*), hand-drawn animation (Robert Breer's *69*), film installations treating celluloid as compositional material (Ernie Gehr's *History* and Paul Sharits's *Episodic Generation* and *Third Degree*), or the opening up of the screen surface to further abstract the image as an intelligible experience (Stan VanDer-Beek's *Steam Screens*). These are not narratives which can be retold or images which can be easily reproduced. They are works which must be experienced, which engage the viewer in the fragility and temporality of the projected image and its instruments: camera, celluloid, projector, screen. The abstract image in the hands of these artists is not a representation of another school of imagery but is created out of the resources of the artist and the sources of the medium. In focusing on this particular body of work I have ignored many artists (Marie Menken, Tony Conrad, Jordan Belson, Ken Jacobs, John Whitney, Len Lye, Sandy Moore, Nathanial Dorsky, and many others). However, by highlighting this work I hope to demonstrate how film is different from video and yet how, through an engagement with abstraction, they come to share certain principles. Film is a handmade art form, it is a strip of film which can be held up to the light and must be manually edited. In the works I have discussed, artists have consciously sought to explore these physical parameters and directly engage the viewer in the reception and completion of the work when it is shown. In their abstract play of light, color, black and white, sound and image, these works test both our language of description and the language of filmmaking. This engagement in the temporality of the screening process and the direct acknowledgment of the viewer also come into play in the work of artists working in video from the early 1960s to the present.

In a publication accompanying his one-artist exhibition at the Smolin Gallery in New York and his concurrent performance in the Yam Festival in New Jersey in 1963, Wolf Vostell wrote this *décollage* performance instruction: "Throw a big whipped cream cake to the TV and smudge it on the surface of the TV while the program is going on."[3] Here Vostell enjoins the viewer to participate in disrupting the flow of television entertainment by covering the screen and making it into an abstract, fractured image. Fluxus and happening events in the early 1960s, when artists first appropriated the television set into their artmaking, also extended to altering the electronic patterns of the cathode ray tube. Nam June Paik's celebrated *Magnet TV* (1965) does not employ videotape or broadcast images but shows a moving abstract pattern created by a large magnet moved about on the surface of the television set. Here Paik, a seminal figure as artist and activist in the history of this art form, was able to fashion a new abstract, kinetic image from the unique capacities of the television set.

In the 1960s Nam June Paik created a number of videotapes based on electronically disrupting the received broadcast signal, changing both sound and image to create an abstract alteration of the recorded image. An example is *Variations on Johnny Carson vs. Charlotte Moorman* (1966), in which we see Moorman on the Johnny Carson television show in an impromptu performance which Paik transforms into a chance event through a video image which constantly breaks down. These works predate Paik's own image-processing and colorizing system, the Paik-Abe Video Synthesizer, and the various other image-modifying and synthesizing tools created in the early 1970s.

As in the case of my discussion of abstraction in film, I have chosen to highlight a specific body of works which focus on the chance occurrences and unique properties of the electronic medium unmediated by image-processed or post-production technologies; thus, I have not included the Rutt-Etra Synthesizer, the Paik-Abe Video Synthesizer, or the works of Shalom Gorewitz, Stephen Beck, Eric Siegel, Ed Emshwiller, Barbara Buckner, Peer Bode, or Matthew Schlanger, among others. As in the case of film I have chosen to focus on a specific selection of artists and video art works which explore the medium itself, the very quality of the electronic image, and do not employ image-processing and post-production technologies, computer graphics, or the array of artist's tools, commercial and quasi-commercial resources used to create a more processed and produced language of abstraction. These works, predicated on chance and the abstract imagery that emerges from the impermanent electronic image, disrupt the normative codes and production processes to discover within the chance operations of the video imaging system a challenging abstraction which resists codification.

An important distinction between film and video is that the video image is immediately viewable as it is recorded: the image is created on the cathode ray tube, onto its

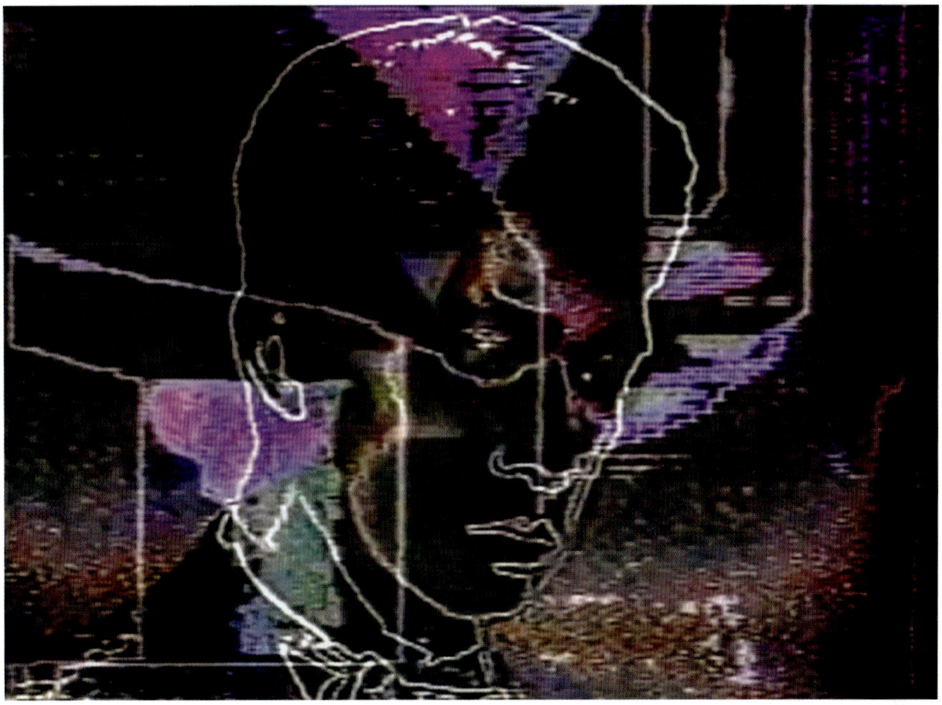

FIGURE 2.1
Nam June Paik, Still from *Nam June Paik: Edited for Television,* 1975. Video, color, sound; 29:24 min. Camera / Supervising Engineer: John J. Godfrey. Produced by the TV Lab at WNET / Thirteen (VTR series). Courtesy of Electronic Arts Intermix (EAI), New York.

own screen, and does not have to be processed and projected before the image can be seen. This creates an active dialectic between artist and process and viewer, a profound cognitive relationship which allows an abstraction unique to the medium. The artists I am discussing here—Nam June Paik, Bill Viola, Woody Vasulka, and Al Robbins—have each created work which explores issues related to those I have discussed within the avant-garde film. By relating to the unique properties of the medium and engaging the viewer in the reception of the work, these artists deconstruct the technology of their art form by playing with and creating a unique set of possibilities out of their respective medium

In 1973 while working in a studio, Bill Viola chanced to make a videotape entitled *Information.* Like Nam June Paik's *Variations on Johnny Carson vs. Charlotte Moorman* it is a work predicated on chance, the unexpected occurrences that create a unique art work. *Information* is the product of a breakdown in a video system. "It is the result of a technical mistake made while working in the studio late one night, when the output of a videotape recorder was accidentally routed through the studio switcher and back into its own input. When the record button was pressed, the machine tried to record itself."[4]

This process created patterns of noise and interference. Unlike videotapes made for broadcast, which are processed through a time-based corrector to make the image fit into the window of the broadcast signal, *Information* has a non-conforming signal and plays back differently on every monitor. It is never seen the same way twice. In other words, the video remakes itself when played, the image is always decoded differently.

The chance operations that composed Viola's and Paik's early abstract image making projects also informed the explorations of the pioneering video artists Woody and Steina Vasulka. Instead of determining what inputs would create what effect, they sought to create not synthesizers but "open-ended boxes"[5] in which abstract imagery could be freely developed through a self-exploring technology. In such works as *Noisefields* (1974), what we see is the visual representation of an audio signal; through the use of an audio synthesizer the Vasulkas were able to manipulate the electronic waveforms of the audio and video signals. Thus the imagery is entirely electronic. "They have all been made artificially from various frequencies, from sounds, from inaudible pitches and their beats."[6] These visual images then flowed from the temporal dimension of sound. As Woody Vasulka noted, "At the time, I was totally obsessed with this idea that there was no single frame anymore. I come from the movies, where the frame was extremely rigid and I understood that electronic material has no limitation within its existence. It only has limitation when it reaches the screen because the screen itself is a rigid time structure."[7] Thus, like the filmmakers discussed earlier, the Vasulkas sought to break through the parameters of the medium and discover the chance combinations that would emerge from its basic materials.

Perhaps no artist was as dedicated to freeing video technology from the imposed systems of the manufacturer as the late Al Robbins. The experience of Bill Viola in making *Information* was the operating challenge in all of Al Robbins's work. It was not created out of synthesizers nor did it go through a time-base corrector to make it suitable for broadcast; it was a raw work which existed only in the time in which one experienced it. Robbins's installations and videotapes did not exist as copies permanently preserved in an inviolable construct; instead, their random abstractions, energies, and bursts of color, shapes, and noise were creating and destroying themselves in the very process of their presentation. Robbins's struggle to purify the signal and image, to let it speak the poetry of its own raw imagery, occupied his life. As a poet and artist, he made work and wrote tirelessly of his quest to get through the toils to realize new outputs.

Robbins's installation such as *Anticata/Strophe* (1980) placed cameras and monitors throughout the gallery space so that images circulated according to the triggering of sequences through the "glitch" sound of the camera. As Robbins wrote, his installations extended "the act of shooting, to evoke a dynamic fluid and intricately expressive as shooting/activating space between images and between image and viewer, as speaking with each other, involving the perceiver in these speakings."[8] As the cameras played off each other and the viewer activated the installation by walking through the "installation space mixed with the like qualities of the videotape, predetermination of recorded tape image is broken by the perceiver's effect, his position when the installation space is intensified: active, physical/kinesthetic, and self-reflective, the installation space is carved according to the world where the tapes were shot and the position of the spectator is brought closer to the posture of the act of shooting."[9] Robbins's abstract images convey the optics of real sight, not the "realism" we draw or photograph nor the safe boundaries we create around our world.

The process of discovery through the optics and electronic recording process of video led Bill Viola to gather abstract images from the desert landscape in *Chott-el-Djerid (A Portrait in Light and Heat)* in 1979. In a sequence of remarkable images recorded through a special telephoto lens adapted for video, Viola shot the mirages that formed during the midday sun in the Tunisian Sahara desert. The colors of light and heat and the uncanny mirage effects create abstract images of real and imagined scenes. Here the landscape gives up images of lyrical and mysterious abstraction created out of natural phenomena. Viola's camera and his ability to create abstraction from the real-time process of image recording convey an immediate sense of discovery, not the distance created through film processing. The light emerging from the screen of the monitor gives a tactical impression of light and color; the abstract electronic image from the world around us has a soft and pointillistic impression. This work offers an interesting contrast to Brakhage's *Anticipation of the Night* and its probing and jabbing abstraction; the flow of video and the editing of film form two very different abstract image compositions. Robbins, Vasulka, Viola, and Paik sought to discover in the abstract image the expressive, constantly present, but impermanent possibilities of video as an artist's medium.

Looking back over the past thirty years of avant-garde film and video art production, it is clear that the artists I have discussed sought to transform their media through chance occurrences and the transaction between their eyes and the world around them. This impulse originated within the film avant-garde and has been carried forward in the video art movement. I have suggested that abstraction, as it came out of either medium, film or video, became a purifying act which saw an idealism within the image wrested free of the logic of capitalism and the production of entertainment. Too often our histories of video art and film approach these media in terms of conventional narratives of mainstream entertainment or as mirror images of the other visual arts. The work of these artists struggling with the abstract image has sought to return technology to the *techné* of radical simplicity and renovation. As these artists pushed the media of film and video through the dimension of the abstract image, they sought to reinvent a poetics of image making.

NOTES

1. Robert Breer, quoted in Marilyn Singer, *A History of the American Avant-Garde Cinema,* catalogue (New York: American Federation of the Arts, 1976), 144.

2. John G. Hanhardt, with artist's statement by Ernie Gehr, *Ernie Gehr: September 27–October 9, 1983,* New American Filmmakers Series 9 (New York: Whitney Museum of American Art, 1983).

3. Wolf Vostell, *Television Décollage & Morning Glory: 2 Pieces by Wolf Vostell* (New York: 3rd Rail Gallery, 1963).

4. Barbara London, ed., *Bill Viola,* catalogue (New York: Museum of Modern Art, 1987), 24.

5. Lucinda Furlong, "Notes Toward a History of Image Processed Video: Steina and Woody Vasulka," *Afterimage* 2, no. 1 (1983): 14.

6. Furlong, "Notes," 15.

7. Furlong, "Notes," 14.

8. Al Robbins, *"Anticata/Strophe"* (October 3–19, 1980), Program Note, New American Filmmakers Series (New York: Whitney Museum of American Art, 1980).

9. René Coehlo and Dorine Mignot, eds., *The Luminous Image: An Exhibition of Video Installations by 22 Artists,* catalogue (Amsterdam: Stedelijk Museum, 1984), 153, 155.

3

JOSEPH KOSUTH'S *THE SECOND INVESTIGATION* IN VANCOUVER (1969)

Art on TV

John C. Welchman

The following discussion of Joseph Kosuth's exhibition at the Douglas Gallery in Vancouver in the fall of 1969 has two important contexts. The first is defined by the situation of this show as one of the exhibitions at "15 Locations" in North and South America, Europe, and Australia that made up *The Second Investigation* (fig. 3.1, left), which Kosuth conceived in 1968. The project was planned during the last months of 1968 and launched at exhibitions put on between December 1968 (Kosuth's exhibition at the Art Gallery of Ontario, Toronto opened December 29, 1968) and January 1969 (the gallerist Seth Siegelaub's *January 5–31* in New York).[1] Each appearance of *The Second Investigation* was based on contiguous text from one of the eight classes Peter Mark Roget established for the Synopsis of Categories for his thesaurus, a "classed catalogue of words" that he first drafted in 1805 and completed half a decade later following his retirement as Secretary of the British Royal Society.[2] Specific sections or subsections from the Synopsis were selected for each "campaign" associated with *The Second Investigation*, typographically transcribed (as necessary), and then relocated into one of more than half a dozen media delivery systems, either by a process of standard submission (such as advertising copy for newspapers and magazines) or by enlargement and reformatting (for display on billboards, for example)—in all cases with the least possible "artistic" interference. The media infiltrated by *The Second Investigation* included national, regional, and local daily newspapers published in a wide range of cities and towns in the United States, the United Kingdom, Australia, Sweden, and Switzerland; weeklies and periodicals such as *The Nation*, *The New Republic*, and *The Village Voice* in the United States; special inter-

15 LOCATIONS 1969/70 JOSEPH KOSUTH ART AS IDEA AS IDEA 1966-1970 15 UBICACION 1969/70 JOSEPH KOSUTH ARTE COMO IDEA COMO IDEA 1966-1970 15 EMPLACE–MENTS 1969/70 JOSEPH KOSUTH L'ART EN-TANT-QU'EN IDEE EN-TANT-QU'EN IDEE 1966-1970 15 PLAATSEN 1969/70 JOSEPH KOSUTH KUNST ALS IDEE ALS IDEE 1966-1970 15 PLATZE 1969/70 JOSEPH KOSUTH KUNST ALS IDEE ALS IDEE 1966-1970 15 LUOGHI 1969/70 JOSEPH KOSUTH ARTE EONE IDEA EONE IDEA 1966-1970

PASADENA ART MUSEUM JANUARY 25 TO MARCH 1; DOUGLAS GALLERY, VANCOUVER OCTOBER 4 TO NOVEMBER 4; MUSEUM OF CONTEMPORARY ART, CHICAGO OCTOBER 31 TO DECEMBER 14; LEO CASTELLI, NEW YORK NOVEMBER 22 TO DECEMBER 20; THE ART GALLERY OF ONTARIO, TORONTO DECEMBER 29 TO JANUARY 10; INSTITUTO TORCUATO DI TELLA, BUENOS AIRES 28 OCTUBRE-8 NOVIEMBRE; NOVA SCOTIA COLLEGE OF ART, HALIFAX OCTOBER 25 TO NOVEMBER 9; COVENTRY COLLEGE OF ART, ENGLAND NOVEMBER 10 TO NOVEMBER 25; CHRIST COLLEGE, OXFORD OCTOBER 21 TO OCTOBER 31; A 37 90 89, ANTWERPEN 31.10-29.11; ART & PROJECT, AMSTERDAM 22.11-30.11; KUNSTHALLE BERNE 8 NOVEMBER-16 NOVEMBER; GALERIA SPERONE, TORINO 9 NOVEMBRE-16 NOVEMBRE; PINACOTHECA, AUSTRALIA OCTOBER 31 TO NOVEMBER 14

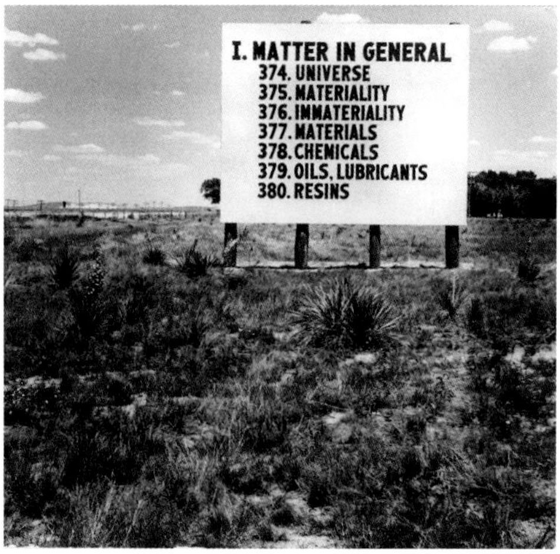

FIGURE 3.1
(left) Joseph Kosuth, *15 Locations, 1969/70, Joseph Kosuth, Art as Idea as Idea (1966–1970),* poster describing exhibition, Douglas Gallery archives. Courtesy of Ace Gallery, Los Angeles. *(right)* Joseph Kosuth, *The Second Investigation (A.A.I.A.I.),* 1968. *Class IV: Matter (I. Matter in General, 374–380),* billboard, Portales, New Mexico, 1969. Courtesy of the artist.

est magazines and journals, including *Women's Wear Daily* and *The New York Review of Books* in the United States and *Exchange and Mart* in the United Kingdom; art magazines, such as *Artforum, Art International, Museum News,* and *Art News;* advertisements in public buses; billboards both in cities (St. Margaret's Bay Road, Halifax, Nova Scotia; Solferino Square, Turin, Italy; Colorado Boulevard, Pasadena, California; various locations in Bern, Switzerland) and in rural areas (Portales, New Mexico, fig. 3.1, right); posters (kiosk advertising in Bern); handbills (distributed in Buenos Aires, Argentina, and Toronto, Canada; dropped from an airplane over Antwerp, Belgium); mailers sent from Amsterdam, the Netherlands; and, finally, TV spots intended to be aired on Canadian national television. *The Second Investigation* also spawned an unauthorized, or at least unplanned, radio component in the form of a broadcast connected to the effort to purchase and air the TV segment, which I discuss below. Most of the distributions were effected in 1969 and 1970, but *The Second Investigation* continued intermittently until February 1974, when what appears to be the final installment was published in a number of Swedish newspapers.

Progressive public and commercial galleries and educational institutions in Canada played a leading role in *The Second Investigation.* Hosting the first exhibition in the series, the Art Gallery of Ontario, Toronto printed five thousand handbills marked with "Sensation. V. Sight" from Class Five of the Synopsis of Categories; these were "placed door-to-door on Tuesday December 30" 1968, during an exhibition that ran from

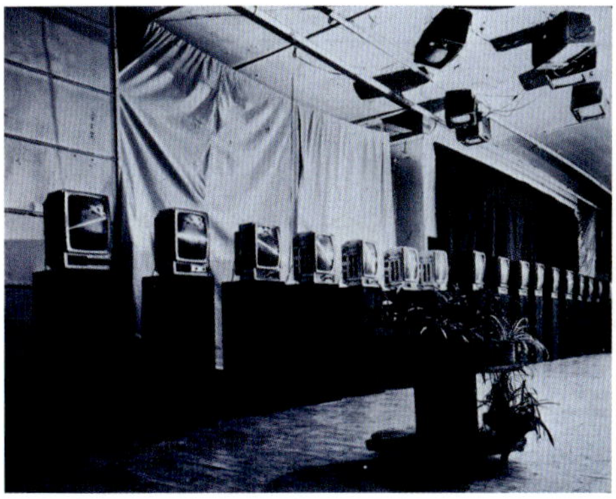
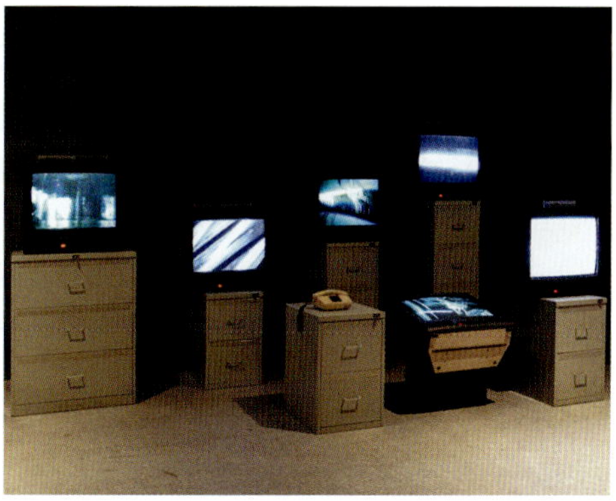

FIGURE 3.2
(left) Nam June Paik, *TV Clock,* 1963. Twenty-four fixed-image color television monitors mounted on twenty-four pedestals, color and black and white, silent; installation dimensions variable, height approx. 76 inches. Courtesy of Nam June Paik Estate. Photograph by Peter Moore. *(right)* Wolf Vostell, *6 TV-Dé-collage,* 1963. Six-channel video (VHS and DVD, black and white, sound; 96 min.) shown on six TV monitors; six office cabinets, a telephone, three photographs (black and white), an exhibition, and six seedbeds with watercress. Collection Museo Nacional Centro de Arte Reina Sofía, Photographic Archives Museo Nacional Centro de Arte Reina Sofía. Photograph © 2014 Artists Rights Society (ARS), New York / ADAGP, Paris.

December 29, 1968 to January 10, 1969.[3] The Nova Scotia College of Art in Halifax put on an exhibition (October 25 to November 9, 1969) featuring four different media presentations from Class One of the Synopsis of Categories, "Abstract Relations. X. Power." Four hundred handbills were printed and distributed; an advertisement was placed in the *Mail Star T.V. Guide* (Saturday, October 25); advertising posters bought for twelve routes of the Halifax city bus network (October 25 to November 1); and a billboard went up on St. Margaret's Bay Road. My focus here is on the third Canadian manifestation of *The Second Investigation,* at the Douglas Gallery in October 1969, which, uniquely, attempted to program Synopsis text on broadcast television.

The second context for the these remarks concerns the relation of television—variously conceived as a physical object or broadcast medium, as entertainment or information, public service or licensed commercial business—to avant-garde art in the 1960s. In what seems like a foreshadowing of debates over dating, innovation, and prioritization during the early years of Conceptual Art, critics and advocates of Nam June Paik and Wolf Vostell, as well as the artists themselves, have made various claims about the incorporation of television in their work beginning as early as the late 1950s (fig. 3.2). Paik was probably the first to offer an extended demonstration of his interest in television in a public exhibition during his first major show, *Exposition of Music—Electronic Television* at the Galerie Parnass in Wuppertal, Germany (March 11–20, 1963), run by the architect Rolf Jährling. Paik's deployment of a dozen variously modified TV sets, which were scattered and stacked in one area of the sprawling exhibition (originally titled *Symphony for 20 Rooms*), bore witness to several valences of the first wave of experimental work with television, the stakes of which were quite different from Kosuth's approach to the medium some half a decade later.

First, as Dieter Daniels and others have argued, Paik seemed to be motivated in part by a critical antagonism towards television flavored by the corrosive skepticism of Guy Debord and manifested in an often aggressive bid to destroy, undermine, or radically repurpose the normal TV signal (at the time Germany had only one channel with limited broadcasting times—which dictated the brief evening opening hours of the Galerie Parnass exhibition).[4] Using both broadcast programs and TV sets themselves as "found" materials, Paik intervened in the consumer-oriented technical neutrality of the "set," or "tube," by rewiring, retuning, and electronically recoding its signals: he thus distorted, as Chris Salter suggests, "both broadcast image and monitor by way of *magnetizers, rectifiers,* and *oscillators*" in order to "defamiliarize and thus transfigure a visual medium into an expressive instrument operating across multiple senses."[5]

Experimental work using or addressing television was present from the very beginning in the diffuse body of work associated with Happenings, Events, and Fluxus, and it was anticipated by developments in the 1950s such as Lucio Fontana's 1952 "Television Manifesto of the Spatial Movement."[6] A photograph of Wolff Vostell's *TV-dé-coll/age (Ereignisse für Millionen, Partitur* [Events for Millions, Score], June 1959), for example, was included as the second item in a list of ten under the heading "1959" exhibited in the *Dokumentationstrasse* (Documentation Street) and published in the catalogue of Harold Szeemann's *Happenings and Fluxus* (Kunstverein, Cologne, 1970). Like Paik, Vostell is a key figure in the early attention to TV as an object and medium. His first Happening, *Theater is in the Street* (Paris, 1958), incorporated auto parts and a TV, and a notebook sketch dated by the artist to 1958 or 1959 (*TV-Décoll/age no. 1*) outlines a project to mount different-sized TV sets behind and against "clean white canvas" to highlight constantly changing, crypto-pictorialist effects produced by "interference built into" the TV sets.[7] Although Vostell's notebooks, dated by the artist to 1958 and 1959, contain sketches for unrealized projects addressing TV more directly, his first public manifestation of these interests was shortly after Paik's Wuppertal exhibition, in May 1963 in New York.

During the 1960s and 1970s, Vostell and Paik subjected television sets, as well as their programs and signals, to a wide variety of appropriations and modifications. Beginning with the presentation of televisions atop filing cabinets in *6 TV-Dé-collage* (1963; fig. 3.2, right), Vostell conscripted them as headboards for the beds in *You* (1964); set them in an arena of broken glass surmounted by found and reconfigured objects, including a bicycle wheel, skis, and various comestibles in *Elektronischer dé-collage Happening Raum* (1968); and used them as molds for concrete sculptures and as units to articulate a fifteen-set-high obelisk in *TV Obelisk* (1979). He even posed two giant TV sets in the center of a freeway intersection in a photo-collaged project for a "Drive-in Museum" (1970).

There are a number of parallels between the careers of Vostell and Kosuth, including their early recourse to plans and diagrams for work that was realized later—Vostell in the late 1950s, Kosuth in the mid-1960s—giving rise to intense debate about the timing and "priority" of their innovations. More tellingly, both also used dictionary definitions during their early investigations (Kosuth in the Photostat definitions of *The Protoinvestigations* and *The First Investigation*, which immediately preceded *The Second Investigation*). The front of the folded invitation card termed Vostell's exhibition at Smolin Gallery in New York (which opened May 22, 1963) a "presentation" of "Wolf Vostell & Television Decollage & Decollage Posters & Comestible Decollage." The inside pages provided an exhibition history and details of the participatory possibilities of the exhibition: an invitation to "eat art and to make art by eating"; a "Do It Yourself" opportunity "to participate in the creation of Décollage at the opening" (along with a telephone number to call to "reserve the area in which you wish to create" and a statement that the gallery would supply the materials). These were flanked by a gridded array of *Life* magazine covers whose axes were labeled with the numbers 1 to 17 (horizontal) and the letters A to O (vertical). The verso of the card was reserved for a photographic transcription (apparently from a French-German dictionary) of the German translation and definition of *décol|age*.[8] Of interest for my discussion here is Vostell's decision to include in his reproduction the first line of the definition that follows next in the dictionary sequence: *décolorer*—to "fade" or lose color.

Commenced before the advent and availability of portable video in the mid- and later 1960s, the interventions of Paik and Vostell were based on the appropriation, modification, supplementation, and re-imagination of television's broadcast contents or of television as a material object. While it often radically refigured or scrambled its materials, the work of Paik and Vostell was predicated on and tethered to the sign system of television as a set of manufactured and broadcast givens—conditions emblematized by the recourse of both artists to devices (Vostell termed them "oscillographs") that recoded TV signals into other visual or sonic forms.

The Second Investigation arrived at the onset, around 1968, of another dialogical mode that would reorganize the relation between art and TV half a decade after the work of Paik and Vostell was first exhibited. In this model artists used portable or commercially available video technologies to make "TV"—shown on monitors, and later screens, outside the purview of broadcast television—or, more occasionally, they produced material by commission, invitation, or collaboration, which aired on one or another of the now-burgeoning array of stations, channels, and programs. While superficially related to this last contingency, Kosuth's recourse to television was constitutionally different from all of these formations, as he was interested in TV only as a public medium and entirely uninvested in the particularities of its programmed content or physical formats. Nor did he wish to introduce his own content into the daily digest of programs in the form of innovative "arts" content. In what follows, the terms and implications of Kosuth's non-auteurist infiltration of the medium of television will hopefully become a little clearer.

Kosuth's Vancouver exhibition was titled *Joseph Kosuth—October 1969* and, according to a title page in the gallery archives, programmed in two chronologically consecutive parts, "Part I Oct 1–29" and "Part II Oct 29–31"; other sources, including the Douglas Gallery "title" label, give "October 4 to November 4," the revised dates suggesting that the media arrangements for the show were being negotiated during, and beyond, the dates originally planned.[9] The contents of the exhibition consisted, first, of a gallery exhibition comprising only the 15 (or, according to another account, possibly a copyediting error, 12) functionally descriptive card labels standing in for the same number of galleries and locations in Argentina, Australia, Belgium, Canada, England, Holland, Italy, Switzerland, and the United States where the labels were also shown.[10] Each card contained information about the sponsoring/exhibiting gallery or institution, along with exhibition dates, the particular thesaurus class and sub-categories, and brief details of the media "presentation" (the newspaper or newspapers and date or dates, billboard location, handbill print run, or other mode of media appearance and distribution). The language used was that of the host gallery with the exception of the label for The Art Gallery of Ontario, Toronto, which was printed in English and French: "Presentation: Cinq-mille imprimé distribuer de porte á porte le Mardi, 30 Décembre." A simple, hand-drawn diagram annotated by Kosuth with "example" at the top and "this is not a drawing" at the bottom offers a layout suggestion in which the "title pieces" are arranged quite close together in a "straight line" (fig. 3.3, bottom). The Douglas Gallery and most other locations followed Kosuth's diagram but spread the title pieces out rather more, in accord with the other directive written onto the diagram: "maybe more space."[11] The second aspect of the Douglas exhibition was to be realized through a media presentation drawn from section "VII. Color" of Class Three of the Synopsis of Categories (see figs. 3.4 and 3.7, bottom right).

In an effort to coordinate the relatively unprecedented collaboration by fifteen venues in nine countries, Siegelaub, acting as the exhibition producer and manager, dispatched planning documents to the participants. Because the undated copy sent to the Douglas Gallery had an attachment containing one of the local newspaper advertisements commissioned by the Kunsthalle, Bern for the exhibition *Live in Your Head: When Attitudes Become Form* (March 22 to April 27, 1969) as an example of a media-situated thesaurus entry, the document was probably produced in the late spring or summer of 1969. Siegelaub's memo provides information about the project concept under several headings. His "General" comments note a focus on "the placement of advertisements in newspaper *[sic]*, periodicals and magazines" and cites examples of works already made, beginning with "*Artforum* (January 1969), 1 of 4 different parts; *Art International* (February 1969), 1 of 5 different parts"; and including "When Attitudes Become Form," as well as "the New York Times, Museum News, the Nation, the New York Post, Variety, Art News, the New York Review of Books, Women's Wear Daily and others." The final aspect of the general description noted: "Each sponsoring Museum or Gallery will underwrite the publication of a work (which may consist of from 1 advertisement up to 7 separate advertisements in as many publications)."[12]

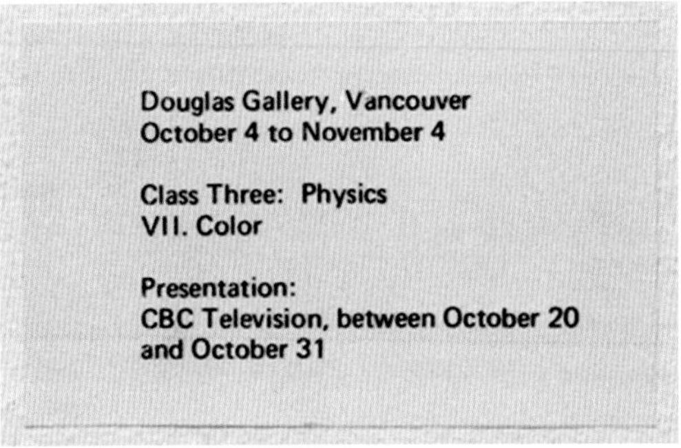

Douglas Gallery, Vancouver
October 4 to November 4

Class Three: Physics
VII. Color

Presentation:
CBC Television, between October 20 and October 31

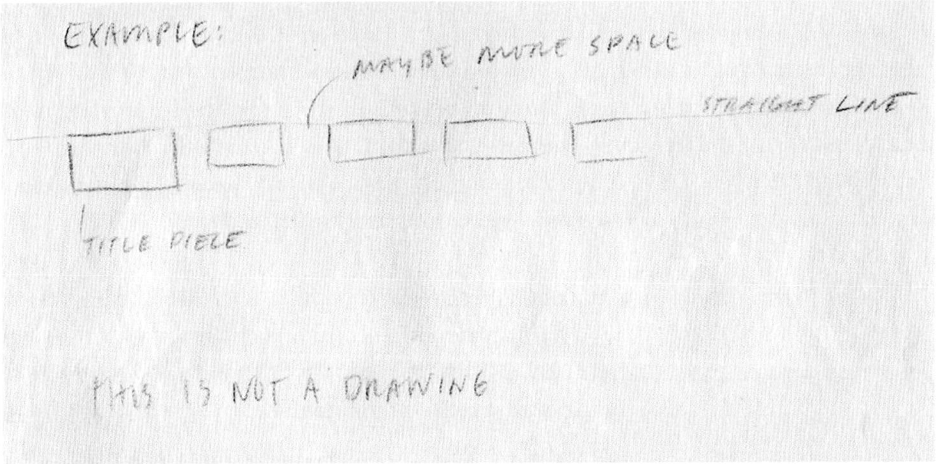

FIGURE 3.3
(top) Wall label for *Joseph Kosuth—October 1969*, Douglas Gallery, Vancouver. Douglas Gallery archives. Courtesy of Ace Gallery, Los Angeles. *(bottom)* Joseph Kosuth, diagram of labels sent to Douglas Gallery, Vancouver, in preparation for *Joseph Kosuth—October 1969*. Douglas Gallery archives. Courtesy of Ace Gallery, Los Angeles.

The second section of the document, headed "Sponsors," lists twelve "Museums and Galleries who have expressed interest in (or have been asked) to participate in the exhibition." That, halfway through the year in which the major initiatives of *The Second Investigation* were realized, several of the listed galleries (Irving Blum, Los Angeles; Illeana Sonnabend, Paris; Yvon Lambert, Milano; Minami ,Tokyo) do not appear to have contributed formally to the project testifies to its logistical contingencies and organizational fluidity. Notes on "The Exhibition" itself comprised two elements: one would be supplied by Kosuth, "the actual advertisements (ready for publications)," and the other by Siegelaub, "a 3 foot square poster (1 meter square)—in as many languages as will be represented in the exhibition—and each sponsor will receive 500 (folded) posters for distribution to their local mailing lists." The second of three attachments sent with the memo was a "(rough) of the poster" featuring headings for the twelve listed galleries, but not the presentational details. Under "Presentation," Siegelaub suggested—but did not mandate—the form outlined above: "The presentation . . . in the exhibition can consist, as some exhibitors are doing, by the entire gallery space being filled only by labels on the wall—with the 10–15 labels listing the data [in the 'native language'] on each piece appearing in the other cities." The layout and spacing of the exhibition of labels was, however, left to each participant: "Theoretically, . . . all the space that is needed is 3 feet in width (the label space) and how it expands from that is up to each individual participant."[13] The final aspect of the presentation notes that each show "should be considered locally as a One-man exhibition, and each Museum or Gallery is free to treat the exhibition in their usual manner."

Siegelaub concludes his circular with a "2-part" note on "Cost," which specifies that "the placement of advertisements . . . in local publications" might "range from $50.00 upwards (this is dependent on the amount of parts in the work, the advertising rates locally, and the size of the advertisements)" and should be "paid directly to the publications by each sponsor." The second allocation of costs, in which specific dollar amounts were not provided in the copy viewed, reads (transcription unmodified)

> 2. To Joseph Kosuth (for Transportation to each Museum or Gallery during the exhibition (October), joint participation in the poster, etc)
>   a. For participation in the exhibition <u>OR</u>
>   b. For participation in the exhibition and the ownership of the work sponsored.

The Douglas Gallery contribution was conceived as a unique media intervention, though when and how the decision was made to book advertising segments on Canadian Broadcast Corporation (CBC), the Canadian national broadcaster, is somewhat unclear. Although including the correct general date for the show ("October")—and thus to this extent at least, customized—Siegelaub's document refers to print media ("newspaper, periodicals and magazines") but does not make reference to television. However, the gallery archive preserves a letter from exhibition coordinator T. Bjornson to Bob Fortune "c/o C B C" in Vancouver, dated September 24, 1969, which offers details about "a show of Joseph Kosuth for Western Canada" taking place "in the latter part of October" (fig. 3.4).[14] It makes reference to conversations "with several people at C B C" who advised Bjornson "that this project should be incorporated into a programme such as 'Hourglass' with Mr. Christmas *[sic]* available to present the piece." The letter duly concludes with a request that "the list of words" (supplied in Bjornson's letter) could be "projected on the T V monitor for 15–20 seconds" during *Hourglass* "anytime from October 20–31st."

It is clear from Bjornson's September 24 letter that the Douglas Gallery attempted with some vigor to place the segment on CBC, was referred instead to programming, and then identified *Hourglass*, the popular, local supper-hour newscast, as perhaps the

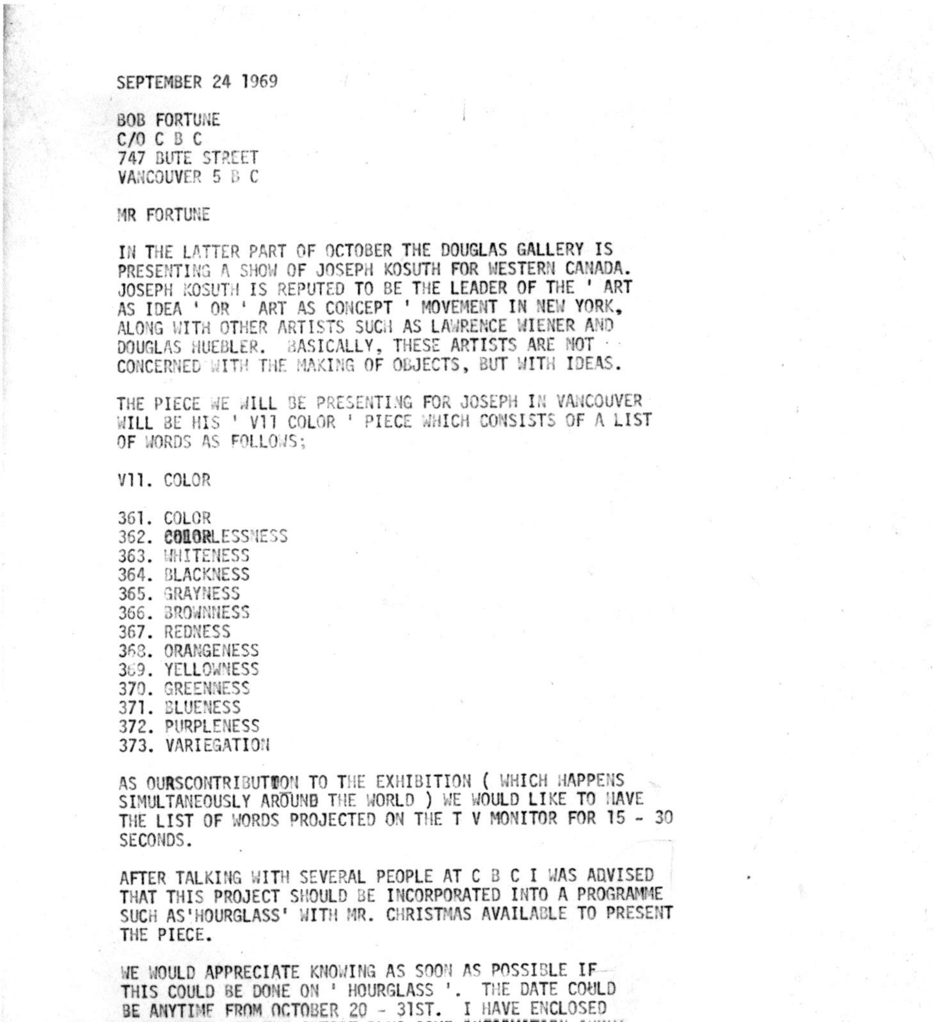

SEPTEMBER 24 1969

BOB FORTUNE
C/O C B C
747 BUTE STREET
VANCOUVER 5 B C

MR FORTUNE

IN THE LATTER PART OF OCTOBER THE DOUGLAS GALLERY IS PRESENTING A SHOW OF JOSEPH KOSUTH FOR WESTERN CANADA. JOSEPH KOSUTH IS REPUTED TO BE THE LEADER OF THE ' ART AS IDEA ' OR ' ART AS CONCEPT ' MOVEMENT IN NEW YORK, ALONG WITH OTHER ARTISTS SUCH AS LAWRENCE WIENER AND DOUGLAS HUEBLER. BASICALLY, THESE ARTISTS ARE NOT CONCERNED WITH THE MAKING OF OBJECTS, BUT WITH IDEAS.

THE PIECE WE WILL BE PRESENTING FOR JOSEPH IN VANCOUVER WILL BE HIS ' V11 COLOR ' PIECE WHICH CONSISTS OF A LIST OF WORDS AS FOLLOWS;

V11. COLOR

361. COLOR
362. COLORLESSNESS
363. WHITENESS
364. BLACKNESS
365. GRAYNESS
366. BROWNNESS
367. REDNESS
368. ORANGENESS
369. YELLOWNESS
370. GREENNESS
371. BLUENESS
372. PURPLENESS
373. VARIEGATION

AS OURSCONTRIBUTION TO THE EXHIBITION (WHICH HAPPENS SIMULTANEOUSLY AROUND THE WORLD) WE WOULD LIKE TO HAVE THE LIST OF WORDS PROJECTED ON THE T V MONITOR FOR 15 - 30 SECONDS.

AFTER TALKING WITH SEVERAL PEOPLE AT C B C I WAS ADVISED THAT THIS PROJECT SHOULD BE INCORPORATED INTO A PROGRAMME SUCH AS'HOURGLASS' WITH MR. CHRISTMAS AVAILABLE TO PRESENT THE PIECE.

WE WOULD APPRECIATE KNOWING AS SOON AS POSSIBLE IF THIS COULD BE DONE ON ' HOURGLASS '. THE DATE COULD BE ANYTIME FROM OCTOBER 20 - 31ST. I HAVE ENCLOSED A BIOGRAPHY ON THE ARTIST PLUS SOME INFORMATION ABOUT THE EXHIBITION. I LOOK FORWARD TO YOUR EARLY REPLY,

SINCERELY, T. BJORNSON (MISS), CO-ORDINATOR.

FIGURE 3.4
Letter from T. Bjornson to Bob Fortune "c/o C B C," Vancouver, September 24, 1969. Douglas Gallery Archives. Courtesy of Ace Gallery, Los Angeles.

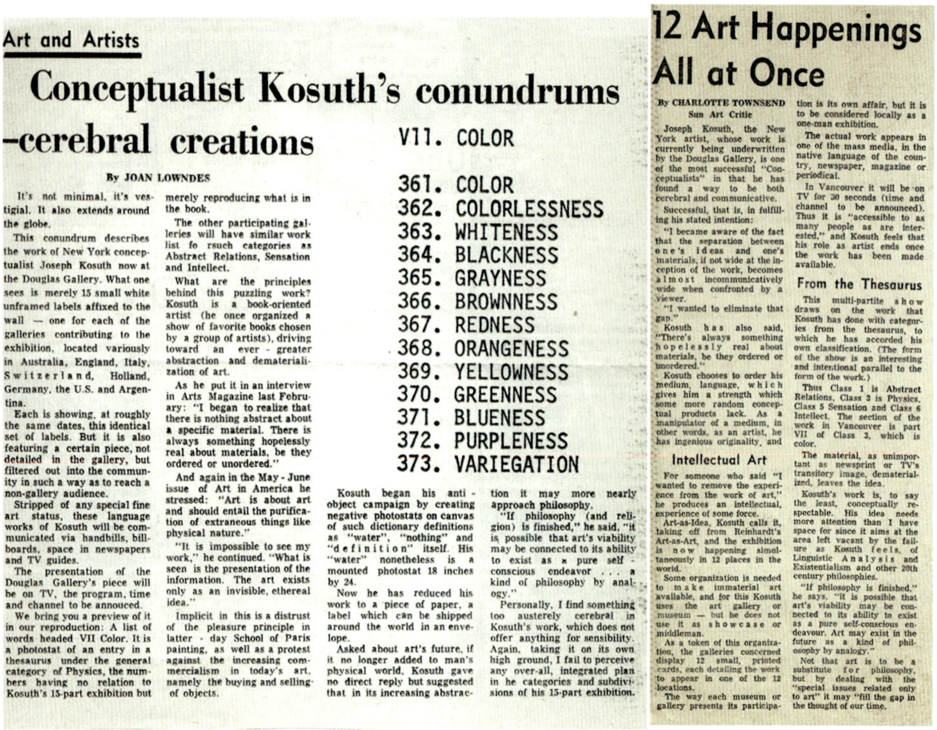

Art and Artists

Conceptualist Kosuth's conundrums —cerebral creations

By JOAN LOWNDES

It's not minimal, it's vestigial. It also extends around the globe.

This conundrum describes the work of New York conceptualist Joseph Kosuth now at the Douglas Gallery. What one sees is merely 15 small white unframed labels affixed to the wall — one for each of the galleries contributing to the exhibition, located variously in Australia, England, Italy, Switzerland, Holland, Germany, the U.S. and Argentina.

Each is showing, at roughly the same dates, this identical set of labels. But it is also featuring a certain piece, not detailed in the gallery, but filtered out into the community in such a way as to reach a non-gallery audience.

Stripped of any special fine art status, these language works of Kosuth will be communicated via handbills, billboards, space in newspapers and TV guides.

The presentation of the Douglas Gallery's piece will be on TV, the program, time and channel to be annouced.

We bring you a preview of it in our reproduction: A list of words headed VII Color. It is a photostat of an entry in a thesaurus under the general category of Physics, the numbers having no relation to Kosuth's 15-part exhibition but merely reproducing what is in the book.

The other participating galleries will have similar work list fo rsuch categories as Abstract Relations, Sensation and Intellect.

What are the principles behind this puzzling work? Kosuth is a book-oriented artist (he once organized a show of favorite books chosen by a group of artists), driving toward an ever - greater abstraction and dematerialization of art.

As he put it in an interview in Arts Magazine last February: "I began to realize that there is nothing abstract about a specific material. There is always something hopelessly real about materials, be they ordered or unordered."

And again in the May - June issue of Art in America he stressed: "Art is about art and should entail the purification of extraneous things like physical nature."

"It is impossible to see my work," he continued. "What is seen is the presentation of the information. The art exists only as an invisible, ethereal idea."

Implicit in this is a distrust of the pleasure principle in latter - day School of Paris painting, as well as a protest against the increasing commercialism in today's art, namely the buying and selling of objects.

VII. COLOR

361. COLOR
362. COLORLESSNESS
363. WHITENESS
364. BLACKNESS
365. GRAYNESS
366. BROWNNESS
367. REDNESS
368. ORANGENESS
369. YELLOWNESS
370. GREENNESS
371. BLUENESS
372. PURPLENESS
373. VARIEGATION

Kosuth began his anti - object campaign by creating negative photostats on canvas of such dictionary definitions as "water", "nothing" and "definition" itself. His "water" nonetheless is a mounted photostat 18 inches by 24.

Now he has reduced his work to a piece of paper, a label which can be shipped around the world in an envelope.

Asked about art's future, if it no longer added to man's physical world, Kosuth gave no direct reply but suggested that in its increasing abstraction it may more nearly approach philosophy.

"If philosophy (and religion) is finished," he said, "it is possible that art's viability may be connected to its ability to exist as a pure self - conscious endeavor . . . a kind of philosophy by analogy."

Personally, I find something too austerely cerebral in Kosuth's work, which does not offer anything for sensibility. Again, taking it on its own high ground, I fail to perceive any over-all, integrated plan in he categories and subdivisions of his 15-part exhibition.

12 Art Happenings All at Once

By CHARLOTTE TOWNSEND
Sun Art Critic

Joseph Kosuth, the New York artist, whose work is currently being underwritten by the Douglas Gallery, is one of the most successful "Conceptualists" in that he has found a way to be both cerebral and communicative.

Successful, that is, in fulfilling his stated intention:

"I became aware of the fact that the separation between one's ideas and one's materials, if not wide at the inception of the work, becomes almost incommunicatively wide when confronted by a viewer.

"I wanted to eliminate that gap."

Kosuth has also said, "There's always something hopelessly real about materials, be they ordered or unordered."

Kosuth chooses to order his medium, language, which gives him a strength which some more random conceptual products lack. As a manipulator of a medium, in other words, as an artist, he has ingenious originality, and

Intellectual Art

For someone who said "I wanted to remove the experience from the work of art," he produces an intellectual, experience of some force.

Art-as-Idea, Kosuth calls it, taking off from Reinhardt's Art-as-Art, and the exhibition is now happening simultaneously in 12 places in the world.

Some organization is needed to make immaterial art available, and for this Kosuth uses the art gallery or museum — but he does not use it as showcase or middleman.

As a token of this organization, the galleries concerned display 12 small, printed cards, each detailing the work to appear in one of the 12 locations.

The way each museum or gallery presents its participation is its own affair, but it is to be considered locally as a one-man exhibition.

The actual work appears in one of the mass media, in the native language of the country, newspaper, magazine or periodical.

In Vancouver it will be on TV for 30 seconds (time and channel to be announced). Thus it is "accessible to as many people as are interested," and Kosuth feels that his role as artist ends once the work has been made available.

From the Thesaurus

This multi-partite show draws on the work that Kosuth has done with categories from the thesaurus, to which he has accorded his own classification. (The form of the show is an interesting and intentional parallel to the form of the work.)

Thus Class 1 is Abstract Relations, Class 3 is Physics, Class 5 Sensation and Class 6 Intellect. The section of the work in Vancouver is part VII of Class 3, which is color.

The material, as unimportant as newsprint or TV's transitory image, dematerialized, leaves the idea.

Kosuth's work is, to say the least, conceptually respectable. His idea needs more attention than I have space for since it aims at the area left vacant by the failure as Kosuth feels, of Linguistic Analysis and Existentialism and other 20th century philosophies.

"If philosophy is finished," he says, "it is possible that art's viability may be connected to its ability to exist as a pure self-conscious endeavour. Art may exist in the future as a kind of philosophy by analogy."

Not that art is to be a substitute for philosophy, but by dealing with the "special issues related only to art" it may "fill the gap in the thought of our time.

FIGURE 3.5
(left) Joan Lowndes, review of *Joseph Kosuth—October 1969*, Douglas Gallery, Vancouver, in *The Province*, Art and Artists, Vancouver. Undated press clipping, Douglas Gallery archives. Courtesy of Ace Gallery, Los Angeles. *(right)* Charlotte Townsend, review of *Joseph Kosuth—October 1969*, Douglas Gallery, Vancouver, in *The Sun*, Vancouver. Undated press clipping, Douglas Gallery archives. Courtesy of Ace Gallery, Los Angeles.

most likely venue. The shift entailed here—from an uncommentaried appearance of the entry on "Color" to a mediated gallery presentation—was surely at odds with Kosuth's consistent advocacy of the "anonymous" presentation of the work in *The Second Investigation*. But it would seem that the gallery had few or no other options. Two reviews of the exhibition (fig. 3.5), presumably published shortly before or after the formal opening, use similar language to note that "program time and channel [were] to be announced," indicating the media presentation had not yet been resolved at this relatively late stage.[15] Although there are no documents accounting for what transpired with the *Hourglass* request (or even if there was a response), three cards in the archive reveal that the gallery successfully pursued its negotiations elsewhere at the CBC, with the assistance of a senior figure in the Vancouver art and media communities (fig. 3.6). The first card, headed "Joseph Kosuth," offers a reformulated production credit: "Vancouver Project co-ordinated in part by Richard Simmins in co-operation with the Douglas Gallery and

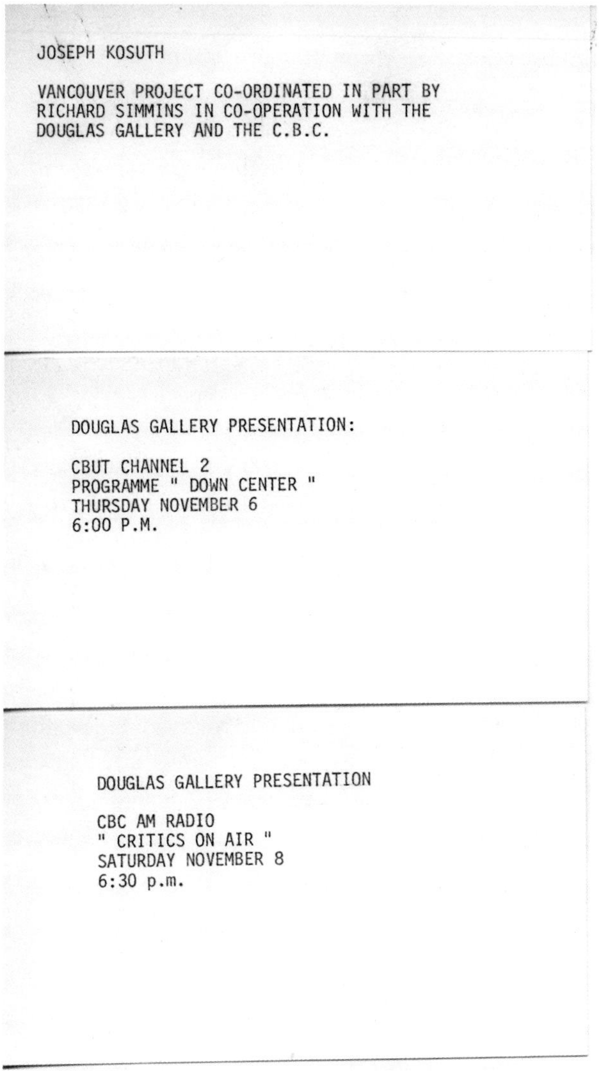
JOSEPH KOSUTH

VANCOUVER PROJECT CO-ORDINATED IN PART BY
RICHARD SIMMINS IN CO-OPERATION WITH THE
DOUGLAS GALLERY AND THE C.B.C.

DOUGLAS GALLERY PRESENTATION:

CBUT CHANNEL 2
PROGRAMME " DOWN CENTER "
THURSDAY NOVEMBER 6
6:00 P.M.

DOUGLAS GALLERY PRESENTATION

CBC AM RADIO
" CRITICS ON AIR "
SATURDAY NOVEMBER 8
6:30 p.m.

FIGURE 3.6
Three cards relating to *Joseph Kosuth—October 1969*, Douglas Gallery, Vancouver. Douglas Gallery archives. Courtesy of Ace Gallery, Los Angeles.

the C.B.C." The second and third cards are both headed "Douglas Gallery Presentation." One reads, "CBUT Channel 2/Programme 'Down Center'/Thursday November 6/6:00 P.M."; the other, "CBC AM radio/'Critics on Air'/Saturday November 8/6: 30 p.m."

It appears that the gallery solicited assistance with the media presentation of "VII. Color" from Simmins, who had been director of the Vancouver Art Gallery (1963–1967) and in the late 1960s and early 1970s worked as an art critic at *Vancouver Province* (1968–1972) before taking up the directorship of the Art Gallery of Greater Victoria in 1973. Several aspects of this arrangement remain unclear: the precise form of the presentation on the topical TV program *Down Centre* that aired on CBUT-DT, the station in Vancouver owned and operated by CBC Television, which still serves as the Pacific

Time Zone flagship of the network; whether Simmins or Douglas Chrismas, the gallery owner, appeared in the broadcast to offer an introduction or other remarks; and how long the thesaurus entry remained onscreen. The second media broadcast raises further questions, because a radio segment was not envisaged in the original plan of presentation. Simmins had connections with CBC's AM radio program *Critics on Air* and was a contributor, so it is possible that he took the lead and may have made the presentation. But it is unclear, again, how this was conceived and executed, whether the Kosuth exhibition was simply discussed by Simmins, Chrismas, and others or was actually "presented," in the presumably unsanctioned form, for example, of a "reading." In any event, the gallery documents affirm that "VII. Color" was either presented in, or the subject of, two media appearances that marked the first use of TV as well as the unanticipated and unsanctioned first radio presentation of the work.

Entry "VII. Color" from Class Three: Physics in the thesaurus's Synopsis of Categories commenced with "361. Color" and was followed by twelve terms, ten of which were nounal color conditions or effects ("-nesses," e.g., "366. Brownness") rather than unassociated adjectival descriptors (e.g., "brown"). Two additional terms—the second, "362. Colorlessness," and the last, "373. Variegation"—invoke the conditions of color absence and color mixtures or combinations (see fig. 3.7, bottom right). It seems clear that in addition to their comment on the constitution of the color spectrum in the form of a conceptual art palette rendered through the black and white of capitalized, typewritten text, the Vancouver-Douglas piece, like others in *The Second Investigation,* carries a subtext that relates to its context. In this case covert reference was made not to the physical location (city or gallery and their associated semantic fields) but to the medium in which the piece appeared: TV itself.

In a note written in 1969 Kosuth pointed to a series of technological feats and their scenes of visual transmission—including "flying to the moon by rocket, or by jet to Los Angeles," "the lights of La Vegas," and "even colored television and movies"—with which a contemporary artist could not hope to compete.[16] The inclusion of TV in *The Second Investigation* in the same year marks, then, a special moment of resistance to the dominance of such spectacles, and almost the only occasion when the artist attempted to strike back against the rhetorical force of big media in kind.[17] The moment of *15 locations* and *The Second Investigation* witnessed a new level of power, penetration, and cultural "believability" in the social diffusion of television in the United States (which, by the late 1960s, had arrived in some 60 million homes), as well as an acceleration

FIGURE 3.7
(opposite top) Color Television by Sylvania, General Telephone and Electronics advertisement, 1969. *(opposite bottom left)* Joseph Kosuth, *Four Words Four Colors,* 1966. Neon and transformer, 78 × 43/10 × 2½ inches. Courtesy of the artist. *(opposite bottom right)* Synopsis category "VII. Color," annotated by Joseph Kosuth, probably early 1969. Detail of a photocopy from the thesaurus. Joseph Kosuth archive, New York. Courtesy of the artist. Photograph by John C. Welchman.

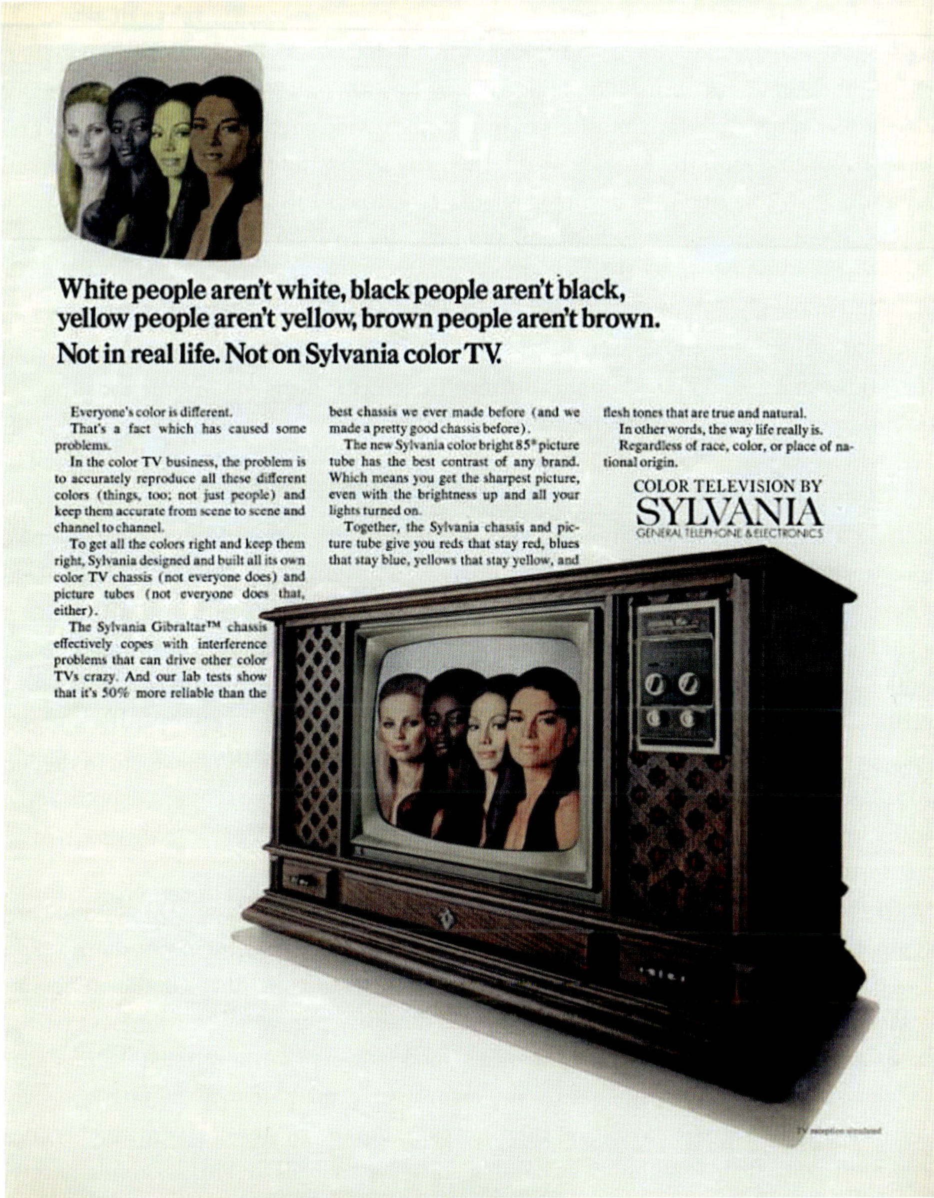

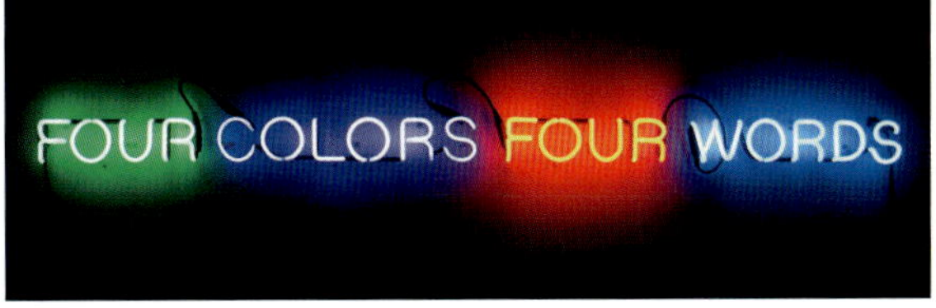

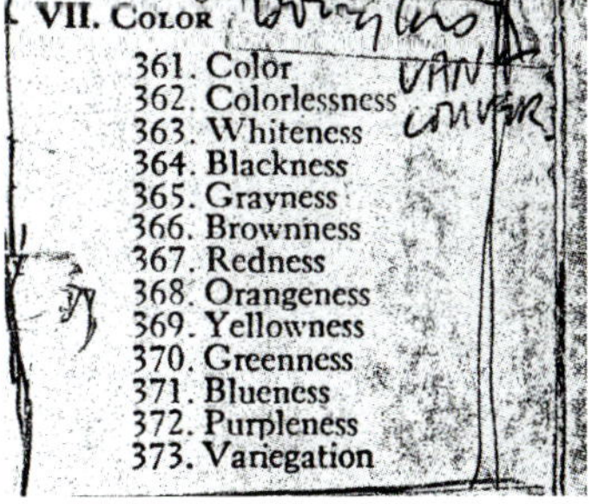
VII. COLOR
361. Color
362. Colorlessness
363. Whiteness
364. Blackness
365. Grayness
366. Brownness
367. Redness
368. Orangeness
369. Yellowness
370. Greenness
371. Blueness
372. Purpleness
373. Variegation

in the intensity of debate about its nature and effects, especially those of broadcast news. The beacon and leading indicator for mass spectacles such as the assassination of JFK, the Apollo moon mission alluded to by Kosuth, and Nixon's visit to China, TV also brokered the first transmissions of live combat, widespread destruction, and fatalities—beginning with the Korean War in the early 1950s and then, more viscerally and repetitively, by imaging the conflict in Vietnam between 1965 and 1975.

Two events can be said to bookend symbolically an interrogatory turn in the discourse around television at the end of the 1960s, crucial, I will argue, for any understanding of the formation and reception of the TV elements of *The Second Investigation*. The first is the notorious speech by Vice President Spiro Agnew in November 1969 to the Midwestern Regional Republican Committee criticizing the orientations, points of view, and liberal or Democratic bias of the staple TV news providers, ABC, CBS and NBC—which precipitated a mass response to the networks. Two years later, the CBS documentary *The Selling of the Pentagon* (broadcast in February, 1971) gave rise to calls for the revocation of station licenses. At around the same time a "truth in news broadcasting" bill was introduced into Congress, occasioning further rounds of debate (though it was not passed). Continuing a truth-denominated, media-critical tradition as old as the United States itself, these legislative and broadcast events should be set in the wider context of a wholesale shift in the social perception of the truthfulness of various media.[18] In November 1968, just under 50 percent of respondents to a Roper poll (published in March 1971) claimed that TV was the most believable form of media, with less than 20 percent offering the same opinion about newspapers. Importantly, advertisements and billboards registered virtually no credibility at all in this particular test case for media-denominated veracity.[19]

Of the many social conditions that inform such developments, several point to conceptual contexts that also underwrite Kosuth's negotiation with media in these years. The first is formed by another horizon of the reflexive criticality that Thomas Jefferson counseled for the sectional restructuring of the newspaper, which now generated circumstances in which even rightist rhetoric—such as Agnew's—lambasted the medium of television and demanded that its purveyors perform their own meta-critique by "turn[ing] their cultural powers on themselves."[20] As the spaces of the media became ever more contested—and politicized—new forms of analysis and infiltration emerged to challenge the old-order perception of the neutrality or objectivity of the airwaves and to draw attention to its dominant codes and discourses, including the provision of "information," the place of "editorial" comment, the montage of imagery, and the calibration of image, text, and voice.

This last interest is sufficiently significant (both for TV and for Kosuth) that it constitutes a second condition in itself. In an article in *Encounter* (May, 1970), British broadcaster Robin Day pointed to one of the defining emergent features of broadcast TV: its reliance on, and domination by, an endless flow of briefly glimpsed but often highly charged images, whose impact eclipses their verbal or textual correlates and is often deemed most "powerful" when silent, or unworded. "Words on TV," Day wrote, "tend to have their own limitations. They tend to be put in the background by the pictures, especially if these are extremely dramatic."[21] Day's notion of words forming a kind of generalized ground on which the figure of the emotive image is superimposed, or, more dramatically, poised to leap forward into the receiving consciousness of the viewer, provides, in its turn, a critical context for Kosuth's gesture of reverse camouflage. Kosuth's texts disturb the priority of both image and voice, driven as they are by the simple imperative that they be consumed by reading alone, or that they pass by the viewer/reader as a textual still life overlooked in the distracted march of the endless syntagm of TV images.

Kosuth's interruption of the iconic valence of the TV image and its sequences and his forced conversion of the viewing experience into either an act of readership or aversion precipitates a moment of counter-televisual resistance. But the TV slots don't, in fact, turn the cultural power of television back on itself, or at least not in terms predicated on the kind of reversibility Agnew and others argued for under the auspices of a political re-adjudication. Instead they arrest and collapse the imagistic flow of TV by putting it on pause so that it becomes, for thirty seconds, something like a cathode ray page. The words it bears are untethered from the customary idioms of TV text—synchronized speech, caption, or voice-over. "On air" for slightly longer than the duration of their literal readability, they stand ready to distribute information that also appears, at first glance, utterly sequestered from the languages of television—that is, it doesn't appear to sell, persuade, entertain, amuse, or even to inform according to the purportedly factographic logic of the "news." At the same time the visible text is not subject to a mode of legibility that is, in a literal sense—or, on the side of appearance—"difficult." That is to say, it is not cluttered, dense, intermittent, provisional, or wild. While mimicking the lineation of a thesaurus entry, it is typographically uninflected and visually stable or neutral.

In 1969, the advent of color TV was a relatively recent phenomenon. The brief era of monochrome-compatible, electronic color television (1946–1953) had been interrupted during the Korean War, followed by the first successful color system, designed by RCA, which began commercial broadcasting after authorization by the FCC in December 1953. Prompted by Disney's *Wonderful World of Color* (which first aired in 1961), the shift from black and white to color was cemented in the mid-1960s, though it was not until 1966 (the same year that color TV was introduced in Canada) that NBC became the first US network to offer color coverage for all of its programming.[22] The Vancouver episode of the *Second Investigation* thus becomes a dissident marker for the infusion of color into TV culture, in dialogue with works that comment on the era of color in print media such as Warhol's *Marilyn Diptych* (1961), which also takes stock of the differences brokered by reproductive technologies between the horizons of color and black and white, overlaying these with questions of celebrity, pictoriality, and the grid (fig. 3.7, top).

The shift in media and entertainment from black and white to color—which was transacted in film in the early 1930s, in magazines in the 1940s and 1950s, and then on TV some years later—took another decade and half (from the point of view of *The Second Investigation*) to effect its popularizing bleed into the format of the daily newspaper. *USA Today,* a national paper introduced by Gannett in 1982, was one of the first newspapers to make heavy use of color in pictures, maps, and graphics—a move that still remains partial in these traditionalist media, as witnessed by the pink sheets of the *Financial Times;* the preference for ink dot drawings, or "hedcuts," rather than photographs of people in the non-lifestyle sections of the *Wall Street Journal;* and resistance to color by many non-tabloid titles until recently. Kosuth's deployment of color categories on television clearly has implications, then, beyond both the video medium itself and the redefinition of color through the pixel, which is one of its most unmistakable legacies. These begin with the introduction of type and faces clearly associated with the printing format onto the image- and sound-denominated screen. But they also include wider contexts for the negotiation with color associated with the strong chromatic regimens of the dominant forms of pictoriality in the late 1960s, notably Color Field painting, and with the new spectra of synthetic hues introduced by the widespread use of plastics and florescent lights among Minimalist artists. Kosuth, himself, of course had already taken up with the neon tube in *One and Eight—A Description* (1965), a piece that typically commented on its own constitution out of light and letters, and *Four Words Four Colors* (1966; fig. 3.7, bottom left), in which color was the subject of the self-affirming statement, among other pieces from the mid-1960s. He also produced an extended body of works using neon two decades later in *It Was It* (1986), *Word, Sentence, Paragraph* (1987–89) and related series, and has more recently used neon in both gallery and publicly sited works, including *ni apparence ni illusion* at the Musée du Louvre, Paris (2009) and *"An Interpretation of This Title": Nietzsche, Darwin and the Paradox of Content,* his contribution to the Edinburgh Festival in the same year.[23]

The neon technology with which Kosuth was one of the first artists to engage went through its own version of the incremental colorization that attended the development of the media of print, film, and TV in roughly the same time frame. The intense, glowing effects of neon were observed in Geissler tubes with the discovery of the element in 1898 (two years after the first public exhibition of projected motion pictures in the United States). Following their commercial development in the 1910s, early neon tubes had a very limited color range until the 1960s, when experiments with phosphor coating materials initiated after World War II generated a spectrum of some two dozen hues. Interestingly, one of the first neon signs—"NEON," purportedly fabricated around 1904 by Perley G. Nutting, founder and first president of the Optical Society of America (1916)[24]—was fashioned in a variant of the self-referential redundancy that Kosuth would later take up under the auspices of the tautological: four neon letters making one neon word that looks forward by implication to *Four Words Four Colors.*

Throughout his experiments with both neon and public media, however, Kosuth maintained his focus on the relations set out between text (black or black reversed into white by the Photostat process), the various "whitenesses" of page, ground, and wall, and the use of (generally) white neon light to formulate, illuminate, overlay, or cancel—sometimes all at once—the appearance of printed letters. These investigations and their specific fields of vision often correlated with enclosed gallery spaces, while Kosuth's earlier public media pieces had been, for the most part, received under the available light of the streets or with the assistance of the illumination devices associated with commercial signage. In "Meaning and Responsibility" (written in 1993), Kosuth reflected on his general commitment to the absence of color: "The elements I use are always achromatic unless there is a reason to use color for counting, as a code, to articulate, or give a functional, organizational order." Even when he used them, then, colors "never function as 'expressive' in the visual sense, simply as meaningful." The rationale for this refusal of chromatic connotation relates to Kosuth's equally indomitable advocacy for the unartlike appearance and anonymity of his work, coupled with a disengagement from "aesthetics" and a "look [that] remains neutral."[25]

Aspects of this orientation were already in place in what was perhaps the first of Kosuth's conceptual projects, *Notebook on Water 1965–66*[26]—which gave rise, in turn, to one of the earliest of the board-mounted Photostats of *The First Investigation—Titled (Art as Idea as Idea)* [*Water*] (1966)[27]—and launched an intermittent but career-long investigation of the morphological nonspecificity of water, what Kosuth termed "its formless, colorless quality."[28] These interests offer another point of contact with, and differentiation from, the work of Hans Haacke, who in the same years took up with the both the physical and "systemic," and the social and ecological implications of water in his first solo exhibition, *Wind and Water* at Galerie Schmela, Düsseldorf, Germany (1965); *Condensation Cube* (1963–65), exhibited the following year at the Howard Wise Gallery in New York; and *Rhinewater Purification Plant* (1972).[29] Several of Kosuth's later public projects, notably *The language of equilibrium / Il linguaggio dell'equilibrio* created on the Island of San Lazzaro degli Armeni, Venice, in 2007, explicitly addressed the aqueous context in which they were sited—in this case by returning to the definition of *water,* which constitutes one of two strands of conceptual intervention in and around the monastic headquarters of the Armenian Mekhitarian Order for which the island is named. *The language of equilibrium* was also marked by a certain loosening of the austerity, if not the focus, of Kosuth's commitment to chromatic neutrality as the neon words appended to four architectural locations—the bell tower, northwest monastery wall, promontory, and observatory—were fashioned in yellow neon, "chosen," following Georg Andreas Böckler's *Ars heraldica* (1688), "because of the symbolic understanding of yellow at the time of the founding of the monastery as meaning 'virtue, intellect, esteem and majesty.'"[30] This is clearly an exception, though possibly one that proves the rule, to David Bachelor's dictum that "to fall into color is to run out of words."[31]

In addition to their reflexive and contradictory relation to the medium in which they appear, the TV segments drop disorienting parentheses of orderly textual abstraction into the seamlessly claustrophobic, serial flow of images and sounds brokered by television.

There is a sense in which Day and other perceptive commentators on the first heyday of TV already saw these segments coming—though not, of course, on the same terms. Day takes pains to point out the defining difference between the image repertoire of death, dismemberment, famine, sex, and violence (in the process of becoming the staples of TV in this era and addressed in their print-media formats by Warhol) and the nature of anything we might understand through conceptualization: the domineering sight of suffering or gratification, he writes, "may have a much more powerful impact than abstract concepts."[32] I want to suggest that a more relentless version of Day's observation, beset by conditions outside his purview as a TV personality and critic, furnished the grounds for Kosuth's intervention. The core of Day's observation—made in overlapping and related language by scores of media commentators over the last half century—surely turns on the sheer unstoppability of the emotive, imagistic run-on of television. How better to catch it off guard or set it up against itself than by administering a thirty-second antidote in the form of an utter reversal of these seemingly inevitable conditions?

Perhaps it takes a philosopher of language who is also a TV viewer and political activist to point up another implication of Kosuth's interruptive infiltration into the spacing system of television: the question of how we can read through, or back against, the infinite ribbon of sound, color, and light excreted by the TV set. For John Searle, whose *Speech Acts: An Essay in the Philosophy of Language* (1969) was published in the same year as the launch of *The Second Investigation,* the uncompromising and ideologically weighted directives of TV could be undermined only by reading between its lines: "I watch TV news," he wrote, "not to find out what's happening, but what *other people think* is happening."[33] The Möbius effect of TV's relation to truth, fact, accuracy—and thinking, or intention, itself—has, of course, become a staple of media theory, with one strand of reflection dating back to Jefferson and another woven from the threads of Searlean discourse. In "Modal Ontology of Television: How to Create Social Objects," Lars Lundsten, for example, uses Searle's terminology to argue that "the facts such as they appear on television belong to different types than the facts we encounter when we take part in the events or observe them on location."[34] Using tactics of infiltration and displacement, backed up by propositional logic, to intervene in the question of site, location, and representation, Kosuth points to a related round of constitutional fallacies in the "makeup" of TV, abetted by its new color compact, underlining its dissembling seductions by brazenly subtracting them from the screen. What stands defiantly in their place is an unexegeticized parable of conceptual variegation, a spectrum analysis pointing to the underlying fact that everything that passes through the tube is truly not just black and white.

NOTES

1. This essay is adapted from my longer text "Ideas Being Given: Joseph Kosuth's Media and Public Projects from *The Second Investigation* (1968–70) to the 2010s," in *Joseph Kosuth,*

Re-defining the Context of Art, 1968–2014: The Second Investigation *and Public Media* (Berlin: Sternberg, forthcoming, 2015).

2. Peter Mark Roget, Preface to the First Edition, 1852, in *Roget's Thesaurus of English Words and Phrases,* new edition, completely revised and modernized by Robert A. Dutch (Oxford: Longman, 1962), xxi. Roget's descendants John Lewis Roget and Samuel Romilly Roget brought out revised and enlarged editions in 1879 and 1936 respectively.

3. This information derives from the wall label presented as part of Kosuth's exhibition at the Douglas Gallery, Vancouver, in October 1969.

4. Dieter Daniels, "Television—Art or Anti-art?: Conflict and Cooperation between the Avant-Garde and the Mass Media in the 1960s and 1970s," Media Art Net, www.medienkunstnetz.de/themes/overview_of_media_art/massmedia/1/.

5. Chris Salter, *Entangled: Technology and the Transformation of Performance* (Cambridge, MA: MIT Press, 2010), 118.

6. The "Manifesto del Movimento Spaziale per la televisione" (Television Manifesto of the Spatial Movement), Milan, May 17, 1952, was signed by seventeen artists associated with the Movimento Spaziale (Spatial Movement), including Lucio Fontana; the manifesto is reprinted in Media Art Net, www.medienkunstnetz.de/source-text/70/. Fontana's visionary attempt to "free" art from materiality, coupled with the proposed presentation of the manifesto during an actual TV broadcast, his interest in other media forms, and his pioneering use of neon, connect aspects of this early invocation of television more directly with Kosuth's *The Second Investigation* than with the work of Paik, Vostell, and others in the early and mid-1960s. See also Anthony G. White, "TV or Not TV: Lucio Fontana's 'Luminous Images in Movement,'" *Grey Room* no. 34 (Winter 2009): 6–27.

7. Wolf Vostell, *TV-Décoll/age no. 1,* 1958–1963, Media Art Net, www.medienkunstnetz.de/works/tv-decowage/.

8. These details are from an invitation card for the Smolin Gallery exhibition addressed to David Tudor and postmarked May 20, 1963, in the Special Collections at the Getty Research Institute, Los Angeles.

9. Douglas Chrismas kindly shared with the author copies of documents from the Douglas Gallery archives, which are now at Ace Gallery, Los Angeles.

10. Two reviews, reprinted as fig. 3.5, of the Douglas Gallery exhibition, one by Charlotte Townsend in *The Sun* and the other by Joan Lowndes in the Art and Artists section of *The Province,* give different numbers: Lowndes states 15, and Townsend 12. Townsend may be citing from a gallery announcement or press release based on the Siegelaub memo described in note 12. The Douglas Gallery archive has photographs of fifteen "title-pieces."

11. The annotated diagram, marked in what appears to be blue crayon, is in the Douglas Gallery archives.

12. Discussion and citations in this and the subsequent paragraph are from Siegelaub's planning document in the Douglas Gallery archives.

13. Few accounts of *15 locations 1969/70 / Joseph Kosuth / Art as Idea as Idea 1966–70* have noted these parameters. A partial exception is Charles Green's discussion of the exhibition at Pinacotheca, Australia (October 31 to November 14, 1969), which gives details about the flier. Green, *The Third Hand: Collaboration in Art from Conceptualism to Postmodernism* (Minneapolis: University of Minnesota Press, 2001), 203, n10.

14. Robert (Bob) Fortune (1925–2006) was a radio presenter with CKMO and CKWX Vancouver in the late 1940s, the CBUT Vancouver weatherman (1954–75), and host of CBC-TV Vancouver's *Hourglass* from the late 1960s. Quoted by his family in an obituary, the self-described left-handed weatherman wrote that in retirement he had "paused to split shakes, probe stars, write (you need a soft cushion), build boats, invent things, sail the oceans, watch barnacles, introduce kids to the magic of the sky, fly in it, carve wood, sweep up, practice Chinese calligraphy (never in the presence of the Chinese), grapple with philosophy, Love the world." It remains unclear whether his earlier philosophical grappling extended to providing a platform for Kosuth's thesaurus entries in late October or early November 1969. Jack Bennest, "Vancouver's First TV Weatherman Passes," RadioWest.ca (blog), June 7, 2006 (7:57 P.M.), http://radiowest.ca/forum/viewtopic.php?f=12&t=129&start=0.

15. Preserved in the Douglas Gallery and the Kosuth archives as clippings without dates, both reviews (see note 10 and fig. 3.5) state that "time and channel [are] to be announced" (Townsend) and "program time and channel to be announced" (Lowndes).

16. Joseph Kosuth, "Footnote to Poetry," in *Art after Philosophy and After: Collected Writings, 1966–1990*, by Joseph Kosuth, ed. Gabriele Guercio (Cambridge, MA: MIT Press, 1991), 36.

17. The first two items on the instruction card for "June 7, Saturday" from *The Fourth Investigation* recapitulate the examples cited in "footnote to Poetry":

1. Take a jet ride to Los Angeles
2. (or) Visit Las Vegas

To these, Kosuth adds two further tasks: "Read at random through the McGraw Hill Encyclopedia of Space. McGraw Hill, N.Y." and "Look at Manhattan from the top of the Empire State Building." Jean-Christophe Ammann and Marianne Eigenheer, eds., *Terza, Quarta, Quinta, Sesta & Settima Investigazione* (1968–1971), vol. 2 (Lucerne: Kunstmuseum Luzern, 1973), 9. Published on the occasion of Kosuth's first retrospective exhibition, May 27 to June 24, 1973, the Lucerne volumes offer the most substantial documentation to date of Kosuth's *Investigations*.

18. As I note in the longer text (see note 1), Thomas Jefferson's persistent criticism of newspapers, the most powerful media form from the birth of the nation until the 1960s, was dominated by what he viewed as their defection from standards of truth and accuracy coupled with abuses of freedom "carried to a length never before known or borne by any civilized nation." Thomas Jefferson to Marc-Auguste Pictet (1803), in Andrew Adgate Lipscomb and Albert Ellery Bergh, eds., *The Writings of Thomas Jefferson: Memorial Edition*, vol. 10 (Washington, DC: Thomas Jefferson Memorial Association of the United States, 1903–04), 357.

19. Irving E. Fang, *Television News: Writing, Editing, Filming, Broadcasting* (New York: Hastings House, 1968), 11–13.

20. Robin Day, quoted in Fang, *Television News*, 20.

21. Day, quoted in Fang, *Television News*, 22.

22. "Color Television History," About.com Inventors, http://inventors.about.com/library/inventors/blcolortelevision.htm.

23. See John C. Welchman, "Histories and Subjects in Contingency," in *Joseph Kosuth, "ni apparence ni illusion,"* catalogue for exhibition October 2009 to April 2010 (French and English; Paris: Musée du Louvre Editions, 2009); and John C. Welchman, "A Crab in the Tree," in *Joseph Kosuth, "An Interpretation of This Title": Nietzsche, Darwin and the Paradox of*

Content, catalogue for exhibition August–September 2009 (Edinburgh: Edinburgh University Library, Georgian/Talbot Rice Gallery, 2009); republished in *Joseph Kosuth, "An Interpretation of This Title": Nietzsche, Darwin and the Paradox of Content* (South Yarra, Australia: Macmillan, 2012), 10–15.

24. John N. Howard, "OSA's First Four Presidents," *Optics & Photonics News* (February 2009), www.opnmagazine-digital.com/opn/200902/?pg=14#pg14. Howard notes that the suggestion that Nutting's "NEON" sign was displayed at the Palace of Electricity at the Louisiana Purchase Exhibition of 1904 has been disputed because it would have antedated by a decade and a half the commercial availability of neon signage.

25. Joseph Kosuth, "Meaning and Responsibility," *Art and Design Magazine,* January–February 1994, 71. This publication served as the exhibition catalogue for *Ad Reinhardt J Kosuth F Gonzalez Torres: Symptoms of Interference, Conditions of Possibility,* Camden Arts Center, London, January 7–March 6, 1994.

26. Kosuth's contribution to the "Artists and Photographs" portfolio (1970), *Notebook on Water 1965–1966,* took the form of a 9½" × 12" printed manila envelope into which twelve individual plates and a folded map were inserted.

27. *Titled (Art as Idea as Idea) [Water]* (1966) was gifted to the Solomon R. Guggenheim Museum, New York, by Leo Castelli in 1973.

28. Joseph Kosuth, quoted in Fiona Biggiero, "Infinitely Reflective Equilibrium: An Introductory Note" in Joseph Kosuth, *The language of equilibrium/Il linguaggio dell'equilibrio* (Milan: Electra, 2009), 5. The catalogue was published in association with the exhibition of the same title curated by Adelina von Fürstenberg on the Island of San Lazzaro, Venice, as a collateral exhibition of the 52nd Venice Biennale (2007).

29. *Hans Haacke 1967,* MIT List Visual Arts Center, October 21–December 31, 2011; exhibition brochure by curator Caroline A. Jones, http://listart.mit.edu/files/Haacke_ed_brochure.pdf.

30. Joseph Kosuth, "The Language of Equilibrium: A Statement by the Artist," in Kosuth, *The language of equilibrium,* 11.

31. David Batchelor, *Chromophobia* (London: Reaktion, 2000), 85.

32. Robin Day, quoted in Fang, *Television News,* 22–23.

33. John Searle, quoted in Fang, *Television News,* 32.

34. Lars Lundsten, "Modal Ontology of Television: How to Create Social Objects," *The American Journal of Economics and Sociology* 58, no. 2 (April 1999), 221–40. See also John R. Searle, *The Construction of Social Reality* (New York: Free Press, 1995), 120–25. For a critique of Searle's views, see Alex Viskovatoff, "Searle, Rationality, and Social Reality: Extensions and Criticisms—John Searle," *American Journal of Economics and Sociology* 62, no. 1 (January 2003).

4

ABSTRACT TRANSMISSIONS

Other Trajectories for Feminist Video

Siona Wilson

A scholarly consensus seems to have emerged that the Korean artist and composer Nam June Paik is the formative figure for our understanding of abstraction in video art. I don't contest this, as far as such narratives go. But the art-historical investment in linear, great-name histories leaves women artists in the margins when it comes to "origins" and establishing "genealogies." In contrast, the idea of the trajectory suggested in my title is intended to be more speculative; it marks the path of a projectile that is thrown across space and time and looked back upon from a later point. The trajectory, in this account, is provisional and tentative—one among several possibilities; it is the occasion for the exploration of an apparent contradiction: how can we reconcile feminism as a social critique, typically understood as a "materialist" mode of inquiry, with the question of abstraction, its apparent philosophical antithesis? Indeed applying the problematic of abstraction to feminist video practice might seem at the outset to be a rather eccentric trajectory, since debates about representation and identity—feminism's *social* address—have typically been at the forefront of established scholarly accounts. But I begin this essay with Paik because his work provides us with an entry point, a staging of the aforementioned contradiction, with his address to questions of abstraction alongside the imaging of female sexuality. If, as we will see, the Paik example seems to establish the relationship between sexual difference and video in terms of an opposition between femininity-as-representation and abstraction-as-form, how, then, do feminist-engaged video artists address and critically displace these terms?

Right from Paik's earliest beginnings in Germany, what we now group unproblematically under the curatorial heading of "video art" was in fact an engagement primarily with television. Before the now-familiar museum experience of the black box with its emphasis on the large-scale projected image, video practices entered the art world in the guise of televisual transmission. Take, for instance, the ubiquitous TV set (e.g., Frank Gillette and Ira Schneider's *Wipe Cycle* [1969] and Paik's *Magnet TV* [1965]), the space/time dynamics of the closed-circuit TV system (e.g., Bruce Nauman's *Live-Taped Corridor* [1970] and Dan Graham's *Time Delay Room* [1974]), the mock or alternative TV show (e.g., Martha Rosler's *Semiotics of the Kitchen* [1975] and Richard Serra's *Television Delivers People* [1973]), and a staple of the late 1960s and 1970s, the various experiments with interrupting or repurposing television transmission itself.

WGBH, a Boston radio station that in 1955 began television broadcasting, was at the forefront of artistic collaboration with televisual broadcast, or what we might more accurately refer to as "Television Art."[1] A particularly controversial work by Paik, *Electronic Opera #1* (1969), raises the question of sexual difference and female sexuality alongside the interruption to the transmission of televisual content, that is, the *abstraction* of the television broadcast. *Electronic Opera #1* is a layering of transmissions from three different cameras and the distorted visual manipulations applied to this footage that produced intense coloristic effects. But the controversy at the network about this work did not arise from Paik's use of "warped perspectives," to use Gene Youngblood's phrase,[2] but rather from a more conventional kind of interruption: his insertion of studio footage of a topless female dancer into the visual layers, distortions, and time-delay effects of his television art. Shot with three studio cameras, the footage from two of the perspectives was subject to the Paik-Abe Video Synthesizer, or "The Wobbulator," that turned the black-and-white television image into deeply saturated color.[3] The final effect is a simultaneous layering of images showing three perspectives on the same figure: the archetypical classical female tri-nude configuration, the three Graces, rendered in psychedelic moving color.

On the one hand, the nude figures, like the representation of "three hippies" and the "national political figures"—the other visual motifs featured in *Electronic Opera #1*—can be understood as distinctly *non*-abstract elements, and the iconographic invocation of the three Graces only further reinforces this view. On the other hand, as Raymond Williams has put it: "*Unlike all previous communications technologies, radio and television were* systems primarily devised for transmission and reception as abstract processes, with little or no definition of preceding content" [italics in the original].[4] Although the development of cinema was defined by production and its distribution networks came much later, the technical potential for television broadcast and the investment in the structure of dissemination, the *form,* came well before the production of content. Williams again: "*It is not only that the supply of broadcasting facilities preceded the demand; it is that the means of communication preceded their content*" [italics in the original].[5] Thus television as a technological formation is bound up with the question of abstraction.

As we have already noted, Paik took the question of media transmission—and its disruption—as the primary field of his artistic inquiry in the 1960s. Although *Electronic Opera #1* does not reach the same kind of zero degree of transmission as works like *Magnet TV,* its representational elements are put to work so that we must constantly confront the question of transmission itself. This is transmission, following Williams, as an *abstract* form. Indeed after the first short sequence of *Electronic Opera #1* showing the dancing woman, a voiceover announcement states: "Please follow this instruction: turn off your television sets." If, in the only remaining act of participation that television allows, we do indeed switch off the set (and as an announcement had already stated, "this is *participation* TV"), the blank screen would provide us with a certain exemplification of abstraction-as-negation, a televisual equivalent, perhaps, of the blank monochrome painting.

. . .

The first video art practitioners of the late 1960s and 1970s took up the Portapak camera after having established an art practice in another medium, so it should come as no surprise that the question of abstraction in relation to video practice would be bound up with current debates related to other established art forms. Furthermore, in the case of Vito Acconci, Richard Serra and Nancy Holt, and Lynda Benglis, their engagement with video was relatively short-lived, so, rather than serving as a hiatus from their other practice, it might be seen as a means of exploring related issues in another form. Take for example Benglis's *Female Sensibility* (1973), which shows fixed-camera head-and-shoulder views of Benglis and a female companion tonguing and kissing each other to a montaged soundtrack of right-wing Texas radio broadcasts. Susan Richmond, in her excellent close reading of this work, analyzes the absence of sensuality in the actions of the figures (for this purportedly lesbian scene) and suggests that Benglis treats her companion less as if she were a lover and more an abstract sculpture in formation: "Their fingers and tongues appear to 'form,' 'press,' 'penetrate,' and 'smooth' out surfaces and crevices—in other words, they imply artistic activities. In a 'sculptural' fashion, the two women foreground the female body as both source and product of their creative gestures."[6] Furthermore, the phrase "female sensibility" used for the work's title was a feminist leitmotif of the period, and Richmond suggests Benglis used it parodically to explore her own ambivalence about the gendered analysis of her abstract sculptural practice. In contrast to the overdetermined representation of the female body, the idea of a "female sensibility" suggests that a feminine mode of expression might be discernably at work at the level of form. Moreover, even though this feminist discourse was about discerning a gendered dimension within artistic form, with a focus in particular on abstract elements, the reference to *sensibility* (i.e., the sensible) suggests the antithesis of abstraction. This alerts us to the complex entanglements of abstraction and representation when sexual difference comes into play.

Benglis is featured as a negative example in an early critical essay on video art, Rosalind Krauss's "Video: The Aesthetics of Narcissism." Krauss argues that reflexivity is a central issue for early video practitioners. Indeed, the discourse of abstraction in 1960s art was focused on conflicts over the critical significance of reflexivity. Reflexivity, the reference to and exploration of the formal properties of a given medium to generate a critical tension between a work's form and content, had displaced the founding antithesis of representation versus abstraction that underpinned early-twentieth-century debates. In Krauss's account, the stakes in early video practice, a decisively *representational* form, lie in the manner in which it negotiates the art world discourse of reflexivity in relation to its mediatic parent, television. While Krauss acknowledges that television broadcast is the "support" for video art (as the canvas is for painting), she places a greater emphasis on the effect of the temporal loop than on the empty distributive form of television itself. In fact she might be said to *abstract* the temporal structure of television in her framing of video practice. As a result she does not refer to practitioners such as Paik, who worked closely with broadcast technology, or Rosler, whose work so insistently foregrounds the TV show format, but rather with video art made and presented within an autonomous art world context.[7]

Video art's reflexive mode, for Krauss and subsequent critics, is temporal.[8] The structure of televisual transmission, of both recorded and live materials, allows for a temporal loop of instantaneous feedback that Krauss understands in psychological terms: "The medium of video art," she argues, "is the psychological condition of the self split and doubled by the mirror reflection of *synchronous* feedback."[9] She uses the psychoanalytic term *narcissism,* suggesting that it is "so endemic to works of video that I find myself wanting to generalize it as *the* condition of the entire genre."[10] Krauss parses her artists in terms of their critical and uncritical relation to the question of reflexivity (with television as the implicitly negative term). The latter she condemns as merely "parodying the critical terms of abstraction"; falling short of reflexivity, these artists are instead only *reflective,* like a mirror. The mirror reflection is the production of symmetry, Krauss explains, whereas reflexivity, by contrast, "is a strategy to achieve a radical asymmetry from within."[11] With negative reference to Lynda Benglis's *Now* (1973)—showing Benglis being taped in a seemingly autoerotic interaction with her prerecorded double—the work, she argues, stages a closed feedback loop that is "bracketing out the text [i.e., history] and substituting it for the mirror-reflection."[12] No past, no history, and, most alarmingly, no subjectivity—*Now,* as Krauss reads it, presents a darkly cynical "displacement of the self . . . transforming the performer's subjectivity into another, mirror, object."[13]

In this essay Krauss articulates the codependences between the work's invocation of the abstract feedback loop of television and the representational depiction of the human body, typically the artist's body on the screen. The accusation of narcissism, clearly used as a negative term, is thus determined just as much by *what* is depicted as it is by the temporality evoked. "The body" she writes, "is therefore as it were centered between two machines that are the opening and closing of a parenthesis. The first of these is the camera; the second is the monitor, which re-projects the performer's image with the immediacy of a mirror."[14] While "the body" in Krauss's essay is not directly addressed in gendered terms (she discusses in equal measure both male and female on-screen bodies), the question of narcissism is, however, bound up with the issue of sexuality and the "riddle," as Freud puts it, of sexual difference.

First addressed by Freud in relation to homosexuality, narcissists, he suggests, take someone like themselves as their object-choice. This notion soon evolves into narcissism understood as a "stage" in sexual development where subjects take themselves as love object: self-love. While this is not the place to gloss the history of psychoanalytic theories of narcissism, a complex and fraught terrain, it should be noted that narcissism, as it is explored in Freud's writings, seems to be, or becomes, a particularly *feminine* condition.[15] This is all very peculiar, given that the mythic figure Narcissus, in Ovid's *Metamorphosis,* was a boy, not a girl. Adored and desired for his beauty by youths and nymphs alike, Narcissus refused all in a denial of sexuality—until, after rejecting the nymph Echo, he finds himself transfixed by the beauty of his own image reflected in a pool of water. Unaware he is looking at himself, he therefore is perpetually unable to attain the object of his desire. Sexuality as such remains beyond his reach. Furthermore, the story of Narcissus includes a female counterpart: Echo. He is trapped by sight, and she by sound, since Echo is condemned to repeat the words of others (in a fragmentary, incomplete form) and never to speak her own. While Freud and later Lacan (whose theory of the mirror stage is a rewriting of Freud on narcissism) do not attend to Echo, Gayatri Chakravorty Spivak has suggested that a feminist reading might yield something valuable from the part she plays. According to Spivak, Echo "is obliged to be imperfectly and interceptively responsive to another's desire."[16] Reading for sexual difference in relation to abstract video, I want to suggest that, following Spivak, we should also look for Echo, not only Narcissus. The story of Echo will help us to unhook the analysis of video from the primacy of the visual, so as to displace the opposition between femininity-as-representation and abstraction-as-form with which, in reference to Paik, we began.

Given that video is a visual medium that also includes sound, we might pay attention to the place of Echo, to the place of sound as well as image in our reflections on sexual difference. In doing so, we will find that the myth of Narcissus is not the "closing of a parenthesis" (and denial of history) that Krauss describes; rather, the repeated partial vocals of Echo keep the parenthesis open at one end. Like the empty, abstract form of televisual transmission, Echo repeats without being able to control the content of her speech. As Spivak argues, Narcissus is caught in a visual trap of "obstinate choice," whereas Echo, ensnared by the other's speech, is subject to "absolute chance."[17] An asymmetrical counterpart, then, he is enslaved to desire without knowledge, and she to knowledge without desire. An instrument of broadcast for an unwitting other's words, Echo, however, gives us repetition with *a difference.* In echoing only the final portion of a speaker's phrase, each repetition generates a singular statement. For example, when, rejecting her advances, Narcissus cries out "Desist!—hold off thy hands;—may sooner death / Seize me, than thou enjoy me."[18] To her mortifying shame, she echoes only the final words "enjoy me," and thereafter "gaunt famine shrivels up / Her skin" and her body perishes, as a result of her sexual rejection by Narcissus, leaving "nought but sound." Within the abstract form that is her mimetic fate, Echo nonetheless adds a complexity to our structure of abstract transmission, making each repetition at once a singular instance of difference.

. . .

Joan Jonas's *Organic Honey's Vertical Roll* (1973–79) (fig. 4.1) calls out for consideration in terms of the gendering of sound and image. Furthermore, the reverberating, asymmetrical relationship between sound and image in this example brings the question of sexual difference, representational forms, and abstraction-as-transmission (repetition and difference) into play with each other in a particularly rich way. Moreover, sound and imagery are carefully articulated in this work as distinctly different kinds of representation that likewise have their own modes of abstraction. *Organic Honey's Vertical Roll* is a videotape of a performance from 1972 that only later became available in the form of a video work itself. Jonas includes video equipment as part of a theatrical set; monitor and camera are used as a kind of prop to catalogue the interaction between various representational forms (pictorial, aural, and theatrical performance) and their abstraction through (partial) televisual transmission. As we will see, Jonas gives us transmission as repetition and difference because the vertical hold on the TV monitors has been altered, fragmenting all transmitted images into a "vertical roll." According to Ina Blom, early video practices with their use of "snow on the screen, uncontrollable vertical rolling of the picture, and the collapse of the image into horizontal bars across the screen testifies to the realm of unmagnetized particles and signaletic slippage."[19] This is the norm of video as an inherently unstable temporal medium that appears as a coherent image only when all the parts of the relay camera, recorder, and monitor—are aligned.

Elements of *Organic Honey's Vertical Roll* are known independently as individual works, including the opening scene, otherwise titled *Mirror Check* (1970). Nude, Jonas stands before the live audience examining the surface of her body methodically, from top to bottom, with a small vanity mirror. The title, *Mirror Check,* places an emphasis on the visual, on the self-conscious staging of the performer's body, under examination. Femininity-as-display is put into tension with the invocation of an everyday self-conscious personal "checking" in the mirror to ensure a flawless mask of femininity for the world. At the same time, an aural framing overwrites this visual training in the maintenance of femininity: *Mirror Check* suggests the technical "testing" of sound equipment, the "sound check" that precedes a musical presentation. "Check, check, one two, one two" is part of the preperformance preparations often conducted in front of the live audience.[20] Furthermore, the soundtrack for *Mirror Check* is the low hiss of white noise. Although we see a visual image, transmission is simultaneously also empty, or, in Williams's terms, without content: abstract. Like Paik's various attempts to disrupt the

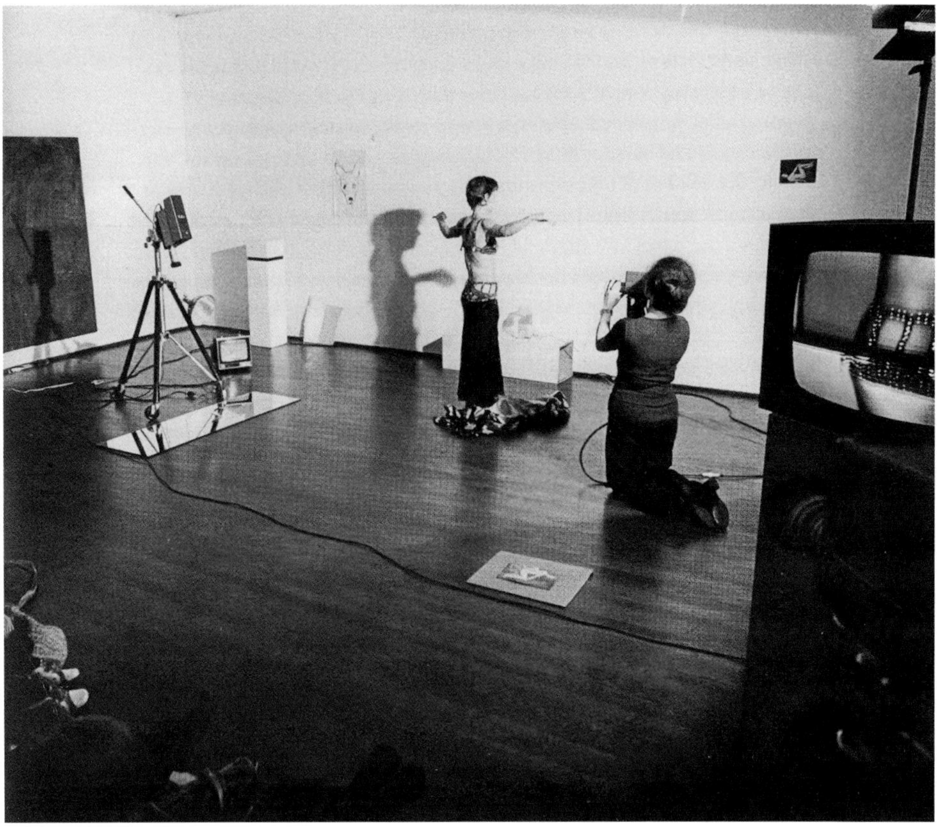

FIGURE 4.1
Joan Jonas, *Organic Honey's Vertical Roll,* 1973–99. Videotape, black and white, sound; 15 minutes. Courtesy Rosamund Felsen Gallery. Photograph by James Patrick.

transmission of televisual content on a visual level, the failure to achieve an aural connection draws our attention to *sound*-as-transmission—the realm of Echo—and this at the same time marks the emptiness of transmission as a form. Thus the female nude is, at the outset, juxtaposed with abstraction-as-transmission in an asymmetrical staging of image and sound. On completing her *Mirror Check,* Jonas walks off stage; the camera shifts stage right to reveal a large television monitor. Two other performers then carry around the stage a mirror that has the same dimensions as the TV monitor; it is walked across the stage facing outward to reflect the audience, before a cameraperson, Babette Mangolte, appears on the stage.

For the rest of the performance, Mangolte films Jonas in different costumes, and the visuals are fed live into the large monitor. Later an additional smaller monitor is also present on stage, and this doubling of the transmitted materials evokes the multiple reception of television as a structure. The mirror is another kind of surface for visual imaging; together with the drawings, photographs, a mask, and various costumes, its representational mode, the shimmering reflection, is subject to the unifying logic of the gray televisual feedback. But transmission is interrupted because of the constantly flickering "vertical roll." Again we are made aware of the question of transmission as the fragmented imagery scrolls and jumps up the screen. All of this appears as an incomplete, partial echo flickering again and again, up and down in the rhythmic folds of the vertical roll.

Rather than Narcissus's mirror, then, I want to suggest that *Organic Honey* teaches us that the logic of video is in the unthinking repetition that is Echo's fate. The partial reiteration of the image in the form of the fragmented vertical roll is also like Echo's repetition in that, as Ovid recounts, she reiterates only the last part of the other's sentence. This is repetition with difference. Furthermore, the end section of *Organic Honey* includes the staging of a clash between Narcissus and Echo. As the notes for the script put it, "Honey hits mirror obsessively with large silver spoon, trying to break her image."[21] This harsh, rhythmic thwacking of metal on glass is visualized by the regular jumps of the monitor's vertical roll. The flickering roll of the image echoes the repeated beat of the discordant, violent sound like an iteration of the trap that Echo is in. With this emphasis on the sonic staging, the feminine in Jonas's video is articulated at the level of form as the open parenthesis of repetition and difference.

· · ·

Most accounts of the proliferation of video art in the late 1960s and 1970s are underpinned by a casually techno-determinist logic. After the Portapak camera entered the commercial market around 1967, video production became more readily affordable to artists. Artists made videos, it seems, because the equipment to do so sat waiting for them in stores. Like most historical accounts of the social development of television, this suggests that the technology, as Williams puts it, is a "self-acting force."[22] Williams also suggests an alternative, social-historical approach that asks how TV fulfills "known social needs, purposes and practices to which the technology is not marginal but central."[23] Attending to the social function of television at the point of reception suggests another important dimension to the gendered coding of video art: the domestic family context. This is the modern theater for the formative experience of sexual difference, Freud's so-called family romance.

Keeping in mind our gendered division of image and sound, Narcissus and Echo, I will draw upon an example by Martha Rosler that evokes sound and femininity in a significant way. Again the question of transmission as abstraction is brought to the fore and bound up with sexual difference. Moreover, Rosler is an artist centrally engaged with TV as *the* dominant visual technology of the time, one that mediates and produces the political world through the experiential everyday. In this particular example, *Domination and the Everyday* (1978) (fig. 4.2), she reveals the extent to which the home is a complex site for the construction of sexual identity in relation to a broader political context.

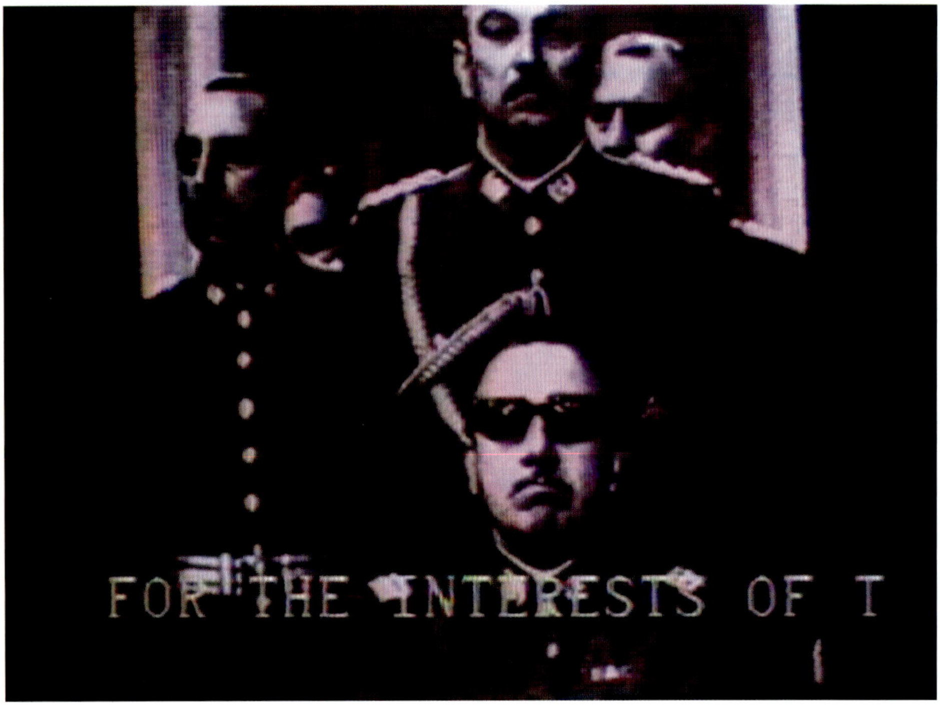

FIGURE 4.2
Martha Rosler, *Domination and the Everyday*, 1978. Videotape, color, sound; 32 minutes, 7 seconds. Courtesy Electronic Arts Intermix (EAI), New York.

Although the development of television can be traced back to communication technologies of the nineteenth century and is one part of the complex social changes brought about by modernity, it did not enter American homes as a domestic commodity until the 1950s. If it were not for the interruption of the Second World War, television would have proliferated a decade and a half earlier.[24] It therefore appeared at the tail end of the radical social transformations brought about by modernity. "An increased awareness of mobility and change, not just as abstractions but as lived experiences," says Williams, "led to a major redefinition, in practice and then in theory, of the function and process of social communication."[25] Television "served an at once mobile and home-centered way of living: a form of *mobile privatization*" [italics in the original].[26] Seen through the lens of sexual politics, Williams's mobile privatization becomes Betty Friedan's "feminine mystique."[27] Privatization is psychologized and politicized in this classic second-wave feminist text into a critique of the social isolation of the middle-class American housewife. The motif of the home as a figure for women's social oppression is especially evident in West Coast feminist practice. In installation art, *Womanhouse* (1972) is a good example; in relation to video art, Martha Rosler is a central figure. Of all the early video practitioners, Rosler is the most thematically engaged with the gendered televisual content. *Semiotics of the Kitchen* (1975) and *The East Is Red, The West Is Bending* (1977) are staged as mock cooking shows; *Losing: Portrait of the Parents* (1977) evokes the television documentary of family tragedy; and *Vital Statistics of a Citizen Simply Obtained* (1977) operates like an alternative game show. While these examples animate different genres of television, *Domination and the Everyday* (1978) engages most directly with television as a form in relation to the domestic context as the domain for gendered-subject formation.

The soundtrack of *Domination and the Everyday* is a recording of Rosler and her infant son at home going about the quotidian routines of a mother and child. This "maternal" everyday contrasts with the "paternal" image-track, which is governed by photographs of masculine political and commercial authority figures and family groups and a scrolling text of political analysis. The relationship between the textual and verbal levels—one analytic and the other not—is complex, and the video turns upon the gender differentiation established between sound and image. The dialogue between mother and child envelops the whole videotape, from the opening color bars (a figure for transmission interrupted) at the beginning to the same color bars at the end. The audio seems to be a completely unedited section of domestic soundscape, a fragment from the continuing flow of everyday life. This maternalized "feminine" realm of sound contrasts with the horizontal scrolling text that demands our intellectual attention: word as logic, analytic, rational. Viewing means reading and comprehending, and in the process Rosler's unremarkable conversation with her son begins to fade into the background: words become noise, a murmuring babble without significant meaning. To follow and comprehend the text renders the soundtrack an aural abstraction of the domestic. The visual domain is disembodied, authoritative, and masculine, and the auditory realm is an embodied sonic space of maternal care. Meaning and cognition are put into a relationship with abstraction as continuous transmission into the domestic space, or as Williams first put it, televisual "flow." In doing so, Rosler raises the question of sexual difference as the backdrop for our process of meaning making. This is abstraction understood as a philosophical question.

"Gender," Spivak has suggested, "is our first instrument of abstraction." "To theorize in the abstract," she explains, "we need a difference. However we philosophize sensible and intelligible, abstract and concrete, etc., the first difference we perceive materially is sexual difference."[28] This insight fundamentally displaces the contradiction with which we began. Although feminism as a form of *social* critique seems to exist at the other end of the spectrum from abstraction, Spivak suggests that gender, as the first perceivable difference, is "our tool for abstraction."[29] Kaja Silverman connects this idea specifically to sound. The mother's voice, she argues, "provides the first axis of Otherness" but, so we do not see this as only a senseless blanket of sound, she goes on to say that it "first charts out and names the world for the infant subject."[30] In *Domination and the Everyday*, Rosler gives us both. Listening to the mother-child conversation, we note her didactic role as parent, but the insistent demand made by the scrolling text also establishes a gendered contrast wherein the maternal voice becomes an abstraction. Susan Hiller's video installation *Belshazzar's Feast, the Writing on Your Wall* (1983–84) (fig. 4.3) also emphasizes the domain of televisual reception and a different, spectral, interruption of transmission. The television monitor is part of an installation that includes the bare bones of a living room space—couch, armchairs, rug, and cushions—all oriented toward the dominant presence of the television set. The wall includes a series of photographs that have been overpainted with abstract scribbles: the sign for writing, but without content or meaning. As in *Organic Honey's Vertical Roll,* in *Belshazzar's Feast* representation and abstraction—both visual and auditory—are put into relation with each other. The screen shows imagery of a fire, evoking the idea of the TV as the new hearth in the modern family home, the center that all of the family members are oriented to.[31] Although the crackling sound of the fire is part of the sound track, it is soon interrupted by an official-sounding voice announcing, "What the fire says: Take One," and three other vocal modes ensue. The first two oscillate between abstract vocal improvisations and a child's faltering explanation of the biblical story of Belshazzar told through reference to Rembrandt's painting of the subject. Jean Fisher describes this shifting back and forth between abstraction and representation as "a lilting glossolalia, or 'speaking in tongues,' . . . and the efforts of a child to relate the fragments of a story into a meaningful whole."[32] Having transgressed God's law, Belshazzar, during a dinner, receives a mysterious, untranslatable message inscribed on the wall by a hand in light. The mystic prophet Daniel later interprets the meaningless words as a premonition of Belshazzar's death. The form of the message is referenced in the video soundtrack through voice and image: the abstract vocals and the illegible scribble, or abstract marks on the images attached to the wall. The biblical myth of a senseless message in light becomes a metaphor for the third vocal mode: contemporary accounts of viewers receiving messages from extraterrestrials through the TV screen after broadcast had shut down for the evening. Like the writing on the wall at Belshazzar's feast, these accounts—found in newspapers and described in whispered speech—also predict coming disasters. The relationship between sound and sense, abstraction and sexual difference is a central component of this work. "There is something archaic, regressive about sound," Hiller has noted. "We hear in the womb before we see."[33] For Hiller, the abstraction of sound into the human voice without meaning—glossolalia, for example—touches upon this early unknowable experience.

Mona Hatoum, in *Measures of Distance* (1988) (fig. 4.4), takes this feminist trajectory into the space of cultural difference and diasporic separation. In this video, Hatoum, a London-based Palestinian artist, describes a period when she was separated from her family because of the Lebanese war. The soundtrack is drawn from the mother's and daughter's letters to each other. These letters, written in Arabic, have been translated into English and are read out by the artist, but the voice of Hatoum as the English-speaking narrator is set against a background recording of female voices (hers and her mother's) chatting in Arabic, her mother tongue. Like Rosler and her son, the domestic

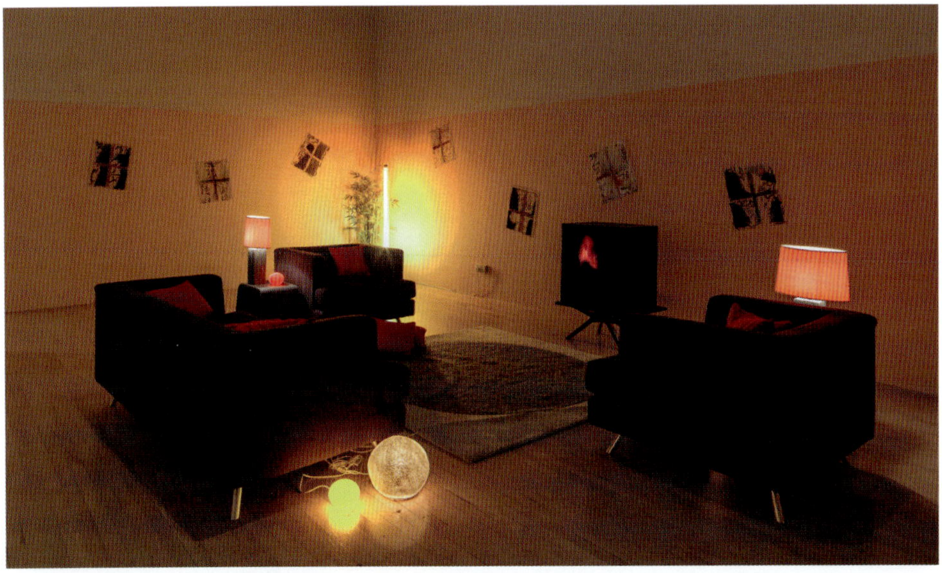

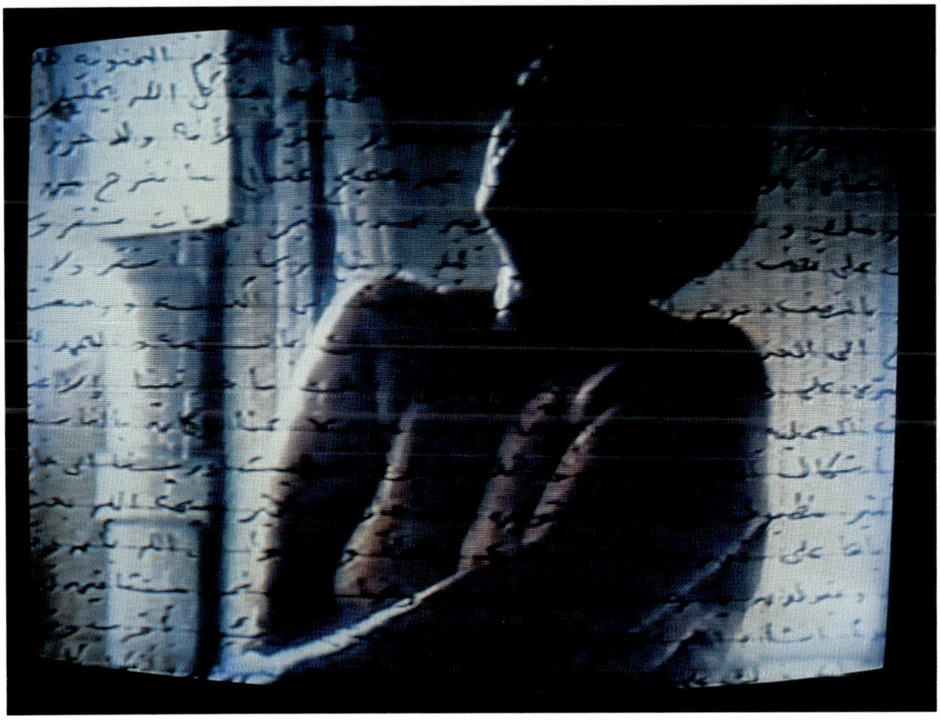

FIGURE 4.3
Susan Hiller, *Belshazzar's Feast, the Writing on Your Wall,* 1983–84. Video installation; 21 minutes, 52 seconds. Copyright Susan Hiller and Timothy Taylor Gallery, London.

FIGURE 4.4
Mona Hatoum, *Measures of Distance,* 1988. Video projection, color, sound; 15 minutes, 30 seconds. Copyright Mona Hatoum. Courtesy of White Cube Gallery.

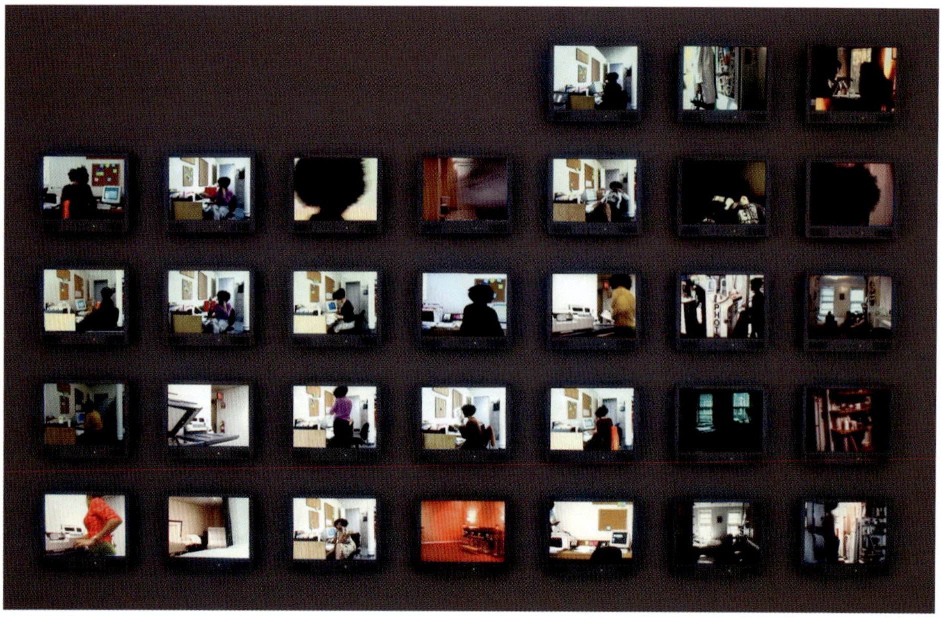

FIGURE 4.5
Lorna Simpson, *31*, 2002. 31-channel video installation, video transferred to DVD, color, sound; 20 minutes. Courtesy of the artist and Salon 94, New York.

everyday becomes abstract voice to non-Arabic speakers (the implied viewer for the piece). For such "foreign" spectators, this sound is abstract; it marks the viewer as an outsider to this intimate mother-daughter relationship. But it also animates the abstract quality in voice as such. As Mladen Dolar has put it, "voice," understood as "the extra linguistic element which enables speech phenomena, but cannot itself be discernable through linguistics," is "the material element recalcitrant to meaning."[34]

My final example, a provisional end point for this trajectory, is Lorna Simpson's 2002 video installation, *31* (fig. 4.5). Unlike her other moving image works—highly filmic in visual codes, large-screen, high production values—*31* maintains a relationship to quotidian televisual transmission. Furthermore, this work brings us back to the question of repetition and difference—to Echo. Laid out in a calendar-style grid of thirty-one flat-screen monitors, *31* shows the same number of different twenty-minute sequences of everyday footage of an anonymous young black female office worker in New York City going about her daily life. With clothing continuities, each monitor suggests that we are viewing segments from the ongoing flow of a particular day in differing combinations of rising, commuting, working, eating, socializing, running errands, and sleeping. No narrative arc is given; instead *31* suggests the repeatable temporal loop. The grid formation of thirty-one black boxes provides the structure for a temporal cycle of abstract transmission. Filled not with notable events or with any sense of character development, instead we barely see the face of the protagonist as she goes about her life. Recalling Krauss's idea of the feedback loop, Chrissie Iles suggests that in *31* the "simultaneity of space and time is given a concrete form in the temporal and spatial grid, within which Simpson's female subject moves purposefully, contained and closely observed."[35] Each box repeats the shape of an unremarkable day, but with a difference. The abstract form of transmission does not produce Krauss's closed parentheses of repetition, but instead, repetition, like Echo, with difference.

As Gary Hill has described, with reference to Robert Smithson, video art is "the nonsite of TV."[36] Anne Wagner elaborates this compelling concept : "Television, in other words, is the site—vast, unmapped, unedited—that video and its attendant mediated performances picture and articulate by negative reversal, as a broken piece of an absent whole."[37] Just as our understanding of video art has transformed with digital technologies into something closer to cinema, TV is no longer seen as the visually impoverished version of film. Furthermore TV exists not only in the home but also on tiny screens for mobile viewing, and in the era of HBO it is no longer the domain of the "surrendered gaze" that was long assumed the hallmark of its mass "distracted" appeal.[38] The parasitic relationship between video practices and TV that I have been tracing in these few examples, as a possible feminist trajectory, thus probably ended at some point in the early 2000s. Since then the social condition of "mobile privatization" that once characterized television has intensified beyond recognition, calling out for other feminist trajectories, other mediatic constellations, redirecting the relationship between sound, repetition, and abstraction that I have tracked in this essay.

NOTES

1. The term "Television Art" is used by Christine Mehring in her account of Paik's earliest work with television, a collaboration with K. O. Götz in Wuppertal, West Germany, in 1963. Mehring, "Television Art's Abstract Starts: Europe circa 1944–1969," *October* (July 1, 2008): 29–64.

2. Gene Youngblood, *Expanded Cinema* (New York: Dutton, 1970), 285.

3. Carolyn L. Kane, "Digital Art and Experimental Color Systems at Bell Laboratories, 1965–1984: Restoring Interdisciplinary Innovations to Media History," *Leonardo* 43, no. 1 (February 1, 2010): 365–66. For a fuller account of this project, see Carolyn L. Kane, *Chromatic Algorithms: Synthetic Color, Computer Art, and Aesthetics after Code* (Chicago, IL: University of Chicago Press, 2014). I am grateful to Kane for sending me a digital copy of a section from *Electronic Opera #1*.

4. Raymond Williams, *Television: Technology and Cultural Form* (New York: Schocken Books, 1975), 25.

5. Williams, *Television*, 25.

6. Susan Richmond, "The Ins and Outs of Female Sensibility: A 1973 Video by Lynda Benglis," *Camera Obscura* 23, no. 3 69 (2008): 91–92.

7. For an early essay on video's relation to television, see David Antin, "Video Art: The

Distinctive Features of the Medium," in *Video Art: An Anthology* (New York: Harcourt, Brace, Jovanovich, 1974). For a later art-historical study, see David Joselit, *Feedback: Television against Democracy* (Cambridge, MA: MIT Press, 2007).

8. Ina Blom offers a different account of the temporal structure of video that connects its feedback logic to Bergsonian notions of time and the archive. Although her account is framed in counterpoint to Krauss, the shared emphasis on the temporal loop is a common feature. Blom, "The Autobiography of Video: Outline for a Revisionist Account of Early Video Art," *Critical Inquiry* 39, no. 2 (January 2013): 276–95. Also see Yvonne Spielmann, *Video: The Reflexive Medium*, English ed. (Cambridge, MA: MIT Press, 2008).

9. Rosalind Krauss, "Video: The Aesthetics of Narcissism," *October*, no. 1 (Spring 1976): 55.

10. Krauss, "Video," 50.

11. Krauss, "Video," 50, 56.

12. Krauss, "Video," 55.

13. Krauss, "Video," 55. For an alternate reading of this work that engages with the question of narcissism in an affirmative manner, see Amelia Jones, *Self/image: Technology, Representation, and the Contemporary Subject* (London: Routledge, 2006). And for an account that historicizes Krauss's interpretation, see Susan Richmond, *Lynda Benglis: Beyond Process* (London: I. B. Tauris, 2013), 78–82.

14. Krauss, "Video," 52.

15. Sigmund Freud, "On Narcissism: An Introduction (1914)," in *The Standard Edition of the Complete Psychological Works of Sigmund Freud*, trans. James Strachey, vol. 14 (London: Hogarth Press and the Institute of Psycho-Analysis, 1957).

16. Gayatri Chakravorty Spivak, "Echo," *New Literary History* 24, no. 1 (1993): 27.

17. Spivak, "Echo," 27.

18. Ovid, *Metamorphoses* (Cambridge, MA: Harvard University Press, 1968), 383–84.

19. Blom, "The Autobiography of Video," 292.

20. Anne Wagner notes the title's reference to the "sound check," although she develops this point in a different direction from my argument. Anne Middleton Wagner, "Performance, Video and the Rhetoric of Presence," *October*, no. 91 (Winter 2000): 59–80.

21. Douglas Crimp, ed., *Joan Jonas, Scripts and Descriptions 1968–1982* (Berkeley: University Art Museum, University of California, 1983), 49.

22. Williams, *Television*, 14.

23. Williams, *Television*, 14.

24. Brian Winston, *Media, Technology and Society: A History from the Telegraph to the Internet* (London: Routledge, 1998).

25. Williams, *Television*, 22.

26. Williams, *Television*, 26. The classic feminist study of the reception and "use" of television within the home is Lynn Spigel, *Make Room for TV: Television and the Family Ideal in Postwar America* (Chicago: University of Chicago Press, 1992).

27. Betty Friedan, *The Feminine Mystique* (New York: Norton, 1963).

28. Gayatri Chakravorty Spivak, *An Aesthetic Education in the Era of Globalization* (Cambridge, MA: Harvard University Press, 2012), 31.

29. Spivak, *An Aesthetic Education*, 31.

30. Kaja Silverman, *The Acoustic Mirror: The Female Voice in Psychoanalysis and Cinema* (Bloomington, IN: Indiana University Press, 1988), 86.

31. Hiller has presented two slightly different versions of this piece, a "living room" version and a "campfire" version. I am describing the former. The latter includes a series of monitors in a circular arrangement; the wall imagery is not present, but the video footage—as described in my text—is the same. For images of the latter version, see Susan Hiller and James Lingwood, *Susan Hiller: Recall: Selected Works 1969–2004* (Gateshead, U.K.: Baltic, 2004).

32. Jean Fisher, "Before Testimony," in Hiller, *Susan Hiller: Recall,* 81.

33. Susan Hiller and Alexandra Kokoli, *The Provisional Texture of Reality: Selected Talks and Texts, 1977–2007* (Zurich: JRP / Ringier, 2008), 235.

34. Mladen Dolar, *A Voice and Nothing More* (Cambridge, MA: MIT Press, 2006), 16; 15.

35. Chrissie Iles, "Images Between Images: Lorna Simpson's Post-Narrative Cinema," in *Lorna Simpson* (London: Phaidon, 2002), 114–15.

36. Gary Hill, "And the Right Hand Did Not Know What the Left Hand Is Doing," in *Illuminating Video: An Essential Guide to Video Art* (New York: Aperture in association with the Bay Area Video Coalition, 1990), 97.

37. Wagner, "Performance, Video and the Rhetoric of Presence," 80.

38. On the idea of the "distracted" appeal, see Williams, *Television;* Stephen Heath, "Representing Television," in *Logics of Television: Essays in Cultural Criticism,* ed. Patricia Mellencamp (London: British Film Institute, 1990). The most sustained critique of this position is found in John Thornton Caldwell, *Televisuality: Style, Crisis, and Authority in American Television* (New Brunswick, N.J.: Rutgers University Press, 1995). For a recent account of these debates, see Amy Holdsworth, "Televisual Memory," *Screen* 51, no. 2 (2010): 129–42.

5

ABSTRACT VIDEO

Jeremy Gilbert-Rolfe

I have suggested elsewhere that nowadays, when thinking of ourselves as part of the world seen from outside and by others who are like us, we think of ourselves as a video image.[1] For a long time we sought to embody the qualities in photography that enhance appearance (lightness rather than heaviness, for example) and before that the same things in painting (wonderful flesh tones and generally intense color, for example), but now the version of both these properties that we like the most is for us found in and through the fact and also the idea of an image that is electronic. When we imagined ourselves as paintings and drawings, both light and emptiness were matters of surface, outline, or implication (the page left white to represent the sky, for example). When imagining ourselves as photographic images, whether still or moving, colored or black and white, we had left the epoch in which all images were layered or made of lines or both, but we were still aware of the image as an impression of light. This was the aspiration that, in the third quarter of the nineteenth century, had caused the Impressionist painters to want to give light and atmosphere as much or more attention than surfaces.

I'm not suggesting they were the first to do this, but I think that their being led in this quest by photography changed everything. Velazquez may have painted the space between things, but when doing so, he did not have in mind a mechanical model of how the physical constituents of that space could be recorded in the sense of being directly transposed, as opposed to summoned up through a procedure that followed from modeling the space conceptually. Vermeer's camera obscura may have given him a glimpse of what it is to mechanically record space as light, but he still did not have in his head what the Impressionists had in theirs, and could hold in their hands as well as in their imaginations: an image that had originated in light but had been developed, to various degrees of tonal range, in a dark room and was now the property of a piece of paper.

Video is much brighter than a sheet of paper, and in itself a bright light from the start. It is not a transposition or record of it. It was never an object. It is an absolutely other space that parallels that of the world as known and, we think, typically perceived, rather than deriving from it in the obvious way that perspective systems do or colored surfaces that are meant to represent depths, and is instead much more like that of the white canvas, which Cézanne described as already deep and only awaiting the painter's decision as to how (in his words) to carve it out. Video depth is immediate and not an end, and not necessarily the beginning of or grounds for the Renaissance perspective of the photograph either. It is a zone of active blankness that, already deep, need not be subjugated to a conceptualized depth. One might also think of Mallarmé presenting a white sheet of paper as a poem: it is already signifying by being an image of what signifies, and in that by being an image which is also the grounds of the image—and too, perhaps, of Charles Peirce's yardstick, at once a sign for a yard and a yard. The video screen is what the sheet of paper once was, and what the film screen never was.

The video screen and the sheet of paper have this in common, and it was never true of the film screen or painting as an art: we see everything on the screen now that we used to see in both books and in the newspaper. Mediums in which everything can happen in that place are not the same as ones of which that is not true. The newspaper began our habituation to the idea that the trivial and the important could both come to us as opening paragraphs in columns presented side by side, both to be continued on page such and such. If one makes a film, it may be shown on television but it is also possible to make one that can only be shown in a cinema for it to really work. One may say that of video when it's an installation rather than something on a console, and I'll discuss two artists who do that. One difference between how we see their work and how we see sculptural installations, for example, is that after seeing it we'll probably go home and watch television, in a way that seems to me similar to that in which Mallarmé's reader might, without moving from her chair, have gone from reading a poem to reading the newspaper. No change of medium in one sense, an absolute change in another. It's all writing. However, in the one, reading might be quite a different thing than in the other. Or different but perhaps not as different as one might suppose, since art borrows from everything including the implications of its medium that it doesn't directly use or address. Mallarmé was influenced by the newspaper's format.

To me, this would suggest that thinking about abstract video would include thinking about its relationship to television in general, and even more to the computer image as such in general, and in particular in both cases, the space abstract video would take place in with regard to what it is as both a sign and an involuntary experience of depth made out of bright light. Its relation to film, while important in some other ways to which I shall come, seems to me less important when thinking about that space than its relation to the computer screen, both as a kind of light and a place and kind of seeing and reading.

I think something similar about the relationship between abstract video and abstract painting, and shall seek to expand on the implications of that in the following few pages. There are two reasons, at least, why I think this.

Abstract or nonrepresentational painting has gone through at least two stages; in the first it sought to free itself from Renaissance perspective, and in the second one—the present and very recent past—it has found that it has, but its detractors haven't noticed. What has happened is, however, very much a matter of painting being influenced by the space, light, and movement of video, in a manner and for reasons directly comparable with the Impressionists' jealousy of photography's capacity to register natural light without lines or turning it into a surface. To compare or relate attempts to make abstract video with an apparent equivalent in painting might prove misleading were one to define the latter in terms not reinvented by its encounter with, or even development out of, the specific properties of the former. I think this is where many artists using computer animation programs shoot themselves in the foot. It would in my view be a bit better if they took from painting what's useful to them but forgot about painting, especially about making it look like a painting. There seems to me huge potential in animating geometry; the algorithm has possibilities denied to the grid on which painting depends. The less we are reminded of stretchers the better, or so it seems to me; it distracts from the pleasure of the already only light and movement(s), at least for me.

Lurking in and around the discussion, and getting in the way, are those who think of abstraction as an endeavor associated with a moment now past. If one thinks that "abstraction" of several kinds played a large part in the visual arts from Cubism to Minimalism but not really since, then a video image that reminds you of abstract painting is by definition an image retrieved from a lost past, nostalgic if only just made. This is an argument that cannot be entirely ignored here as it plays a large part in contemporary art criticism and art history, both popular and academic. However, there is another way of looking at things. I am not concerned here with the place of an art critical, or historical, category called "abstract video" in relation to an agreed-upon version of what has happened in art in the last two hundred or so years. I am interested in that genealogically, as I've suggested already. But this essay will not deal with whether abstract video succeeds anything else and will only compare it with other mediums with a view to getting at what it is or might be, and what that suggests both its potential and its limits might be. I think they're found in what it is in video that comes before anything else as much as in its historical development and origins, in the following sense.

I said that the first phase of abstract painting involved its separating itself from—defining itself as not defined by—the rules of Renaissance perspective, but that abstract painting's detractors haven't noticed. Nor have many or most of its supporters or even most abstract painters if it comes to that. I think this is because most people haven't fully appreciated the effect on painting of video. I am speaking here not of video's, or the video image's, historical relationship to abstract painting as a thing and therefore an experience that came after it, but as something that in the lives of most, if not now all people, comes well before it.

Richard Shiff, a major critic and historian of abstract painting (and also of Cézanne), has talked about how, when he was a kid in New York in the 1950s, he would watch with rapt attention the black and white signal that came on the television screen after programs went off the air at the end of the evening. It was, he noticed, only when something irregular happened that they blurred and warped into pure black and white. The rest of the time it was all grays. It was the first abstraction he would see, and it would remain that for quite a while.[2]

I want to suggest that in the years since Shiff (and I) were young, not only video space but also video light has come to play a part in our consciousness that is comparable to, but perhaps more complicated than, the one played by the light of the film screen in Mondrian's. I think it is probably more complicated than the light of the film projector because of the ubiquity noted above, which causes it to be associated with habits of reading as much as of seeing, as the film screen does not. I think it worth pointing out that, if the first stage of abstract painting's history involves its freeing itself from perspective, it also involves its freeing itself from nature. The video screen displaces both, and as it comes to ubiquity, abstract painting emerges, which has an indeterminate relationship to either but which is, unlike most of what precedes it, scrutinized like an object as much as, or at the same time and to the same extent as, it is contemplated or otherwise encountered as a space. That is to say, we suddenly have abstract painting which is as much—or almost as much—read as a collection of signs as it is apprehended as a phenomenal event, present in the space it shares with its viewer but at the same time discontinuous with it, because it generates another space from within itself, sensed as both outside and also as having invaded that which it seems only to share.

It has been suggested elsewhere that we may think of painting's involvement with light in the last nearly hundred and fifty years as first an infatuation with the weightless image of photography, particularly of people and things in sunlight (Impressionism), but simultaneously with the brightness of the newly invented electric light (the electric light in Manet's *Bar at the Folies-Bergère* is electric light's first appearance in painting and also where the paint in the painting is thickest), and thence to Mondrian and the bright light of the cinema screen, a brightness video exceeds.[3] Painting's infatuation with light soon led it away from nature and towards technology, that is to say, and that is why I think abstract video ought not to be about video artists imitating abstract paintings (or some outmoded interpretation of the concerns thereof) but rather of redefining, or defining for the first time, what "abstraction" might mean to an artist who wanted to work with video (fig. 5.1).

Bearing in mind Richard Shiff's observation, I think it would be well to remember that although photography did not come before painting, it certainly came before

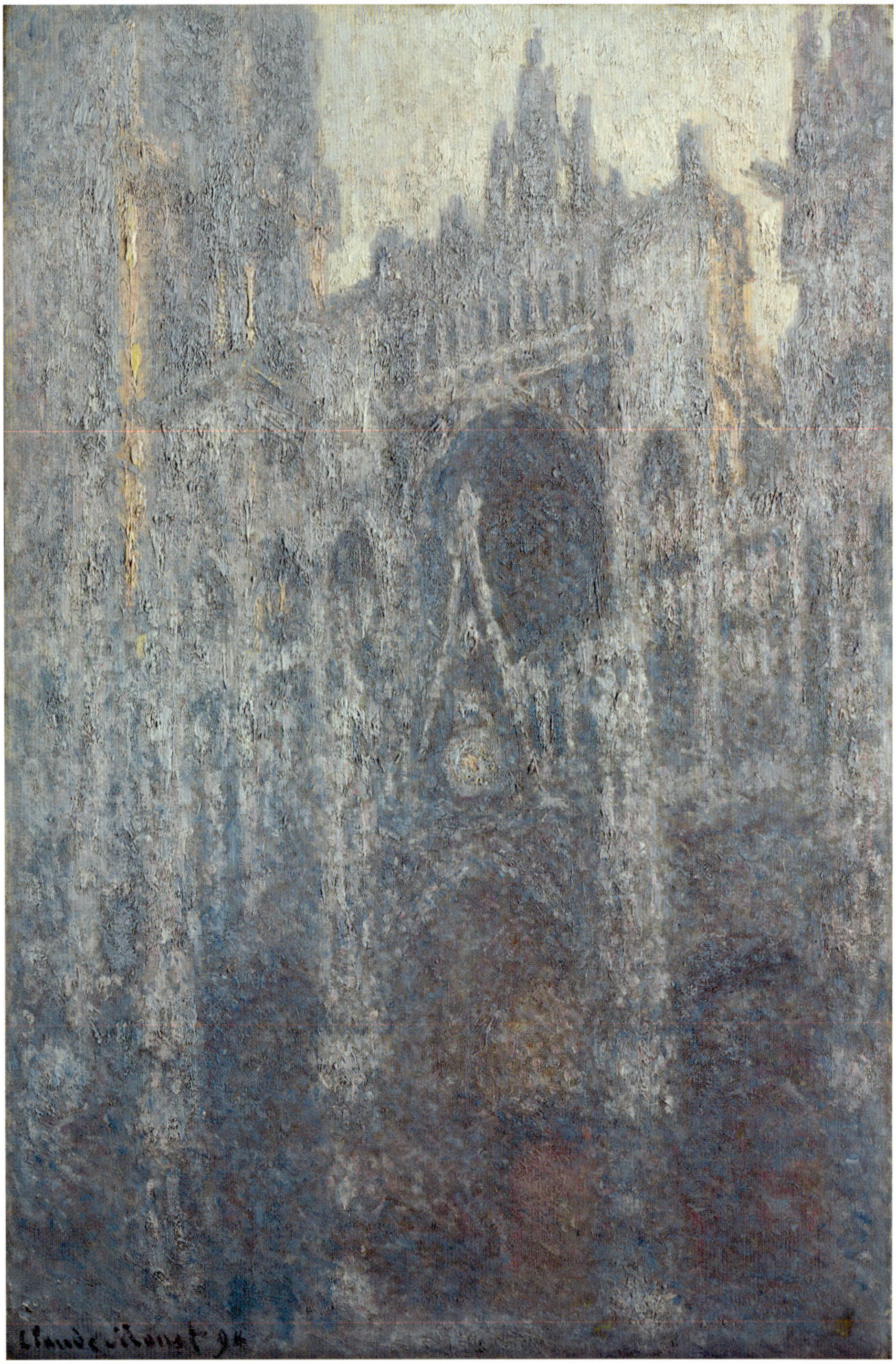

FIGURE 5.1

Claude Monet, *The Portal of Rouen Cathedral in Morning Light*, 1894. Oil on canvas; 39¼ × 25⅞ inches. (99.7 × 65.7 cm). The J. Paul Getty Museum, Los Angeles. Digital image courtesy of the Getty's Open Content Program.

Impressionism. Also the fact that for anyone born after, say, 1980 at the latest, not only did video and the computer come before painting but they were also, like painting, already there, and unlike their limited place in Shiff's childhood world, they were already everywhere. Among other things this means that video already contained nature; it was not a fresh look at it but the usual experience of it. A theory of abstract video needs, I think, to start there if only because ultimately it needs to think about moving beyond it.

Two examples of work by artists who use video, or the kind of light that video and its close relatives produce, seem to me to provide some indication of how such a question might be asked.

James Turrell's *Breathing Light* (2013)[4] is not a successful video work in my view for exactly the opposite reasons that his earliest works, which don't use electricity, are. Shown in the Los Angeles County Museum of Art as part of Turrell's retrospective, *Breathing Light* is a large work that places the viewer in a space lit by LED that changes slowly but not as imperceptibly as the sky, with which natural condition it nonetheless seeks to compete.

The bright white space of video is, I think, most closely identified by now with the computer screen rather than with the video monitor, and likewise video color is as much a general property of colors such as those produced by LED lights as with what one sees in video projection strictly defined or on a monitor. In Turrell's earliest work, and in his massive, and as yet uncompleted, major work *Roden Crater,* he concentrates the viewer's attention on the sky. The sky changes very slowly; one looks at an isolated rectangle of it and gets lost. Video, or actually anything computerized, doesn't seem to me to be able to change slowly enough to compete with that. Standing in *Breathing Light* I become accustomed to, which is to say I come to sense, the rate of change, the pace of what's happening, very quickly. I am in a movement I can perceive. Unlike the sky's imperceptible life, it has no mystery. It rapidly becomes a perfect setting for a bikini advertisement, as the colors are such that they do a great job on tanned skin as they pass through the rainbow. One gets lost less in contemplating a time structured by color than in the skin tones of the prettiest person in the room—not quite the same thing, however closely related one might argue it to be in this or that sense. It is, in contrast to the looking at either the sky or another person in daylight, mechanical. In contrast to the artist's early works' ability to engage us in the almost nonmovement of the sky, of a presence felt to be moving in a way one could not say one actually saw—as one may say one hears the influence but not the precise sound of the very low notes in Beethoven's piano pieces—Turrell's later works instead remind us of Bergson's insistence that the mechanical was for him automatically funny when attached to the human, and in that recalling but this time in reverse, Oscar Wilde's remark about seeing a sunset that was feebly attempting to impersonate a Turner. It is the sky deprived of soul and instead replaced by an entirely manageable version of itself.

This seems to me to indicate a limit on video's relationship to the natural which recalls painting's, but in that suggests that nature as phenomenon with which we're familiar, is perhaps a more difficult limit for the video artist than for the painter because of the presence of perceptibly measurable change in the image that actually moves. In both cases nature can be faked only so far or embodied only in a certain way. However, while Impressionism, faced with proof that nothing man had at his disposal could match the brightness of the sun, had only to turn to complementary colors to make colors "pop," and in that, to simulate sunlight's intensity to an extent that was quite sufficient to the required task (and remains demonstrably so despite subsequent technology's ability to provide much brighter pictures), Turrell is defeated not just by the sky but by the body.

Video would have to be much slower than Turrell lets it be to simulate the speeds in which he wants to locate us; as it is, what he achieves seems much too knowable. It moves much faster than the sky in most conditions, at a slow speed I quickly come to calculate. If it refers to what he has elsewhere done with natural light, what kind of reference it makes is not clear. If it does something else altogether, then I should like to know more about why it is the length it is as opposed to any other, whether shorter or longer. As it is, it reminds me of an essay by Gregory Flaxman, in which he quotes Deleuze musing that "It is strange that aesthetics (as the science of the sensible) could be founded in what could be represented,"[5] and goes on from there to recall immediately that the origins of this thought are in Kant's devastating announcement in the *Critique of Pure Reason,* and in contradistinction to previous notions of aesthetic judgment, that "speculative reason must begin by cleansing judgment of the taint of all empiricism. For this reason, he adds, we must disavow the tradition of aesthetics that sought to reflect upon actual sensation under the auspices of taste."[6]

Here, I want to suggest that a video art that seeks to be abstract would be one that would do better to begin with the never represented, thus avoiding two reasons for finding Turrell's *Breathing Light* unsatisfying on its own terms: it impersonates the affect of a sunset too clumsily and quickly, and it is too unambiguously grounded in judgments of taste to which we are already habituated. The difficulty is less that it reminds one of a bikini ad than that it does nothing with that recollection, perhaps failing to make our reminiscence of such ads more thrilling than they already are.

As an alternative I'd suggest Diana Thater's *Dark Matter* (2003) (fig. 5.2). It shows us a signal representing a light that is and never will be, available to the naked eye, as an experience only available through video. *Dark Matter* was part of an installation in which Thater presented, better to say, used, video in a variety of ways, beginning on the ground floor with a video console with an image of a movie marquee on it. As exhibited when I saw it, *Dark Matter* is a horizontal screen on which one sees an ultra-red video signal that is a telescope recording of dark matter: anti-light, impossibly far away from us, imaginable any way you like, but visible only through a telescope and only as an electronic recording of a light band invisible to the unassisted eye. It is an image of something that could never be an image, in that it refers to a concept unknowable as a physical sensation

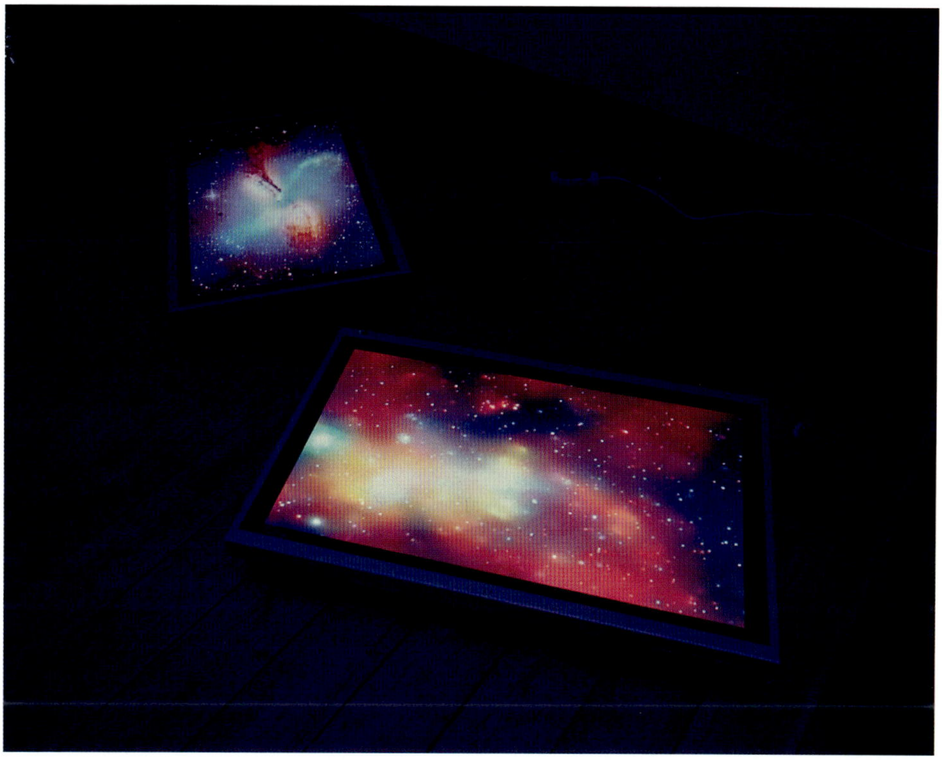

FIGURE 5.2
Diana Thater, *Dark Matter,* 2003. Video installation: two flat screen monitors, two DVD players, two DVDs and Lee filters; dimensions variable; loop. Courtesy of the artist.

despite being made out of matter. It is like an abstract painting in that what it gives one is a physical presence that is not a picture, but crucially unlike one in that it has no surface. This is crucial because it keeps the video one step away from materiality of the sort we associate with painting, instead concentrating on movement and color, suspended in or communicated through the implacable plastic surface that is inseparable from video except when it's projected.

Pace Deleuze on Kant, Thater's piece re-presents only through an elaborate transcription that makes what was hitherto not present except as something known to be there but not seen, available to vision as a sensation—as opposed to being available as a code that could be read and interpreted, but that would not have a visceral effect as does the presence of swarming. We are indeed moved by knowing what it is, but can only compare it to an idea, not to anything we have already seen. If it is a representation, then it represents forces, which are by definition invisible. It is not a representation in the sense of being a picture or reduction of an extant visual form. In *Dark Matter* Thater brings into view forces that certainly move us because of their connotations, but our bodies as well as our minds are moved far more by the swarming infrared movements that they become in the work itself. The content is implicitly exciting, but the formless motion and intensity that are its manifestation in front of us are explicitly exciting.

· · ·

This is also why the Thater is sexier than the Turrell, I think: swarming infrared is a body driven by its interior. David Reed has made paintings that invoke a comparable effect. Turrell's work seeks to be contemplative and manages at most to be dreamy, but Thater's is hot and intense, and this in no small part because it's photographic but its movements are not calculable in a straightforward way. Swarming is less a progression than a condition. Where Turrell's *Breathing Light* takes us through a progression, in which we don't so much get lost as suspended, Thater's *Dark Matter* presents us with another body on which we can't help but concentrate and in which it is not clear that we get lost but by which we are certainly, I think, transfixed. In a way we are back to Richard Shiff staring at the video signal, because Thater has us looking at just that, a video signal that does not refer back to an experience we've had of something else. In comparison, Turrell cannot do with video what he does with the sky because while fulfilling our (culturally induced) desire to be a part of a video image—detached from our sense of gravity as surely as we'd be in a green-screen image—he doesn't make it do anything to us but fails to simulate the pace of nature because it's too fast, therein denying the opportunity for contemplativeness it might seem to promise while not giving us any turmoil instead.

· · ·

I have suggested that abstract video ought not to be involved, or at least too involved, in looking for something to do in other mediums. Rather, to my mind it is more exciting from the point of view of art, and from the point of view of cultural exegesis in general, when it brings the energy and possibilities for signification of video, as at once a ubiquitous presence and a kind of image, into the gallery or museum or some other space where it does something it doesn't do in the world at large. That gives one an opportunity to see what it is, as opposed to what kinds of already extant modes of communication or affect-production it might be applied or help to support.

Turrell's *Breathing Light* offers several very obvious sources in, or opportunities for comparison with, the work of the Minimalist artists of his generation. *Breathing Light,* in detaching one from a clear sense of one's relationship to the floor, recalls Carl Andre's *Plains* (1969). *Plains* is a large grid made out of two metals, one denser than the other, and the lighter one seems to be levitated by the denser, so that when one stands in the middle of it, one's sense of where the floor is becomes ambiguous. It may exist (or may have existed) in more than one version, but the most well-known is the one shown at the Guggenheim, where one can see even in a photograph how it introduced uncertainty to one's sense of the floor's flatness. Likewise, the colors Turrell uses and the space in which they situate the viewer will remind some, or most, of Dan Flavin's corridors and Robert Irwin's use of scrim. It is, then, arguable that his *Breathing Light* may be seen as quite continuous with a sixties' view of how sculpture might be expanded to include its viewer within its own space by following painting and seeking to undermine, or eliminate, the difference between the space of the work and the space of the viewer. I should argue that this genealogy, which locates the work firmly within art history but takes no account of television, dates the artist in a way that doesn't help. Thater's work is in no way as firmly grounded in art history, although it is certainly grounded in art, which is in practice never a matter of genealogy alone. Not only was Victor Schlovsky obviously right to suggest that art is not a matter of fathers and sons but of uncles and nephews (the former being an academy while the latter suggests criticality derived from difference and distance), but I think it also true that art is a matter of chance encounters as much as of genealogy—and of course the two can be the same thing, and very often are.

However, to make art out of video as such runs an obvious risk, to which I now turn. In saying that an abstract video that did something would, perhaps, be a kind of art that brought the ubiquity of video into play and moved freely within it, I have made a case for Thater as an exemplary practitioner of the medium, but in bringing up the possibility that what's exciting is a condition rather than a progression, I have also brought us to the difficulty that was once faced by abstract painting in one way and has dogged abstract film and by extension, and also in practice, abstract video from their inception. It is central to what I'm arguing here because it is the prejudice, or arguments, against presenting a condition without a story in the way that Thater's *Dark Matter* does. *Dark Matter,* as noted, may be compared to a painting by David Reed in regard to how forces are being deployed through similar colors and movements—but it is the painter who's seeking to imitate the flawless surface of the photographic, which is simply a property of the video screen. The painter strives for what in video is simply a given, painting helpless before the photographic surface as it was once in awe of its light. Other works of Thater's may be compared to other kinds of paintings by other painters—she looks at art a lot and has a degree in art history—but none of these comparisons situate her in the history of painting, or in any special relationship to it, in the way that comparisons with his contemporaries identify Turrell with Minimalist sculpture.

Instead, we have to look at her work as a presentation of a selected version of the possibilities of video as a kind of event. The difficulty her work revives is the one that abstraction in film faced from the start. If abstract painting was dogged by critics who still wanted a picture rather than an event, abstract film was dismissed by critical thinkers who similarly had no interest in the expressive or communicative potential of the medium itself when not trapped in that aesthetic of representation about which Deleuze mused. Here is Roman Jakobson, founder of Prague Structuralism, sometime collaborator with Lévi-Strauss, and the man who sought to identify as specifically as possible where affect could be located in poetry (especially), on why abstract film is a nonstarter. Note *en passant* that he finds film itself a dubious enterprise:

> There is a striking difference between a primarily spatial, simultaneously visible picture and a musical or verbal flow which proceeds in time and successively excites our audition. Even a motion picture continually calls for simultaneous perception of its spatial composition. The verbal or musical sequence, if it is to be produced, followed, and remembered, fulfills two fundamental requirements—it exhibits a consistently hierarchical structure and is resolvable into ultimate, discrete, strictly patterned components designed ad hoc. . . . No similar components underlie visual sign sets, and even if some hierarchical arrangement appears, it is neither compulsory nor systematic. It is the lack of these two properties that disturbs and rapidly fatigues us when we watch an abstract film, and which inhibits our perceptive and mnestic abilities.[7]

Jakobson's essay was written in 1963 (in Cambridge, Massachusetts) and seems to us very archaic. He seems not to have noticed Jackson Pollock, whose paintings take to an extreme what was an obvious component of modern painting from at the latest, Manet: the impossibility of seeing a painting as a simultaneity rather than a perpetually unfolding duration. However, his insistence that film should follow an order reducible to that of either narrative or music is by no means restricted to him, or to those whose youth predates the art of America since World War II. Roberta Smith called my friend Paul Sharits's films "moving wallpaper" some fifteen years later (fig. 5.3). Her critical reputation was (and is) grounded in her work on Minimalist sculpture, in particular, on Donald Judd's. Why should sculpture that does not obey a hierarchy, but rather seeks not to, and that has no associations through which it seeks to exercise the mnestic, save in terms of references to ideas about art history and certain properties considered as values (such as the industrial versus the handmade), somehow be OK, while film that engages in repetition without iconography (the first condition of Minimalism) be casually dismissed?

Clearly the answer is that Smith expected all film to follow Hollywood and tell a story, rather as if a green painting by Brice Marden (about whom she wrote the earliest essay of any length) was a landscape into which the artist hadn't yet put any farm hands. This was at a time when finding a way of rethinking film from before Hollywood was a preoccupation of such filmmakers as Hollis Frampton and Michael Snow, friends of, for example, Andre as well as of Sharits. An abstract video that seeks to be abstract will surely face similar skepticism.

One reason for the persistence of such skepticism resides in what Thater's *Dark Matter* makes us see. Jakobson, who championed and explained the work of the Russian and Czech avant-garde at its most advanced, has no use for a form—abstract film—that makes you feel the force of a technology. He is happy to feel the force of the body mediated by grammar and the other rules of a language, both spoken and written, and not

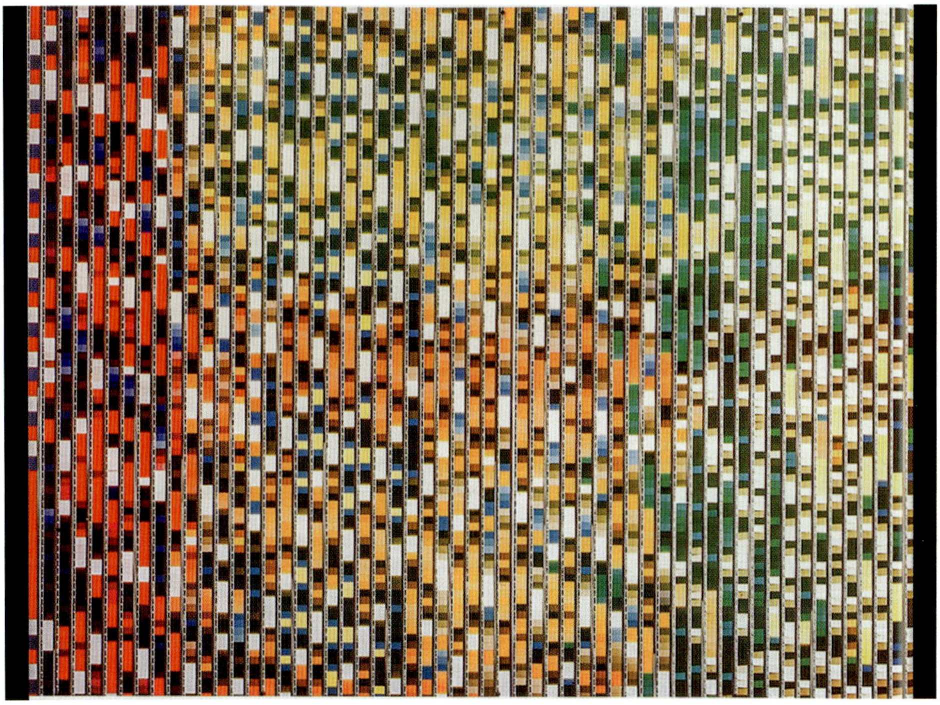

FIGURE 5.3
Paul Sharits, *Specimen*, 1975. 16mm film, color, sound. Courtesy of Christopher Sharits.

so keen on the machine when it's literally that, rather than an apparatus made more completely out of conventions. I don't think he ever says anything about Mallarmé and paper. Smith, almost similarly, is more than happy to champion work that is all about activating its own physicality—supposedly in the service of getting beyond the illusionism inherent in painting—when such work stands still. Work that is not still and made of metal but made of light and movement—there not as a thing but as a projection, but no less there for all that—is somehow automatically a matter of the peripheral. I wrote a whole book about how what art history wants to regard as peripheral is nothing of the sort, and began this essay with a reference to it. Neither Jakobson nor Smith grasped about film what Shiff grasped about the video signal. Both found film as a medium, not subjected to the rules of narrative or music, either tiring or trivial (depending, I suppose, on whether you tried concentrating on it). I am quite sure that in the contemporary situation, where we languish under a critical fashion preoccupied with the revival of social realism at the expense of an interest in the logic of the senses, abstract video will encounter the same old silly opposition as it develops.

Shiff's video signal and Thater's *Dark Matter* bring us up against video, as a thing that can be only an abstraction, a materiality that has no substance but electricity. Most of Thater's work involves the recognizable, beautiful coordinations between the musical and film or video time, and everything that Jakobson requires to stimulate the memory as well as perception. In *Dark Matter* she, perhaps as an aside to her main work, which is after all to do with animals, has made a piece that fills the video signal with reference to what is at once an idea and an actuality, and of which there's no memory, and here is where we may say it's abstract in some way, which, possibly, returns us to Deleuze's musing about representation and the aesthetic. Such works, like abstraction in general and music rather than painting in particular, connect the body involuntarily to movement. Abstract video is the activation of the condition of video as a movement, a field of light always already moving. The late-at-night signal in New York showed the way, just like a sheet of paper showed the way to competing with the sun and also to asking what lies beneath words given that what we see there is a sea of white. Television and the computer screen set the terms. *Dark Matter* points to a video art made out of force and movement and the not-there, from which, no doubt, painting will seek to derive this and that kind of lead, while television will equally without doubt use what it can of it and leave the rest.

NOTES

1. Jeremy Gilbert-Rolfe, *Beauty and the Contemporary Sublime* (New York: Allworth Press, 1999), 89: "(I)n the twentieth century people above all want to inhabit the photographic rather than use it. Go to a shopping mall and what one sees are people wearing video-colored clothes eating video-colored food in a video-colored environment."

2. Richard Shiff, "The Undecidable," (paper presented at the Art Center College of Design biannual conference, "40 Years of Unexplained Change: Art, History, Subjectivity since 1973," Pasadena, November 9–10, 2013).

3. Jeremy Gilbert-Rolfe and Rebecca Norton, "Awkward × 2: What We Think We're Doing," (paper presented at the School of the Art Institute of Chicago, Chicago, October 25, 2011); reprinted as "Lecture for Chicago," *Brooklyn Rail,* Artseen, October 2012, www.brooklynrail.org/2012/10/artseen/lecture-for-chicago.

4. James Turrell has refused permission to reproduce the image for publication; for reference, please see www.lacma.org/art/exhibition/james-turrell-retrospective.

5. Gregory Flaxman, "Transcendental Aesthetics: Deleuze's Philosophy of Space," in *Deleuze and Space,* ed., Ian Buchanan and Greg Lambert (Edinburgh, Scotland: Edinburgh University Press, 2005), 162.

6. Flaxman, "Transcendental Aesthetics."

7. Roman Jakobson, "Visual and Auditory Signs," in *Roman Jakobson: Selected Writings,* vol. 2, *Word and Language* (The Hague: Mouton, 1971), 336.

PART TWO

INTERFERENCE

6

VISUAL MUSIC'S INFLUENCE ON CONTEMPORARY ABSTRACTION

Cindy Keefer

If it's not abstract it couldn't be great.

OSKAR FISCHINGER

Contemporary abstract media artists as diverse as Björk, Jeremy Blake, Scott Draves, Steve Roden, Robert Seidel, Scott Snibbe, Vibeke Sorensen, Jennifer Steinkamp, and Jennifer West share the influence of historical Visual Music films, specifically those by German American Oskar Fischinger (1900–1967). Most of these artists have publicly acknowledged Fischinger's impact on their work, as have generations of Visual Music filmmakers including Len Lye, Norman McLaren, Jordan Belson, James Whitney, Mary Ellen Bute, Jules Engel, and Harry Smith. Fischinger is the most important and influential filmmaker in the history of Visual Music. After Walther Ruttmann and Viking Eggeling, Fischinger pioneered a new language of abstraction in film. He produced fifty short films and eight hundred paintings and is recognized as the father of Visual Music, the grandfather of music videos, and the great-grandfather of motion graphics.

Interactive artist Scott Snibbe's "Motion Phone" iPad and iPhone app (2012) is a tool for abstract visual communication, first influenced by Fischinger's film *Studie nr. 8* (1931): "Fischinger's work became the fundamental inspiration for what I had been calling 'useless programs,' works of interactive computer graphics that had no more use than, say, a poem, a song, or a work of art. Soon after seeing Fischinger's film, I began writing a program called Motion Phone that let people create Fischinger-like abstract films in real time, collaboratively over a network. That work of art became my entrée into the field of interactive art, and the launch of a career that later spawned million-selling apps . . . and visual music collaborations with Björk."[1]

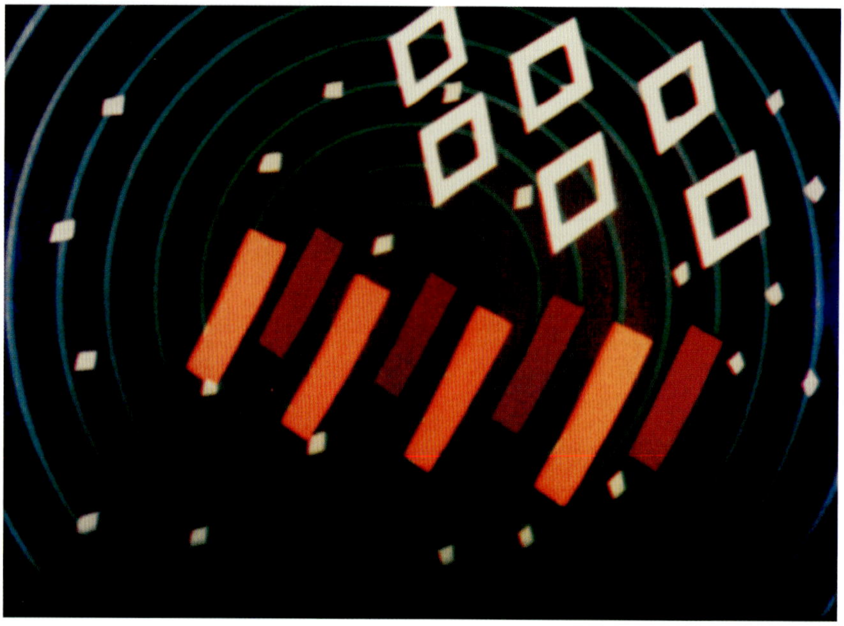

FIGURE 6.1
Oskar Fischinger, *Allegretto,* 1936–43. 35mm film, color, sound; 2 minutes, 30 seconds. © Center for Visual Music.

Oskar Fischinger was born in Gelnhausen, Germany in 1900. He studied music, drafting, and organ building and began his animated film experiments around 1920, first experimenting with wax, silhouettes, and hand-drawn animation. He invented apparatus beginning with a wax-slicing machine, in order to realize his visions. Fischinger became extremely successful in Europe with his series of abstract *Studies* films synchronized to music, his famous waltzing cigarette commercials, and color abstract films.

With Paramount Studio's help, Fischinger emigrated from Berlin to Hollywood in 1936, thus becoming the direct link from the European avant-garde film community to West Coast experimental filmmaking. He worked briefly for Paramount, Disney, and MGM, but was not successful in the studio systems. He did manage to make several film masterpieces in America—*Allegretto* (1936–1943) (fig. 6.1), *An Optical Poem* (1937), *Radio Dynamics* (1942), and *Motion Painting no. 1* (1947)—as well as some advertising films and hundreds of oil paintings. As Snibbe notes, "Fischinger understood something deep and primitive about the human brain. His films represent a crystallization, a super-stimulus of form, movement, and color that bores down to the fundamentals of how we perceive."[2]

Fischinger's work continues to affect and influence today, and his films are still screened worldwide in museums, festivals, and cinematheques. An HD reconstruction of Fischinger's *Raumlichtkunst* multimedia shows is touring internationally. Artist Doug Aitken hand-picked one of Fischinger's early abstract films, *Spirals* (c. 1926), for inclusion in his *Station to Station* (2013) art project touring American cities. In 2005, Fischinger was the most prominently featured filmmaker in the blockbuster *Visual Music* exhibition at the Hirshhorn Museum and Sculpture Garden (Washington, DC) and MOCA Los Angeles and attended by nearly 300,000 people. This exhibition also featured work by Belson, John and James Whitney, Lye, Thomas Wilfred, and other artists, and was partly responsible for the rapidly growing interest in Visual Music in recent years.[3]

Contemporary artist Jennifer Steinkamp's installation *SWELL* was also included in this exhibition. While at Art Center College of Design in Pasadena, Steinkamp took a class taught by media historian Gene Youngblood, where he screened Fischinger and other films. "Inspired by the visual music created by her predecessors," reports JoAnn Northrup, the curator of a recent retrospective exhibition of Steinkamp's work, "she began making her own films, working with computers."[4] Also in California, several generations of film and video artists at California Institute of the Arts' Experimental Animation program were introduced to Fischinger, Belson, the Whitneys, and Visual Music films by instructors Jules Engel and William Moritz, until their deaths in 2003 and 2004. At Cal Arts, Engel mentored Richard Baily (1953–2006). Baily made computer films in the 1970s before working at the legendary visual effects company Robert Abel & Associates. Baily's nebulous atmosphere (created by his company Image Savant) outside the windows of the space station in the film *Solaris* (2002) owes allegiance to the abstract cosmological imagery in *The Right Stuff* (1983) created by Jordan Belson (1926–2011). Indeed, Baily acknowledges Belson as a major inspiration: "For me, personally, this whole field of visual music starts and ends with his work. Everyone else, including me, are just hobbyists. . . . I keep looking for the humanity in abstraction, cosmic snapshots, fractured glimpses of the larger unseen world that we live in. No other filmmaker has even come close."[5]

California artist Christina McPhee refers to the significance of both Belson and Stan Brakhage films in regard to her video work, citing especially Belson's "color-space and atmosphere [and] the fluidity of edges" and Stan Brakhage's *Dog Star Man* (1961–64).[6] These influences can be seen in her recent abstract video projections for *Carbon Song Cycle* (2013–14); the colorful, layered, three-screen *Bird of Paradise* (2011–12); and the spectacular *MEAT OIL JOY PAINT* (2010), a tribute to artist Carolee Schneemann's performance from 1964, *Meat Joy*. In these videos, McPhee draws from Belson's and Brakhage's use of color and superimposition and their explorations of the nature of light.

Belson is known for his abstract films woven with cosmological imagery, exploring consciousness, transcendence, and light. His major films include *Allures* (1961), *Re-entry* (1964), *Samadhi* (1967), and *Chakra* (1972). Trained as a painter, Belson began making films after seeing Fischinger, McLaren, and Hans Richter films at the San Francisco Museum of Art in the 1940s. He continued making abstract films until 2005, though he switched to video for the postproduction work (done by editors). Belson is also often remembered for his work in the 1950s Vortex Concerts in San Francisco, discussed later in this essay. His films continue to inspire artists today, particularly younger artists just discovering his work. Selected films are shown in museum and gallery exhibitions, most recently at Raven Row, London in 2013, and the DVD *Jordan Belson: 5 Essential Films* (2006) is in distribution.

The work of Norman McLaren (1914–1987) continues to inspire filmmakers today. Beginning in April 2014, four digital video artists' works influenced by McLaren were screened across walls of the city in Montreal, part of a unique competition, *McLaren Wall-to-Wall,* celebrating McLaren's centennial. Scottish-born McLaren founded the National Film Board of Canada's animation studio, where he worked for decades creating classics of experimental animation. The invitation to the competition went out to "filmmakers and creators from the four corners of the Earth to celebrate his legacy by submitting original creations inspired by his work."[7] The original work submitted was required to incorporate, "like quotations," brief excerpts from a specific McLaren film: *Spheres, Neighbors, Begone Dull Care,* or *Synchromy* (three of these are abstract). This is a unique case of a site-specific installation requiring use of an excerpt from a historic Visual Music film to create a new work, in what the call for work refers to as a dialogue with McLaren's work. The new works, called "architectural video projections" in the guidelines, were to be screened on specific structures.

Clearly, abstract video today owes an enormous debt to the Visual Music films of the past. But what actually *is* Visual Music? Animation and film historian William Moritz has called it "a music for the eye comparable to the effects of sound for the ear" and asks, "What are the visual equivalents of melody, harmony, rhythm, and counterpoint?"[8] In 2006, when we were jurors for an exhibition, I wrote an essay with artist-scholar Jack Ox that clarified definitions of Visual Music. We identified the following different kinds of visual structures that can be called Visual Music:

- A visualization of music which is the translation of a specific musical composition (or sound) into a visual language, with the original syntax being emulated in the new visual rendition. This can be done with or without a computer. This can also be defined as intermedia.
- A time based narrative visual structure that is similar to the structure of a kind or style of music. It is a new composition created visually but as if it were an aural piece. This can have sound, or exist silent.
- A direct translation of image to sound or music, as images photographed, drawn or scratched onto a film's soundtrack are directly converted to sound when the film is projected. Often these images are simultaneously shown visually. Literally, what you see is also what you hear. (An early example is filmmaker Oskar Fischinger's *Ornament Sound* experiments c. 1932.) There are many examples in Visual Music film of this process, e.g., McLaren, Spinello, Damonte and other contemporary filmmakers. . . . This method has been called a "pure" type of Visual Music.

- A visual composition that is not done in a linear, time-based manner, but rather something more static like a 7' × 8' canvas. However, as in Klee, the movement of the painted elements can and have achieved a kind of *Visual Music,* serving as an artist's visual interpretation of specific music.[9]

We noted that definitions are expanding as the field grows rapidly. While not exclusively so, most Visual Music works tend to be abstract. In this essay, we also discussed the history of Visual Music:

> The origins of Visual Music can be found in the theories of Pythagoras and Aristotle, then in Goethe, Sir Isaac Newton, and numerous other texts on the correspondences of the color spectrum and sound waves, music and color, and sound and light. The color organ tradition—machines constructed to project colored light in rhythmic structures borrowed from music, and sometimes specifically to visualize accompanying music, began with Castel. . . . There was a plethora of color organs at the end of the 19th century, and many more throughout the 20th century—first mechanical and electronic versions and then computer versions. . . .
>
> Perhaps the better-known history of Visual Music is its rich body of abstract film, a history originating with painters who turned to film and animation in order to bring movement to their artworks. Abstract Visual Music film developed beginning with the c. 1910 work (now lost) of Italian Futurists Arnoldo Ginna and Bruno Corra, then received much attention with the German Absolute Film movement of the Twenties (Viking Eggeling, Walther Ruttmann, Oskar Fischinger, Hans Richter). Visual Music films include work hand-painting and scratching on film (Len Lye, Norman McLaren, Harry Smith, and numerous contemporary artists), and a wide variety of cinematic, optical, and animation techniques. Notable historical movements in Visual Music film include the European avant-garde of the Twenties and Thirties, the California School of Color Music beginning in the Thirties; the San Francisco filmmakers associated with the Beat Era; a substantial tradition of spiritually influenced work; a group affiliated with The Museum of Non-Objective Painting in New York in the Forties; work in Fifties and Sixties light shows; early computer graphics beginning in the Sixties; and video synthesis work in the Seventies.[10]

COLOR MUSIC

From the Jesuit priest Father Castel in the 1730s to present day, there is a long tradition of artists creating a type of Visual Music called Color Music, using color organs—machines of their own invention using moving colored lights to compose and perform visual compositions. Some were designed to perform colors silently, others were performed with music. Color Music, the art of projected light and color, is a predecessor to today's VJs and live cinema artists and much ambient video work. Generations of video and light artists working with light and color stem from this tradition, and some were influenced by the work of Danish American Thomas Wilfred (1889–1968). Wilfred performed his Clavilux color organ in concert halls in the early 1920s and in 1930

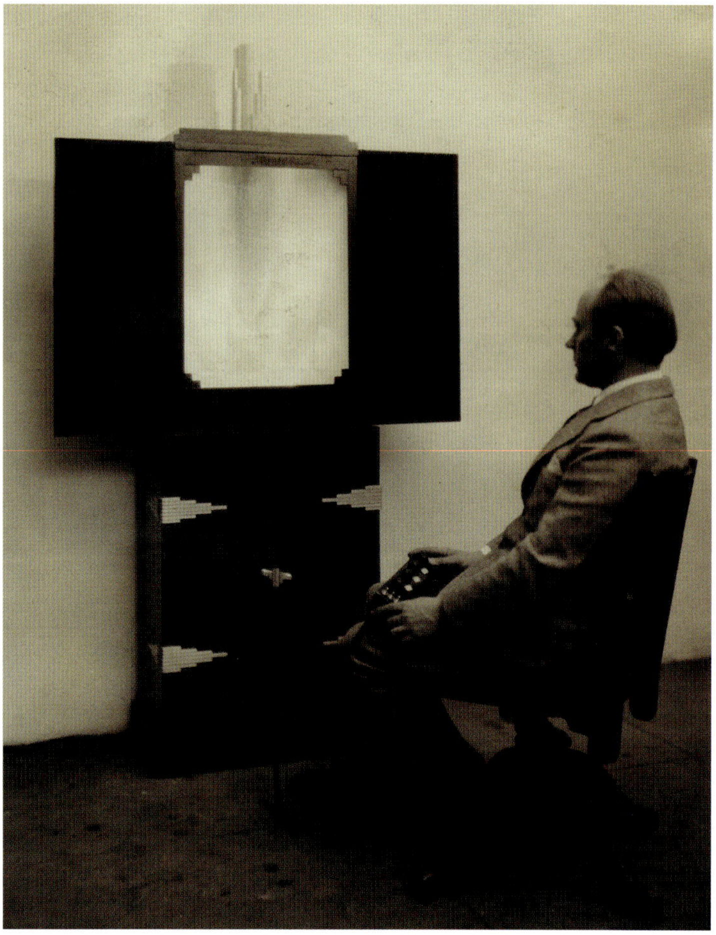

FIGURE 6.2
Thomas Wilfred, *First Home Clavilux Model,* 1930. Thomas Wilfred Papers (MS 1375), Manuscripts and Archives, Yale University Library.

established the Art Institute of Light in New York for research and demonstrations of Lumia, his name for the art of light (fig. 6.2).

"After 1926 Wilfred concentrated on creating self-contained, programmed 'lumia compositions,' many of which, with a two-foot square screen in a decorative cabinet, resemble modern television sets," explains William Moritz.[11] Moritz describes the imagery of a later lumia composition, Wilfred's *Vertical Sequence II, Opus 137* (1941): "The attack and decay of colors as they fade in and out, the metamorphoses of brilliant reds into rich wines and saturated purples that dissolve into luminous white, the intense gold of a sunset refusing to blend with a simultaneous apparition of a green or peach streak, the subtle directional flows with slight curling or bending just as they leave the screen, the interaction between nearly palpable veils and clouds of turbulence boiling up."[12]

Contemporary artists from a myriad of practices have Visual Music in their backgrounds. James Turrell, for example, encountered Wilfred early: "As a child, my aunt, a New Yorker, [took] me to MoMA, and they were showing this light artist who made a light box, Thomas Wilfred. He used mechanics that make reflections, so in his work things are constantly changing, and that was fascinating to me. It was the only thing that seemed up-to-date."[13]

Belson too acknowledged the influence of Wilfred's Lumia, which he'd seen at the San Francisco Museum of Art. New York artist George Stadnik has been involved in a restoration project for Wilfred's Clavilux, and Stadnik's *Flame* (2006) evokes the sensuous, ever-evolving silent imagery of Lumia. Stadnik notes,

> The art of Lumia has inspired my work since 1968. Creating mechanical light boxes for thirty years enabled me to explore many aspects of the properties of light. In 1998, my work became digital. I started making Lumia compositions using commercial optical simulation software. I create Lumia machines inside the computer. These machines simulate the manipulation of the properties of light over time to generate silent compositions of movement, color and transformation. Seeing the work of the 20th Century Lumia artist, Thomas Wilfred, at the Museum of Modern Art motivated me to experiment with light as an art form. Watching the colors move, blend and change was a unique and captivating experience.[14]

EARLY ABSTRACT VIDEO IN VISUAL MUSIC FILM

New York filmmaker and media artist Jud Yalkut (1938–2013) worked with Nam June Paik, John Cage, and the collective USCO. An early pioneer of the use of abstract video *on* film, Yalkut explored methods of recording imagery from a television screen onto 16mm film. This is seen in his work with Paik and in films such as his *Turn, Turn, Turn* (1966), described as "a kinetic alchemy of the light and electronic works of Nicolas Schoffer, Julio Le Parc, USCO, and Nam June Paik . . . a film of the eye-shattering, flashing, rotating light sculptures programmed by USCO."[15]

In the 1950s, Mary Ellen Bute (1906–1983) in New York and Hy Hirsh (1911–1961) in San Francisco shot patterns from an oscilloscope screen and printed these images into their films, layered with their abstract animation (fig. 6.3). Bute was a pioneer of electronic art and music visualization. She made *Abstronic* (1952) with oscilloscope imagery, which she called electronic animation.

Artist-engineer Stephen Beck invented the Beck Direct Video Synthesizer (built 1968–1972), which allowed him to "play" and manipulate color video in real time. His 1970s work includes the film *Cycles* (1974) made with Jordan Belson. Beck was an artist in residence at the National Center for Experiments in Television at KQED, San Francisco, where he worked with his Direct Video synthesizer. Belson and Beck collaborated to create *Cycles,* wherein Belson's film sequences and original video created by Beck were fed repeatedly through the Direct Video synthesizer, and the artists transformed the imagery with each pass.

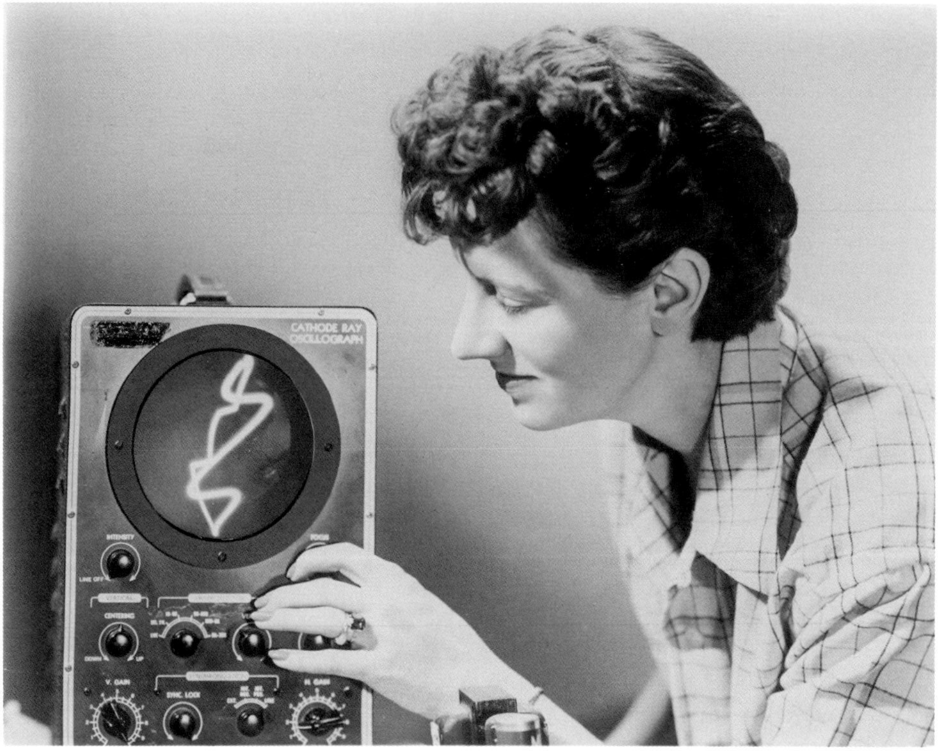

FIGURE 6.3
Mary Ellen Bute with her oscilloscope. Courtesy of Center for Visual Music.

Beck's *Video Weavings* (1973–76) is still exhibited in galleries today, recently at the Getty Museum, Los Angeles, and the Museum of Contemporary Art, San Diego. His *Illuminated Music 2* video was included in the 2005 *Visual Music* exhibition at MOCA and the Hirshhorn Museum. Beck's recent work includes ambient video sculpture and the exquisite *NOOR Part 1* (2011). Beck explains that "NOOR is the Arabic (and Farsi) word meaning Light. NOOR seeks to build bridges between cultures, and is an exploration of Spiritual Technology."[16]

Stephen Beck and Vibeke Sorensen bridge the historical to contemporary; both are renowned Visual Music artists known for their pioneering abstract video work in the 1970s, and they continue to create abstract media work today. Sorensen is an artist, professor, and long-time fan of Fischinger's work. She has created dozens of abstract Visual Music installations and videos, as well as digital multimedia works and performances. She considers her video *NLoops* (1988) an homage to Fischinger, and for decades has exposed her students at the University of Southern California, the Department of Media Study at SUNY Buffalo, Art Center College of Design, California Institute of the Arts, and Princeton, among others, to Visual Music films. In 2013 Sorensen presented her installation *Illuminations* at ZKM, Karlsruhe, Germany, as part of the BEYOND 3-D Festival. The festival's webpage described the work: "*Illuminations* is a real-time computer generated visual music installation that employs 12 6 × 8 foot screens, 12 computers and projectors, a multichannel sound system, and a large mirror. A stereoscopic version of this piece requires 3D projectors. The music, animation, installation, and Pure Data programming are by Vibeke Sorensen."[17]

EARLY ABSTRACT FILM IN MULTIMEDIA AND EXPANDED CINEMA

Multiple-channel projections and multiscreen installations are increasingly popular now in the gallery and site-specific settings. There is a long list of historic Visual Music filmmakers who either proposed or created abstract multiple projector and multiscreen work, starting with Fischinger, Belson, Stan VanDerBeek (credited with originating the term "expanded cinema" in the 1960s), McLaren, Bruce Conner, Harry Smith, Hirsh, and the three sons of John Whitney Sr. One can add to this list numerous light-show creators who used abstract imagery on multiple screens in the 1960s and 70s (Joshua White, Elias Romero, Bill Hamm, Glen McKay, Tony Martin, Scott Bartlett, Tom DeWitt, Ben Van Meter, and Single Wing Turquoise Bird). McLaren, Hirsh, Smith, and Dwinell Grant also made 3-D films, and Fischinger made a short 3-D test.

As I wrote in an earlier essay, the origins of immersive media environments, multiple-projector Expanded Cinema performances, and 1960s psychedelic light shows can be traced to the early experiments of film artists Oskar Fischinger and Jordan Belson. These filmmakers expanded their work outside the rectangular film frame and beyond traditional screens, using multiple cinematic projections far surpassing anything previously attempted. They covered rooms and domes and planetariums with abstract imagery, creating sophisticated illusions and combining cinema with other art forms to create a greater experience.[18]

The earliest Visual Music filmmaker to use abstract film in a multimedia event is Oskar Fischinger, first in Alexander László's *Farblichtmusik* (Color-Light-Music) shows (c. 1926) and then in his own cinema performances in Germany called *Raumlichtmusik* (Space-Light-Music) (fig. 6.4). In 1925, László presented concerts performing music accompanied by projected colored light from his color organ and by painted slides. László wanted a more modern element, so he asked Fischinger for some of his abstract films. In Munich, March 1926, Fischinger and László joined forces to perform *Farblichtmusik* concerts, combining Fischinger's abstract 35mm films with projected colored lights, music, and painted glass slides. For various reasons their partnership soon dissolved, but Fischinger continued his own cinema performances (c. 1926), called *Raumlichtmusik*, and then *Raumlichtkunst*. For these performances he used up to five projectors, colored filters, and painted slides. The accompanying music appears to have been avant-garde percussion. From reviews and Fischinger's notes, we understand these shows as

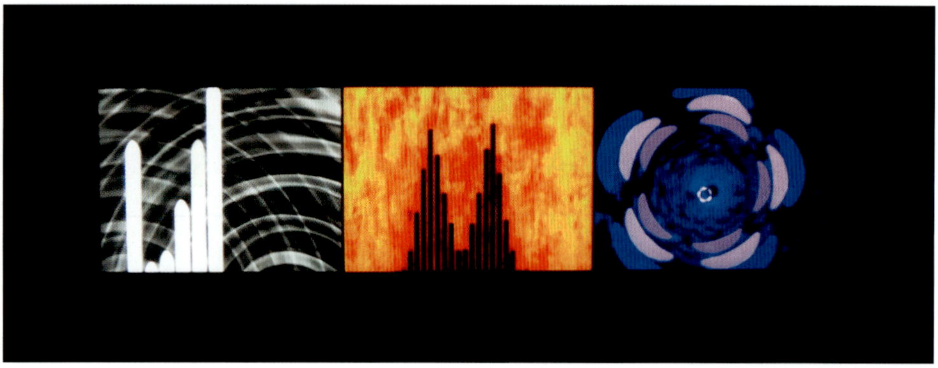

FIGURE 6.4
Oskar Fischinger's *Raumlichtkunst*, c. 1926/2012. Three-screen HD video installation reconstructed by Center for Visual Music from 35mm film; variable loops. Installation view at Whitney Museum, New York. © Center for Visual Music.

attempts to create some of the first cinematic immersive environments, and they are a clear precursor to light shows and expanded cinema performances decades later.

For a new reconstruction project, nitrate film from *Raumlichtkunst* was restored and transferred to HD with added digital color, by Center for Visual Music. It has been presented as a triptych, a thirty-foot-wide, three-screen, high definition installation accompanied by Edgar Varèse and John Cage soundtracks, at major museums (Whitney Museum of Art, New York, 2012; Tate Modern, London, 2012–2013; Palais de Tokyo, Paris, 2013; other exhibitions pending at this writing). The author was the archivist and curator for this project.[19]

This translation of historical Visual Music cinema to a contemporary, abstract, HD museum installation has been immensely popular, and *Raumlichtkunst* was named in *Artforum*'s Best of 2012 lists. An *Art in America* review described "a syncopated barrage of light, color, and movement: sudden eruptions, languidly swirling liquid, solar systems of spinning dots, disks that materialize and dissipate, pickets that march stolidly across backdrops of whirling circular patterns, an expanding and contracting globe. . . . The unpredictability of organic shapes and patterns plays against the comfort of geometry; fast contrasts with slow, and all is enhanced by the cacophony of percussive audio accompaniment."[20]

THE VORTEX CONCERTS AND DOME THEATRE PREDECESSORS

Within the last eight years, there has been a rapid increase in artists composing abstract visuals for planetariums and domes—and in new festivals screening this work. In this practice, early influences may again be traced to Visual Music artists Fischinger and Belson. In the 1940s, Fischinger briefly received support from the Museum of Non-

Objective Painting in New York (now the Guggenheim Museum). Plans were under way for the new museum, with Frank Lloyd Wright working on designs. The museum's curator, Hilla Rebay, proposed the creation of a Film Center in the museum, discussing it extensively with Fischinger, who likely would have headed this Center. In 1944, Fischinger proposed building a dome theatre in the museum: "I would like to suggest to you a bigger theatre—half spherical—like a big planetarium. The Machines in the center. The spheric projection-surface of a planetarium . . . is a cosmic-feeling of endless endless space without perspective. Images projected in such a sphere become far distant. . . . The people (a few hundred) are sitting in a big circle around the projection machines. The Sound comes (ideal) also from the Center like the lightbeams of the projectors."[21] Sadly, this dome theatre was never built.

The first use of abstract moving images combined with experimental music in a planetarium was in San Francisco's Morrison Planetarium in 1957, with the legendary Vortex Concerts. Featuring new electronic music from avant-garde composers worldwide curated by sound artist Henry Jacobs, five Vortex series were held at the Morrison through January 1959, with over thirty-eight performances. In the blackness of the planetarium's sixty-five-foot dome, visual director Belson created spectacular illusions layering abstract patterns, lighting effects, and cosmic imagery. He recalled "working in an environment representing the heavens . . . a full-bodied experience with stunning visual effects."[22]

The Vortex 4 program notes announced that "Vortex is a new form of theater based on the combination of electronics, optics and architecture. . . . The elements of Vortex are sound, light, color, and movement in their most comprehensive theatrical expression. These audiovisual combinations are presented in a circular, domed theater equipped with special projectors and sound systems. In Vortex there is no separation of audience and stage or screen; the entire domed area becomes a living theater of sound and light."[23]

Vortex was immediately popular; this type of immersive environment had never been created before. Two or three performances a night became necessary. The press loved Vortex and showered positive reviews. A *Time* magazine article in early 1959 discussed its popularity. Vortex became a direct predecessor to the 1960s light shows in the San Francisco Bay area (many created by artists who'd attended Vortex) and other multiscreen and immersive works.

As Vortex continued, the visual effects evolved in their sophistication. Belson would use up to thirty projection devices including the planetarium's thirteen-foot starfield projector, kaleidoscope, and rotating projectors; strobes; slide projectors; 16mm film projectors; a flicker machine; and interference pattern projectors.

Despite the concerts' popularity, friction with planetarium management continually increased. Finally the management cancelled Vortex. The final series (Vortex V) was performed in early 1959. Despite efforts by Jacobs and Belson, Vortex was never performed again. Belson deemed an assistant's later attempt to re-create a version of

Vortex unsatisfactory. Years later, Belson rejected all offers (even from major museums) to remount Vortex, stating it was impossible to re-create. Though others have used the name Vortex for various contemporary projects, they have no relation to the original series.

JOHN WHITNEY SR. AND THE DAWN OF COMPUTER ANIMATION

For computer graphic and software artists today, a major influence is filmmaker John Whitney Sr., whose experiments building early analog computers and motion-control devices resulted in his computer-animated films, notably *Catalog* (1961), *Permutations* (1968), *Matrix I—III* (1971–72), and *Arabesque* (1975). Whitney is remembered for his work with Saul Bass on the opening credits in *Vertigo* (1958), and his slit-screen effect was used by others in Stanley Kubrick's *2001: A Space Odyssey* (1968). Whitney worked with Charles and Ray Eames to prepare the seven-screen *Glimpses of the USA* film for the 1959 American National Exhibition in Moscow, where it was shown in a dome theatre, though not specifically formatted for dome projection.

There is a long tradition of groundbreaking experimental imagery by artists such as Fischinger, Whitney, and Belson being appropriated by Hollywood, pop culture, advertising, and design. In a few cases, these filmmakers were credited for their work or actually paid, although usually minimally (except for Belson, who was paid well): Hollywood used Visual Music filmmakers for *Fantasia, Vertigo,* and *The Right Stuff*—Fischinger, John Whitney Sr., and Belson, respectively. *Fantasia* shows Fischinger's influence but none of his actual work, and he requested his name be removed from the film. He was paid minimally and treated with little respect. More recently Terrence Malick studied the work of Jordan Belson, Richard Baily, and other Visual Music filmmakers before creating the abstract sequences in *Tree of Life* (2011). Several shots from Wilfred's Lumias are in the film.

CONTEMPORARY ABSTRACTION: ROBERT SEIDEL

Beginning as an abstract video artist after studying at Bauhaus University Weimar, Berlin-based Robert Seidel creates installations, single-channel videos, and abstract projection sculptures now featured in museum and gallery exhibitions throughout Europe. His lush abstract imagery folds, caresses, and floats over plaster sculptures, water, and other surfaces. Seidel's recent site specific installations were commissioned in Germany and Korea, and his videos and projections have exhibited at ZKM, LACMA, MOCA Taipei, the Royal Museum of Fine Art Antwerp, and festivals and galleries worldwide.

Seidel wrote about his discovery of Fischinger's work, "The sheer extent of conceptual and formal ideas overwhelmed me. Fischinger's ceaseless research—laying a bridge between imagination and realization with every step—is still unparalleled today. Whether it was static or motion painting, image-creating machines or silhouette and wax animation, each work clearly followed his vision, despite innumerable technical, financial, and personal obstacles."[24]

Regarding music, Seidel notes, "Musical-wise I'm not searching in pinpoint synchronisation; I think the works of Fischinger or Richter get strongest when there is a slight shift, an off-beat or a broken connection with the sound. Here, as a viewer, I'm challenged the most and it becomes my 'personal' film. These moments of uncertainty are what make these films immortal masterpieces."[25]

Seidel laments that Fischinger's influence has not resulted in more success for the abstract film today. He notes, "At present one rarely encounters maturely formulated abstraction, in part because the advertising and event industries have appropriated abstract visual images and projection, misusing them as ornamental filler. These examples are often rendered with a high level of technical skill, but are nevertheless soulless, inconsiderate forms of perfection."[26]

INTERACTIVE AND GENERATIVE ABSTRACTION

Björk's *Biophilia* interactive app album (2011) is rooted in Visual Music culture, literally making music visual with a special nod to Fischinger. Collaborator, interactive artist, and app developer Scott Snibbe gave Björk the *Oskar Fischinger: Ten Films* DVD at an early stage of research, and Björk has long been a fan of abstract film and artists' films. As noted earlier, Snibbe's own work is strongly influenced by Fischinger.

New York-based artist Scott Draves creates single-channel work, apps, and multiscreen installations with his Electric Sheep creations, a networked collective intelligence using algorithms to create generative abstract animation. In 2014, his *Generation 245* (fig. 6.5) was exhibited as a thirty-two-screen installation at Microsoft Research headquarters in Seattle. His abstract digital videos are in collections worldwide, including Google's, and he is part of MoMA New York's permanent online exhibition *Design and the Elastic Mind* (2008). Additionally, Draves's abstract *Dreams in High Fidelity* has screened in planetarium domes, as a twenty-five-projector installation, at a TEDx conference, at MoMA, on nineteen Jumbotrons at BBC's Big Screens project (2010), at LACMA and the Redcat Theatre in Los Angeles in Center for Visual Music's curated programs, and at numerous galleries and venues worldwide.

Draves acknowledges his debt to Oskar Fischinger: "Fischinger's work has been with me for many years and I'm still discovering it today. . . . He influenced me, and he also influenced artists working across the spectrum (as he did himself). Just the other day I was watching Roger Waters' *The Wall* on tour again in 2012. I was struck by the images of goose-stepping hammers, and how similar they are to Fischinger's Muratti cigarette commercial *Muratti Greift Ein* (*Muratti Gets in the Act*). When I went online to look it up, I discovered my memory was actually of a Lucky Strike commercial which was knocked off from Fischinger fourteen years after his 1934 original. And so the story grows."[27]

UK-based artist Bret Battey composes exquisite, intricate, algorithmically generated

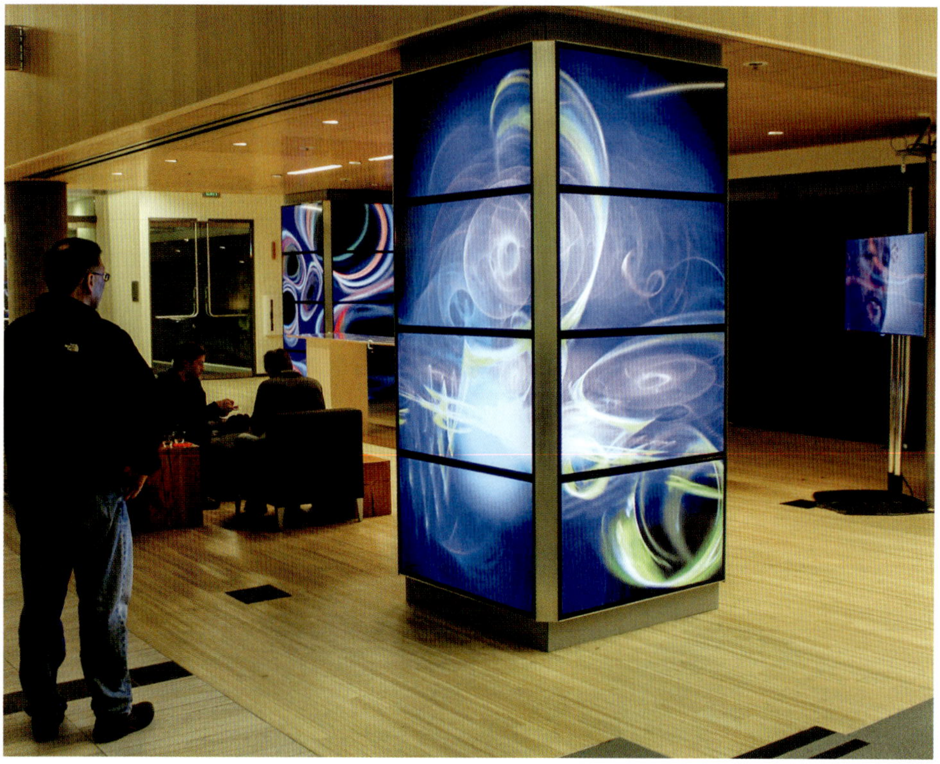

FIGURE 6.5
Scott Draves, *Generation 245*, 2014. Custom software, Internet-wide collective intelligence, "Electric Sheep," 111 GB, 1080p; thirty-two–screen digital video installation; variable lengths. Studio 99, Microsoft Research HQ, Redmond, WA. Courtesy of the artist.

Visual Music films. His *Luna Series 1: Mercurius* (2007) can be viewed in part as a subtle homage to James Whitney's films *Yantra* and *Lapis,* not only in the visual structures consisting of thousands of dot points but in several quiet musical phrases evoking a theme from the soundtrack of *Yantra.*[28] Battey wrote about *Mercurius,* "Three-dimensional rotation algorithms create the spiral forms in this work. In the visual music tradition, the spiral or mandala form has been used to evoke the unity of a meditative state—James Whitney's *Lapis* (1966) being an extraordinary example."[29]

James Whitney (1921–1982), the brother of John Whitney Sr., made several visionary, spiritual abstract films that are classics of experimental animation and Visual Music. Battey explains, "How powerfully I was struck when I first saw some of the early Belson films . . . certainly by James' *Lapis.* . . . Perhaps *Lapis* seeded my perception and encouraged me to be receptive when my experiments with visual code started resulting in the mysterious coherent patterning of tens of thousands of tiny points."[30]

MATERIALITY AND NEW FORMATS

By default, abstract filmmakers still working in celluloid will all become abstract digital video artists, because they'll soon be forced to adapt to these formats. The tools for production of cinema on film, indeed the celluloid film itself, appear bound for extinction in the approaching future. "Coming from a computer-driven interest in images and film," said Robert Seidel, "the Visual Music pioneers showed me the beauty of conscious and random errors in the process of filmmaking. Scratched and hand-painted film, jittering stock as well as optical sound expanded my artistic palette by not emulating these techniques, but finding similar approaches in the digital medium."[31]

Historic Visual Music filmmakers pioneered techniques such as loops, scratching on film, and flicker effects (Jordan Belson's *Allures,* 1961). Many attribute the first use of loops as a device to *Ballet Mécanique* (1924), a well-known classic of experimental cinema by Fernand Léger (made with Dudley Murphy and Man Ray). Though not abstract, it's often included in the canon of Visual Music due to its highly rhythmic structure and image/sound synchronicity. Fischinger used looped imagery in his circa 1926 *Raumlichtkunst* films; from the 1960s onwards loops were widespread in experimental film. Unfortunately, many people working in Visual Music are unaware of the rich heritage of experimental and abstract films that came before them. In the 2011 catalog of the International Festival of Animated Film at Stuttgart, an introduction to a screening of new Visual Music works claimed that looping originates with VJs!

The scratching on film (e.g., *Free Radicals* and *Particles in Space*) of Len Lye (1901–1980) has influenced numerous artists, as have films painted directly on the film stock (e.g., Harry Smith's *Early Abstractions Films 1–3,* McLaren's *Begone Dull Care,* Lye's *A Colour Box,* and many Brakhage films), and the use of physical items affixed to the film itself (e.g., Brakhage's *Mothlight*). Despite misrepresentations on YouTube, Fischinger did not make hand-painted films, only a few painted shots in his early *Raumlichtkunst* (c. 1926) project.

In 2004, Jud Yalkut spoke of his mixture of "film, video, and digital manipulation, and the complex tactilities that this affords me. . . . By tactilities, I mean the unique texture which each medium has, whether it is the beautiful reflected light of film, the direct eye-brain projection of electron/photons in video, or the magical iterations of digital delay, feedback, and electronic coloration. The contrast between 'real' color in imagery and the otherworldly richness of electronic color is highly beautiful and fascinating to me, as are the confluence of pixels in digital work, raster lines in video, and grain in film. They each have a unique beauty that cannot be found in other forms."[32]

It's becoming increasingly difficult to view these important Visual Music works in an accurate context or to experience anything close to Yalkut's "tactilities," even as these works have become more influential today. Unauthorized, degraded online versions don't represent the works correctly, and sometimes museums unknowingly present works improperly (e.g., with incorrect aspect ratios, color, or speeds). Often historical film and video are shown in substandard conditions—inferior copies, too-bright rooms—or displayed as moving wallpaper with little care regarding sound or viewing environment. Paradoxically, museum and gallery exhibitions are where so many discover these works, and will continue to spread their influences widely across future generations. Thus it's essential that those interested in these historical works seek out accurate copies and demand that museums present the work properly. To paraphrase a statement by Fischinger in the 1947 *Art in Cinema* catalog, the only hope for this type of media is that the art museums develop increasingly greater interest and care in presenting this work properly.

NOTES

1. Scott Snibbe, Testimonial, in *Oskar Fischinger (1900–1967): Experiments in Cinematic Abstraction,* ed. Cindy Keefer and Jaap Guldemond (Amsterdam and Los Angeles: EYE Filmmuseum and Center for Visual Music, 2013), 224.

2. Snibbe, Testimonial, 224.

3. The Center for Visual Music consulted and provided most of the films for the 2005 *Visual Music* exhibition. See Center for Visual Music, "About the Films: Films/videos in *Visual Music* exhibition, MOCA LA and Hirshhorn, 2005," www.centerforvisualmusic.org/VMFilms.htm.

4. JoAnn Northrup, "Jennifer Steinkamp," in *Selections: The San Jose Museum of Art Permanent Collection,* ed. Susan Landauer (San Jose, CA: San Jose Museum of Art, 2004).

5. Richard Baily, quoted in posts to VisualMusicPlus online discussion list, September 24, 2003, administered by Center for Visual Music and archived on Yahoo Groups.

6. Christina McPhee, e-mail to the author, February 10, 2014.

7. "McLaren Wall-to-Wall," National Film Board of Canada and Quartier des Spectacles Montreal, www.mclarenwalltowall.com/en/competition/. Accessed December 18, 2013.

8. William Moritz, "Toward an Aesthetics of Visual Music," *ASIFA Canada Bulletin* 14, no. 3 (December 1986), http://centerforvisualmusic.org/TAVM.htm.

9. Jack Ox and Cindy Keefer, "On Curating Recent Digital Abstract Visual Music" (essay for *Abstract Visual Music* project, New York Digital Salon, School of Visual Arts, New York, 2006); revised, 2008, www.centerforvisualmusic.org/Ox_Keefer_VM.htm.

10. Ox and Keefer, "On Curating."

11. William Moritz, "Abstract Film and Color Music," in *The Spiritual in Art: Abstract Painting 1890–1985,* ed. Maurice Tuchman et al. (New York: Abbeville Press, 1986), 299.

12. Moritz, "Abstract Film and Color Music," 300.

13. James Turrell, quoted in "In Conversation: James Turrell with Alex Bacon," *The Brooklyn Rail,* September 4, 2013.

14. George Stadnik, "About Lumia," The Art of Lumia, www.photonlightguitars.com/aboutlumia.html.

15. *Film Quarterly,* quoted in description of *Turn, Turn, Turn,* Film-makers' Coop, n.d., http://film-makerscoop.com/rentals-sales/search-results?fmc_filmid=3527.

16. "Noor," SteveBeck.tv, n.d., www.stevebeck.tv/noor.htm.

17. Beyond 3D Festival, Art: Installation, http://2013.beyond-festival.com/en/art/installation/.

18. Cindy Keefer, "'*Raumlichtmusik*'—Early 20th Century Abstract Cinema Immersive Environments," *Leonardo Electronic Almanac,* Creative Data special issue, 16, no. 6–7 (October 2009), www.leonardo.info/LEA/CreativeData/CD_Keefer.pdf.

19. For more on *Raumlichtkunst,* please see "Oskar Fischinger's *Raumlichtkunst,*" Center for Visual Music, www.centerforvisualmusic.org/Raumlichtkunst.html.

20. "Oskar Fischinger, New York, at Whitney Museum," Reviews, *Art in America,* November 6, 2012.

21. Oskar Fischinger to Hilla Rebay, April 24, 1944, Fischinger Collection, Center for Visual Music, Los Angeles.

22. Jordan Belson, telephone conversation with the author, December 2002. This quote and other Vortex information here are derived partly from Keefer, "*Raumlichtmusik.*"

23. Original program notes, Belson collection, Center for Visual Music archive, Los Angeles.

24. Robert Seidel, Testimonial, in *Oskar Fischinger,* ed. Keefer and Guldemond, 223.

25. Robert Seidel, e-mail to the author, February 9, 2014.

26. Seidel, Testimonial, in *Oskar Fischinger,* 224.

27. Scott Draves, Testimonial, in *Oskar Fischinger,* ed. Keefer and Guldemond, 221.

28. The soundtrack for James Whitney's film *Yantra* is an edited version of the longer *Cain and Abel* score by Dutch composer Henk Badings. Jordan Belson did this edit in 1959; then Whitney approved it for the soundtrack of *Yantra,* which had previously been released silent.

29. Bret Battey, Bat Hat Media, www.mti.dmu.ac.uk/~bbattey/Gallery/merc.html.

30. Bret Battey, e-mail to the author, February 7, 2014. For information on James Whitney's films and use of dot patterns, see William Moritz, *Enlightenment,* www.centerforvisualmusic.org/WMEnlightenment.html.

31. Robert Seidel, e-mail to author, February 9, 2014.

32. Sabrina Gschwandtner, "Between Film and Video—the Intermedia Art of Jud Yalkut: An Interview with Jud Yalkut," in Video: Vintage and Current, *Millennium Film Journal,* no. 42 (Fall 2004).

7

GETTING MESSY

Chance and Glitch in Contemporary Video Art

Gregory Zinman

> We speak of messy abstraction and of clean abstraction (or sometimes biomorphic and geometric abstraction), but this applies not only for the "works themselves" but also our approach to them. Abstraction is not only an idea of form but also a matter of defamiliarization and derangement. Abstraction is in equal measures theatrical and performative, absorptive and ideal.
>
> CHARLES BERNSTEIN

"The digital," a phrase that pervades present scholarship in the fields of film and media studies, is often employed as shorthand for a set of conditions—and even aesthetics—encompassing that which is programmatic, precise, automated, and endlessly replicable. These notions of the digital are also often set in relation or opposition to analog technologies, "the real," and the humanistic. To be sure, many strains of contemporary digital art and design embrace the use of the computer to create seamless animations constructed from ever-more-complex algorithmic modeling. Certain digital practitioners, however, employ computational tools and techniques in order to illuminate imperfections, making visible the components of the work's construction, questioning the expected use of technology, and creating new kinds of abstraction in time-based media.

This essay seeks to examine such works, works that exist between media and whose creators explore the collisions, slippages, and juxtapositions produced by the admixture of analog and digital technologies, allowing chance operations to inform both their methods and their creative output. Borrowing from poet Charles Bernstein, I locate these works on a sliding scale of "clean" to "messy" abstraction, both in the artists' approaches and in their resulting imagery. A "clean" abstraction might involve blocks of color and hard-edged geometric forms, while a "messy" abstraction may appear as a seemingly random array of fleeting flecks and sprawling lines skipping across the screen. These terms may also be applied to the methods that produce these abstractions: a "messy" artist may stain a filmstrip with her own bodily fluids; expose her film to the elements, thereby letting chance operations and the environment determine the ensuing patterns caused by wind and rain; or rely on the kinesthetic scratching of the film emulsion to achieve a jittery, dancing line. An artist's "clean" methodology, on the other hand, might involve the precise manipulation of code or the strategic disruption of a video codec's ability to decode a data stream. And yet it is easy to see how these methods and outcomes may not necessarily exist only as binaries but also as mutually informing ideas regarding the nature of abstraction. Those "messy" stains and specks may be the performative offspring of a meticulous conceptual plan that would otherwise be considered "clean," and that careful application of lossy data compression may similarly result in a continuously fractured image that manifests as total chaos.

Clean and messy alike, these abstractions in time seek to make strange the familiar and prompt us to reconsider and re-view the ways moving image technologies alter our relation to the everyday. Jennifer West, Lynn Marie Kirby, and Takeshi Murata all make moving image work that eschews the photographic in favor of an exploratory and direct manipulation of filmic and digital materials, producing a set of effects that calls into question the presumed or "correct" use of the tools and technologies employed. These works share the quality of being hybrids, operating between older and newer media forms—bypassing medium specificity in a search of a syncretic alterity resulting from encoding and transcoding processes. Kirby takes cameraless photochemical light exposures of specific geographical locations and then shapes them digitally into stuttering geometric displays of form and color. West transfers her analog, direct film works to digital looping projections. Murata repurposes footage from '80s film and television commercials to make compression artifact art.

Of the three, Murata is the only artist explicitly aligned with "glitch," a contemporary aesthetic characterized by data compression, loss, and error. As a concept, glitch has been discussed and debated in the media arts community online, although it has not yet received sustained scholarly attention.[1] Several media artists have suggested that a study of glitch should attend to the practice as a material mode of expression, as well as a means of seeing and thinking about the world. Most notably, Dutch artist-theorist Rosa Menkman, in her *Glitch Studies Manifesto*, advocates for a "critical transmedia aesthetics": "Dispute the operating templates of creative practice: fight genres, interfaces and expectations!" In her glitch feminism manifesto, writer/artist/curator Legacy Russell calls for an embrace of the error in "breaking from the hegemony of a 'structured system' infused with the pomp and circumstance of patriarchy."[2] Extending these statements from the art world to the academy, this essay aims to show how glitch, as a concept, allows scholars to better understand the unique practices of Kirby, West, and Murata.

In general, we understand a glitch as something that indicates a technology's inability to perform its assigned function—a scratched groove that causes a record to skip; a torn sprocket hole that creates a film jam, freezing the image onscreen as the celluloid frame begins to burn up in the projector; the repetitive, catching "tick tick" of a hard drive failing to mount. In their purest form, glitches occur by malfunction, through age and consequent deterioration, or as the result of poor programming. But artists across media find ways of forcing the issue, of manufacturing glitches by pushing their technology to fail productively or by coercing that technology to perform in ways that fall outside of its normative uses. Kirby allows light and other elements, including dust, wind, and moisture—elements that would otherwise be considered to cause imperfections—to shape the images that form the basis of her films. Before she digitizes her work, West subjects her film stock to all manner of chemical, biological, and environmental stresses in order to achieve unforeseen patterns and colors. And Murata manipulates video codecs to upset and reshape the linear progression of digital moving images into a mutant mosaic of runaway pixels. Taken together, these video artists show how media disruptions on the level of materiality can foster new kinds of abstraction. They also show the degree to which those disruptions make use of and rely on chance operations to achieve their diverse effects.

While these artists' effects may be new, their heavy reliance on the play of chance and choice, as well as accident and intention, also places their work in a long line of moving image art that manufactures, employs, or intervenes in new technology to make new kinds of abstraction, from Walter Ruttmann's paint-on-glass apparatus for *Lichtspiel: Opus I* (1921), the first publicly screened abstract film, to Len Lye's hyperkinetic, directly painted and scratched films; from the real-time overhead projections of oils and dyes performed by psychedelic light outfits such as the Joshua Light Show to the design and construction of unique video synthesizers, such as one designed by Nam June Paik and Shuya Abe. These contemporary digital works, like their forerunners in moving image abstraction, are best understood not only in relation to the photographic moving image but also in relation to painting. What follows is an examination of how these elements—the painterly and the automatic, the aleatory and the programmatic—combine and reconfigure our understanding of the moving image after the advent of digital filmmaking.

LYNN MARIE KIRBY: SHIFTING LIGHT FROM SUBJECT TO MATERIAL

Lynn Marie Kirby's *Latent Light Excavations* (2003–2007) (fig. 7.1) are film–digital video hybrids that begin as cameraless films. She makes her "site-specific" works without a camera, exposing the film stock to the available light in a particular place. For the *Latent Light* series, Kirby captured the light from three locations in and around San Francisco: under a jacaranda tree in a botanical garden, beneath the Golden Gate Bridge, and inside

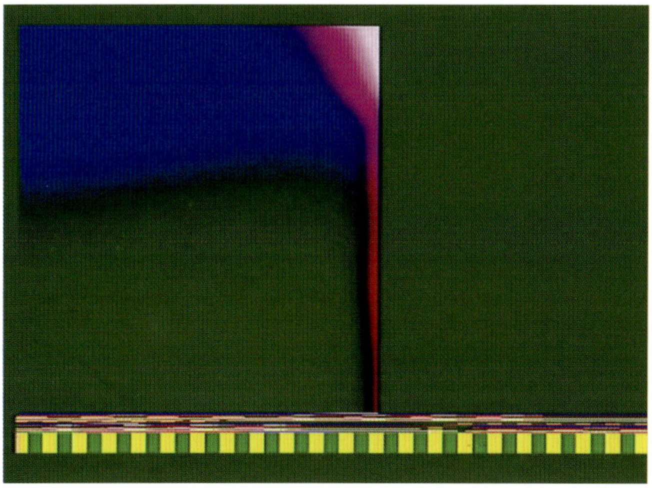

FIGURE 7.1
Lynn Marie Kirby, *Jacaranda Tree Chalon Road Exposure: Brazilian Export, From Refracted Case Histories*, 2004. Film to digital transfer; 4 minutes, 30 seconds. Courtesy of the artist.

St. Ignatius Church. These pieces are therefore predicated on the chance operations of how the light will behave in the chosen spaces and of how the light will subsequently interact with the exposed film. After the initial exposure, Kirby takes the colorfield-like originals and edits them digitally, composing "clean" abstractions of quickly shifting color that at times resemble paintings by Arthur Dove, Ellsworth Kelly, and Barnett Newman. Kirby segments and recrops her frames, composing hard-edged landscapes of vibrant color that still carry elements of grain and surface detail that speak to their analog origins. At the same time, the pieces also betray their video format, displaying interlaced artifacts and stuttering rhythms, as if the conversion from film to video was placing a mechanical burden on the resulting moving images. Many frames are segmented into rectangular sections and grids, and multihued triangles and halated circles skip across the surface of the image. A number of these geometric abstractions are in fact Kirby's incorporation of the digital editing icons from the program she employs. Placing these icons within the field established by the initial light capture, Kirby thus negotiates the digital and analog, allowing each to inform and reinterpret the other. Editing software here becomes both a tool for shaping and a subject of the image. The artist explains that the "resulting work is the 'residue' of a real-time performance on the film to digital transfer deck." The indexical trace that putatively inheres in the photochemical process—the record of the place captured, the dust and light that leave an impression on Kirby's film—is transferred into and persists throughout the digital field that she describes in the editing process. In these works, the performance of light is reinscribed and reshaped by the "performance of invisibility" that glitch artist Evan Meaney ascribes to the functioning of digital systems.[3] Both Kirby's analog and digital handiwork remain obscured to the uniformed viewer, even as she brings the characteristics of each to bear on the final image.

The title of Kirby's series alerts us that these films are inherently intermedial and polysemic—they are *excavations,* a mining or digging up of light that was hidden and, quite literally, to borrow additional construction terminology, waiting to be developed. But what does it mean to dig for light? In one of the works in the series, *St. Ignatius Church Exposure: Lenten Light Conversions,* Kirby recorded light in the titular building over the forty days of Lent.[4] The work's site and its spiritual theme connect Kirby's vibrant abstract moving images to the ages-old practice of painting religious icons, and it evokes the scintillating light play of the stained glass often found in churches. The title plays off a number of "conversions," including phrases of spiritual revelation ("beginning to see the light") as well as changes of material character—of one kind of light (sunlight) into others (artificial, backlit, and/or projected) and of analog to digital. This last mode of conversion provides a way of seeing St. Ignatius's light as it has never been seen before. The recasting of the church's light into pure abstraction brings to mind painter Robert Motherwell's insistence that modern abstract art came into existence not merely as a response to photography's purported technologically superior ability to represent the world, but also, and more importantly, as a means of constructing an experiential, sensuous bridge between the individual and the world. As Motherwell put it, abstraction arrived "as the consequence of a most profound, relentless, unquenchable need. The need is for felt experience—intense, immediate, direct, subtle, unified, warm, vivid, rhythmic."[5]

Mining the physical site of the church for its light, Kirby provides a "felt experience" that gives the viewer a sense of place without recourse to conventional representation. Her upending of cinematic conventions might be said to be constituted by her making use of both automatic and performative qualities in the analog without ever snapping a picture. She expresses craft and style through her meticulous manipulation of the digital, presenting a number of knotty conceptual—and formal—twists. Kirby intervenes into the materiality of the image only after having first put it through an operation of chance. And yet many of the resulting abstractions, composed horizontally, recall natural landscapes and thus perform a series of associations between artistic forms and practices—from architecture to painting to filmmaking. The film also combines representation with abstraction so that it serves both as a depiction and a re-visitation of a physical place. The filmic exposures are documents of the time and places in which they were made. The trace of the physical structure persists as light and color and then is subjectively re-viewed and rearranged by the artist's manipulation of the digital video. Kirby's capture and restructuring of light enacts a play of dematerialization and rematerialization—of space into light, and light into digital code that manifests onscreen. Film theorist P. Adams Sitney locates the primary desire of the abstract filmmaker in creating "a work which aspires not to refer, but *to be,* which attempts to challenge the ontological priority of the object."[6] Through abstractions in time, Kirby does not merely record or represent the world that we know but instead creates a new world from the old, a world that was previously hidden.

JENNIFER WEST: TRANSFERRING ANALOG AESTHETICS

In contrast to Kirby's analog-digital work, in which light is revealed and concretized into material, Jennifer West embraces a referential approach to her direct films. She employs bodily fluids, drugs, cosmetics, foodstuffs, and kinetic acts such as skateboarding to create gestural handmade works on 35- and 70mm film that are subsequently shown as silent digital loops in gallery spaces. West's application of "messy" materials via chance operations allows viewers to see the ways glitch art illuminates the beauty of happenstance. Using analog methods and digital displays, Jennifer West's handmade films thus also function as litanies of their making. West, who studied with Diana Thater and Mike Kelley at the Art Center College of Design in Pasadena, expresses a closer affinity to visual art than to experimental film. Describing her process, she explains, "I'm coming at it more as a mark-maker and a painter."[7] West's handmade films combine cameraless techniques with self-shot footage of herself, her family, and her students. The films reference and appropriate art-historical, cinematic, and pop-cultural works, and engage with a number of alternative youth cultures, including skateboarding and snowboarding, riot grrrl, and grunge. West's films also play on the tension between the images made by the materials placed on the filmstrip, the materials themselves, and the photographed footage. She creates multiple pieces simultaneously, allowing the film stock of one to decompose or "marinate" while she attends to various aspects of other works-in-progress. Upon completion, she transfers her work to digital and projects the film as a silent HD loop. Her work is most often shown as such in a gallery setting, with the image projected onto a white wall rather than onto a screen.

The titles of West's allusive works always contain the ingredients used to make their images, and those elements usually play off the piece's name in some thematic way. Her first film, *Marinated Film—the Roll of 16mm That I Had in the Fridge for Over 10 Years* (2004–05) was displayed with fourteen recipe cards describing each of the marinades used, including wine, Pop Rocks, urine, gasoline, hair dye, and blueberries.[8] This mélange of items illustrates a desire to compare and combine the image-making capabilities of the natural and the manufactured, the ingested and excreted, and the bodily with the cosmetic. *Marinated Film* also plays with the idea of cinematic time. The piece runs just over nine minutes but took a decade to produce, as the various materials were left to "work," continuing to shape celluloid images on a nearly imperceptible time scale.

After *Marinated Film*, West began incorporating the laundry list of materials used in her films' construction into the titles themselves. For example, *Nirvana Alchemy Film (16mm black & white film soaked in lithium mineral hot springs, pennyroyal tea, doused in mud, sopped in bleach, cherry antacid and laxatives—jumping by Finn West & Jwest)* (2007) runs for just under three minutes, and the ingredients all refer to lyrics and songs by the titular grunge band. As indicated, these materials are applied to film that West shot of herself and her son jumping on a trampoline. The camera is positioned below the jumpers, so that their landing feet almost seem to produce the reticulated blood-red swathes and pockmarked neon green lines wavering across the screen. The overall sensation is of restless and relentless motion, even agitation. Again we see the intersection of choice and chance: West establishes the parameters of the piece but cannot anticipate the particular kinds of marks and colors that may be produced by the application of the chosen materials. The trampoline footage reinforces the idea of play, and the structuring rules laid down by West (that the materials must explicitly make reference to the theme) thus take on a ludic quality. As with many abstract films, language is a complicating factor here, and West takes the use of the title-as-explanatory-possibility to its very limit. The language of West's titles at once intrigues and informs the mind's eye and ear and cues us to see and hear things that are implied but not necessarily present. (It is difficult not to think of Nirvana's music once one has read the title to the film.) In this way, West creates tension between what is represented (Nirvana's music and pet themes) and what is real (the materials used to create the painterly smears that we see).

In *Skate the Sky Film (35mm film print of clouds in the sky covered with ink, Ho-Hos, and Melon—taped to Tate Turbine Hall ramp and skateboarded over using ollie, kick flip, pop shove-it, acid drop, melon grab, crooked grind, bunny hop, tic tacs, sex change, disco flip—skateboarding performed live for Long Weekend by Thomas Lock, Louis Henderson, Charlotte Brennan, Dion Penman, Sam Griffin, Jak Tonge, Evin Goode and Quantin Paris—clouds in the sky shot by Peter West)*, West transformed the Tate Modern's cavernous Turbine Hall into a skate park and asked her riders to skate directly on filmstrips. The ensuing residue and scratches became the visual stuff of the film, thus combining the handmade hallmarks of chance, direct image making, and the melding of gestural performance with rigorous conceptual planning. West obviously enjoys the handmade tactility—the "messiness"—of making films, but she is also meticulous about extensively documenting her process with her collaborators in photographs. By highlighting production through the display of production stills, she creates art documents that nod to classical Hollywood press materials—a pulling back of the curtain and a demystification of the process. West publishes these photos in zines that are given away at her shows, an acknowledgement of DIY culture, and a practice emblematic of West's bridging of subculture and gallery worlds.[9]

West's savvy extends to her simultaneous embrace and parody of her art-historical antecedents. Her *Lavender Mist Film/Pollock Film 1 (70mm film leader rubbed with Jimson Weed Trumpet flowers, spraypainted, dipped and splattered with nail polish, sprayed with lavender mist air freshener)* (2009) (fig. 7.2) attempts a feminist intervention into the masculine field of action painting in a breezy forty-six seconds. She carefully replicates Pollock's color palette while using everyday materials, tossing in some hallucinogenic flowers that evoke the self-mythologizing grandeur of the Abstract Expressionists. Formally, West's splatters and drips recall the style of much postwar American art. She even seems to be appropriating critic Harold Rosenberg's conception of the AbEx canvas as the "space of an event" and relocating it on a celluloid strip, a cramped space that is then blown up to overwhelming proportions though projection. However, West's practice,

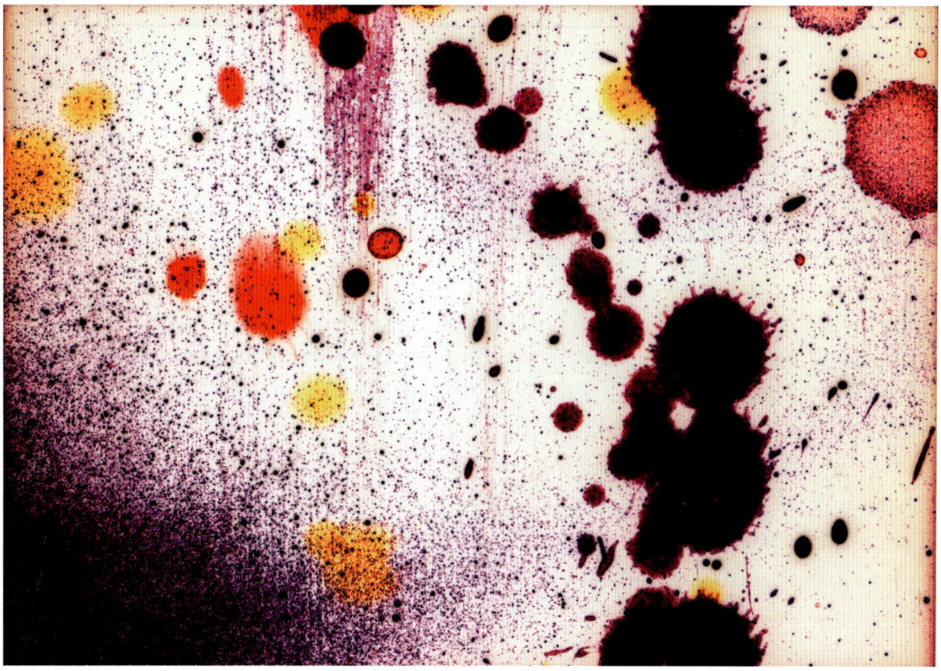

FIGURE 7.2
Jennifer West, *Lavender Mist Film/Pollock Film 1*, 2009. 70mm film transferred to digital video, silent; 46 seconds. Courtesy of the artist, Marc Foxx Gallery, Los Angeles, and Vilma Gold Gallery, London.

which fosters collaboration, playfully undercuts that era's tropes of heroic individualism. Furthermore, her methods are also related to the color field paintings of Helen Frankenthaler and Morris Louis, in which the artists stained their canvases, letting color spread and seep into the pictorial ground rather than build up skeins or layers of paint.[10]

Even though her films are suffused with a longing for the past—for older music, for the lysergic hippie culture of Southern California, for youth—West chooses to project her films digitally because the analog whir of the projector is "too nostalgic," and the digital aspects of her work ensure that "the subjects are considered in the medium of their time."[11] The insistence on projection, rather than displaying the piece on a monitor or flat screen, is in keeping with cinema's increased reliance on modes of digital production, dissemination, and projection and maintains certain qualities ascribed to the cinematic experience. The looping strategies of West's display harken back to some of the earliest conventions of cinematic exhibition, in which exhibitors would often show their wares multiple times while bringing to mind the perpetual repetitions seen in online moving images such as GIFs and Vines. More recently, West made eighty of her films publicly accessible on Vimeo, encouraging viewers to informally gather at their schools, homes, and offices and "drift" through her oeuvre by using phones, tablets, and laptops in order to create uniquely curated multiscreen installations. The potential messiness of ceding programming control to her audience was balanced by the clarity of West's "instructions" indicating ways people could participate in the project. Called *Warm Bodies in a Room,* the show shifted the time and sites of the work's reception from a brick-and-mortar gallery to a dematerialized, globally networked simultaneity, all while valorizing the idea that the work should be consumed communally, among people in a shared space—real or virtual or both.[12]

West's combinatory aesthetics productively complicate readings of her work. The use of digital projection in the gallery space also situates West's work in the more lucrative art-world sphere of "artists' films," rather than in the realm of experimental film. Her exhibition practices place her in the white cube rather than black box, and her work circulates through the world of art fairs, installations, and commissions. West's wordy titles describe an effort to make her "messy" abstractions more legible to both casual viewers and art world denizens. In that sense, it may further be argued that West's films are, in fact, too literal and lacking in mystery—too "clean" in their final presentation as describable, graspable, and collectible art objects. The manner in which she lists the friends and collaborators who have contributed to the final project speaks to her actual social network. In that respect, West's films present perfect specimens of contemporary digital media: data-rich, pre-Googled, and reference-ready. On the other hand, her Vimeo experiment indicates a populist desire to reach a public positioned beyond the gallery wall. In this light, it is possible to see that even though West's titles immediately circumscribe a certain level of critical response, they also perform the task of removing a literary or even linguistic reading in order to heighten the viewer's experience to an affective response to the play of movement and color that operates beyond the limits of language.

TAKESHI MURATA: GLITCHING CINEMA'S ANALOG PAST

West's and Kirby's interventions into materiality demand that we rethink the presumed functions and purposes of the media they are exploring. For West, this means eschewing photography in repurposing the celluloid as a canvas on which to paint, spray, or stain a variety of materials. For Kirby, this means rethinking the relationship between capturing and shaping light without ever having filmed anything. The cinematic image thus becomes a site of production rather than reproduction. Digital artist Takeshi Murata extends this concept, engineering error in order to display a cascade of ghostly imagery that reworks representational images into a riot of color. While Murata's video work is exclusively digital, encompassing abstract psychedelia as well as 3-D character animations, several of his pieces have relied on analog film sources as their foundation. In his glitch-induced abstractions, Murata also relies on chance operations in a variety of ways.[13]

Murata's techniques involve a form of data compression known as datamoshing or "pixel bleeding." Its very name bespeaks the organic-computer hybridity that typifies Murata's work. The use of video compression artifacts is a subset of glitch art in which artists exploit technological error so as to create new images and sounds. Murata creates his glitch video from software packages such as AfterEffects and the DivX codec (a program used to read or write media files), though the pixel bleed effect has become so popular that developers and artists have recently introduced datamosh plug-ins for existing software. Datamoshing involves the removal of an encoded video's I-frames ("intra-coded picture," also known as key frames—a frame that does not require any information regarding another frame to be decoded), leaving only the P- ("predicted picture") or B- ("bi-predictive picture") frames. P-frames contain information predicting the changes in the image between the current frame and the previous one, and B-frames contain information predicting the image differences between the previous, current, and subsequent frames. Because P- and B-frames use data from previous and forward frames, they are more compressed than I-frames. The results are artworks of complex construction that are nevertheless predicated on material absence and difference.

It is important to note that Murata's work makes use of technical errors; his videos are not errors in and of themselves. As artist and theorist Iman Moradi explains, the visual glitch is "an artifact resulting from an error. It is neither the cause, nor the error itself, it is simply the product of an error and more specifically its visual manifestation."[14] Errors are the result of mistakes in process, and although it may be "impossible to deliberately make a mistake," as Norwegian curator and sound artist Per Platou observes, it is still possible to be surprised by what an error engenders.[15] "Data-bender" and audio glitch artist Benjamin Berg (aka stAllio!) explains the reasons for this surprise:

> You had painters who were more concerned with exploring the nature of paint and canvas than with "representing" some physical object or scene. Glitch practices are like that stuff, but because digital structures are more hidden, you can do things where even if you know pretty much what's going to happen, you don't really know what the end result will look or sound like. It's not really chance, because there are rules governing it, but it feels like chance because you don't understand those rules. Even if you have a good grasp of something like JPEG compression, you probably can't look at the code and tell what the image is going to look like. So it's a way of creating things that you wouldn't have thought of yourself, just as in the tradition of John Cage, Bryon Gysin, etc.[16]

Compression artifact works such as those made by Berg, Murata, animator David O'Reilly, Sven Köing, Paper Rad, and others demonstrate that it is possible to incorporate those unexpected results into a work in order to effect that same sense of surprise, astonishment, or befuddlement in the viewer.

Purposeful mistakes may be an oxymoron, but happy accidents are an essential facet of moving image abstraction. Lynn Marie Kirby, for instance, can't know what will happen when the light on a specific day interacts with her photochemical film. Jennifer

West's splashes of paint or melting foodstuffs may appear one way on a frame-by-frame basis and completely transform when put into motion and blown up by projection. Similarly, Murata may have a good idea of what his compression artifacts—his enforced errors—may produce but may be nevertheless pleasantly surprised by the particular movement resulting from the removal of certain key frames. As in most art-making, Murata's works entail a play of trial and, yes, error—of experimenting with his tools and materials in order to see what he is capable of producing under set parameters or to hone his practice in order to produce a desired effect.

With Murata's glitch art, previously unseen computational processes bubble up and burst though the surface of the image, indicating the material underpinning of the image—not unlike the scratches in Kirby's work or the paint-on-film applications in West's. These aesthetics are not entirely sui generis. As early as 1947, computer animation pioneers James Whitney and John Whitney invoked Marcel Duchamp's "irony of indifference" in advocating for an aesthetic of "machine-realized" art.[17] This indifference is both a resignation and a strategy, a form of trust in the automated process of the machine to do what it does. And yet, we also know that a computer will not do what it does without having first been given a command by a human.

Glitch also offers a perverse delight by allowing us to see technology fail. Technology fails people all the time—a memory error wipes out a finished essay, a software update erases one's catalog of music files—and it often registers as cruel, unfair, or unwarranted. Datamoshing allows us to enjoy the disruption of the technological object that is supposed to perform flawlessly. In other words, it is a thrill to see technology fail at its most basic tasks and allows us to reassert human authority over the machine.

This animus toward the machine, while understandable, may nevertheless be misplaced. Code, after all, is written by humans. With respect to glitch, however, what results is not a resurgence of the trace of the human hand, but rather a synthesis of the human mind—the artist's—that intervenes in the code and the computer's rule-based logic that allows the code to be run. Within this synthesis is a curious push-pull of authorship and control between computer and artist. The challenge with glitch art is how to limit error, producing a desired effect without sacrificing the functionality of the program. In other words, the computer needs to *malfunction properly* in order to produce the abstracted image.

With most computer imagery, legibility is at a premium. Clarity might allow the viewer to process information more quickly; sharpness can enhance game play or render video in crystalline detail. In an age of high-definition precision, blurred images recall the censorious—images of sex and violence considered too graphic for polite or even public consumption, news reports of an exploded IED's bloody aftermath, a pixilated visage preserving the anonymity of a corporate whistleblower. Murata's *Monster Movie* (2005) (fig. 7.3) offers a continual rupture of the legible in order to both demonstrate the extent to which computer-generated imagery is an assemblage of discrete parts and to ask us to become active viewers, engaging our eye in a screen that most often serves as a

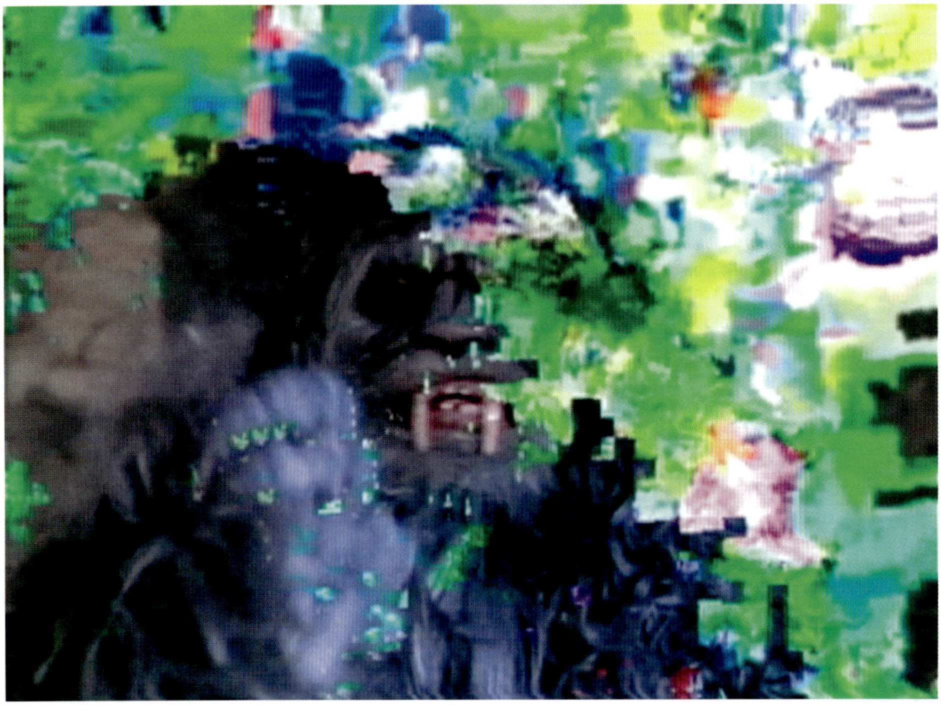

FIGURE 7.3
Takeshi Murata, *Monster Movie,* 2005. Digital video, color, sound; 3 minutes, 55 seconds. Courtesy of the artist and Electronic Arts Intermix (EAI), New York.

site of information reception or passive pleasure. In *Monster Movie,* Murata uses a series of select frames from the B-movie comedy *Caveman* (Carl Gottlieb, 1981) to transform an abominable snowman into a whirling dervish of pixels that re-form and break apart thirty times a second, resulting in over 7,200 discrete images. The emphasis in the four-minute video is on movement and kinetics, the gestures of the costumed actor and the colorful maelstrom unleashed by machine software. Here is the smeared flotsam and jetsam of cinema's past, re-presented in a way that complicates our ability to see the moving image—or its history—clearly.

However, Murata's digital occlusions connect to an entirely different history—that of painterly abstraction. Impressionism challenged viewers to see how time and light might be collapsed into what Meyer Schapiro described as an "unconventionalized and unregulated vision" that rebuffed consumer culture.[18] Futurist painting's fascination with modern machines and velocity resulted in works that blurred simultaneity and speed. Futurism's forerunner, Divisionism, was a Neo-Impressionist school in which colors were broken down into dots that are then brought together and visually harmonized in the eye of the viewer. Divisionism was a scientifically informed kind of painting, but Murata's dots are pixels, which coalesce and blur within the blink of an eye.

Unlike Divisionism, which engineers pictorial elements into a cohesive whole, Murata tears his images apart before allowing them to come back together.

Murata's resultant abstractions thus appear messy, but they are not so much concerned with disorder as they are with a reordering: quite literally, telling the video software to reorder a sequence of images. Viewers first see the yeti emerging from a dark pool, mirroring the almost immediate eruption of digital chaos that transforms the image. *Monster Movie* does not move from cut to cut, as in traditional cinematic editing, but rather morphs and stretches from one image to another. The viewer can barely distinguish the sequences of the beast emerging from a body of water, swinging its long arms akimbo as it advances toward the camera, gesticulating in front of fiery torches, lurching to one side, and writhing on the ground. Set to a briskly percussive soundtrack by Plate Tectonics, consisting of drum-kit scatterings and vocal yelps, the images of the flailing monster unravel into a perpetual riot of pixilated efflorescence—the image shimmers, twists, and cartwheels around the frame, often all at once. The figure of the snowman is played for cheap laughs in *Caveman,* and yet the effect of seeing this inhuman apparition in *Monster Movie* chase the deliquescent trail of his own image, his mouth open in an unheard scream, is indeed strange, unstable, and monstrous. Viewers first see the beast emerging from a dark pool, mirroring the almost immediate eruption of digital chaos that ensues, transforming the image from one of representation to one of abstraction.

Murata's appropriation of a cinematic afterthought like *Caveman* resonates on both technical and thematic levels. With regard to the former, layers are one of the elements that make up the construction and manipulation of digital imagery. With regard to the latter, Murata resuscitates fragments from the largely forgotten film featuring ex-Beatle Ringo Starr in order to demonstrate how memory itself is layered, filtered, and fragmented. Memory—both the human and computer kinds—is nonlinear and, as demonstrated by Murata's digital flaying of *Caveman* to create *Monster Movie,* susceptible to influence and even corruption. Experimental filmmaker Hollis Frampton described nostalgia as "the wounds of returning," and Murata processes the return to even the most anodyne cinematic past through images of violence and rupture. As Murata reroutes his clips of the staggering snowman back for yet another dispersal, through looping and reversals, he engenders a perpetual return that nevertheless never repeats—the digital morass we see isn't what we saw before, even if the source material remains the same.

Chance plays a role here, not in that Murata's compositions are accidental or random, but that because it is difficult to precisely envision what will happen to a digital video file when the key frames are removed, the artist's process necessarily involves an element of experimentation and refinement. In his analysis of John Cage's use of chance, art historian Branden Joseph observes how Bergson's *Creative Evolution* seems to suggest that if the notion of memory and absence were removed from the perceiving subject, the only remaining concern would be the perception of the discovery of objects, though not necessarily the ones that were being sought.[19] This relationship between absence and unexpected presence could also easily describe the production and reception of Murata's compression works. The absent object—here a key frame—lingers in ghostly outline or movement through the remaining presence of the frames that precede and follow it, resulting in a surprising synthesis of image and afterimage, kinesis and digital shadow—a newly perceived object realized by the combination of the artist's careful manipulation of the frames and the computer's performance of its orders. Murata's order is not necessarily pitched in relation to disorder so much as it is to another order that is not yet been fully understood.[20]

Wendy Chun and Tara McPherson have written on the development of software (Chun) and operating systems (McPherson) as design progressions intended to elide human presence and, in some cases, explicitly intended to foreclose the possibility of human intervention.[21] And yet, Murata's probings into video software's algorithmic functions illustrate the degree to which digital media art is still subject to art historical concerns of style, authorship, form, and composition. Murata himself seems less interested in his work's self-reflexive qualities than in something like an authorial signature. He explains, "Ultimately, I hope that the work inherently shows that there's a human behind it and that people can have an emotional response from watching it."[22] What the artist seeks is not a didacticism derived from pulling back the cover on computational functions but an affective response to the work. His is a remark spoken by an artist who understands the degree to which computers are the handiwork of humans.

MEDIA CULTURE'S MESSY, LOSSY MEMORY

What Murata's art throws into relief—or, more precisely, makes real out of the virtual—is how our digital environment is suffused with traces of the cinematic past. In his transformation of *Caveman,* Murata succeeds in making kitsch strange. Kitsch's lack of restraint, its ebullience, is evident in the apparent disintegration and proliferation of the image, an image that pours itself out and makes itself multiple, all while undergoing the defamiliarization that Bernstein speaks of in this essay's epigraph. Murata makes schlock uncanny, and, in so doing, asks us to reconsider our relationship to the marginalized and trashier aspects of our culture: how have our cultural cast-offs shaped us? Why do their monstrous, or uncanny, reappearance disturb us? What else has been forgotten? What else has been lost?

One of Murata's most recent datamoshing pieces, *Shiboogi* (2013) (fig. 7.4), takes media detritus as its subject, and in so doing, makes use of chance in another way entirely. Against a colorful, constantly undulating background of brightly pixilated horizontal waveforms resembling nothing so much as a radioactive sandpainting, the viewer sees a blue frame emerge. Within this smaller frame appears a close-up of a hand slicing a baguette, images of coffee being poured, and a woman nodding in approval as she takes a sip from her cup. The frame collapses into the colorful muddle, replaced by what appears to be a car advertisement with Western actors and Japanese chyrons. More ads

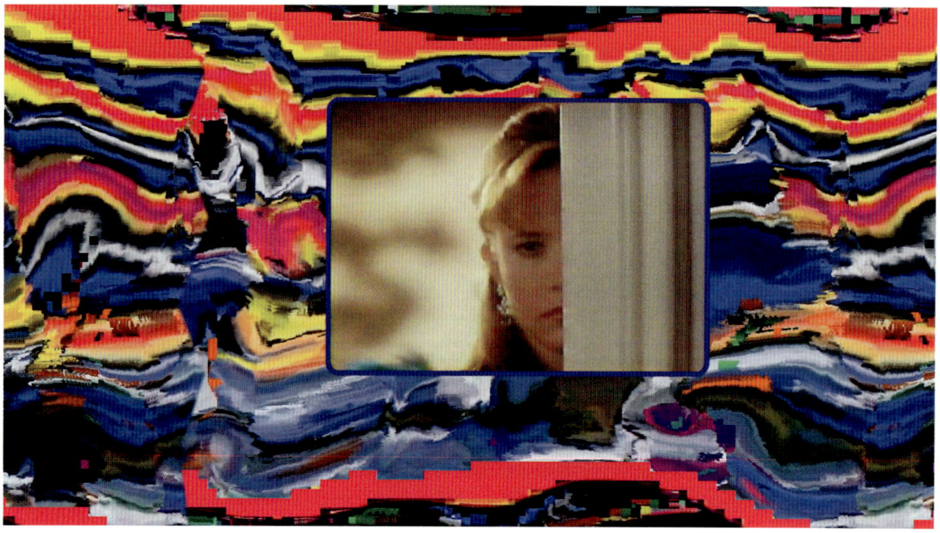

FIGURE 7.4
Takeshi Murata, *Shiboogi*, 2013. Digital video, color, silent; 8 minutes, 18 seconds. Courtesy of the artist, Salon 94, and Ratio 3.

follow, each in its own frame, replacing the ones that have drained into the digital soup, which seethes and pulses, altering its direction and tempo. A snail emerging from an egg oozes by a fashionable woman and shoots lasers from its antennae; an elegant woman in evening dress spies on a man in a white suit who transforms, in a cut, into a unicorn. A Mickey Mouse–themed soft drink is proffered, and clunky translations for spots selling "sound cooking" and "stick coffee" manifest through the electric haze.

The ornate moving background, it turns out, was inspired by Australian fashion brand Coogi, whose densely patterned, multicolor knitwear was most famously sported by rapper The Notorious B.I.G., who was murdered in 1997, at the apex of his career. The artist happened upon the commercials in *Shiboogi*'s frames-within-a-frame by chance in a Japanese record shop. The piece's title is likely a play on Shibuya, Tokyo's hip shopping district.

Shiboogi engages issues of identity and memory, influence and absence. The appearance of occidental actors in these commercials, taken with the Coogi's cultural journey from Melbourne to the streets of Brooklyn, indicates a concern with transversing and negotiating national boundaries. For the Chicago-born Murata, this could be read, at least in part, as a meditation on the artist's identity as a Japanese American, but *Shiboogi* also addresses a larger theme of how media, and particularly media online, is presented not programmatically but rather in flow or flux, constantly changing, unstable and ahistorical in the extreme. These forgotten Japanese commercials, presumably unfamiliar to Western audiences, emerge and recede into the "fabric" of Murata's media flow, joining the tide of similarly obscure ads, fashions, games, and movies that make up global

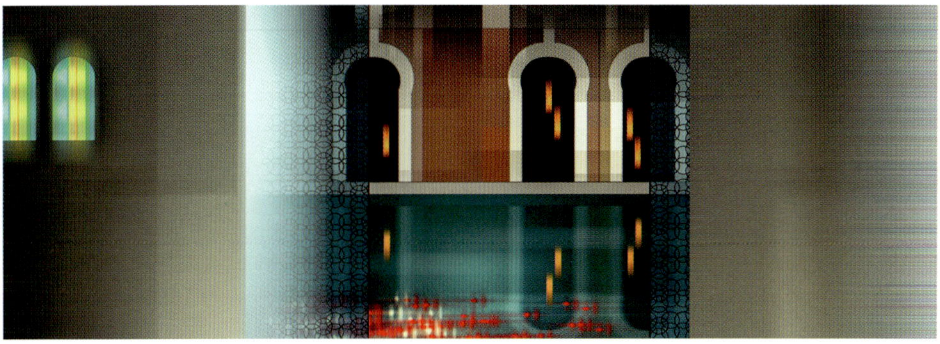

FIGURE 8.1
Jeremy Blake, *Liquid Villa,* 2000. Digital animation with audio; 7 minutes, 30 seconds, continuous. Courtesy of Kinz Fine Art.

Thanks to its mention in a text by Ed Halter, I read *Digital Material: Tracing New Media in Everyday Life in Technology,* which references Lyotard's exhibition *Les Immatériaux,* and I realized that I'd forgotten about his use of the plural form in the title ("the immaterials," not "the immaterial").[3] In an essay on the exhibition, Lyotard explains the selection of this term by saying that "the message cannot be dissociated from the support (material), and the code itself is inscribed in the support."[4] I understand this to mean that objects and processes in an information society cannot be fully divorced from a more traditional understanding of material; even something as intangible as a digital file is inseparable from the more tangible objects or systems in which it is inscribed. Lyotard intended the term *immaterials* to be ambiguously positioned within and against the traditional understanding of the relationship between human and material—as both material and not. The discourse surrounding digital art has often emphasized the latter understanding over the former, which is what sparked my interest in thinking about digital materialism.

It's strange, in a way, that this would have led me to Blake's work. Blake certainly didn't foreground his use of digital materials, as he described himself as a painter. I suppose it was *Winchester* (2002) that I was thinking about; I remember not being able to just walk past those glowing colors whenever I saw the piece. In painting as in digital video, color is a material effect, and this idea is fully present in Blake's work. Seeing *Winchester* was a visceral experience of digital display, of software-controlled electrical impulses passing through liquid crystals in order to generate fields of color. I've come to think of Blake's assertion that he was a painter as a way of calling attention to the materiality of his digital media works.

A full materialist analysis of Blake's works might consider the context of the artifacts of DVD compression, flat-screen or projector-based display in the gallery, image editing and motion graphics software, and his work-in-progress materials. Unfortunately, the Fales Library (which holds the Blake archives) currently does not offer research access to its digital collections, which I think would be necessary to such a study. However, I think it is a fruitful perspective to bear in mind when looking at Blake's work, even if he often downplayed his use of digital media, because his screen-based works have such important implications for a society that is conditioned by digital technology.

JG: Though you were initially drawn to *Winchester,* the centerpiece of the exhibition ended up being a slightly earlier work by Blake, *Liquid Villa* (2000). Both *Winchester* and *Liquid Villa* have to do with architecture, either real or virtual, but in both cases, protean and rather delirious. What made you look to *Liquid Villa* instead of the later, better-known work?

MC: It should be noted that *Liquid Villa* is also from a period in which Blake was working somewhat serially. It's quite similar to the works shown in his 1998 exhibition *Bungalow 8* at Kinz + Tillou and to the later *Station to Station* series. All these works depict architectural interiors of a fantastical nature; the one shown in *Liquid Villa* is an Alhambra-like exterior. In the context of Blake's work, though, I think of it as a nod to the excitingly poor taste of some Los Angeles homes, the Orientalist retreat of some studio exec, pressed into service as a filming location from time to time.

As far as why I chose this work, there are several answers. One is that the pre-*Winchester* work is much flatter, and this interested me. Around the time he made *Winchester,* he told an interviewer, "Formally, I prefer flatness in painting, and film-people who use cinemascope as a canvas hold great appeal."[5] Particularly when shown on a flat screen, the denial of pictorial depth in Blake's earlier work brought the materiality of the digital image to the fore.

JG: How do you understand flatness as pointing to the materiality of the digital image?

MC: By materiality, I'm referring to the material of bits and bytes as well as the material of liquid crystals and DVDs. In my text for the Honor Fraser exhibition, I mention the glowing orange torches visible in the dark alcoves of *Liquid Villa* as a moment in which the image asserts itself as being digital. They resemble the low-resolution artifacts of a too-large digital image, reminding us that such images are constructed from a limited grid of pixels. In that text, I suggested that these traces of digital materiality function in a way that is analogous to facture in painting.

If Blake had amplified these traces further and introduced more noticeable "glitches" into the work, as many other artists have done, then that would have been a very different project, an attempt to foreground the apparatus that generates an image, calling attention to its limitations. Instead, he called attention to them only insofar as he presented the image as a flat surface. This allows us to pay particularly close attention to the construction of the image rather than its figurative content, and as we do so, we see not only Blake's precise forms, we also see the visual "noise" that appears in a field of solid color or the jagged edge within an otherwise smooth gradient. Blake once described his work as "mark making resolving itself onscreen in a kind of time based painting,"[6] which suggests to me that this process of "screen resolution" and its attendant artifacts was not outside Blake's understanding of his work, but integral to it. As Ceci Moss wrote of Gilbert Simondon's conception of communications systems, "form (as signal) is never abstracted from matter (as noise)," and I think this is very applicable to *Liquid Villa*.[7] If signal cannot be abstracted from noise, nor form from matter, then Blake's emphasis on digital form foregrounds his digital matter.

To return to your question about why I chose the work: a related answer is that *Liquid Villa* has less of a binary division between architecture and abstraction. In *Winchester,* the abstractions interrupt and obscure the imagery of the house. There's something threatening about their intrusion into the cinematic image; they overturn a symbolic order and introduce entropy. In *Liquid Villa,* there are moments and passages that slip between representations of architecture and pure abstraction. It is much more liminal.

In one of the articles you suggested that we refer to as part of this exchange, Daniel Birnbaum, writing about *Les Immatériaux,* says that Lyotard argued that "the works [in the exhibition] demonstrated a highly fluid present where everything solid was not only evaporating but liquefying into some other state, perhaps even . . . information."[8] One could think of the state changes in *Liquid Villa* as synecdoches of such a larger cultural shift, but they refer as much to an inner, mental world as they do to an external reality.

So Blake's work could be seen as a later reflection of this paradigm shift, of a "fluid present" and of all that is solid "liquefying," but one that uncovers a psychic charge within the technoscientific apparatus.

JG: Both *Liquid Villa* and *Winchester* make reference to analog technology through their soundtracks—in the former, we hear the faint crackle of static on a vinyl record, and in the latter, I think I hear the soft whir of a film projector. Is this one way materiality haunts Blake's work—as acoustic ghosts?

MC: I can't say for sure, but the *Winchester* soundtrack does sound like a film projector, and Blake also has said that the film was shot on a Super 8 camera.

Despite the analog parallel, these soundtracks work in very different ways for me. In *Winchester,* the sound of the film projector points more directly to the material apparatus of film, to the process by which the footage was originally shot. In *Liquid Villa,* the soundtrack seems to be diegetic at times, setting the scene: the party ended a few hours ago; the guests are sprawling somewhere off camera; and someone forgot to turn off the last LP. However, the diegetic sound is accompanied at times by a low, rather ominous tone or joined by somewhat grating mechanical noises. Later, what sounds like faint shouting from deep in an echoing corridor can barely be discerned under the sound of rain. Like the images in the work, the sound in *Liquid Villa* oscillates between competing interpretations.

I like your suggestion that the ghosts of other media haunt Blake's work. This somehow seems appropriate for a music- and movie-obsessed painter who has turned to digital materials.

JG: Thinking of the sound in *Liquid Vill*a as diegetic brings me to another question about the relationship between Blake's work and the techniques and conventions of narrative cinema: specifically, his use of the dissolve. *Liquid Villa,* for instance, is punctuated by a series of slow, almost languid dissolves. In a conversation between Blake and John Baldessari published in *Artforum,* Blake said, "For me, the dissolve is a device that formally supports time-based abstract imagery."[9] I'm wondering how this might apply to *Liquid Villa* or other works in the show?

MC: It's really interesting that you picked up on this. A dissolve is a device inherited from cinema, and its use in dominant media is quite linear: one image comes in, and another goes out. At the start and finish, we have an unbesmirched photorealistic image and a steady transition between the two.

There are few traditional dissolves in the more recent works in the exhibition. Sara Ludy's *Dream House* (2014) is a slide show that cuts from still image to still image; Travess Smalley's piece *Third Trance* (2011) is a fluid abstraction that loops, employing a hard cut between each repetition; Jeff Baij's *The Mind's Eye and the Sequel to the Mind's Eye* (2013) uses abrupt, jarring edits to transition between short animations. The only more or less traditional dissolve is in the work of Chris Coy and Jon Rafman, *Unexpressed Resentment* (2014), and it goes on for minutes, as a wash of color gradually appears on a black screen.

However, one could think about the dissolve in a more expanded sense as just one template among many for the deployment of semitransparent layered images. So, someone like Travess Smalley is using the basic elements of the dissolve—layers and transparency—even if his use of them does not follow the temporal structure of the dissolve. Similarly, Petra Cortright's *mp3 +skins +download +winap +patra* (2013) is an abstract composition created from webcam images that were layered together in Photoshop. Although this work is a static image (until the silk it is printed on catches an air current, that is), it's the layering process that transforms presumably figurative video imagery into a colored, gestural abstraction.

Rafaël Rozendaal's website *Into Time .us* (2012) makes use of a related technique: the gradient rather than the dissolve—a technique that also appears in *Liquid Villa*. The work is presented as a two-channel projection with two trackpad input devices and broken mirrors and consists of a shifting field of colored gradients; when a user clicks on a point in the image, it breaks up the screen into a series of differently shaded planes that intersect at that point. One could argue that the gradient is a kind of dissolve that plays out in the space of a single image rather than in time, shifting from green at one end of an image to blue at the other, for example. However, a digital gradient is unlike a dissolve in that it is not literally generated from multiple images. Thus, when the colors in Rozendaal's website shift over time, the computer is not generating a transition between layered images but calculating intermediate color values. This technique is also used in *Liquid Villa,* most notably when what Blake described as a "golden ray" bisects the screen.

Colored gradients also form the basis of Rozendaal's lenticular print *Into Time 13 11 27* (2014). Here, we have a different process for layering multiple images and transitioning among them: the images are divided into vertical slices or stripes, and a plastic prism sheet is placed over the top of them. The elongated grooves of the prism sheet allow us to see only one slice of image at a time, but as we move in space, our perspective alters. Thus we see different images from any given vantage point, but most of the time we're seeing part of one image and part of another. The effect of these transitions in Rozendaal's work bears certain similarities to both the dissolve and the gradient as a means of combining images, but the underlying means of creating them is very different.

So I agree with Blake, but I think his comment about the dissolve reflects a skeuomorphic way of thinking about digital abstraction that derives from narrative cinema, while many of the other artists in the exhibition mobilize similar techniques to very different effect. However, the word *dissolve* is, in particular, highly appropriate to the liquid qualities of Blake's work.

JG: I wonder if this speaks to the historical gap between *Liquid Villa* and the other works in the show—even if it is a difference of only a decade, sometimes even less. For Blake, working in the late 1990s and early 2000s, narrative cinema was a key frame of reference, whereas the artists working today face a different situation, technologically and culturally. I hope you'll excuse me for ventriloquizing Blake once again, but I think his statements help us get to some of the issues raised in your show. In the conversation with Baldessari, Blake said: "The philosophical discussion around painted abstraction has, I think, deteriorated lately, leaving abstraction as a kind of style. I want abstraction to be more than a style, or a backdrop, so I try to build a context for it in my work—often I make a kind of fantasy architecture to house the abstraction."[10]

Do you think of *Liquid Villa* as a "fantasy architecture" used to support time-based abstraction? Or is it risky to take Blake at his word? How might this help us understand some of the other works in the show, such as Sara Ludy's *Dream House* (2014), a 3-D model of an architectural space the artist saw in a recurring dream?

MC: That Blake quote was from 2004, and I think it relates more to *Winchester* than to *Liquid Villa*. But if the fantasy architecture of *Winchester* was intended to "house" Blake's abstraction, then it was a failure. The abstraction is not contained within the house; it obliterates it.

There are many ways in which architecture—particularly domestic architecture—is thought of as analogous to the mind, or to memory. The Winchester mansion, interestingly, is a dramatic enactment of this analogy. Built by Sarah Winchester as a kind of apotropaic labyrinth designed to entrap vengeful spirits, it can be seen as an architectural defense against deep-seated guilt or anxiety, or as a symptom of the same. Likewise, it's tempting to read Blake's use of the house along similar lines, as some kind of object of introjection, particularly because the abstractions in *Winchester* can be so unnerving.

Liquid Villa is different. The architecture doesn't house the abstraction, it *becomes* the abstraction. The architecture isn't overwhelmed; it is liquefied, to use Birnbaum's terms. One could read this liquefaction in psychological terms or in relation to a broader situation, a "highly fluid present." I'll have to double down on the ventriloquism here—in a 2006 e-mail interview with Coy, Blake described the work as a reaction to his experience of late 1990s New York, the time of the first dot-com boom: "New York in the nineties was very work driven and there was a lot of economic optimism. I loved the ambition and the powerful energy I sensed in that, but at the same time I also felt like maybe life was going by a little too fast in some ways. So as a reaction I made this slow meditative work that reflected some of the dream-like pleasures and fears of the culture at that time as I saw it."[11]

For me, the phrase "a fluid present" is useful to describe a time in which the reach of digital technology was expanding exponentially, as was the data-driven financial system, and I think the quote supports my contention that the liquefaction seen in Blake's work moves beyond a purely formal device to attain psychological and societal resonance.

Sara Ludy's *Dream House,* which is included in the exhibition, is worth discussing here. Despite its sterile surfaces and mathematically perfect lines and shading, her dream-based 3-D model somehow conjures an oneiric intensity but in comparison with the protean architecture of Jeremy Blake, Ludy's dream house is profoundly lucid. Perhaps *oneiric* is the wrong word; dreams are characterized by instability, and her dream house is stable. Perhaps we should understand this piece purely in psychological terms, or perhaps it reflects a different technological milieu, one in which a general sense of fluidity has been supplanted by rigid structures. Ludy's *Dream House* is as carefully ordered as the USS *Discovery One* before it goes through the Stargate.

JG: Blake's architecture is liquefying, dissolving before our very eyes, and obdurately flat, whereas Ludy's is crisp, rigid, and three-dimensional, and yet, I think both works conjure a kind of architectural uncanny; we aren't meant to feel at home in these spaces, even if they seem eerily familiar.

I'd like to return to your comment about Lyotard's *Les Immatériaux* as an inspiration for *Liquid Crystal Palace*. In the mid-1980s, Lyotard was interested in how works of art can "present the unpresentable" and therefore provoke the disorienting, potentially violent aesthetic experience of the sublime. Birnbaum notes that one of Lyotard's aims during this period was "to restore the sublime as a central aesthetic category of the avant-garde." *Les Immatériaux* was thus part of Lyotard's broader theoretical elaboration of the "postmodern sublime," which describes the violent transmutation of matter into data during the information age.[12]

Considering the influence of Lyotard's exhibition on your thinking makes me wonder whether we should talk about the work in *Liquid Crystal Palace* in terms of a "postmodern sublime," or perhaps even "sublime data." Or rather, do you think they have a greater affinity with the sublime aesthetics of modernist painting—I'm thinking here of the numerous vertical "zips" seen in *Liquid Villa,* which immediately recall the heroic canvases of Barnett Newman, a champion of the sublime. Blake's liquid swirls of color have also been compared to Color Field painting, such as the work of Morris Louis and Jules Olitski. Do you think *Liquid Crystal Palace* shows us something about how contemporary artists invoke the sublime?

MC: Earlier, I wrote about the unstable architecture of *Liquid Villa* as a kind of visualization of what Birnbaum called "liquefaction" and what you describe as "violent transmutation." This certainly connects with the idea of the sublime, although I think the abstractions in *Liquid Crystal Palace* are also variously rooted in gesture, the mind, and the body. They may resemble the modernist paintings you cite, but have different stakes.

We were just talking about the relationship between architecture and abstraction; Lyotard's article conveniently begins with a reference to Leon Battista Alberti, an architect and painter, and painting's participation in establishing a social order. "In the centuries that followed, [painting] contributed its share toward realizing the metaphysical and political program of visual and social order. Optical geometry, the ordering of colors and values according to a hierarchy of Neoplatonic inspiration, and the pictorial rules that captured and crystallized the heydays of religious or historical legend helped instill a sense of identity in the new political communities."[13] The phrase that sticks out for me here is "the ordering of colors." It makes sense to use such a phrase in relation to the work of someone like Alberti, for whom color's function was pretty strictly representational, but can one honestly stand in front of the work of someone like Titian and describe it as an "ordering of colors" in support of the rise of the nation state and the proto-capitalist social order?

In his article "Color, the Formless, and Cinematic Eros," Brian Price situates Blake's work in relation to a different Renaissance narrative. He mentions Titian as one of several sixteenth-century Venetian painters who challenged the privileging of line over color, citing the work of science writer Philip Ball on this topic. Price writes, "The pleasure of the [line drawing] is thus owed to the perceptual certainty and formal mastery of the pictorial field. By contrast, color disrupts order; it promises to undo the gestalt effected by line and form."[14]

Line is the province of the draftsman and the architect, and it plays no small part in Blake's work, but it is always set off against formless expanses of color. Price's argument gives us another way of understanding the relationship between abstraction and architecture in Blake's work—as a playing out of a tension between form and the formless, between the increasingly vast project of ordering of the world rationally and the impossibility of this task.

JG: I think these tensions you've identified—between line and color (rooted in the Renaissance discourse of *disegno* versus *colorito*), form and formlessness, reason and the irrational—help us understand Blake's approach to abstraction. His comment to Baldessari, "That's what abstraction means to me: the visual demonstration of philosophical nuance," would seem to confirm this.[15]

MC: It's perhaps easiest to try to define this philosophy of abstraction in relation to other works in the show that also deal with line and color.

Rozendaal's work has a particular exuberance about line. In his web-based installation *Into Time .us,* the projected color fields of dissolving gradients are shattered into geometric patterns each time a visitor clicks on the image via a nearby trackpad, creating patterns that resonate with shards of broken mirror on the floor. Rozendaal's work is often line-based: he frequently uses vector graphics, which are based on mathematical equations that, in principle, generate perfect lines. Vector graphics are different from the raster graphics used by Blake or any JPEG or TIFF, in which grids of pixels are assigned particular values. If a raster image is scaled up, one can see the resulting loss of quality; a vector graphic can be executed at any size, and it will always be perfect. Of course, as Rozendaal has lamented, a vector graphic must always be displayed on some kind of screen; it can never truly be perfect. This is already in contrast with Blake's position—as I discussed above, I don't think he expected this kind of perfection of the digital image.

So Rozendaal is excited by the vector's potential for mathematical perfection and disappointed by its material realization. There's nothing in his work that suggests that the project of ordering the world through reason should be oppressive, or incompatible with lyrical, emotional experience. Perhaps one could even read his work as the supposedly unquantifiable—color and emotion—contained within perfect mathematical forms.

Vector graphics are schematic, and they are the province of the draftsman (used often in the real world for applications such as CAD drawings). Raster graphics perhaps have something more painterly about them. Where Rozendaal expresses a longing for the perfect line, Cortright celebrates the imperfection of the raster graphic. If there are vague hints of raster graphics' imperfections in Blake's work, they are much more evident in Cortright's works in *Liquid Crystal Palace*. In *mp3 +skins +download +winap +patra*, still frames from a consumer-grade webcam—images of her, presumably—have been layered and blended in Photoshop and printed on silk. *fuzzy love clams* (2013), a print on aluminum, was hand-painted in Photoshop, each machine-transferred colored mark pointing back to the gestural motion of the artist's hand on the computer input device. Cortright's work overtly makes use of very default technology—technology that makes her work, in Lyotard's terms, "at first glance not much more than the consummation of the machine's image-making capacities."[16] But if Lyotard saw in this a glimpse of the "infinite dialectic of ideas in the process of being realized,"[17] Cortright's use of color emphasizes the disruptiveness of the individual within an overdetermined techno-social framework. The colors of *mp3* and *fuzzy love clams* are the by-product of a body in motion that does not experience the unblinking eye of the webcam or the constrained space of the trackpad as a technical limit.

If we think of the line as a way of structuring the world through reason, particularly through digital technology, and color as a means of accessing realms of emotion or experience that cannot quite be contained within this structure, then distinct philosophical positions can be seen in the work of Rozendaal, Cortright, and Blake. For Rozendaal, there is no emotion or experience that cannot be described within the rational systems of digital technology; if there is a limit, it is that mathematically ideal form, and color cannot be precisely realized with the imperfect materials of printers or displays. Cortright also works within highly ordered systems. Her work foregrounds her tools and their limitations but finds within them ample room for the unboundedness of color and free gesture. In Blake's work, though, the conflict between line and color, form and formless, has a more dramatic character, and I think it points back to his own ambivalence about digital technologies and a data-driven world.

One final note on this phrase "the ordering of color." Coy's aforementioned work *Unexpressed Resentment*, which takes the form of a long dissolve to a pink and orange abstraction, is based on the color used in the Scientology emotional tone scale for "unexpressed resentment."

JG: So, once again, color is used as a kind of psychological index for an internal, affective state—one that remains unruly, and outside of, or perhaps prior to, reason. This brings me to my next question, about the therapeutic and narcotic effect of psychedelic aesthetics. In your essay on *Liquid Crystal Palace,* you note Blake's fascination with the use of abstraction as dystopian decor in François Truffaut's *Fahrenheit 451,* especially on the Big Brother–style screens that infiltrate and surveil domestic space. Truffaut's film was released at the height of the psychedelic counterculture, in 1966, the same year Timothy Leary coined "Turn on, tune in, and drop out," the year before the "summer of love." Blake's reference to Truffaut made me think of his other, better-known connection to mainstream narrative cinema—that is, his hallucination sequences in Paul Thomas Anderson's *Punch-Drunk Love* (2002). In some sense, Blake's druggy, hypnotic style suggests a therapeutic or even soporific function of abstraction—lulling us into a kind of somnambulatory state or waking dream. I also see a kind of therapeutic psychedelia at work in Travess Smalley's *Primordial Trance Puddle* (2011), which resembles the work by him you chose for the exhibition, *Third Trance* (2011). Overall, the discussion of dream states like "trance" and "hypnosis" bring to mind critic Parker Tyler's description of the durational experience of watching Warhol's early films, which he says oscillate between the monotonous distension of "dragtime" and the psychedelic absorption of "drugtime."[18] Do you think these terms have some utility in talking about works in the show?

MC: Yes, that's a nice phrase, I hadn't read that text before. What I think is so interesting about Tyler's argument is that Warhol's early films—*Empire* for example—were as factual as one can get. If we've been setting up a dialectic between rational ordering and the unknowable or irrational within the individual and in the world at large, Warhol's films manage to collapse this dialectic: psychedelic actualities. The closer we look, perhaps, the more everything seems unknowable.

JG: So, following Tyler, Warhol's dragtime-drugtime works to radically defamiliarize us from mundane activities like eating and sleeping, resulting in utter boredom, or fascination, or some combination of the two. I think Blake's work tends more towards the drugtime of psychedelic absorption—but to what ends?

I think you hint at it towards the end of your essay, where you start out by describing how, in *Fahrenheit 451*

> geometric abstraction and other modernist styles are held up as failures: reduced to mere ornamentation, and offered to the masses as a sense-tingling but mind-numbing panacea via the technology of the flatscreen. But the decorative, sensory, psychedelic weave of images that physically affect the sensorium of the body were never really outside of the project of modernism; they were merely its flip side. Haunted by the perceived failure of geomet-

ric abstraction, and fascinated by technologies that are often written off as mundane, flat, and lacking in affect, Blake found in digital abstraction and prosumer tools not dystopia, but a "dystopic potential.[19]

I think this contrast—between the avant-garde's utopian aspirations for abstraction and the "dystopic potential" that Blake found in digital technology and mobilized for abstract painting—is key.

MC: By the time of Truffaut's film, the social ills of postwar housing had, I think, linked geometric abstraction with technocracy and all its failings; geometric abstraction can be seen in the set design as well as in the onscreen passages that Blake references. Maybe one could see this as painting paying the price for architecture's sins to some extent. I suppose that *psychedelic* is a slightly anachronistic term to apply to early-twentieth-century artists, but in the way that Mondrian was able to attach such spiritual significance to and invest such craft in highly ordered paintings, in the way that Malevich was able to propose an art that left the world of objects behind—there were many ways in which modernist painters suggested a direct passage from the sensory experience of the artwork to some sort of altered mental state. Unlike the architects of many housing estates, their work functioned less as a reification of the social order than as a way to move beyond it.

Utopia is a place, and it has rules and order and organization. In other words, it has architecture. Dystopia is a disordered no-place, a place with no architecture, and perhaps this is one reason why the dystopic imaginary might be appealing to an artist working against the backdrop of the dot-com boom of late-nineties New York. We live in a world of carefully designed systems, and Blake's embrace of dystopia was a way of stepping outside of these systems, probing the limits of order and reason. Today, these limits increasingly look like a hard, apocalyptic historical horizon, but this is itself a kind of fantasy, the flip side of utopia. The dystopia of *Liquid Villa,* in contrast, found these limits by presenting digital architecture as abstraction.

Dystopia is not only the longed-for but feared destruction of our highly ordered systems by uncontrollable events, it is also the irrational and formless within these very systems. And this, I think, was Blake's dystopia.

NOTES

1. *Liquid Crystal Palace* was an exhibition curated by Michael Connor and Nate Hitchcock at Honor Fraser Gallery in Los Angeles in 2014.
2. Bruno Latour, *Pandora's Hope: Essays on the Reality of Science Studies* (Cambridge: Harvard University Press, 1999), 304.
3. Ed Halter, "The Matter of Electronics," *Vague Terrain,* February 2010, http://vague

terrain.net/content/2010/02/matter-electronics; and Marianne van den Boomen, Ann-Sophie Lehmann, Sybilles Lammes, and Joost Raessens, eds., *Digital Material: Tracing New Media in Everyday Life and Technology* (Amsterdam: Amsterdam University Press, 2009). *Les Immatériaux* was an influential exhibition curated by French philosopher Jean-François Lyotard at the Centre Pompidou in Paris in 1985.

4. Jean-François Lyotard, *"Les Immatériaux," Art & Text* 17 (1985), 47–57.

5. Jeremy Blake, quoted in Melanie Crean, "Interview with Jeremy Blake," *The (Re)Structured Screen,* December 2002, http://integr8dmedia.net/viralnet/therestructuredscreen/interview05blake.html.

6. Blake, quoted in Crean, "Interview."

7. Ceci Moss, "Expanded Internet Art and the Informational Milieu," *Rhizome,* December 19, 2013, http://rhizome.org/editorial/2013/dec/19/expanded-internet-art-and-informational-milieu/.

8. Daniel Birnbaum, "Subliminal Messages: Daniel Birnbaum on Jean-François Lyotard's 'The Sublime and the Avant-Garde' (1984)," *Artforum* 51 (September 2012).

9. Jeremy Blake, "In Conversation: John Baldessari and Jeremy Blake," *Artforum* 42 (March 2004): 160–65.

10. Blake, "In Conversation," 162.

11. Jeremy Blake, e-mail interview with Chris Coy, April 4, 2006.

12. Lyotard developed his theory of the postmodern sublime in a series of related writings: Jean-François Lyotard, "Presenting the Unpresentable: The Sublime," *Artforum* 20, no. 8 (April 1982): 64–69; "The Sublime and the Avant-Garde," *Artforum* 22, no. 8 (April 1984): 36–43; and his defining treatise on postmodernism, *The Postmodern Condition: A Report on Knowledge* (Minneapolis: University of Minnesota Press, 1984).

13. Lyotard, "Presenting the Unpresentable," 64.

14. Brian Price, "Color, the Formless, and Cinematic Eros," *Framework: Journal of Cinema and Media* 47, no. 1 (Spring 2006): 22–35.

15. Blake, "In Conversation."

16. Lyotard, "Presenting the Unpresentable," 66.

17. Lyotard, "Presenting the Unpresentable," 66.

18. Parker Tyler, "Dragtime and Drugtime; or, Film à la Warhol," *Evergreen Review,* April 1967.

19. Michael Connor, "Liquid Crystal Palace: Jeremy Blake and His New Peers," *Rhizome,* http://rhizome.org/editorial/2014/feb/28/liquid-crystal-palace/.

9

ABSTRACT VIDEO

net.video.abstraction

Tilman Baumgärtel, Sarah Cook,
Charlotte Frost, and Caitlin Jones

In this roundtable conducted across four time zones and via several platforms including e-mail and Google Docs, four theorists, historians, and curators of media art attempted to come to grips with Internet abstraction. It might be fair to say that the asynchronous nature of the discussion itself at times demonstrated some of the forms of abstraction we sought to discuss. For example, Sarah Cook chose to focus on an artwork that develops our understanding of how online spaces bring together seemingly disconnected elements. In trying to establish a framework from within which to discuss "abstraction," we all experienced degrees of disconnection from one another and the writing tasks at hand. Although each of us is extremely familiar with discussing art in online spaces, representing the nature and scope of abstraction after the Internet was somehow defamiliarizing. That is not to say the subject matter was foreign, but that something in the action of discussing it seemed to play out the very features we sought to explicate. The group started using Google Docs to create a more dedicated discussion space, given that with the sheer weight of e-mail everyone gets these days, an e-mail–based discussion can seem like an unwelcome interruption in a space where we often feel we're losing a battle with correspondence. What follows then, is an edited version of the various elements of our conversation. We each chose a piece of web-based art that deals with an aspect of abstraction and moving imagery, though we grappled with understanding the two central notions of our subject matter, "video" and "abstraction," in an online context. And so it was by disconnected discussion, varied interpretation, routine interruption, and theoretical dissociation that we came to gather our thoughts.

INTERPRETATION—TILMAN BAUMGÄRTEL

CONTEMPORARY ASCII

http://www.ljudmila.org/~vuk/ascii/

The works I want to discuss are the different iterations of the ASCII Video project by the ASCII Art Ensemble (a group that included the Slovenian artists Vuk Ćosić and Luka Frelih and Dutch artist Walter van der Cruijsen), as it was one of the more notable works of "video net art" and at the same time made reference to a practice that was part of net culture long before net art.

Since 1998, the ASCII Art Ensemble has used a process one could call "ASCIIfication" to turn moving images into dancing rows and columns of numbers and characters in the characteristic absinthe green of the monochrome cathode ray tube (CRT) monitor. In the following year, the first *Matrix* movie turned this look into a cinematic aesthetic in its own right, one that has since become a staple of postmodern pop culture. The best-known series of works that the ASCII Art Ensemble developed took scenes from movies such as *Battleship Potemkin, Psycho,* and, most famously *Deep Throat* (see fig. 9.1), and turned them into moving ASCII code. There was the *Instant ASCII Camera* (shown at the *net.condition* show at the Zentrum für Kunst und Medientechnologie in Karlsruhe, Germany, in 1999, one of the first large-scale museum presentations of Internet art) that printed out ASCII versions of photo portraits of the visitors. In the piece *ASCII history for the blind,*[1] a text-to-speech-program read the ASCII characters and turned canonic artworks into "text pictures." (Ironically, this piece has become a victim of "bit rot," as it works only with the now-outdated RealPlayer software.) Another iteration of the same concept was an ASCII level for the Unreal game engine. Finally, Vuk Ćosić projected green ASCII characters on the walls of St. George's Hall in Liverpool. The group also collaborated with other media art practitioners such as Times Up, Gebhard Sengmueller, and Alexei Shulgin to ASCIIfy even more audiovisual data.

In a way, the ASCII Art Ensemble was an example of how artists anticipate practices that become much more common than their own endeavors. Today, countless programs and apps (often filed under "Fun" on Internet websites) do the same as the software that the ASCII Art Ensemble developed—even though, arguably, with much less aesthetic rigor than the Java and Java Script Applications of the group. And if you search for "ASCII video" on YouTube, you will be confronted with countless examples of ASCIIfication of moving images.

But why is the strange and mystifying visual mode of "representation" that ASCIIfication allows such an important subject in both net art and the general Internet and computer culture? The answer is twofold: ASCII is an important element of net culture, which—especially in its beginnings—was not particularly visual, a shortcoming that ASCII Art tried to overcome. And at the same time, ASCIIfication allows for an interrogation of the relation between the real and the code, the object and its digital representations, which are entirely dependent on a senseless machine logic—more on that later.

Let's first look at the historic relevance of ASCII Art, which snuck into our contem-

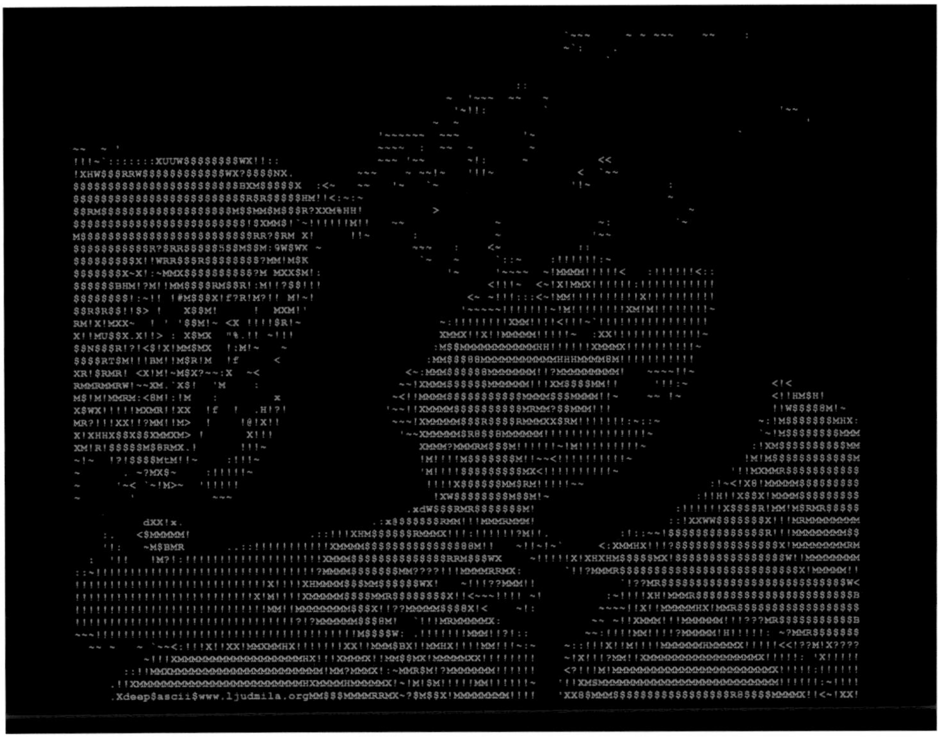

FIGURE 9.1
Vuk Ćosić, *Deep ASCII*, 1998. Internet art, video and online, silent; 55 minutes. Programming by Luka Frelih, produced at Ljubljana Digital Medialab. © ASCII Art Ensemble. Courtesy of Vuk Ćosić.

porary visual culture through the servants' door. The high art of deconstructing images and then piecing them together again from the printable characters defined by the international ASCII Standard was developed by anonymous amateurs, obscure tinkerers, kids with too much time on their hands and a computer. Like computer games, it is a folk art of the digital age, and no Dürer or Warhol of the form has been identified so far—even though early computer artists like Ken Knowlton aspired to nothing less. Apparently, the now largely historical UNIX system included a program called TOASCII, which "prints textual characters that represent the black and white image used as input."

This is an art form that supposedly was invented by bored telegraph operators and was refined by equally bored teenagers too young to vote or to buy alcoholic beverages at the corner store. At the same time, it has points of contact with some of the most refined artistic uses of the written word, from hieroglyphics to concrete poetry.

On the one hand, ASCII Art is merely an unlikely by-product of the technical necessity to allow digital devices to communicate with each other and to process, store, and distribute alphabetical characters, numbers, and a handful of symbols without error between different machines. On the other hand, the art form bred a competitive scene of practitioners who—unknown to the world at large—pushed the limits of the form in a ruthless, high-pressure environment, where only the most innovative would survive. In the process, they developed a particular look that has become an identifiable cipher for something vaguely retro, vaguely digital.

ASCII Art takes the concrete and translates it into abstractions, into letters and numbers that entail only a ghostly shadow of the real that they encode. ASCII Art is about this kind of metamorphosis, not unlike the abstract video works that artists such as Eric Siegel, Stephen Beck, and Woody Vasulka created in the 1960s and 1970s with the video synthesizers they built. Although the best-known of these art machines is the Paik-Abe synthesizer from 1969, Dan Sandin's videotape *Five-Minute Romp through the IP* (1973) might be the most accessible introduction to this type of analog image manipulation. However, what they have in common with the ASCII video experiments of the ASCII Art Ensemble is that they are about the process of turning representational graphic images into something abstract.

When Vuk Ćosić and the ASCII Art Ensemble took on the form, it was on its way from being a widely practiced digital folk art to a kind of visual shorthand for the dated, outmoded visuality of early computer culture. In a recent e-mail interview, Ćosić pointed out that he wanted to stage "an alternative evolution of computer graphics as if we didn't have rasters or vectors. Also it was valuable to me because it was a continuation of visual poetry and all other formative literary experiences in my growing up. The third unavoidable tangent was of course the hacker folklore."[2] According to Walter van der Cruijsen the group was originally inspired by a demonstration by a programmer of a video format for the blind based on ASCII characters converted to a braille pad.

In an Internet catalogue to accompany a virtual exhibition of works of the ASCII Art ensemble (which to my knowledge never took place in physical space), Lev Manovich writes: "The result [of the works of the ASCII Art Ensemble—T. B.] is as satisfying poetically as it is conceptually—for what we get is a double image, a recognizable film image and an abstract code together. Both are visible at once. . . . Here the code and the image coexist."[3]

Photography and film are regarded as indexical media—media that just record what was in front of the lens of the camera. In the discussed pieces, the ASCIIfication serves as a kind of "alienating effect" à la Brecht. And it turns the living, the vital, the body and the flesh into (not so) dead letters. Vuk Ćosić was open about the reasons for using a porn movie as one of their first (and most popular) examples to make this process visible in 1998: "First the decision was made to work on a porno film because of the close-ups."[4]

How could the most physical movie genre, pornography, be turned into the most abstract kind of visual rendering in the work of the ASCII Art Ensemble, with just a greenish and ghostly return of the real? Well, as the final, unsettling sentence of André Bazin's ode to realism in his famous essay "The Ontology of the Photographic Image" has it: "On the other hand, of course, cinema is also a language."[5]

CJ: The first thing that comes to my mind when reading this is the connection between code and abstraction. In a way, depending on your level of familiarity with programming languages or binary code, anything driven by code is in essence driven by abstraction. And I think this is why the ASCII Art Ensemble's work was so influential, and JODI's *%Location* or *404* web works as well, because it made the abstraction of code representational, or is it vice versa—as you say, Tilman, "about the process of turning graphic, representational images into something abstract"?

DISCONNECTION—SARAH COOK

TEMPLATE CINEMA

http://www.templatecinema.com/

I've chosen a work that deliberately complicates the idea of abstract video by not being abstract in a visual sense but rather by the way in which the video image has a disconnection from its "original" meaning or source. The project is *Template Cinema* (2003) by UK-based artists Thomson & Craighead. They describe the work as "low-tech networked movies made from existing data appropriated in real time from the World Wide Web."[6] Thomson & Craighead have long used webcams in their work, choosing them as much for their location on the globe (i.e., what time it is where they are) and the stability of the technology or connection as for what appears on them or happens in front of them. *Template Cinema* as an online work includes three different movies—one with a webcam in Sweden, one in Saint-Malo, and one called *Five Ghosts* with an initially indistinct location but with a sound track that includes a recorded telephone conversation involving crossed wires. An earlier related gallery-based work, *Short films about Flying* (2002), combined webcam footage with intertitles from chat rooms and sound tracks from Internet radio stations. In all cases, the works start with a piece of stock footage of a film leader (also sourced from the web), and the source of the material is always visually present in some form—as end credits, captions, or, in *Short films about Flying* as informational metadata presented on a second, smaller screen—with the "film" projected in the space. Considering that the *Template Cinema* project is over a decade old, it is remarkable that it still works so well on contemporary browsers as a work of net-based art. This is testament to the practice of the artists, which is based in part on an algorithmic way of working, on establishing a set of rules or instructions, and on allowing the content of the work to be modifiable or updatable once those mechanisms of the work's creation are in place. Thomson & Craighead continue to use webcams and other sources of found footage and imagery in many of their gallery-based installations. Their series of "desktop documentaries," including the *Flat Earth* trilogy made primarily for gallery-based exhibition, in collaboration with writer Steve Rushton, are constructed with material found entirely online and recombined, sometimes presented on two screens: one of footage or images and the other of the metadata indicating the source of the material.

I've chosen *Template Cinema* because I think it still tells us something about video

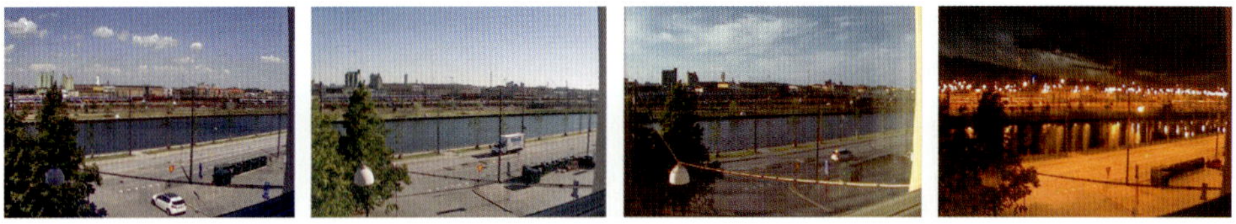

FIGURE 9.2
Thomson & Craighead, *Template Cinema, Somewhere in Sweden,* 2004. Internet art. Courtesy of the artists.

on the web in terms of the proliferation of live video in the form of webcams. I think of webcams as a different order of online video from other live moving-image-watching experiences we have on the Internet (television shows, performance such as theatre or sports live streams, and conference proceedings). Webcam feeds are without commentary and without editing—though sometimes they allow control of camera angle from the viewer. The abstraction that shows up in the piece is thus one from the original context of the material. Removed from its original website framing (by which I mean that you come upon it not because you have clicked through to it from, say, a holiday booking website, knowing where the camera is based and why), the video image appears momentarily "abstract" as you wonder while watching it where it is, if it is live or prerecorded, if the edits are deliberate. You may have noted the opening title of the film, which listed today's date and time (the date and time of your viewing), but it is not until you get to the end credits or note a caption within the image (as in the case of *Somewhere in Sweden,* fig. 9.2) that you acknowledge both the "liveness" and the dislocation of the video image. The piece engages in a process of recombination, of chance. No two movies are the same, because of the live nature of the video image. The viewer logging in and clicking on one of the short films of *Template Cinema* is faced with a mini-movie whose contents, structure, plot, and outcome are completely unknown in advance. I would argue that this abstraction is an essential part of the aesthetic process in the creation of the work and in the practice of the artists. The work's abstraction is not nonrepresentational—because at times the work is figurative, as when the video feed resolves itself into something meaningful (a skyline), some action happens (a woman pushes a baby stroller along the street), or in the case of *Five Ghosts* the soundtrack of the telephone conversation suggests a recognizable action. There is no "appearance" of the abstract, but rather the disconnect, so that meaning is abstracted from usual expectation.

CF: Though it's not a web-based piece, I couldn't help but also think about Thomson & Craighead's *The Time Machine in alphabetical order* (2010) with regard to your point about disconnection as abstraction.[7] The effect of watching this piece is of all the constituent parts of the film flashing across the screen disconnected from their original contexts. It places database culture where visual narrative once stood.

TB: I like *Template Cinema*—and I am surprised that it still works!—but how is this abstract video?

SC: Again, by choosing a work in which the image content of the video itself is not abstract in a figurative sense, I am trying to problematize how the data of online video (the video) relates to its metadata (such as "where" it is online). Perhaps I can connect it, as Charlotte points out, to *The Time Machine in alphabetical order*. In that work, the viewer experiences time travel in a linear sense, within the timeline (narrative arc) of the film, with clips ordered alphabetically by first letter of each word spoken in the dialogue—allowing you to view the arc of the film from beginning to end. You need only watch the sequence of clips for any letter or any repeated word, arranged in chronological order, to learn there is a man, a machine, a monster, and a girl—all the classic elements of a Hollywood movie plot. In *Template Cinema* the video footage itself is similarly unmoored from its original "location" (in space rather than in time perhaps, though webcams are already time-disconnecting devices) and is subject to a new rule, a new ordering, and thus abstracted. In computer programming, programmers talk of abstractions and their opposite: implementations, concretizations, or reifications. To simplify (and quote Wikipedia), "The abstraction principle can be generalized as the 'don't repeat yourself' principle, which recommends avoiding the duplication of information in general, and also avoiding the duplication of human effort involved in the software development process."[8] This is exactly what *Template Cinema* does, by using a live webcam video feed to ensure that no single mini-movie is ever a repeat, no two are the same, no two viewing experiences are the same.

CJ: I'm happy that the issue of metadata has come up here. As with Tilman's ASCII example, there is this idea that the underlying structures add an additional layer of abstraction. While the ASCII works conflate the two visually, in the work of Thomson & Craighead the underlying code is always present but invisible. With the growing importance and influence of metadata, cookies, and other forms of tracking algorithms, this way of thinking about abstraction online seems more relevant and pressing than ever.

SC: Thomson & Craighead are, however, becoming more interested in visual and figurative forms of abstraction in their work and in relation to their use of webcams. They are creating light boxes (sculptures) displaying screen grabs taken from broken webcams. Some of the images are captured from a moving image stream and then output as stills layered atop one another to create a lenticular image that moves as you move in front of it. The brokenness of the webcams is curious—they are continuously transmitting, so they are physically present but informationally absent. Perhaps this connects to Charlotte's chosen work in terms of glitch.

INTERRUPTION—CHARLOTTE FROST

THE COLLAPSE OF PAL

http://videoscapes.blogspot.com/2010/07/collapse-of-pal.html/

On May 25, 2010, Dutch glitch artist Rosa Menkman staged a live work about the death of the PAL (Phase Alternating Line) television signal. Her work was broadcast live on Danish television and though that performance, like the PAL signal, is now consigned to history, it is still possible to watch an eight-minute online video of "part 1" of *The Collapse of PAL* (fig. 9.3) and it is this video to which I will primarily refer. I have chosen it because glitch art is a steadily growing genre that clearly fits with the idea of online "abstract video." For example, the visuals we encounter are far from being high-definition images of the real world. Following the stabilization of the title page, a distorted image of a woman's head and shoulders dominates the screen. She is made of diagonal lines of blue and lilac, and her features—eyes, nose, mouth—are just patches of light and dark, frilled at the edges by the stripes that form the image. As she fades from the screen, a typed narrative begins. It tell us: "The angel of history had television. . . . She witnessed the termination of PAL. . . . And when the PAL signal was muted . . . its chance to clarify smothered . . . a brutal but silent execution had taken place." Then we see what might be a landscape with a lake, the woman's head again, and rogue shapes that interfere with the images (which eventually appear to be of a moving landscape shifting in front of us like the view from a car or train).

The idea behind much of this type of work is to deliberately distort communication signals for visual effect. In an interview with Andrew Rosinski, Menkman offers a useful definition, remarking that "glitch art is a practice that studies and researches the vernacular of file formats in exploitative manners to deconstruct and create new, brutalist (audio) visual works."[9] Indeed, in this section of the work, as Menkman explains on her website, she "used a NES, some image bending and a broken photo camera (CCD chip is loose) & for the sound [she] used a cracklebox, feedback, Eurosignal, and a couple of DV-compressed videobends."[10] And so I'd argue that somewhat akin to types of painterly abstraction (Pollock, DeKooning, even Rothko perhaps), glitch involves an intense focus on form, medium, and gesture—almost to obfuscation. However, I would also argue that the abstraction in glitch is more than just an interrupted aesthetic—even if I might try to make a case for abstract painting somehow interrupting the signal of paint. While it might be the aesthetic interruption we notice first in the *Collapse of PAL*, the work also demonstrates a very literal disturbance in signal. The Vimeo-based footage, by virtue of being available online, is no longer made of PAL. In the original broadcast, it was a dying signal, but the material we watch is archival footage of something already dead. PAL has ended, its signal permanently interrupted, and yet here it is being somehow resurrected for us in a work that speaks to its physical specificities from beyond. Indeed, Menkman interrupts the signal and our understanding of it to somehow make it more present to us.

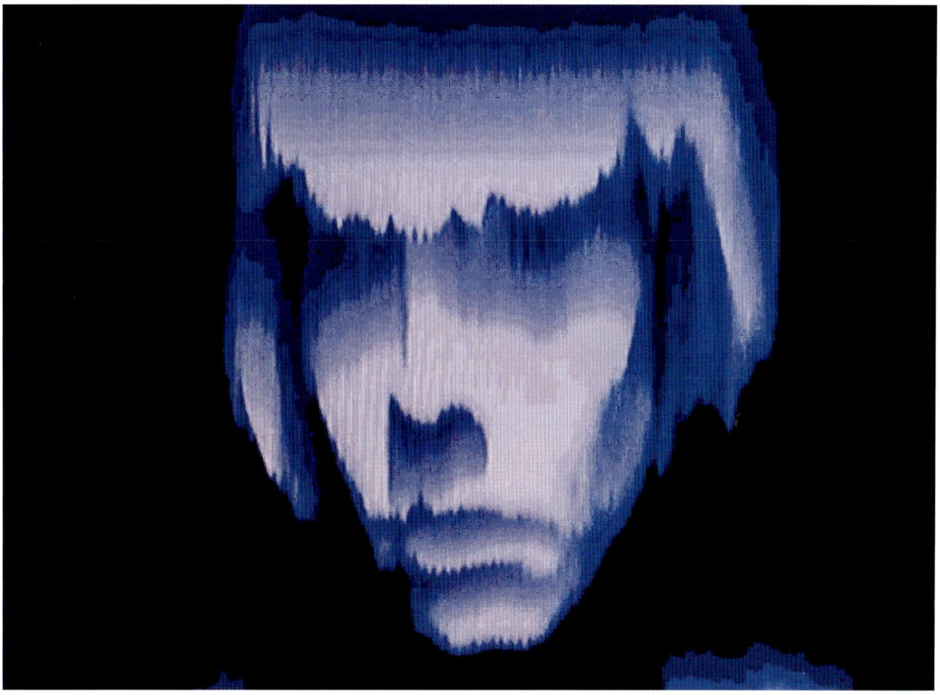

FIGURE 9.3
Rosa Menkman, *The Collapse of PAL*, 2010–11. Audiovisual performance, video, color, sound; 30 minutes. Courtesy of the artist.

TB: Is glitch art already a genre in its own right? I sometimes feel that the Iman Moradis of this world are selling old wine in new bottles and deliberately ignore the history of this approach in, among other things, abstract video art from the '70s. For me, one of the greatest pieces of glitch art is Joan Jonas's *Vertical Roll* (1972).

CF: Tilman, I think that's a great example of early glitch, but I'm confused by your surprise that after forty-odd years, glitch is finally starting to appear as a genre in its own right. My other thought on this would be that rather than ignoring its history, glitch is often precisely driven by a desire to process history. In the piece I have offered as an example, this happens both literally and metaphorically, and I'd argue that the similarities between Menkman's and Jonas's work are connective threads Menkman might even be deliberately weaving.

SC: Maybe this is too much of a tangent for this discussion, but here in the United Kingdom in 2012 (and in Australia in 2013), there were numerous projects about the end of analog television and the switch from "terrestrial" to digital transmission (which happened at different times in different parts of the country). Many of these artworks embraced a glitch aesthetic, drawing attention to the historical moment of the switch-over or switch-off, when the screen turned to the static—the white noise, or "snow," of having no signal. Interestingly, all the projects I saw, by artists including David Hall, sought to formally frame the work in the 4:3 ratio of the old CRT monitor, not the flashy flat 16:9 of the LED screen, which is how most people now watch television. I wonder if any net-based works were made with this same content, or if the works were screened online in any form? I do know that Sneha Solanki's collaborative project *Analogue Is not Digital* collected and released video clips from the last moments of terrestrial broadcast to create a kind of archive of that moment, with information on how artists could reuse that material in the creation of new video artworks. Perhaps this connects to Caitlin's choice of work, in addressing how the popular culture throwaway moment can be captured, or how the aesthetics of older formats can be celebrated over time (as Tilman suggests with his discussion of ASCII art).

DISSOCIATION—CAITLIN JONES

LORNA MILLS: VISUAL ART, IMAGES & ANIMATIONS

http://www.digitalmediatree.com/sallymckay/LornaMillsImageDump/pageback/60891/

Through my choice I'd like to address two thoughts related to abstraction and the moving image online: the enduring importance of the animated GIF and our current culture of total image saturation—with *saturation* meaning the sheer volume of images existing on the web almost completely dissociated, or "abstracted," from their original context, form, and meaning. Whether it's through Reddit, Tumblr, 4chan, or another, unattributed images have become a common currency of the web. An artist who I think addresses both of my concerns simultaneously is the Canadian Lorna Mills. Her prolific, profane, hilarious, and often disturbing animated GIFs represent a different take on the notion of abstraction and the moving image.

The Graphics Interchange Format (GIF) was an early animation format with limited color and low resolution. These attributes made it easy to create and distribute moving images regardless of processing speed or bandwidth. Wildly popular, artists of the early net.art era relied on it heavily, and it has continued to be used by a range of artists. Most significant, however, is the use of animated GIFs in what Internet art pioneer Olia Lialina refers to as part of the Vernacular Web, the web of amateurs "soon to be washed away by dot-com ambitions, professional authoring tools, and guidelines designed by usability experts."[11] But GIFs didn't wash away; in fact, they have only risen in popularity.

As an artist, Mills has obsessively and deliberately been working in this format since 2005. Combining shot footage (which she shoots herself) with found images, she refers to herself as "ravingly formal and very precise" with her compositions.[12] Although in some cases they can be shown offline as video, her GIFs are deeply imbedded in the Internet from both a technological and sociological perspective.

While Mills has created more prototypically "abstract" images, what is interesting to me in the context of this discussion is her blog, which can be read as a whole entity/artwork. The forced compression of the GIF format, the hard pixelated edges and the images' complete removal from their original context (they are both known and foreign to us) represent another way of thinking about abstraction—that of dissociation. In a blog format, her varied subjects—"vehicular accidents, men and women wanking with rubber dolphins, masturbating kangaroos, animals humping inanimate objects, animals who smoke, people fighting, animals fighting, pro wrestling, and owls doing absolutely anything"—juxtaposed and seemingly eternally scrolling, create a disorienting viewing experience that adds another layer of abstraction.[13] Even though GIFs are created out of representational images, they are radically abstract.

A post from December 20, 2013 shows three images (fig. 9.4).[14] One, a composite of tongues, teeth, and water, creates a moving monochrome, identifiable but disembodied; it is abstracted on almost every level. In the next, pixelated, flapping dragons hover around a roast chicken with jiggling human female breasts (a sub-meme found on the web), abstracting and then conflating elements of three major Internet classifications—fantasy, food, and porn—into a single image. The final image depicts a snake swallowing its own tail, a crude and jagged overlay on an image of an inconsistently rotating earth.

Mills's work is representative of and highly prescient in relation to a range of emerging contemporary art practices (some of which are known, much to my chagrin, as "post Internet") that deal with the circulation and corruption of online images. Hito Steyerl's essay "In Defense of the Poor Image" also responds to this particular moment. In this influential and often-cited text from 2009, Steyerl discusses how compression, low resolution distribution, and questionable "quality" have created a new image economy of sorts. In her introduction, Steyerl states, "[The poor image] is passed on as a lure, a decoy, an index, or as a reminder of its former visual self. It mocks the promises of digital technology. Not only is it often degraded to the point of just being a hurried blur, one even doubts whether it could be called an image at all. Only digital technology could produce such a dilapidated image in the first place. . . . The poor image tends towards abstraction: it is a visual idea in its very becoming."[15]

TB: In a recent forum on post-Internet art, JODI argued that this kind of stuff was simply "digital pop art," and I tend to agree. But then again, is their *MY%Desktop* (2002–2010) piece *not* digital pop art, because it uses just desktop icons—which are kind of pop art in themselves? (Oh, how I wish I had taken on this piece now!)

CF: Tilman, tell us more about the connections you see between Lorna Mills's work and JODI's *MY%Desktop*? I'm also interested to hear more about the concept of "digital pop art." It sounds as though you (and perhaps JODI) are using

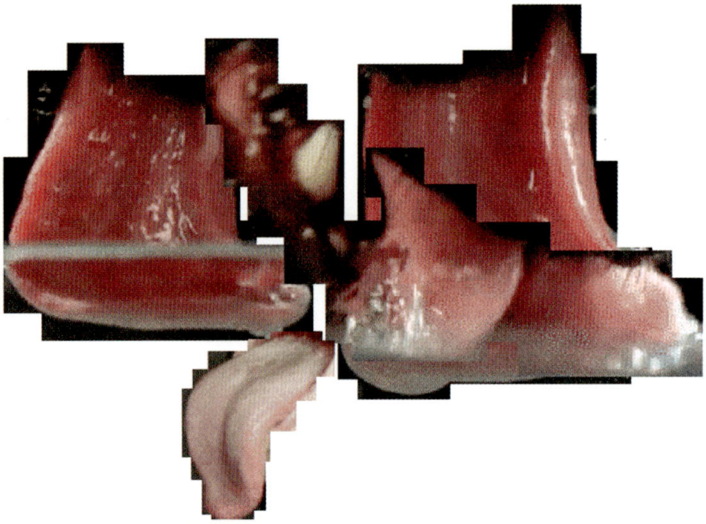

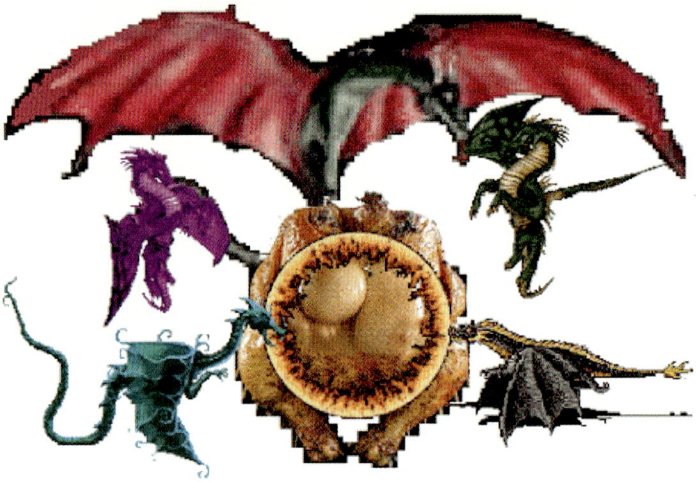

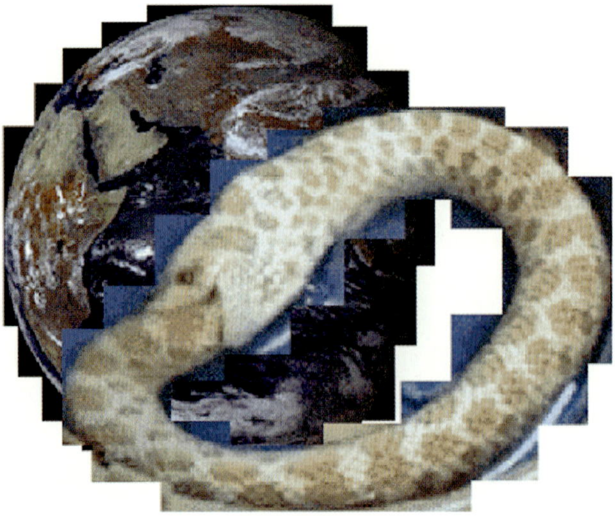

the term negatively. But isn't our immersion in the imagery of popular culture intensified by our wired lives, and doesn't that make works that comment upon such phenomena all the more compelling? Though I don't think it represents "abstraction" in any way, I would have loved to write about the work of Jeremy Bailey. In videos such as *The Future of Creativity* (2012; http://youtube.com/watch?v=/FZgfiWTwfgA), he uses kitschy digital aesthetics and the all-too-familiar tech demo format to critique web cultures. I raise it as an example because I think it could also be termed "digital pop art," but I wouldn't see that as a bad thing. In fact, I think Bailey's work so compelling precisely because he deals with such large (and popular) topics as web-based, post-Internet creativity and uses such iconically webby visuals.

SC: In an earlier edit of this conversation I did mention JODI and the pop-up, glitchy, out-of-control aesthetic as a key factor in our identification of characteristics of work falling under the category of net.video.abstraction. Made up of screen grabs of what it seemed Joan and Dirk were doing on their own computers, it is in fact cleverly programmed/created, the glitches being deliberate. The work is now primarily known through its projected or screened form, as if it were a prerecorded work, though it bears a close resemblance to current machinima (a category of "video" work, predominantly distributed online on platforms such as Vimeo, which we haven't discussed but could have, given how much of the good machinima art is about the glitch, such as the work of GoTo80 or Baden Pailthorpe). That aside, I am curious about the question of pop-cultural appropriation (key to JODI's, Mills's, and Bailey's practices) of existing imagery, and how that might relate to the Thomson & Craighead and Vuk Ćosić's examples also. All the works we've chosen are connected in this way, are they not?

TB: *MY%Desktop* was shown as a single monitor piece from the beginning. I know, because I curated the exhibition. I think the "pop art" comment, which definitely was meant to be negative, is about the fact that these days artists work with all kind of debris from the Internet while JODI first and foremost works with material that is "native" to the net, and the computer and programming is an important part of their artistic work. I have to say that with a lot of recent work, I also start to feel that it seems a little bit too easy to just endlessly repurpose stuff that you found on the net and then claim that it is (a) critique or (b) a celebration of net culture. There just is so much of this stuff.

FIGURE 9.4
(opposite) Lorna Mills, *Garden Variety (series)*, 2013. Internet art, three animated GIF collages from blog post of 12–20–2013, 10:10 A.M. http://www.digitalmediatree.com/sallymckay/LornaMillsImageDump/pageback/60891/. Courtesy of the artist.

CJ: Always happy to have Pop come into any conversation! But I see Mills's work more in the way, Tilman, that you yourself describe ASCII—as "folkloric." GIFs are Pop, in that they're a wildly popular form of communication on the web, and they're free; they don't require huge amounts of skill or bandwidth to create. As they are used by artists like Mills, however, I see them as hugely subversive, as she takes their Popness (often in a very abject way) as the subject itself. Ironically, I see it very much like I see the work of JODI (and I think it's worth noting that although none of us chose to use JODI as our example, we've come back to them again and again). Like JODI and how they subverted ideas of techno-utopianism, Mills does much the same—and abstraction is the thing that pulls this out.

CF: I have another thought I wonder if we might all consider. This chapter has been difficult to write for all of us. Partly that has been because—as is the way with the arts—we are all overloaded with work and struggling to find the time to fully engage in a rigorous discussion. However, I wonder if our issues also relate to the ideas of "abstraction" and "video" in the context of online art. In discussing *The Collapse of PAL* by Rosa Menkman, I found myself grappling with what constitutes video in an online space, and then I was perplexed by abstraction. Computer graphic user interfaces represent abstractions that we live our lives through every day. It therefore seemed extremely difficult to draw a line around moving image works that are historically and aesthetically—if not physically—part of the video art family tree, let alone consider how abstraction is represented through media and platforms that already manifest themselves in abstract representation. So I'd been keen to hear your thoughts on the difficulties of considering both these concepts today and whether you think it is precisely because we are living in age of almost ubiquitous moving abstraction that we need artists who consider this critically.

SC: I think Charlotte's metaphor of "drawing a line around" is good. Artists' works can point us to unusual or alternative viewpoints, framing different viewing experiences into aesthetic or artistic ones, or, perhaps most interestingly to me, politicizing the content of the view by changing its frame or context. So Mark Napier's work *Feed* (2001), once described as abstract action painting, does exactly that (or did, but I can't get it to work in my browser anymore) by highlighting the computer graphic user interface, all pop-up windows, grids, graphs, and color swatches, defamiliarizing us from the experience of browsing a website. At the time, we didn't have nearly the information overload experience on the web we have now, so the work feels a bit like it was a warning of how our browsing habits would be parsed and the information presented back to us. I'm running off on another tangent here, but there is something to be said about all of the works we've talked about—that their relationship to "video" could be, as Charlotte pointed out earlier, in their deliberate attempts to distort communication signals.

CF: The mention of the work *Feed* reminds me that Menkman pointed me to another discussion that had recently unfolded on net-art critic Josephine Bosma's Facebook page. Bosma invited people to compare Peter Luining in 2004: http://www.ffff00.com/ and Anthony Antonellis in 2011: http://www.dfff00.com/.[16] The two URLs lead to static webpages composed entirely of slightly different shades of yellow—the former a chrome yellow, the latter almost a lime color. In discussing the works on Bosma's page, Menkman points out that Luining's work is made out of entirely different code from Antonellis's just because it was made seven years earlier. So the different colors stand out now as entire histories and cultures of programming distilled, reduced, abstracted even, into one simple color (and therefore set of letters and numbers). Luining's yellow simulates the lost age of web-stable color remits—a time when web designers were required to work with a very reduced palate for cross-browser consistency. Menkman's *The Collapse of PAL* doesn't reduce the PAL signal to one color but rather removes it from its original context, so its fabric becomes clearer and twists it somehow so we can see its very fibers.

CJ: It seems as though each of us individually decided to approach the idea of abstraction in nonformal aesthetic terms. In all of the examples, the underlying technological frame drives the abstraction, be it the code, the compression, or the method of distribution. In the Ćosić, Thomson & Craighead, and Menkman examples, it's the code and, moreover, the metadata or signal that is dictating the level of abstraction. In the case of Mills, it is perhaps the broader cultural context that creates the abstraction. But in none of our examples is true aesthetic abstraction really exhibited in "the image" or even the moving image itself.

SC: I wonder if it is a matter of taste. As Gabrielle asked in her introductory provocations to us, why has online video art enjoyed less attention or associated theoretical writing than other forms of net-based art practices, and the practice of abstraction in this realm even less? The fact that we have struggled to put our finger on how abstraction plays out in the online moving image is indicative—we each chose very different works based on our different (and personal) aesthetic sensibilities. There is so much art to choose from online, so many works using the moving image in different ways according to different strategies—some not even identified as Art yet. Add to this the fact that the readings of the works change over time (as our dialogue evidences) and that many more of them are now "born digital" rather than having become digital in some part of their expression or sharing—and, well, perhaps the visual ceases to be the most important or interesting aspect of the work? I'm sure we could have this same conversation again another time—say, five years from now—when we are even more post-Internet or post-digital than we are now, and with our new understandings of technology or cultural contexts, we might find new criteria by which to judge our chosen projects. Maybe we should do just that. Who's in?

NOTES

1. "The Official History of Net.art, volume IV," *ASCII history of art for the blind,* http://www.ljudmila.org/~vuk/ascii/blind/.

2. Vuk Ćosić, e-mail message to Tilman Baumgärtel, March 6, 2014.

3. Lev Manovich, *The Language of New Media* (Cambridge, MA: MIT Press, 2001), 331.

4. Josephine Bosma, "The ASCII Art Ensemble," Heise Online, July 9, 1998, http://www.heise.de/tp/artikel/2/2458/1.html.

5. André Bazin, "The Ontology of the Photographic Image," *Film Quarterly* 13, no. 4 (Summer 1960), 4–9.

6. *Template Cinema,* http://templatecinema.com/.

7. Thomson & Craighead, *The Time Machine in alphabetical order,* http://www.ucl.ac.uk/slade/slide/docs/thetimemachine.html.

8. "Abstraction Principle (Computer Programming)," *Wikipedia,* http://en.wikipedia.org/wiki/Abstraction_principle_%28computer_programming%29.

9. Andrew Rosinski, "Interview with Rosa Menkman, Dutch Visualist," DINCA, http://dinca.org/interview-with-rosa-menkman-dutch-visualist/5323.htm.

10. Rosa Menkman, *"The Collapse of PAL,"* 2010, http://videoscapes.blogspot.hk/2010/07/collapse-of-pal.html

11. Olia Lialina, "A Vernacular Web," 2005, http://art.teleportacia.org/observation/vernacular.

12. Lorna Mills, quoted in Sky Goodden, "The Newest New Media: Lorna Mills on the Evolving Niche of GIF Art," *Artinfo,* October 19, 2013, http://www.blouinartinfo.com/news/story/973600/the-newest-new-media-lorna-mills-on-the-evolving-niche-of-gif.

13. Goodden, "Newest New Media."

14. Lorna Mills, *Garden Variety (series),* Lorna Mills: Visual Art, Images & Animations (blog), December 20, 2013, http://www.digitalmediatree.com/sallymckay/LornaMillsImageDump/?60818.

15. Hito Steyerl, "In Defense of the Poor Image," *e-flux journal #10,* November 2009, http://www.e-flux.com/journal/in-defense-of-the-poor-image/.

16. From a discussion on Josephine Bosma's Facebook page, February 13, 2014.

10

INTERACTIVE ABSTRACTIONS

Between Embodied Exploration and Instrumental Control "Underneath Your Fingertips"

Katja Kwastek

This essay discusses abstract moving images generated or shaped by means of real-time audience interaction. As such, they differ from prerecorded compositions as well as from generative works based on preprogrammed operations, which cannot be influenced while being executed. The focus on audience interaction also excludes animations reacting exclusively to other (nonhuman) forms of data input, such as music, environmental data, or Internet data streams. Although such systems may rightly be determined as interactive, the focus of this essay is on humans' real-time interaction with abstract moving images.

Interactive video does not necessarily have to be abstract. It may make use of preexisting assets, which the recipient is encouraged to select or arrange, and these assets may well be figurative or even narrative. Since the 1980s artists like Grahame Weinbren or Lynn Hershman Leeson have experimented with such forms of interactive storytelling, and interactive television remains an undercurrent in mainstream media. And even if no preexisting assets are used, interactive video may be mimetic, as is the case in so-called closed-circuit video installations, which capture and replay the live image of visitors. So why would artists produce abstract interactive video, and what does the concept of abstraction entail when it comes to interactive imaging processes?

INTERACTIVE ABSTRACTIONS IN EARLY EXPERIMENTAL VIDEO, TV, AND COMPUTER GRAPHICS

While the real-time generation and manipulation of electronic images was an important aspect of early experimental video, there is little evidence of artists having granted control of the respective systems to their audience. Mostly, artists working in the field of experimental video wouldn't even perform live; they would record their experiments on film or present them by means of representative photographic stills.[1]

One early exemption was Nam June Paik.[2] Like many artists of the 1960s, Paik was greatly interested in exploring the aesthetic potential of indeterminacy. Heralded by Marcel Duchamp's interest in unintentionality and followed by John Cage's fascination with chance operations, the artistic exploration of the relationship between chance and control had become an important topic of the arts by 1960. Like Cage, Paik experimented with the inclusion of everyday material and technology into his works. In the early 1960s, he started to manipulate the electromagnetic signals of television sets to the point of full abstraction. In 1962 he claimed that "as the next step toward more indeterminacy, I wanted to let the audience act and play itself."[3] In fact, at his groundbreaking *Exposition of Music* (1963), visitors were invited to use a foot pedal and a microphone to operate two manipulated televisions (while other television sets had been prepared to react to radio programs and audio tapes). Paik continued to pursue these explorations in the different versions of his *Participation TV* (1963–1966) and *Magnet TV* (1965).[4] However, in his later work with the Paik-Abe Synthesizer, which, like other video synthesizers built in the 1970s, allowed for a sophisticated montage and electronic manipulation of moving images, he wouldn't surrender control to the audience.

The 1960s also saw the first phase of computer art. Computer scientists like A. Michael Noll and Frieder Nake started to explore the artistic potential of computer graphics, creating abstract compositions based on elaborate computational algorithms. The results of these operational processes were exhibited as printed images, each of which was seen as an exemplary sample out of a whole class of possible results of the programmed operation. The common visual output medium of early digital computers was the plotter.[5] It was only in 1963 that the electronics engineer Ivan Sutherland presented Sketchpad, the first user interface that allowed graphics to be immediately manipulated on a display screen by means of a light pen.[6] Earlier on, computational real-time operations had to rely on input devices like phone dials or buttons and knobs. Nevertheless, we might count early game-based demonstrations of these interfaces, such as Noughts and Crosses (1952) and Tennis for Two (1958), as the very first computer-based interactive abstractions.[7]

VISUALIZING INTERACTION

It took until the 1970s for interactive computer graphics to enter the realm of the arts. In 1971, Myron Krueger, who is considered a pioneer of interactive media art, created

Psychic Space, an interaction environment that detected the movements of the visitors by means of a touch-sensitive floor. In *Maze,* an application designed for that environment, recipients could use their own movements to steer a square through an animated labyrinth displayed on a vertical projection screen. As they did so, they had to deal with a complex and occasionally bizarre set of rules. Krueger wanted to explore and reveal the laws and conventions of interaction. Like the early video games, *Maze* was a symbolic environment within which abstract graphics served to visualize its underlying rule systems and to direct user interaction. In *Videoplace,* however, a system which Krueger developed subsequently, the visitor's silhouette was recorded via video camera, then digitally manipulated and projected. Though the silhouette significantly simplified the visitor's image, it still iconically referenced it, as opposed to the symbolic representation as a simple square in *Maze.* Even today, systems based on motion capture via video camera are one of the main means of interactive installation art. Similarly, the depiction of the user's image as an abstracted silhouette is still common.

In Krueger's works, the silhouette as well as the depiction of the objects and surroundings it could interact with were rather simple in terms of visual definition. One of Krueger's key statements concerning *Videoplace* is that "it is the composition of the relationship between action and response that is important. The beauty of the visual and aural response is secondary. Response is the medium!"[8] While one might suspect that Krueger's attitude was a rhetorical trick to downplay the fact that early real-time computer graphics were technically clumsy, it is all the more astonishing that we find comparable arguments in very recent statements, even concerning the video game. In a series of interviews published around 2007, Yoshikazu Yamashita, one of the lead developers of Nintendo's Wii, defends the simple appearance of the so-called *kokeshi* (which represent players in video game actions) as follows: "The kokeshi might be simple, but your mind helps make it more real. In Wii Sports Baseball, even though the arms and legs aren't shown when the fielders move, it feels realistic when you see them in motion."[9] Abstraction here serves as a means to facilitate the player's identification with his virtual counterpart. The schematism of the representation enhances its universality as a placeholder, to become meaningful only through individual interaction.

In other contexts too, visual minimalism has been used as a means to focus attention on the process of interaction itself. Andrew Hieronymi, in his installation entitled *Move* (2005) (fig. 10.1)—again based on motion capture via video camera—exposes the basic actions carried out by participants in video games, which he identifies as Jump, Avoid, Chase, Throw, Hide, and Collect. To enable and provoke the recipient to perform these actions, Hieronymi sought out very simple visualizations based on moving red and white geometric forms and dots. They are projected onto the floor to visualize core rules and tasks, which are easily deducible and challenge the participant to act. By separating the core mechanics of video game actions from their usually narrative context, Hieronymi puts these actions, their underlying rules, and respective user attitudes on center stage.[10] In this case, action is literally abstracted from any narrative content.

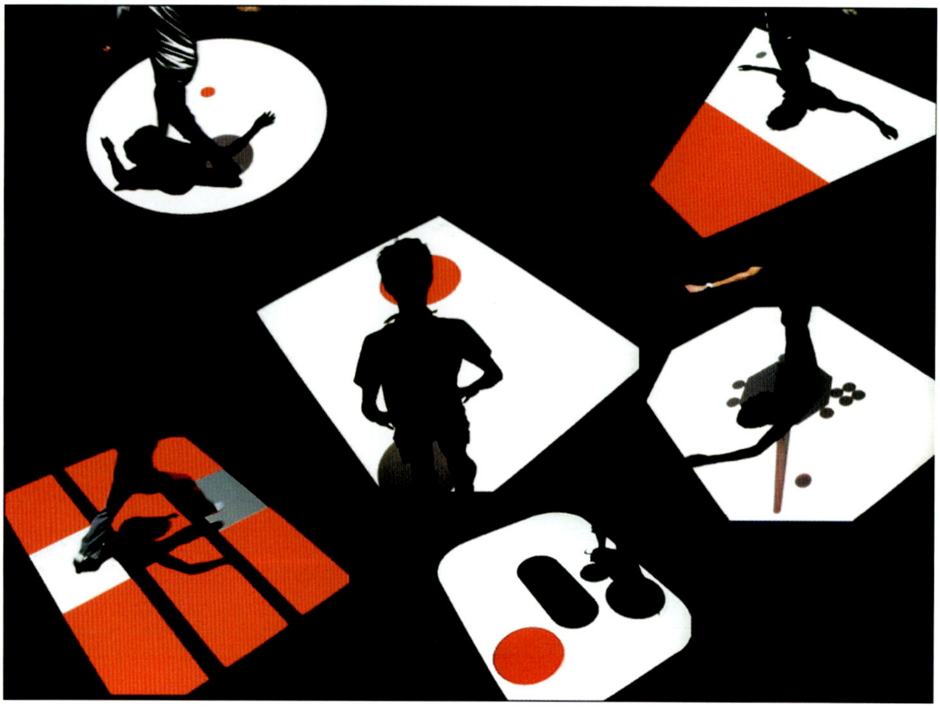

FIGURE 10.1
Andrew Hieronymi, *Move,* 2005. Interactive installation. © Andrew Hieronymi; assistant, Togo Kida.

In interactive works, abstract animations may thus serve to make visual the system's interaction potential and channel the resulting interaction. Often, such works feature rule systems with clearly identifiable goals and thus show close parallels to video games. However, while the video game started as an abstract symbolic system, with the increasing perfection of computer graphics, the tendency was towards seeking a maximum degree of realism, providing illusionistic game environments that mimic real physical settings. The underlying assumption was that games should be immersive and that immersion was facilitated by visual illusionism. As shown, this assumption has recently been questioned by, among others, the Wii developers. Katie Salen and Eric Zimmerman, in their book entitled *Rules of Play,* use the term "immersive fallacy" to denote the still widespread and dominant belief that game worlds should be as realistic as possible. They argue that an intensely pleasurable play experience by no means requires the illusion that one is actually part of an imaginary world.[11] Salen and Zimmerman emphasize that the main goal of games should be to create meaning for players and that such meaning arises through processes of meta-communication—that is, an attitude that is connected to but distanced from the real world.[12] In the same vein, interactive abstract video may offer behavioral systems that reference real-world rules or actions but actually highlight or scrutinize their workings by abstracting or isolating them. Abstraction, in this context, is a means of visualizing structural conditions or generalizing phenomena by representing their core characteristics. This clearly relates to the original, philosophical notion of abstraction, denoting the generalization of the particular and the concentration on the essential as well as, within the arts, the depiction of general, immaterial or theoretical concepts.

VISUALIZING INTERPERSONAL RELATIONS

Scott Snibbe's *Boundary Functions* (1998) (fig. 10.2), another interactive installation based on camera monitoring and floor projection, also follows a minimalistic approach, this time aimed at directly visualizing interpersonal relations. As soon as more than one visitor enters a demarcated area, straight graphic lines are projected onto the floor so as to partition the area in such a way that each participant is assigned a section of equal size. In geometry, this kind of construction, which is based on distance calculations, is called a Voronoi diagram. As participants move, join in, or leave, the partitioning lines immediately shift to adapt to the new situation. The result is an abstract, dynamic line structure inextricably linked to the people it encircles as they trigger the lines that constantly adapt to their movement.[13] However, as opposed to the rule-based systems of Krueger and Hieronymi, *Boundary Functions* does not present a clear goal but invites recipients to freely explore the visualization and to reflect upon concepts and perceptions of personal space.

Another and more recent example of how abstract graphics can serve as a means to visualize interpersonal relations is Sonia Cillari's *Se Mi Sei Vicino* (If You Are Close To Me), first presented to the public in 2006. Upon entering the dimly lit room containing Cillari's interactive installation, the visitor's attention is immediately captured by a female performer standing motionless in the middle of the room and by two large abstract graphics projected onto two of the walls. Each of the graphics depicts a three-dimensional vertical structure—a spindle-shaped, flexible grid that stretches from the bottom to the top of the projection area. While the upper and lower extremities of this structure are fixed and immobile, the grid itself is in a state of constant, wave-like motion. The nodes of the grid are highlighted as white triangles resembling force arrows. When a visitor approaches the performer, the grid begins to expand sideways and to sprout horizontal peaks. At the same time, an arrangement of metallic sounds begins to play. Touching the performer intensifies the effect. The spaces in the grid begin to fill up, first with gray tones and then with colors. The sounds become louder and turn into a sizzling reminiscent of newly lit fireworks. Thus, the audiovisual feedback can be interpreted as an abstract representation of the performer—specifically, as a visualization (and sonification) of her reactions to people approaching her. These reactions are represented as structures that enter into motion, in the form of uniform rhythms, or momentary peaks or eruptions, accompanied by a crescendo of sound.[14]

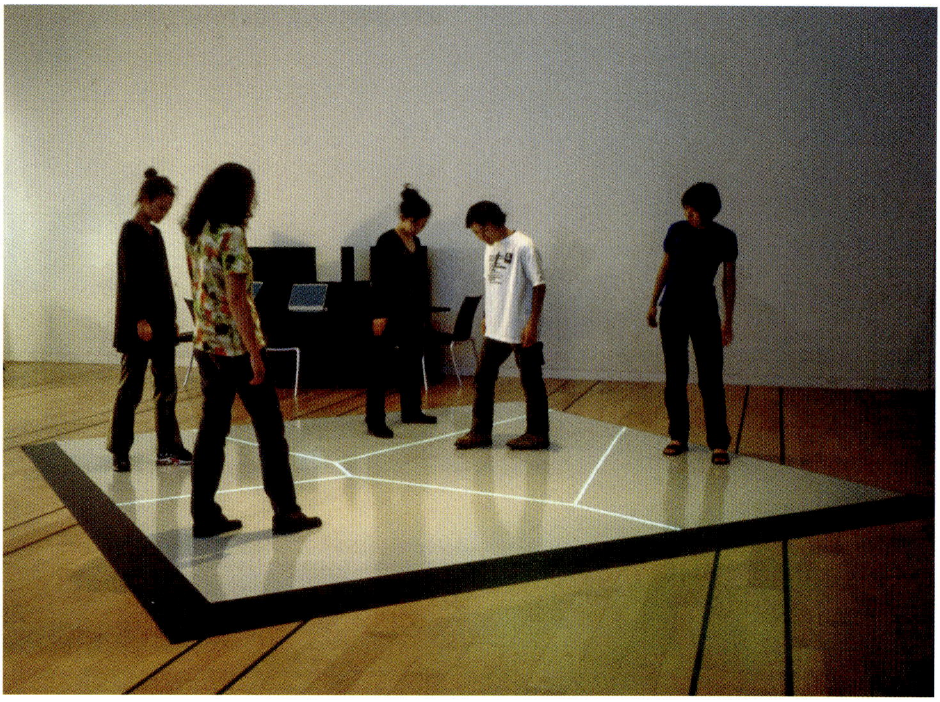

FIGURE 10.2
Scott Snibbe, *Boundary Functions*, 1998. Interactive installation. Courtesy of the artist.

Again, though these audiovisual formations are abstract in the sense of being nonfigurative, they are nevertheless representational in that they represent or symbolize the invisible emotional as well as physical tensions that arise in interpersonal encounters.

IMMERSIVE ENVIRONMENTS

Cillari's example clearly evidences that formal reduction is not the only means of interactive abstraction. Interactive abstract video may also be formally elaborate and visually complex. It may even offer overwhelming, visually immersive experiences. The ultimate impossibility of a convincing and fully illusionistic visual imitation of the "real world" also led to concepts of virtual reality that focus on visionary worlds or imaginary environments.[15] Within these, abstract forms are not results of simplification or reduction but result from alienation or pure fantasy. Early and very famous examples are Charlotte Davies's *Osmose* (1995) and *Ephémère* (1998), three-dimensional immersive environments that allow recipients—which Davies calls "immersants"—to navigate virtual worlds. They are equipped with a head-mounted display and a motion-sensitive

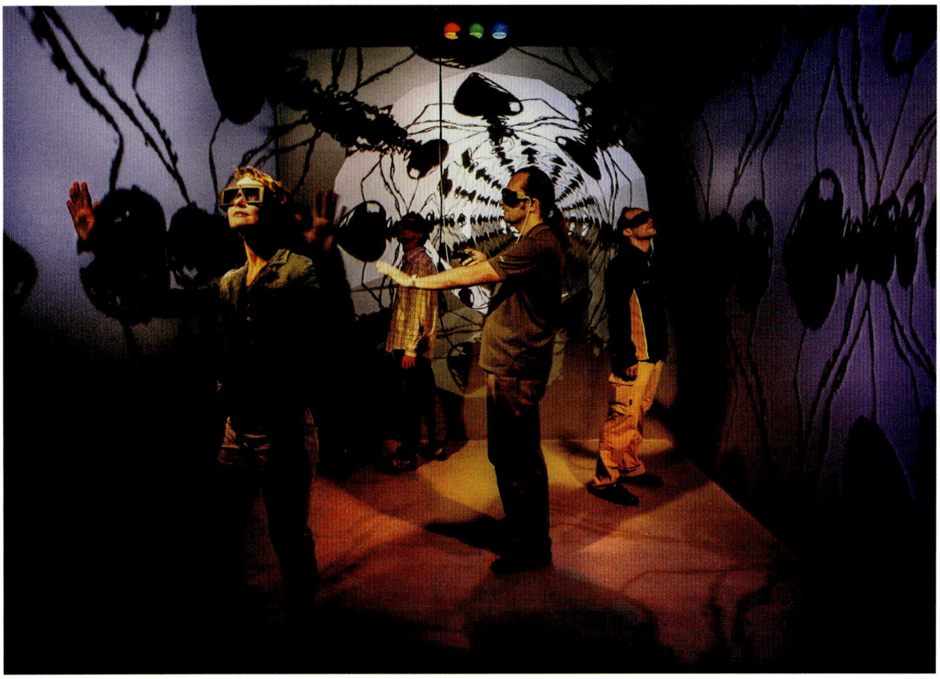

FIGURE 10.3
Peter Kogler, *Cave,* 1999. Immersive interactive environment. Computer animation in cooperation with Ars Electronica Future-lab; sound by Franz Pomassl. Courtesy of the artist and Ars Electronica. Photograph by Pilo Pichler.

chest harness and can navigate the environment by means of their own breathing and movement. Though the displayed worlds loosely resemble forests, underwater worlds, or clouds, and—in *Ephémère*—also the interior of the human body, they are far from being realistic representations. These environments are independent of any material constraints or Cartesian rules. They appear blurry, painterly, immaterial, transparent, and ephemeral. As Christiane Paul emphasizes, "one of the extremely effective strategies Davies employs is to avoid representational realism in the creation of her worlds."[16]

While Davies worked with references to the organic and created vague and uncanny realms, Peter Kogler and Franz Pomassl realized an equally immersive, interactive virtual environment, which is, however, nearly exclusively based on graphic patterns and geometric structures and makes no attempt at triggering familiar environments. Their 1999 *Cave* (fig. 10.3) application was produced for the Linz Ars Electronica Center's CAVE environment, a space with rear-projection screens on five surfaces, within which three-dimensional effects could be experienced through special glasses. Kogler and Pomassl's work invited visitors to immerse themselves in a labyrinth of graphically patterned tubes, pipes, and passageways, accompanied by an impressive soundscape. By means of a joystick, they could navigate this immersive system, inhabit and explore it.[17] While the visual style of this environment has few commonalities with Davies's organic shapes, both projects apply abstracted or nonfigurative compositions to heighten their respective visually immersive qualities, transporting the recipients into wholly artificial realms.

Interactive abstractions, as we have seen so far, may thus visualize processes of interaction, or they may invite recipients into a three-dimensional, navigable world. Both categories are aimed at modes of aesthetic experience that I have elsewhere denoted as experimental exploration. The recipient explores an artificial environment or a rule-based setting by means of experimental navigation or testing interaction. In the remainder of this essay, I will introduce another category of interactive abstraction and discuss works that encourage recipients to actually become expressive themselves, and to "create" abstract animations.[18]

(AUDIO)VISUAL INSTRUMENTS

Even before exploring the potentials of full body interaction in his installation pieces, Scott Snibbe's fascination with early experimental and abstract film had prompted him to devise screen-based installations that enable recipients to directly engage with visual forms. In 1989, he presented his first interactive application, named *Motion Sketch,* a kind of painting software for animated geometric forms, which resembled those used by Oskar Fischinger in his early films. *Motion Sketch* allowed users to select forms from a menu, control their size, color and speed, and set them into motion on the screen. In 1995, Snibbe also presented a multi-user version of *Motion Sketch,* entitled *Motion Phone.*[19]

Although *Motion Sketch* and *Motion Phone* were exclusively visual, the 1990s saw the development of several applications that aimed at audiovisuality, at a mapping or reciprocal control of electronic sounds and abstract graphics. Media artist Golan Levin has identified three metaphors that guide such mapping processes: scores, control panels, and "interactive widgets."[20] The reference to musical scores is evidenced in many works of Toshio Iwai. Between 1992 and 1994 Iwai developed a system called *Music Insects* in which recipients could use a mouse to create drawings on a monitor. The system assigned musical notes to the drawing's pixels, based on the colors in which they were drawn. These notes were activated by preprogrammed "insects" representing different musical instruments, which ran across the screen and functioned as pick-ups. As soon as an insect made contact with a pixel, the corresponding note sounded. In 1995, Iwai created *Piano—as Image Media,* an installation in which visitors used a trackball to draw shapes and patterns that were projected onto transparent gauze and animated so that the individual pixels of the patterns moved line by line toward a real piano, which—controlled by a computer—interpreted them as musical notation and played the corresponding notes. The pixels then appeared to traverse the keyboard, only to stream out of the piano and head upwards, changing into colored geometric objects as they flow.[21]

The second metaphor identified by Levin, the control panel, was widely applied throughout the 1990s but has more recently reached a high level of technical and artistic sophistication with a device entitled *reacTable,* a highly complex music table conceived and developed since 2003 by a research team at the Pompeu Fabra University in Barcelona. It is a round table on which various cube- and disk-shaped building blocks tagged with markers can be positioned. They function as sound generators, sound filters, and sound controllers, while the computer graphics displayed on the table visualize the current activity of the blocks as well as their interplay by means of circular graphics surrounding the blocks and connecting, dynamic lines indicating frequencies and rhythms.[22]

The third category of interactive audiovisual systems makes use of what Levin calls interactive widgets, "a group of virtual objects . . . which can be manipulated, stretched, collided, etc. by a performer in order to shape or compose music."[23] One example for such systems is *Small Fish.* In 1998 and 1999, Kiyoshi Furukawa together with Wolfgang Münch and Masaki Fujihata created this screen-based system consisting of fifteen different audiovisual applications. They all present predesigned geometric forms or painterly shapes, which trigger sounds while moving across the screen or encountering moving "pick-up-dots." The user can shift the sounding elements around in order to manipulate the composition.[24] The results are colorful animations of geometric or organic forms, some of them resembling abstract paintings of the classical avant-garde—Paul Klee or Joan Miró for example. However, while the user may influence their arrangement and movement, the shapes of the forms themselves do not change. This is why Levin criticizes the poor granularity of control of such systems, within which "canned ingredients, all too inevitably, yield canned results."[25]

Therefore, in 1997, he collaborated with Scott Snibbe in developing new kinds of visual instruments, aimed at creating "phenomenological interfaces that engage the unconscious mind directly."[26] They were searching for aesthetic solutions that, instead of relying on geometric or clear-cut predesigned forms, would reference the process of drawing, as pioneered by the abstract films of Len Lye. They acknowledge that in Lye's films, "for the first time the hand and the spontaneous mind are visible on celluloid—like watching the inner thoughts of the artist."[27] Fascinated by this effect, Levin and Snibbe sought out ways to make the process of drawing itself the direct point of departure for animation. In *Escargogolator,* for example, the user's mark (set via the cursor) was animated based on the geometrical construction of so called evolutes, which resulted in a twisting and curling, expanding and shrinking of the original mark. Thus, the user created a dynamic mark that determined the conditions of animation. One could then "witness how those conditions evolve and disintegrate over time."[28]

In their subsequent individual works, Levin and Snibbe each explored a further aspect of interactive abstractions. While Levin continued to elaborate on the "painterly metaphor" and started to develop audiovisual systems, Snibbe further experimented with algorithms referencing geometrical figures or physical laws, creating dynamic systems whose parameters can be controlled by the users. One example is *Bubble Harp* (1997), which, like *Boundary Functions,* is based on the idea of a Voronoi diagram. This time, in addition to setting singular dots on the screen to cause enclosing lines, the user can also draw lines, generating a sequence of dots each of which continuously repeats its initial movement and provokes enclosing lines to continuously adapt. As dots can be added endlessly, the animation may develop into a very complex, dynamic network. A further work of Snibbe, entitled *Gravilux* (1998), takes gravity as a point of departure. Here, the cursor serves to attract or repel the elements of an artificial grid of dots, whose color, proximity, and size can be controlled via a menu. The grid thus expands or shrinks, bends or curls, and dots may accumulate or diverge dynamically.

While Snibbe thus focused on allowing users to influence and play with systems that feature physical laws and properties (or at least reference them), Levin further explored the "idea of an inexhaustible, extremely variable, dynamic, audiovisual substance which can be freely 'painted,'"[29] creating a series of works entitled *Audiovisual Environment Suite* (1999–2000). In one application of the suite, named *Yellowtail,* shapes drawn by means of a mouse are animated as if backwards, reenacting the impulse that informed the act of drawing. In addition to the direction of movement, also the speed of the user's mark is measured and informs the breadth and animation speed of the shapes. Sonification of the shapes is achieved through the overlay of the animations with an inverse spectrogram, which interprets the graphics as sound notation. Thus the dynamics of drawing are represented and animated audiovisually; the generated animations actually represent indexical traces of the user's expressive actions, which may then be contemplated and studied, facilitated by the fact that the animations are looped continuously.

At the end of the 1990s both Snibbe and Levin abandoned the work with standard interfaces to create large-scale interactive installations. Snibbe started to explore the aesthetic potentials of the human silhouette, inviting recipients to perform movements that were replayed, collected, and countered with graphic animations on a big screen projection.[30] Levin continued to develop audiovisual systems but explored interface solutions that enabled gestural input, and thus more intuitive interaction. The so-called *Manual Input Workstation,* which Levin created together with Zachary Lieberman in 2004, allows the recipient to create and manipulate sounding shapes by using hand gestures in a kind of shadow play. Visitors can place cardboard shapes on the glass top of an overhead projector so that shadows of the shapes are projected onto the facing wall. A computer system records the shadows via a video camera, analyzes them, and generates animated audiovisual objects that are superimposed via a video projector onto the original overhead projection, the sound being played through adjacent speakers. Visitors can use hand movements and gestures to discover more sophisticated ways of creating dynamic shapes. The work offers different program modes. One of them, entitled *NegDrop,* invites the recipient to create closed contours that the system then fills with colored shapes. If the contour is opened, the shape inside drops to the bottom of the screen and bounces repeatedly, each time triggering a sound. The sounds vary, depending on the size, the form, and the speed at which the shapes fall. The factors that contribute to the generation of notes (volume, pitch, and timbre) are directly assigned to the characteristics underlying shapes (volume, contours, and position). Thus, the possibility of manipulating the sounding objects in real time allows the recipient to observe the interplay between shape and sound precisely.[31]

MERGING OF INTERACTIVE AND GENERATIVE IMAGING

While Levin had thus shifted to focus on audiovisual interactions, the exploration of a painterly metaphor was restated in the 2000s by Camille Utterback, whose *External Measures Series* not only takes the idea of interactive abstract painting to the realm of full body interaction but also significantly advances the complexity of the resulting composition.[32] As opposed to the applications of Levin's *Audiovisual Environment Suite,* the works of the *External Measures Series* concentrate exclusively on visual expression. They elicit a wide variety of painterly marks within one composition, as if resulting from the use of different brushes, colors, and drawing and painting techniques, merging into one complex dynamic composition. Technically, the works are again based on an overhead camera recording the movement of people in space, which is processed and shapes a wall projection displaying the resulting composition.

In *Untitled 5* (2004) (fig. 10.4), the fifth installation of the series, the movement of a filigree network of black lines is controlled by the body movement of the visitor. The user's path is marked by a thin, curved red line, while it also effects blot-like forms at its contours. Once they have appeared, these blots start to move away from their point of origin and leave traces resembling brushstrokes.[33] Also the next work of the series, *Untitled 6* (2005), starts with a filigree network of lines controlled by the visitor's silhouette.[34] In addition, his direction of movement is represented by a sequence of small cartoon-style clouds. These cloudlike marks "store information" about the movements they represent. Utterback explains that "[a] second movement over these marks releases them to continue moving with their stored momentum."[35] Their prior direction of movement now triggers monochrome forms that extend like irregular stripes or ribbons, effecting openings within the picture plane. When these stripes or ribbons once again cross the path of the filigree network of lines controlled by visitor movement, they accumulate and bleed out into semi-transparent blots that seem to flow like watercolor, resulting in clouded contours.

We can see that, in these works, the impact of the recipient's action is not restricted to the actual moment of interaction, because the composition is also influenced by prior movements, thereby adhering to a complex and only partially controllable, generative process. As such, the works of the *External Measures Series* represent a merging of generative software and interactive abstractions, which had been heralded by works like Snibbe and Levin's *Escargogolator,* but are expanded here so as to result in a fully fledged painterly and dynamic composition.

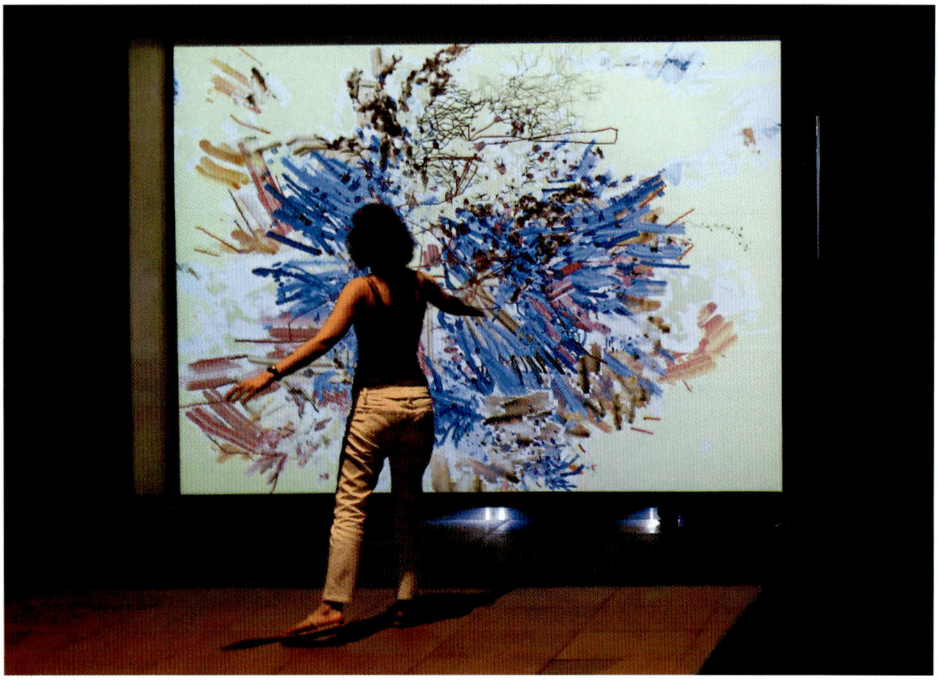

FIGURE 10.4
Camille Utterback, *Untitled 5*, 2004. Interactive installation. Installation view. Courtesy of the artist.

But again, the painterly aesthetic is only one possible option for interactive abstractions including generative elements. Austrian artist LIA has been working on comparably complex applications that, however, instead of presenting organic shapes, focus on graphical elements and structures. In her works—some of which were freely available as online applications early on—a multitude of gossamer lines may grow, curl, or meander; geometric shapes may multiply, build formation, and wander across the screen, while the user can influence their evolution by selecting starting points or formal parameters.[36]

FROM SCIENCE MUSEUM TO APP STORE

Until recently, works like those discussed so far have been presented nearly exclusively in museum and exhibition contexts, notwithstanding early attempts to distribute them online or on CD.[37] Some artists have furthermore attempted to market their developments as audiovisual instruments. Toshio Iwai, for example, has created such an instrument together with Yamaha, called *TENORI-ON*,[38] and the *reacTable*, too, is available as a market-ready device. Another ambitious attempt to commodify this form of art was the *softwareARTspace* inaugurated in 2005 by Steven Sacks, director of the Bit-

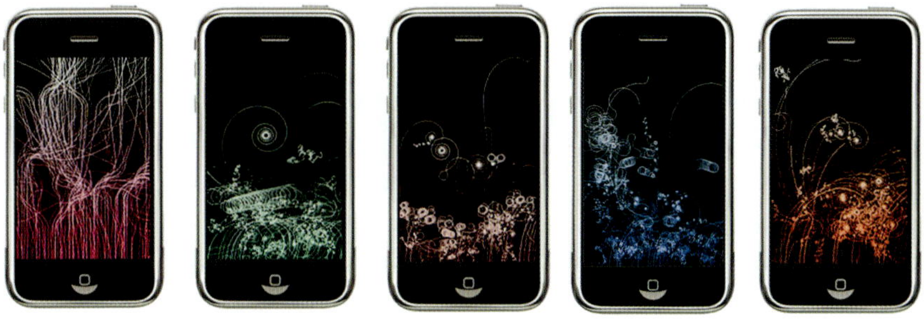

FIGURE 10.5
LIA, *Sumo5*, 2012. iPhone/iPad application. © LIA, www.liaworks.com.

forms Gallery in New York. While distributing each piece as a limited edition of 5,000, he imagined a software art station in private households on which "you can easily switch amongst your collection."[39] However, the blog to this initiative contains only one entry, and no new works have been added to the initial selection, indicating that this attempt did not prove successful. Supposedly, this was also due to the launch of the App Store, a platform that, though mainly intended for purposes that lie beyond those of the art world, actually revolutionized the distribution of interactive abstract art.

Scott Snibbe recounts that he had switched to full-body interaction systems suitable to serve as museum exhibits, abandoning his early screen-based works, because he didn't see a way to distribute the latter. But with the advent of the iPad, "all of a sudden there was a direct channel to individual human beings, to offer them something seemingly absurd and useless and yet that would give them intense amounts of joy and pleasure. . . . With the iPad, I could just go directly to people and say: check this thing out."[40] The iPad enables an easy distribution of applications that provide "interactivity underneath your fingertips."[41] Snibbe thus reprogrammed his early screen-based applications to work as apps—as did Levin and LIA. In 2010, Snibbe released, among others, *Bubble Harp* and *Gravilux* as apps, followed by a relaunch of *Motion Phone* in 2012. By August 2010, the first apps Snibbe launched, together, had been downloaded more than 400,000 times.[42]

This success obviously attracted the attention of Icelandic artist Björk. Björk had worked with audiovisual instruments before and used the *reacTable* in some of her performances. For her album *Biophilia*, she commissioned Snibbe to direct the creation of an app for each song, released subsequently in the second half of 2011. In addition to the lyrics, each app contains an interactive play mode, accompanied by an "animation" (essentially a graphic visualization of the song) and the score of the song. Most of the play mode variants enable the user to explore or alter a sound layer that is closely related to the actual song, by manipulation or control of interactive graphics that allude to the theme of the song. They vary from visualizations of microbiological processes like blood flow or virus attacks to astronomical references and abstract geometric compositions.

Some of the *Biophilia* apps make use of the tablet PC's new features, enabling an operation via multitouch (*Thunderbolt*) or a control by means of tilting the device (*Crystalline*). Also LIA is experimenting with the integration of new control features provided by the iPad and has implemented combinations of multitouch, tilting, and shaking in her iPad apps (*Sum05* [2012], fig. 10.5, and *PhiLIA 01* [2009]). The tablet PC thus not only provides a promising new distribution platform for interactive abstractions, but its technical features also allow for the implementation of new ways of control or manipulation. The following years will show how far and within which contexts these potentials will be extended. Possibly, they may further push the merging of visual arts and music, while also challenging the boundaries between art and entertainment, as well as between the arts and graphic and interaction design.

As has been shown, abstract video has played a central role within the development of interactive imagery. It is perfectly suited to channel or invite interaction with computer-based systems, be it in the form of visualizations of interactive operations, virtual worlds to be explored, or expressive tool. It is, however, important to note that, though such interactive abstractions are not necessarily narrative nor figurative, they may well be representational, in that they may reference reality in various ways, scrutinizing them by means of isolation or alienation. As such, they often provide models of visualizing real-world phenomena, theoretical concepts, or musical compositions that elude mimetic representation.

NOTES

1. For an overview of early experimental video, see, among others, David Dunn, ed., *Eigenwelt der Apparatewelt: Pioneers of Electronic Art* (Linz, Austria: Ars Electronica, 1992); and Woody Vasulka and Peter Weibel, eds., *Buffalo Heads: Media Study, Media Practice, Media Pioneers, 1973–1990* (London/Cambridge: MIT Press, 2008).

2. See also John Hanhardt's essay reprinted in this volume, discussing installation pieces presented in 1979 and 1980 by Stan VanDerBeek and Al Robbins, which involve the audience in various ways.

3. Nam June Paik, "About the Exposition of Music," *Décollage* 3 (1962).

4. Edith Decker, *Paik Video* (Cologne: DuMont, 1988), 60–66.

5. On early computer graphics, see the excellent study by Christoph Klütsch, *Computergraphik: Ästhetische Experimente zwischen zwei Kulturen: Die Anfänge der Computerkunst in den 1960er Jahren* (Vienna/New York: Springer, 2007).

6. Ivan Edward Sutherland, *Sketchpad: A Man-Machine Graphical Communication System*, PhD thesis, Massachusetts Institute of Technology, www.cl.cam.ac.uk, 17.

7. Tristan Donovan, *Replay: The History of Video Games* (Lews: Yellow Ant, 2010), 6; and Stefan Höltgen, Johannes Maibaum, and Matthias Rech, "Tennisspielen mit Physik," *RETRO Magazin* 24 (2012), 32–37.

8. Myron Krueger, *Artificial Reality II* (Reading, MA: Addison-Wesley, 1991), 86.

9. Yoshikazu Yamashita, quoted in "Wii Sports 2: A Question of Realism," Iwata Asks, www.nintendo.co.uk/Iwata-Asks/Iwata-Asks-Wii/Iwata-Asks-Wii-Sports/2-A-Question-of-Realism/2-A-Question-of-Realism-217824.html.

10. See Andrew Hieronymi, *MOVE*, http://users.design.ucla.edu/~ahierony/move/.

11. Katie Salen and Eric Zimmerman, *Rules of Play: Game Design Fundamentals* (Cambridge, MA: MIT Press, 2004), 450. This critique of visual illusionism as a hindrance to interaction may even lead to a total rejection of visual representations in interactive art. Canadian artist David Rokeby believes that the reproduction of a recipient's body on a projection screen is incompatible with its physical perception: "When playing with Myron Krueger's work . . . where you . . . had a visual shadow avatar on the screen, your feeling of being in your body was blasted away by negotiating the manipulation of an avatar separate from your body." Rokeby himself thus neither depicts nor represents the human body, instead using acoustic feedback to encourage physical movements and enable enhanced self-awareness. Lizzie Muller and Caitlin Jones, "Interview with David Rokeby," question 11, *Very Nervous System:* Documentary Collection, Daniel Langlois Foundation, 2010, www.fondation-langlois.org/html/e/page.php?NumPage=2187.

12. Salen and Zimmerman, *Rules of Play*, 450–53.

13. See "Boundary Functions, 1998," Scott Sona Snibbe: Projects, www.snibbe.com/projects/interactive/boundaryfunctions.

14. See my extensive analysis of this work in Katja Kwastek, *Aesthetics of Interaction in Digital Art* (Cambridge, MA: MIT Press, 2013), 241–48.

15. See my detailed discussion of the concept of immersion in interactive art in Katja Kwastek, "Immersed in Reflection? The Aesthetic Experience of Interactive Media Art," in *Immersion: Historical and Current Perspectives on a Key Term in Art and Media Studies*, ed. Burcu Dogramaci and Fabienne Liptay (Amsterdam/New York: Rodopi, 2015).

16. Christiane Paul, *Digital Art* (Thames and Hudson: London 2003), 127.

17. Pascal Maresch, "Peter Kogler / Franz Pomassl, CAVE," in *Lifescience*, ed. Gerfried Stocker and Christine Schöpf (Vienna: Springer, 1999), 364–66.

18. See my discussion of modes of experience in interactive art in Kwastek, *Aesthetics of Interaction*, 128–34.

19. Scott Sona Snibbe and Golan Levin, "Interactive Dynamic Abstraction," in *Proceedings of the First International Symposium on Non-photorealistic Animation and Rendering*, Annecy, France, June 5–7, 2000 (New York: ACM, 2000), 21–29, www.snibbe.com/download/publications/academic/2000Dynamic_NPAR.pdf.

20. Golan Levin, "Painterly Interfaces for Audiovisual Performances," MS thesis, MIT Media Laboratory, 2000, 34, www.flong.com/storage/pdf/articles/thesis300.pdf.

21. Toshio Iwai, "A Short History of the Works," Doors of Perception, 1993, http://museum.doorsofperception.com/doors1/transcripts/iwai/iwai.html; and Toshio Iwai, "Piano—as Image Media," *Leonardo* 34, no. 3 (2001), 183.

22. See Sergi Jordà, Günter Geiger, Marcos Alonso, and Martin Kaltenbrunner, *The reacTable: Exploring the Synergy between Live Music Performance and Tabletop Tangible Interfaces*, Music Technology Group, Pompeu Fabra University, Barcelona, Spain, http://mtg.upf.edu/files/publications/reactable_tei2007.pdf.

23. Levin, "Painterly Interfaces," 34.

24. See the project documentation at http://hosting.zkm.de/wmuench/small_fish.

25. Levin, "Painterly Interfaces," 46.

26. Levin and Snibbe, "Interactive Dynamic Abstraction."

27. Levin and Snibbe, "Interactive Dynamic Abstraction."

28. Levin, "Painterly Interfaces," 66.

29. Levin, "Painterly Interfaces," 56.

30. See Scott Snibbe, *Visceral Cinema: Chien,* exhibition catalogue (Los Angeles: Telic Gallery, 2005).

31. See my detailed analysis of the work in Kwastek, *Aesthetics of Interaction,* 225–34.

32. Camille Utterback, *"Untitled 6,"* 2005, http://camilleutterback.com/projects/untitled-6/.

33. Utterback explains that in *Untitled 5,* "animated marks are both pushed away by, and collect around the edges of people's silhouettes." Utterback, *"Untitled 6."*

34. This time, these lines are red and described as vein-like by the artist. Utterback, *"Untitled 6."*

35. Utterback, *"Untitled 6."*

36. See LIA's website at www.liaworks.com.

37. See, among others, ZKM's *artintact CDROMagazine,* issued yearly from 1994 to 1999.

38. Iwai also developed an early application for the Nintendo DS game console entitled *Electroplankton.*

39. Software{ART}space (blog), www.softwareart.blogs.com/.

40. "Scott Snibbe, Interactive Artist." *CNN,* The Next List, December 18, 2011, http://vimeo.com/39725809, 4 min.

41. "Scott Snibbe, Interactive Artist," 4 min.

42. Reyhan Harmanci, "For Digital Artists, Apps Provide New Palette," *New York Times,* August 19, 2010, www.nytimes.com/2010/08/20/us/20bciart.html?_r=0.

PART THREE

RECEPTION

11

REAL TIME, SCREEN TIME

Lumi Tan

For visitors to any major museum in the past two decades, the process of viewing contemporary video art is one that is familiar. You round a corner or step through a curtain into a darkened space, starkly separated from the white cube of the galleries exhibiting objects. Temporarily displaced as your eyes adjust, you follow the light until you're faced with one or more large-scale, projected, high definition moving images. The wall label before entering has stated the running time of the video work, but you decide the length of your stay. You settle in and take a seat on a bench or the floor, but most viewers linger on the sidelines only long enough to get a general impression of what they are watching. The allotment of attention for many is akin to looking at a painting or a sculpture for a few seconds, whether the video lasts a few minutes or over an hour. The choice of many artists to show videos in a seamless loop, with no marked beginning or ending, accedes to the viewer in that it affirms there is no correct entry point; it is an invitation to enter at any time. This strategy has become so expected that to have to endure thirty seconds of credits or to have to return for a prescribed start time can seem burdensome. Classics of the genre such as Douglas Gordon's *24 Hour Psycho* (1993) seem to be custom-made for this viewership, where even the iconic violent shower scene of the original film is slowed down enough to appear no more or less captivating to a viewer than any other. The blockbuster reception of Christian Marclay's *The Clock* (2010) gestures to the same convenience but with the benefit of speed; viewers stayed for hours, at all times of day, to see what film clip would come next, knowing the video would deliver minute-by-minute change.

In the contemporary moment, time is more malleable and self-determined than ever before. This can be attributed to a multitude of reasons, from the demands of a late capitalist society as described by Jonathan Crary—"One of these [normative] conditions can be characterized as a generalized inscription of human life into duration without breaks, defined by a principle of continuous functioning. It is a time that no longer passes, beyond clock time"[1]—to alternative notions of time set apart from dominant narratives such as Judith Halberstam explores in her influential book *In a Queer Time and Place: Transgender Bodies, Subcultural Lives*. This essay will discuss how time functions as an abstract material in recent video art, utilizing temporalities of performance, engaging a contemporary viewer who has already experienced the diversity and evolution of the moving image through film, television, and the Internet, and through individualized and communal viewing experiences. Instead of appearing formally abstract, these works reveal their abstraction *through* time, undermining familiarity by altering the viewer's relationship both behind and in front of the camera. Also under consideration is the current preoccupation with "liveness," perpetually mediated through personal methods of documentation such as smartphones or tablets. As Philip Auslander points out in his extensive writing on the term, this hybridization of performance and film was pursued early on in Sergei Eisenstein's works of the early 1920s, as well as in Erwin Piscator's epic theater of the same period; it is nothing new.[2] However, it is *how* these shifts in time are understood in the present moment, where the mediated or fragmented perception of time is so established and commonplace that not only does it distinguish itself from prior modes of viewership, but indeed it asserts an unprecedented dominance over our lived experience.

The history of video art stands as a record of how its contemporaneous public adapted to the consumption of time-based art and entertainment. In Paul Sharits's 1974 manifesto "Statement regarding Multiple Screen/Sound 'Locational' Film Environments—Installations," he stated that one provision for the development of his locational film works would be to not "prescribe a definite duration of respondent's observation (i.e., the respondent may enter and leave at any time)."[3] Sharits, a key figure in American Structuralist film, was one of the first to create film *as* space in the types of installations that are now commonplace (almost to the point of cliché), showing projections in an exhibition context. This was a call for a certain independence from the defined start and end times of the movie theater or performance hall, which infer that the viewer is at a disadvantage if entering late. The audience, referred to by Sharits as an active "respondent" rather than an implicitly passive "viewer," is privileged and autonomous in this new paradigm. This line of thinking corresponded to the audience's role in Minimalism and Conceptual Art, in which the viewer is required to "complete" the work. This breaking down of the traditional audience-performer dichotomy was also well-established in performance by this time. Whether these performances took place in a formal gallery setting or the myriad of informal loft spaces, they allowed the audience to be autonomous, moving freely rather than being tied to a seat, and to determine the beginning and end of the experience. Already in the 1960s, the Judson Dance Theater had removed theatricality and spectacle from the downtown New York dance scene; Allan Kaprow had started his Happenings; and Vito Acconci, Joan Jonas, Carolee Schneeman, and Jack Smith (to name a few artists among many) had debuted now-canonical live works. Viewers could choose to interact with durational performances as they would an object, a concept that has continued well into the present with the museum's embrace of both video installation and performance (best exemplified in the incredible success of Marina Abramovic's *The Artist Is Present* retrospective at MoMA in 2010). Bruce Nauman, in describing his work *Mapping the Studio I (Fat Chance John Cage)* (2001), which clocked in at forty hours and fifteen minutes when counting all seven video channels, explained, "I wanted the feeling that the piece was just there, almost like an object, just there, ongoing, being itself."[4]

The histories of performance art and video art are inextricably tied—early performance works were disseminated only because of the then-nascent technology, resulting in their tremendous influence over younger generations. Nauman was a seminal figure in the crossover between video installation and performance; whereas artists such as Acconci and Jonas began with live performance and then incorporated film or video or edited documentation of performances to be shown as stand-alone works, Nauman's early works existed only on video (or 16mm film, in some cases) and his audience was found only on the other side of the screen. As a genre, early video art was well-positioned, in Christine Ross's words, to "disrupt dominant conventionalities of time, notably acceleration and temporal linearity."[5] However, the viewers' experience of the work in the gallery setting has not changed much in the past few decades; it is still shown on monitors where, again, viewers have the choice to leave when they want. Due to the prevalence of television as a form of entertainment in the 1970s, this passive mode of watching moving images became habitual to the general public. The one-to-one relationship with a television, rather than the communal relationship of the movie theater, in addition to the technical and physical limitations of the appliance itself made television monitors a natural venue for experimental video art. Television also provided generative material for artists such as Dara Birnbaum and Mike Smith, and artists were often commissioned to make work specifically for television, as Nam June Paik and Stan VanDerBeek did for WGBH in Boston. With broadcast television, the viewer had a few, limited options—when to turn it off and on, what channel to watch and when. The advent of the VCR in the early 1980s radically changed the viewers' control over their time. The cinema was brought into the home, enabling viewers to watch and rewatch programming at any time, regardless of the networks' schedules. Currently, the Internet is the site of entertainment in which the viewer is the programmer, consuming unlimited video content, wherever and whenever, with the additional possibility of creating that content and sharing it at an increasingly accelerated rate. Not only is the content accessible, but so are the modes of production. Wipes, cuts, compositing, special filters—these strategies of controlling time in the moving image are available to anyone with a computer or a smartphone. Apps like Vine and Instagram offer portable collections of six- or fifteen-second videos; this brevity has bred a new culture of performers who use these constraints to their advantage. The scroll is the new loop, an endless feed of content that extends infinitesimally.

But how does this heightened moment of individualized production and consumption translate to video art in the institutional exhibition space? The museum remains a communal site intended to draw in the general public by offering a distinct alternative to quotidian ways of processing media—and simultaneously, to display and narrate a linear history. How does the presence of the apparatuses of production shift the perception of time in an institutional space? Mika Tajima, New Humans, and Charles Atlas explored this question in two recent projects: *Today Is Not a Dress Rehearsal* (fig. 11.1) at the San Francisco Museum of Modern Art in 2009 and *The Pedestrians* (fig. 11.2) at South London Gallery in 2011. Tajima, a multidisciplinary artist with a solo practice, started New Humans in 2003 as a collaboration with a rotating group of artists, musicians, and designers; in these installations, the group comprised Howie Chen and Eric Tsai. Atlas is celebrated for his seminal videos with dancers and performers including Leigh Bowery, Michael Clark, Yvonne Rainer, and most famously Merce Cunningham, with whom he worked for over thirty years and exuberantly transformed the genre of contemporary dance for video. The live-editing process that was featured during these collaborations with Tajima and New Humans was the latest iteration of his subjective approach to documenting performance. Atlas first brought it into his practice in a 2003 exhibition, *Instant Fame,* at the New York non-profit Participant Inc, in which he live-edited video portraits during short interviews, updating the concept of the portrait studio. He has since brought the process into large-scale performance such as concerts with Antony and the Johnsons and *MC9,* an exhibition and series of performances at the Tate Modern Tanks in 2013.

In *Today Is Not a Dress Rehearsal,* Tajima's sculptures doubled as scenery flats, a strategy seen in earlier exhibitions such as *Disassociate,* at Elizabeth Dee Gallery in 2007, where the panels' positions were changed during the run of the exhibition to delineate private working space such as that seen in a recording studio or cubicle office. This resistance to static positions endowed the objects with performative roles, which she further examined in her 2009 exhibition at X Initiative in New York, which opened during the global recession. Tajima emptied her studio and storage space and placed all her works on view under the title *The Extras,* grouping them in scenarios as if they were performers waiting for their moment in the spotlight next to seamless backdrops, or leaving them in storage racks to be pulled out at a later time. In *Today Is Not a Dress Rehearsal,* the sculptures did finally get their time on stage; silkscreened with graphic images inspired by SFMOMA's architecture, they formed a film set in which Tajima, New Humans, and Atlas shot for three days. The installation was programmed as part of the museum's Live Art performance series under the theme of speech as the most basic performative act; invited speakers included the philosopher and theorist Judith Butler (well-known for her work on subject formation through speech) and members of the

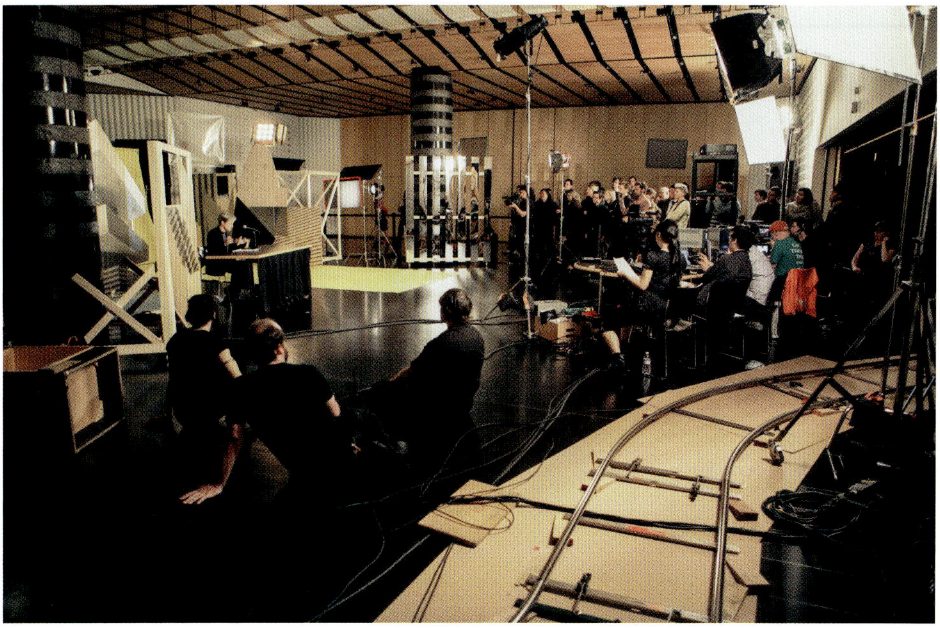

FIGURE 11.1
Mika Tajima/New Humans and Charles Atlas, *Today Is Not a Dress Rehearsal,* 2009. Multimedia performance installation. Courtesy of the artist and SFMOMA.

local chapter of Toastmasters, the public speaking association. New Humans manipulated the sound during recording and also participated with a noise performance; Atlas live-edited the footage, which was simultaneously projected onto the scenic elements and in a separate theater at the museum.

The installation was billed as "film production as performance," and the public was invited to see all stages of the production, with or without performances taking place, or to experience time more flatly in the theater. Tajima explained that she wanted to address "anticipation: we're ready and excited and want to see some kind of action. We want that theatrical experience of a fast, quick spectacle, but the idea of film production itself is actually this elongated, almost mundane activity that happens over extended periods of time. There's a lot of activity, there's a lot of people working on projects and moving things back and forth, but it's that intangible aspect of work itself."[6] Multiple temporalities were made visible to the audience, who could move between them by choosing which situation to take part in: the inefficiency of film production that is intended to create a finished product that erases the labor put into it; the live speeches that were constantly interrupted by Tajima's directions to change the set and lights and thus never completed; the instant video mixing; the displacement of that product to another physical space; and the exhibition that is left when the artists and performers are not present. These actions were then repeated at the start of each day—Suzanne

Hudson identified this temporality as "in use, used, to be used again."[7] Since Atlas's mixing was live, and each part of the process was no more or less important or essential to the performance as a whole, there was no exhibited "result" or conclusion, no summary of activity. This predilection towards process over product is also referenced in the title, a motivational aphorism to make every moment count. (Edited footage of the performance was shown in a later group exhibition at SFMOMA entitled *Stage Presence,* in 2012; however, both Tajima's and Atlas's versions were shown, again addressing the idea of individualized experience even on the part of the makers.) Exposing the "action," as banal as it may be, allows the audience to feel as though they are witnessing a parallel time, one that is typically left behind in the editing room. In the conception of these productions as performances, Tajima has referenced Jean-Luc Godard's 1968 film *Sympathy for the Devil,* which combines documentation of the Rolling Stones rehearsing the eponymous song in a recording studio, interspersed with fictionalized scenes of revolutionary actions. The lateral, 360-degree tracking shot used in the film is a strategy to flatten time; a corollary to the video loop; it exaggerates the lulls in time, the redundancy, and the confinement that production entails.

This mise-en-scène was expanded in *The Pedestrians* two years later, where the artists had ten days to film, with the ensuing videos and installation on view for another ten days. Rather than being behind the scenes as in *Today Is Not a Dress Rehearsal,* viewers were instead circulating *within* the scene; the press release termed the walkway that cut through the space as "at once arcade, exhibition, passage, runway, and stage." Themed around the politics of walking in public space, the installation at South London Gallery included a dolly track that circled the entire gallery, defining the limits of a set/stage inside. Atlas's live video edits were projected high onto the walls above the set/stage, and the program of performances was broadened to address sound, speech, and movement and included video artist John Smith, choreographer Gaby Agis, and talks by Richard Hornsey and Nina Power. Atlas explained, "The only way for spectators to see it was to walk through it, to traverse the length of the gallery, so that the film set became a stage or a tracking-shot vector. Also, the live mixes being projected into the installation space created a visual feedback loop that heightened awareness of what was being produced from within the action in the space."[8] Tajima added, "The audience, performers, and technicians were producing and being produced simultaneously, depending on where they were located."[9] In Smith's performance, he read excerpts from texts in his past videos (in which he often acts as unreliable narrator controlling the viewer's perspective), interspersing his narration with his bellowing instructions through a megaphone as New Humans provided an ambient sound track. This demonstrated a deliberate disorientation of the audience, who sat on the floor in the center of the room; even though the "action" in this later exhibition was more explicit, it was still unclear where to look or what to do: At Smith playing the role of director (but not directing other performers)? At Tajima being the "actual" director? At Atlas's videos, or at your fellow audience members? At the musicians? Tajima has often spoken of this absence of a focal

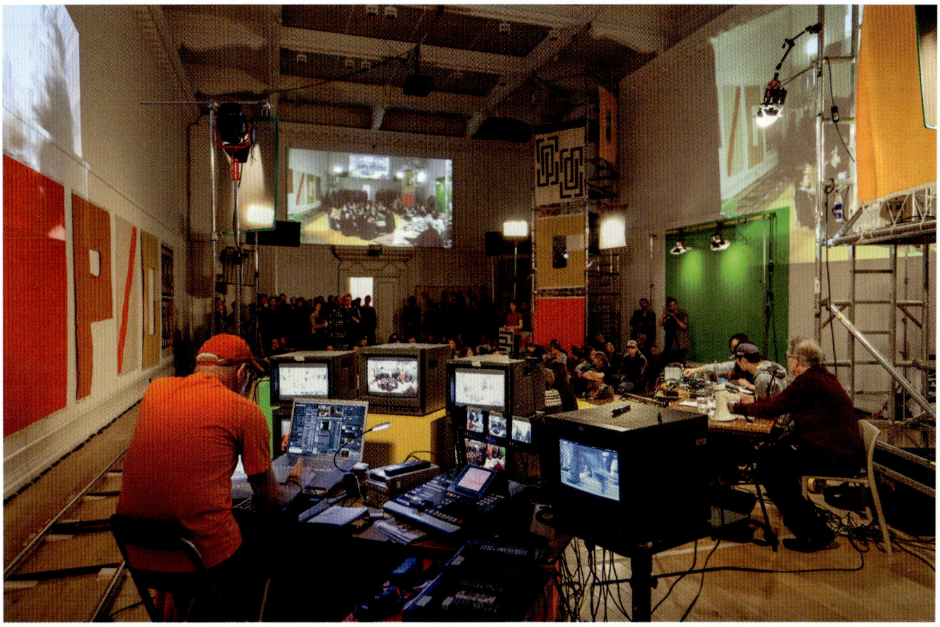

FIGURE 11.2
Charles Atlas, Mika Tajima, and New Humans, *The Pedestrians,* 2011. Multimedia performance installation. Courtesy of the artist and South London Gallery.

point: "There's a constant shifting of where you should actually look. If you're watching one of the videos, you can easily get distracted by the other video or the sculptures."[10] One could read these multiple viewpoints as their own type of abstraction, where each viewing experience becomes disjunctive, removed from any linear trajectory or proper viewing etiquette. Moving the audience onstage, surrounded by a dolly track that acts as a significant barrier between the set and the "real" world, allows another level of direction not integrated into *Today Is Not a Dress Rehearsal.* These two installations are works-in-progress that revel in the lack of finality, instilling an abstracted timeline into the presupposed linear narratives of institutions.

Tajima, New Humans, and Atlas's installations made explicit the idea of the film set as an isolated environment where time does not exist, where it is instead produced and reproduced by a set of technical controls like lighting and editing. In his essay "Toward a Non-Bourgeois Camera Style," Brian Henderson writes that "Cinema, like painting, is a two-dimensional art which creates the illusion of a third dimension. . . . Cinema escapes the limits of two dimensions through its own third dimension, time. . . . Cinema overcomes two-dimensionality through its 'walk-around capability,' which is also a prime feature of ordinary human perception."[11] Published in *Film Quarterly* in 1970, the text analyzes Godard's use of the lateral tracking shot in *Sympathy for the Devil* and *Weekend* (1967).

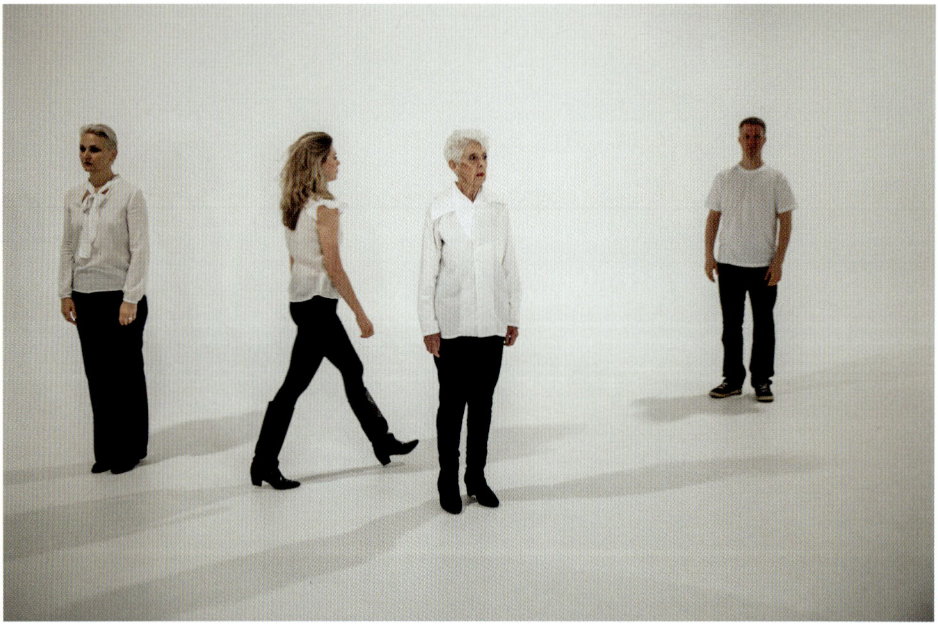

FIGURE 11.3
Alix Pearlstein, *Moves in the Field,* 2012. Single-channel, HD video, color, sound; 20 minutes. Courtesy of the artist and On Stellar Rays, NYC.

Alix Pearlstein's work is unparalleled in its "walk-around" capability; her camera is liberated from the established rules of illusion in regard to the objectivity of the camera or the person holding it. Although the camera moves in *a* space, that space often remains undefined, even if the set may be entirely specific to the institution where the videos are shown. For Pearlstein's 2008 exhibition at The Kitchen, she shot three video works—*After the Fall, Goldrush* (both 2008), and *Two Women 2* (2007–2008)—in the black box theater to be shown in the white cube gallery (painted black in this instance). While this particular site is charged with a history of experimental theater, one could argue that to the general public, it is a void like any other empty set. For *The Dark Pavement,* her 2013 exhibition at the Atlanta Contemporary Art Center, she shot in the institution's cellar, parking lot, and gallery space; yet, even for a viewer watching these videos inside the exhibition space, the sites can still remain anonymous or foreign. Pearlstein's videos usually refute any immediate references to the outside world but can draw upon other historical video or film works; many writing on her work have observed that the videos feel like laboratories for human experimentation, a sealed world of her own design. Even though artifice, in the expected theatrical or cinematic sense, is removed from the work, this affective tension between her performers is what keeps the viewer fully engaged in Pearlstein's world and convinced by the abstracted time depicted within.

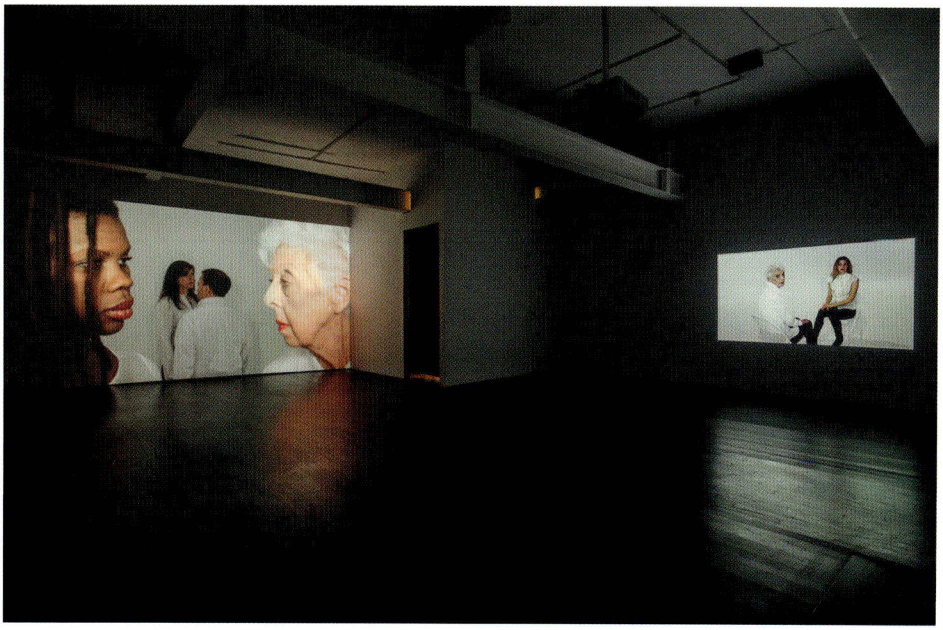

FIGURE 11.4
Alix Pearlstein, installation view: *Moves in the Field*, 2012 (single-channel, HD video, color, sound; 20 minutes), and *The Drawing Lesson*, 2012 (single-channel, HD video, color, sound; 7 minutes, 13 seconds). Courtesy of the artist and On Stellar Rays, NYC.

In *The Drawing Lesson*, Pearlstein's 2012 exhibition at On Stellar Rays gallery, two videos with shared sensibilities, *The Drawing Lesson* and *Moves in the Field* (both 2012) (figs. 11.3 and 11.4), were shown in one space. Both pieces share casts diverse in age, race, and gender, dressed in white tops and black pants; both were filmed against a white cyclorama typically used for commercial photography shoots. There is a complete absence of mise-en-scène in these spaces, and when any hint of a physical space is revealed, it comes as a relief to the viewer that these characters are in a "real" space. In *Moves in the Field*, there is no soundtrack, only the diegetic sound of footsteps, the actors' breathing, or the air against the microphone as it accompanies a fast-moving camera. The term "moves in the field" is from figure skating and refers to basic skating skills and edge control—essentially, the smoothest and fastest way to travel around the rink. This motion is reflected in the freehand camera work and delivers the perspective from eye level, mimicking a human manner of observation. This human quality is enhanced in moments when the camera pans too quickly from side to side, so that the field of vision blurs, or when it moves uncommonly close to an actor's face so that light bounces off skin, or when it is allowed to shake. Responding to instructions by Pearlstein, the actors shift from facing each other in pairs to gathering in seemingly random groups, to moving off camera and suddenly appearing in another, unexpected spatial plane.

Crucial to Pearlstein's videos, the performers are professional theater actors or other performers who are able to express psychological intensity without any narrative framework; they are neither actors playing a part or amateurs being natural. In a 2012 interview in *BOMB* magazine, Pearlstein quotes another of Henderson's observations in reference to *Moves in the Field:* "His [Godard's] camera serves no individual and prefers none to another. It never initiates movement to follow a character, and if it picks one up as it moves, it leaves him behind haphazardly."[12] At first encounter, the movements feel improvisatory or random, but repetition and pattern slowly become apparent. The performers often look directly into the camera, reciprocating the careful observation by the viewer. Halfway through the video, a performer jogs through the set as if he missed his cue and is trying to hit his mark; this seems to indicate a point when the action diversifies. Hand gestures and expressions of smiles or disappointment begin to occur, and performers even make physical contact—an act that feels radical in this scenario. Other small actions become monumental: a female performer has a costume change into a black dress, runs towards the camera barefoot, repeats this action minutes later, and then eventually appears back in her white shirt and pants. A fog emitted from a noisy machine rolls into the scene and then disappears without affecting the performers. The effect here is highly theatrical; the tight framing of the camera allows the viewer to imagine that the actors move off stage, exiting and entering the scene as directed. However, this effect is disturbed by Pearlstein's seamless editing, in which the video appears as one single continuous take. In each of her works, this tension between the expectations of theatrical and cinematic constructions of time are complicated by the illusion of real time. Pearlstein has remarked, "As soon as you're working with duration, you're working with contingency. Working with longer durations allows the sense of the immediacy of a live performance (that it's never the same from one performance to the next) to be translated into a mediated situation."[13] The viewer has a trust that the camera is capturing what we are *supposed* to see, even when the camera's point of view is completely disorienting in terms of space and depth.

In *The Drawing Lesson,* the action is far more simple, consistent, and repetitive. The camera begins by circling around a female performer sitting in a white folding chair, who at first looks straight ahead, ignoring the camera. On subsequent tours around her, her look follows the camera, swiveling quickly to catch it, similar to a dancer "spotting" while turning. Although the camera here is also freehand, the movement is significantly smoother, simulating a camera on a track, with a calming rhythm to how it negotiates the room. As the camera captures the off-stage areas, it exposes the edges of the cyclorama, rooting the action in the physical space and hinting that the set is on a proscenium stage. The camera returns to find a different configuration, adding one performer at a time until the group reaches four, then removing an actor until only two remain. The effect is not theatrical here as in *Moves in the Field;* the viewer does not imagine that there is a stagehand scrambling to reset the chairs before each cycle, and there is no sound of footsteps to denote this off-stage action (which is especially noticeable since this video also features diegetic sound). Additionally, the viewer can predict the action in a way not possible in *Moves in the Field*. The camera approaches the group with a long shot and then zooms in as it approaches the performers; by establishing this set trajectory, the camera differentiates itself from the viewer's perspective. Thus, the piece is more illusionistic and establishes itself in the realm of cinema. When taking *The Drawing Lesson*'s reference point into consideration, Pearlstein can be seen as literalizing Henderson's idea of cinema's third dimension of time; the video is based on a sculpture based on a painting. Giulio Paolini's *Tre per tre (ognuno è l'altro o nessuno)* (Three by three [each is the other or no one]; 1999) is a life-sized sculpture that thrice replicates the artist figure depicted in Jean-Baptiste-Siméon Chardin's *The Drawing Lesson* (1734). However, in Paolini's work, only one of these figures actually functions in the role of the artist with pencil and paper in hand. One figure is the model being observed by this artist, and the third merely observes the two others, off to the side. This unusual configuration of artist, model, and viewer was somewhat mirrored in the installation of *Moves in the Field* and *The Drawing Lesson* at On Stellar Rays; the viewer was physically caught between inclusion and exclusion and the structural differences within each scenario, which, at first encounter, seem extremely similar.

This analogy can also be extended to the transposing of performative roles within the works of both Pearlstein and Tajima-New Humans-Atlas. Tajima said of *The Pedestrians*, "Charlie [Atlas] has a seminal film, *Hail the New Puritan*. It has a lot of elements that I wanted to translate for the new situation: the director as actor, viewers as performers, musicians as extras, artworks as props."[14] Pearlstein has said, "The focus is on the actor, and that's a focus on us—they stand in for us, for the viewer, for everyone. That focus animates the relationship between performance, theater, and film. These forms all trade places in my work: film acts like theater, performance acts like film."[15] Each of these shifts between the roles of artist/director, performers, audience, and setting is echoed in the perception and production of time as well and points to the instability of any of these positions in contemporary art or even culture at large.

No longer is it as simple as believing that performance is live and anything on a screen is edited or mediated, as it may have been at the start of the intersection between video and performance. Even the "live feed" is almost never as labeled; even though the Internet makes a live feed relatively simple to achieve, audiences expect regular minor or major delays in the transfer of the image or the buffering of video. These delays are thus delays in communication, clarity, and comprehension. An act like Atlas's live mixing complicates this dynamic further; this act is quite performative in itself (his presence on stage is akin to a DJ at a club, a conductor who is slightly removed from the center of attention), and these effects are overtly synthetic, making a live experience less realistic, more processed, while adding another layer of temporality that is as instantaneous to the audience as the live performance. Is either experience more "live" than the other? Although these effects are more common now with digital imaging, that these viewing experiences can overlap without conflict speaks to a common expectation of immediacy. More often than not, at least one mediated image is apparent in our field of vision, and we're able to differentiate between these multiple temporalities with ease—think of how effortless it has become to absorb an automatically updating feed of words or images on a phone while holding a conversation with a person sitting in front of you. Pearlstein's use of professional actors or performers has the same effect as Atlas's act but with opposing means, subtlety heightening the degree of reality or liveness in her performers' behavior. The performances are able to capture the tension between natural and affected, improvised and directed, announcing their own mediation the longer one watches. The artificial environment of the cyclorama (or the black box theater or the white cube gallery) limits the conception of time; the artist's camera further delineates it. Both performers and viewers are made exceptionally aware of the camera's presence as a simultaneous interloper and enabler. Time truly unfolds in these works, only to be collapsed back onto itself as the video loop starts again with no warning.

In Godard and Anne-Marie Miéville's *The Old Place* (1998), a video essay on the history of art commissioned by the Museum of Modern Art, Miéville states, "Art was not sheltered from time. It was the shelter of time." As has been demonstrated over the last forty years, video art has generated more fluid perceptions of time but has also absorbed more dominant forms of media in order to reflect them back to the viewer. Whereas the audience for early video art could effortlessly understand their intimate rapport with the television monitor, the contemporary audience has become increasingly removed from the immediacy of the experiences depicted in the works discussed in this essay. Though we as a culture are more invested in the moving image than ever before, we are more accustomed to the portable small screen than the wall-sized projection, to handheld cameras in lieu of camera crews and dollies, to abbreviated videos instead of ones of long duration, to viewing alone instead of among a crowd.

We can now coerce time into being accessible; it stops and starts to fit the contours of our daily lives, leading to an adaptation of time that has become absolutely quotidian and automatic. The works by Pearlstein, Tajima, and Atlas disturb this ease, putting forth individualized versions of abstraction formed through their gestures towards a sense of reality but never settling there. This reality is not subverted through narrative or illusory images seeking to deceive, but rather through our relationship to time and its production—particularly through the use of the camera. These works do not ask us for a suspension of disbelief but grant a deeper investigation of how temporal abstraction has become the new standard. Bringing about this awareness has been the priority of video artists since the origins of the genre, concurrently debunking the chronological tropes of film and television while providing innovation in the conception and reception of time. It may be the case now that in order to be displaced, to remove ourselves from our present tense, we need the elements particular to video installation: the darkened room or the contained set, the physicality of an installation where other bodies, real or projected, look back at us, move next to us. Ultimately, it remains the viewer's choice to exit the gallery at any point, leaving the work to be "just there, ongoing, as itself," existing in its own particular temporality.

NOTES

1. Jonathan Crary, *24/7: Late Capitalism and the Ends of Sleep* (New York: Verso Books, 2013), 8.

2. Philip Auslander, "Liveness, Mediatization, and Intermedial Performance," *Degrés: Revue de synthèse à orientation sémiologique* (Spring 2000): 1.

3. Paul Sharits, "Statement regarding Multiple Screen/Sound 'Locational' Film Environments—Installation," *Film Culture* 65–66 (1978): 79–80.

4. Michael Auping and Bruce Nauman, "1,000 Words: Bruce Nauman Talks about Mapping the Studio," *Artforum* (March 2002): 121.

5. Christine Ross, "The Temporalities of Video: Extendedness Revisited," *Art Journal* (Fall 2006): 83.

6. Mika Tajima, quoted in Patricia Maloney, "Interview with Mika Tajima," *Art Practical*, August 2, 2012, www.artpractical.com/column/interview_with_mika_tajima/.

7. Suzanne Hudson, quoted in Charles Atlas, Suzanne Hudson, and Mika Tajima, "1,000 Words: Charles Atlas and Mika Tajima Talk about *The Pedestrians*, 2011," *Artforum* (May 2011): 259.

8. Charles Atlas, quoted in Atlas, Hudson, and Tajima, "1,000 Words," 260.

9. Mika Tajima, quoted in Atlas, Hudson, and Tajima, "1,000 Words," 260.

10. Mika Tajima, quoted in Maloney and Tajima, "Interview with Tajima."

11. Brian Henderson, "Toward a Non-bourgeois Camera Style," *Film Quarterly*, Winter 1970–71, 10.

12. Henderson, "Towards a Non-bourgeois Camera Style," 2, quoted in Alix Pearlstein and John Pilson, "Alix Pearlstein," *BOMB*, Winter 2012–13, 133.

13. Alix Pearlstein, quoted in Pearlstein and Pilson, "Alix Pearlstein," 133.

14. Mika Tajima, quoted in Atlas, Hudson, and Tajima, "1,000 Words," 261.

15. Pearlstein and Pilson, "Alix Pearlstein," 126.

12

THE SPREADABILITY OF VIDEO

Christine Ross

In the fall of 2013, the Centre Pompidou in Paris held an exhibition eponymously entitled *Pierre Huyghe*.[1] Although the exhibition was conceived as a mid-career retrospective of Pierre Huyghe's artistic production, it took the form of an ecosystem—a living environment that evolved according to the performance and media experiments that took place throughout the duration of the show. These transformations were reinforced by the exhibition design. Installed in the small space of the South Gallery, more than fifty artworks dating from the 1980s to 2013 were presented in such proximity to and juxtaposition with each other that their distinctiveness was easily disrupted when perceived by viewers. The sound components of the video and performance works continuously overlapped, effectively contaminating each other. When entering the gallery, viewers were randomly exposed to at least three intersecting sounds: the voice of the announcer declaring the names of the incoming visitors (*Name Announcer,* 2011); a sound extract from a 1988 discussion about Duchamp at the Institut des hautes études en arts plastiques; and the voice of Kate Bush while she is signing *Wuthering Heights*—from the soundtrack of *The Host and the Cloud* (2010) (fig. 12.4)—emerging from the back of the gallery. As they walked deeper into the space, the viewers were exposed to the layering of a variety of video sound tracks, including Lucie Dolène (the voice of Disney's French version of Snow White) humming "Someday My Prince Will Come" from *Blanche-Neige Lucie* (1997) and the buzzing bees from *A Way in Untilled* (2012). The permeability of the works' boundaries was facilitated by the curatorial and artistic decision to build the exhibition from the partitions left behind by the previous exhibition, a Mike Kelley

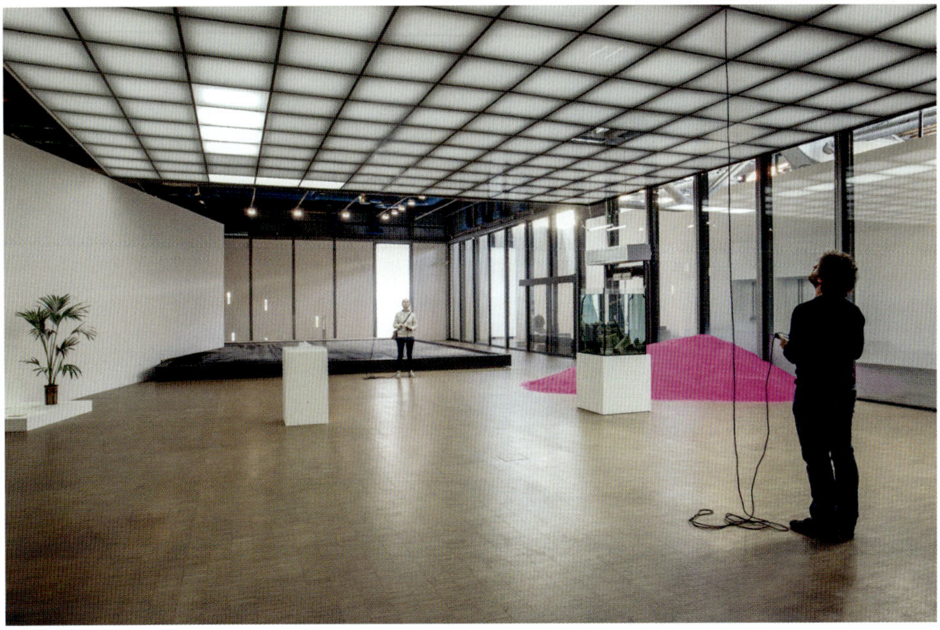

FIGURE 12.1
Pierre Huyghe, *Atari Light,* 1999 (computer game program, interface, two joysticks, halogen lamps, ceiling construction), and *L'Expédition Scintillante, Acte 3: Untitled (Black Ice Stage),* 2002 (black ice rink, female skater, programme; Music: *Music for Airports # 4* by Brian Eno [1978], 13¾ × 403⅛ × 304¾ inches [35 × 1024 × 774 cm]). Installation view: *Pierre Huyghe,* Centre Pompidou, Paris (September 25, 2013–January 6, 2014). Courtesy of the artist and Esther Schipper Gallery, Berlin. Photograph © Andrea Rossetti.

retrospective. This setup, which had only one closed soundproof room, was explored not only to maximize the circulation of sound throughout the exhibition space but also to give spectators the possibility of seeing images from different artworks *at the same time,* thereby creating new image combinations. The spectators' interpretation of individual artworks was consequently discouraged in favor of their exposure to the aural and visual mixing of images.

This chapter examines the pivotal role of video in *Pierre Huyghe*'s unique redefinition of the retrospective format, with the understanding that video here is mostly combined with 16mm or 35mm film, usually transferred to digital beta, or consists entirely of a digital beta work. It asks how, in the age of the digital mixing of media, the vanishing of video as a specific medium can be explored to rethink the aesthetic function of the image. How does this vanishing affect spectatorship and the exhibition format? Can this vanishing be understood as a form of abstraction? How and why does video still matter? My main claim is that the innovativeness of current video art (or at least one of its main fields of innovativeness) lies in the exploration of the *spreadability* of its images and sounds in the gallery space, even beyond the spaces constructed to contain them. Media scholar Henry Jenkins has recently used this term to define the technical and cultural potential of the emerging media landscape—a digital mediascape that favors the circulation of content more than its distribution—in which audiences are encouraged to share and reframe media content.[2] By spreadability, however, I refer not so much to the ways in which participatory cultures are emerging from the sharing of media content as to the ways in which the digital mediascape technically and culturally encourages the circulation of sound-images. In *Pierre Huyghe,* that circulation is certainly technically and culturally conditioned by the evolution of new media, but its modality and impact are not tied to the participatory ethos. Spreadability consists here in the circulation of sound-images *in space.* The effect of that circulation is to create porous, intensified situations.

The Pompidou retrospective was a pivotal mobilizer of this type of investigation—one that not only problematized the conventional view of the retrospective exhibition as a coexistence of discrete artworks organized chronologically but one that also dethroned the hierarchical position of the spectator in relation to the artworks. Exploring Manuel De Landa's Deleuzian notion of intensity as the process by which things individuate *differentially* (by which things become different as they interact), this chapter argues that in the retrospective the spreadability of video images and video sounds abstracted the exhibition space by turning it into an evolving situation. It showed abstraction to be not simply the abandonment of representational or figurative imagery, nor what art historian Lucian Krukowski has identified as the nonobjective route of abstraction: "the disengagement from both the mimetic and analytic responses to natural objects in favor of inventions in which the visual elements are conceived on linguistic or notational models."[3] My hypothesis is the following: as video sound-images spread through space and spread space, they abstract the exhibition space by making its unperceivable intensities manifest. In that process, the exhibition space is requalified as a situation, an ecosystem, or something like a garden (terms I will be using from now on). In *Pierre Huyghe,* video representation persists, but its mimetic, indexical and analytic functions are significantly marginalized. The video sound-images are produced and experienced by viewers as fictions, narratives, and documents—and they are surely interpreted. But their main function rests elsewhere. They spread. They are not so much abstract in themselves. Rather, they have abstracting effects. Their spreadability abstracts the environment in which video keeps evolving. Spectators are exposed to that abstraction: they don't control it; they are part of it.

The objective of this chapter is to understand this abstractive mechanism. To do so, it starts by briefly situating video in relation to the emerging digital mediascape, positing that video has lost its medium specificity but that it still persists aesthetically. It then investigates Huyghe's evolving video practice in relation to that change. My investigation mainly proceeds by contrasting *The Third Memory* (1999)—one of the pivotal video installations that established the artist as a major figure of video art in the late 1990s and early 2000s (an installation shown at the Centre Pompidou at the same time as, but separately, from the retrospective)—with the *Pierre Huyghe* retrospective. Finally, it analyzes the spreadability function put into play in the retrospective by situating the Pompidou show within the speculative turn in the humanities and social sciences (a turn invested in the thinking of potentiality) from which the abstraction effects of video—explored as an intensification practice—can be better explained and comprehended.

AFTER THE THIRD MEMORY

The becoming digital of video happened rather quickly if we compare video to film and photography, whose analog lives were long enough to establish them as true institutions. Media theoretician Philippe Dubois has splendidly analyzed this state of affairs. As Dubois maintains, video art has only occupied a fragile, transitory and intermediary position between two moving image technologies: analog film and digital imagery (to which we should add a third non-moving-image technology, photography).[4] Video art has always been at the threshold of the before and the after, the "too soon" and the "too late," with not much time between these two extremes. Its history as an analog medium is about forty years old and began with the availability of the first portable recording systems in the late 1960s. But from its beginnings, analog video was fundamentally proto-digital insofar as artists used a variety of electronic tools to transform the electronic signal—adding synthetic colors; mixing images; creating holes in the image to fill them with other images (keying); sequencing images to create effects of image superimposition, juxtaposition, and dissolution; disrupting image and sound synchronization. They abstracted the image-sounds of television. The electronic tools also enabled the circulation of images within the screen and from one screen to the other, inside but also beyond the gallery space. These transformations were invented before the full array of digital image-manipulation. If video persists today, it is precisely because its aesthetics has influenced and continues to fit the image-circulation potential of the emerging mediascape.

However, although video persists in some form or another, the history of the moving image unfolds now "after video." By this, I do not mean that we are in a post-video moment but that we are "after" video in the same sense that art historian David Joselit speaks of "after art." For Joselit, "after art" signifies that the notion of the medium (even of the post-medium) has ceased to be a productive analytical tool to understand artistic practices. The idea of the medium presupposes that the art object is a distinct, relatively stable, and localizable object. It denies the fact that since the 1990s, digital technologies have become predominant in their capacity to convert all work (sound, image, or text) in a digital sequence.[5] These technologies activate the reproduction, reframing, and circulation of images. They allow for the spreading of sounds and images. Hence, it is not that we are living the end of art or the end of video art, but that sound-images

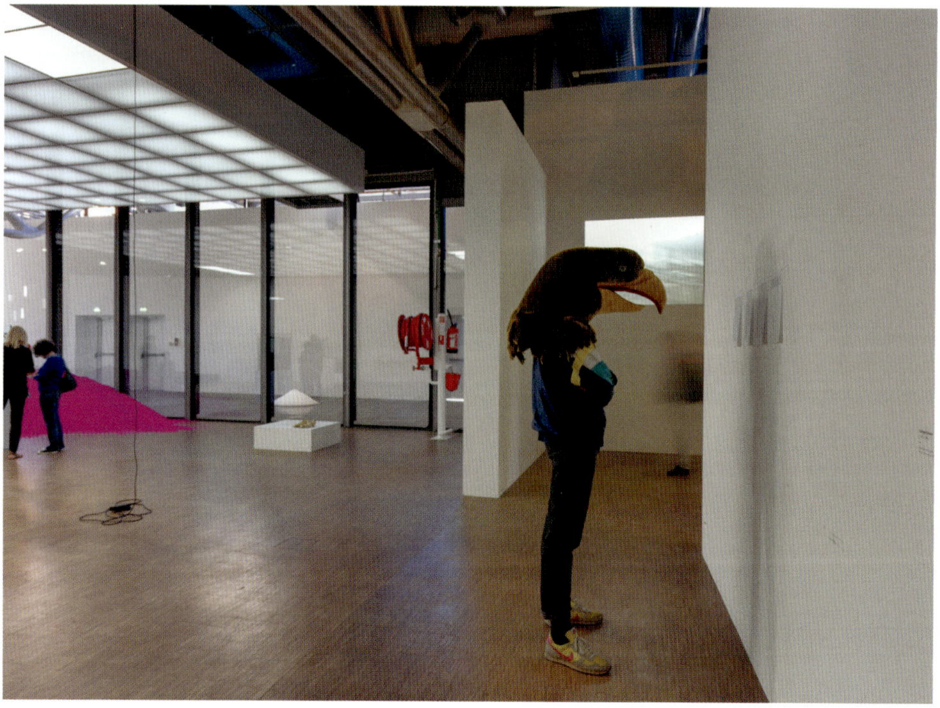

FIGURE 12.2
Pierre Huyghe, *Atari Light*, 1999 (computer game program, interface, two joysticks, halogen lamps, ceiling construction), and *La Toison d'Or*, 1993 / 1999 (performer with mask from original event, Jardin de l'Arquebuse, Dijon, France, April 16, 1993). Installation view: *Pierre Huyghe*, Centre Pompidou, Paris (September 25, 2013–January 6, 2014). Courtesy of Marian Goodman Gallery, New York, and Esther Schipper Gallery, Berlin. Photograph by Philippe Migeat, Centre Pompidou, Paris.

in general and notably those explored by artists persist only through their capacity, just about inexhaustible in the digital age, for reproduction, remediation, proliferation and circulation.[6] Interestingly, regarding the point I am trying to make here about the spreadability of video in Huyghe's practice, Joselit sees Huyghe's videos of the 1990s and 2000s as highly representative of the "after," emphasizing how his works function not as mediums but as "reformatting processes" (a term used by Huyghe) whereby a video, for example, can become a celebration, and an amusement park can become a garden. "After video" corresponds to a unique moment in the history of media. For the sake of clarity, it is useful to characterize that moment by referring to its three main aesthetic operations: the ending of video art as a distinct (medium tape-based) practice; its spreadability; and the persistence of the main aesthetic constituent of video art: temporal exploration (let us simply recall here Nam June Paik's famous statement: "In video there is no space [no delimited frame] there is only time [lines with no thickness]. . . . Video is essentially time.")[7] In light of this last feature, it is imperative to emphasize that time has consistently been a deep concern for Huyghe, at least since his founding in 1995 of l'Association des temps libérés (The Association of Freed Time), an association to "develop unproductive time, for a reflection on free time, and to cultivate a society without work."[8]

Huyghe is primarily known for his video installation remakes, retakes, and reruns (notably, *Blanche-Neige Lucie* [1997], *L'Ellipse* [1998], *No Ghost Just a Shell* [1999–2003], and *The Third Memory* [1999]) that stage individuals reappropriating their voice over their stolen, neglected, or fictionalized life stories. These works recirculate modified versions of film narratives constitutive of the history of cinema. In *L'Ellipse,* for example, the actor Bruno Ganz was invited to replay his role in Wim Wenders's *The American Friend* (1977) by walking in real time the distance between two scenes originally connected by a jump cut: a moment of wandering and introspection through Paris—the manifestation par excellence of unproductive time. In *Blanche-Neige Lucie,* Lucie Dolène hums the Snow White song in an empty studio while subtitles reveal that she sued and won her case against Disney Voice Characters to gain the copyright to her interpretation. *The Third Memory*—one of Huyghe's best known video works—was presented during the *Pierre Huyghe* retrospective but was shown separately on the fourth floor of the Centre Pompidou, in the permanent collection galleries. Accessible, but to be looked at independently, its presentation there highlighted the important shift in Huyghe's video production. *The Third Memory* is a video installation. That format was made clear in its isolated display. It revolves around Sydney Lumet's film *Dog Day Afternoon* (1975), whose script was based on a famous hold-up of a bank held by John Wojtowicz in Brooklyn in 1972. Huyghe invited Wojtowicz (by then out of prison) to play his role as the main actor of the story—a role played by Al Pacino in Lumet's film. More than twenty-five years after being dispossessed of his story by media (not only by film but also television), Wojtowicz reconstitutes the event with other actors. As video curator Christine Van Assche stipulates, in *The Third Memory* Wojtowicz "becomes the hero again" as "he reactivates every day, at each instant, the memory of this news item and gives it a central place in the story of his life."[9] The two sections of the work are installed in two adjacent rooms: the first room presenting newspaper articles and archived televisual documents of the event, and the second room presenting a two-channel video projection juxtaposing images from the reconstitution with footage from *Dog Day Afternoon.* The juxtaposition discloses how much Wojtowicz's memory has been influenced and altered by the film. The reconstitution produces a story that is not entirely his. Fiction and reality bleed into each other.

In the retrospective, there is a sense that for Huyghe the remakes, retakes, and reruns structuring his previous videos were not enough anymore to guarantee the recirculation of images, even the reconstitution of fictional/factual life stories. Referring to his current work, Huyghe states that "I am interested in the vitality of the image, in the ways in which an idea or an artefact leaks in a biological or mineral reality. . . . I am interested in things and operations in themselves, contingency, the creation of form which cannot be exhausted by the sedimentation of discourse. . . . I'm trying not to define the relation between the subjects but only to set the early conditions for potential porosity."[10] This vitality is inseparable from the notion of unproductive time sustaining the Association of Freed Time—a temporality that becomes effective in long duration and in the absence of control: not only the time it takes to allow for the contingency of the human/nonhuman interactions to take place but the actual dynamism of these interactions. Vitality lies more precisely in the production of porous situations whose occurrence and fate are never secure. At least since the garden he made for *dOCUMENTA (13)* in 2012, Huyghe's artistic intervention consists predominantly of a Duchampian act of selection: he selects elements (video images, living organisms) most likely to interact so as to augment the situations' capacity for porosity.

As stipulated in my introductory remarks, my claim is that video is a major player in that vitalist, situational dynamism. In the *Pierre Huyghe* retrospective, the remake/retake/rerun functions of video (operations that support the recirculation of images and the reappropriation of rights related to expression and interpretation) have been reoriented to act biologically. Video is now projected to lose in media specificity: it is nearly dissolvable and thus spreadable. Video images and video sounds spread in space as they spread the space: in so doing, they do not merely circulate but gain in permeability and interactiveness. As Emma Lavigne, the curator of the Pompidou show, specifies, the prerequisite for that type of spreadability is to break the *"dispositif"*—the apparatus—of the installation format; it is both to reformat video installations into situations and to discontinue the art milieu's medium-guided perception of Huyghe as a *video* artist mostly dedicated to the critique of the history of *cinema*.[11] For Lavigne, a key example of that break was in the renewed display of the video *Streamside Day* (2003). Normally projected on a wall in a large (10 × 8 m) enclosed room with a tree in its box installed nearby, it was reformatted for the retrospective into a smaller wall projection. The video documents Huyghe's invention of a ritual that celebrates the birth of a community in Streamside Knolls in New York's Hudson Valley. The inhabitants at the time did not know each other because they had just moved into the new housing development. They all wanted to preserve something of the natural environment surrounding the estate. The nature and culture celebration took the form of a ceremony held on October 11, 2003. It included a parade of members of the community led by a flute player, as well as speeches, a meal, and a show, with children disguised as animals making cardboard houses; domesticated animals circulated freely. The video is mainly about the capacity of inhabitants to build rituals (rituals that can be repeated accordingly) and the consolidation of communities by rituals. In the Pompidou retrospective, *Streamside Day* was projected on the wall of an open corridor and its scale was significantly reduced to a format that recalled an 8mm family movie setting, to be watched by family or community members. In this setting, the intimacy provided by the scale of the image was expanded (spread, as it were) to include any passerby in the exposed, public space. In this setting, *Streamside Day* ceased to be the re-creation of a site (an installation) and became a celebration potential (a situation)—the potential for any visitor to set up his or her own ritual.

Philosopher Giorgio Agamben, expanding on Foucault's discussion of the term, has defined the "dispositif" (*dispositivo*) as "anything that has in some way the capacity to capture, orient, determine, intercept, model, control, or secure the gestures, behaviors, opinions, or discourses of living beings."[12] This includes prisons, mental health facilities, and factories, but also the pen, computers, and language itself. For Agamben, apparatuses constitute us as subjects but in so doing they desubjectify us. Even if one doesn't agree with the austerity of his assessment, it is interesting to point out that he sees *profanation*—"the restitution to common use" or "the free use"—as a means to reduce the desubjectifying effects of apparatuses.[13] Huyghe's breaking of the dispositif through the reformatting and spreading of video must be understood as a form of profanation: it frees, restores, publicizes, and vitalizes images and sounds by augmenting their potential to interact with other images and sounds, transforming them both semantically and materially in that very process.

INTENSITY

The spreadability of video as a practice of abstraction is mobilized by a speculative approach to art. In many recent interviews, Huyghe has stated and restated his interest in that turn, especially in intensity, one of the pivotal concepts of speculative realism. Speculative realism is a response to the limits of Kantian and post-Kantian antirealism, which affirms that reality ("all that exists") is fundamentally mental—a "variation of mind or spirit."[14] Antirealism (which is in fact a form of idealism) is grounded in what philosopher Quentin Meillassoux terms *correlationism:* "the idea according to which we only ever have access to the correlation between thinking and being, and never to either term considered apart from the other."[15] Such an ontological stance, in its numerous variations, holds that humans can never access, know, or speak about the world as a realm independent of thought or language. The world, reality, and the existence of reality are mind dependent. The origins of correlationism (which speculative realism seeks to oppose) lie in Immanuel Kant's critical philosophy—a philosophy that rejected the possibility of knowing a noumenal realm beyond the human mind. In such a philosophy, objects conform to the mind; human knowledge of the perceived world is structured and made possible by mental a priori categories and forms of intuition. That correlationist tradition persists in any philosophy or artistic practice—including phenomenology, neo-Marxism, deconstruction, postmodernism, criticality, relational aesthetics and participatory art—whose ontology affirms that consciousness, ideas, power, discourse, text, representation, or culture constitutes reality. In speculative philosophies and artistic practices, the purpose is to reflect not so much upon *what is* as *what can be*—a realm accessible through speculation. Speculative realist philosophies (which are realist philosophies) maintain that the antirealist (correlationist) stance has reached

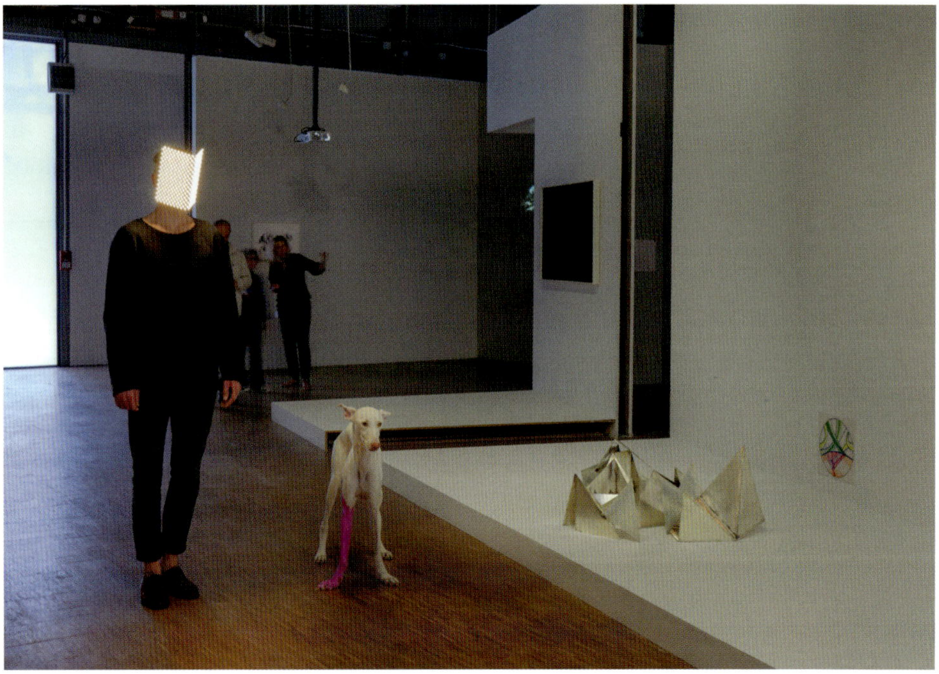

FIGURE 12.3
Pierre Huyghe, *Player,* 2010 (LED, brass, hand controller, mask; 15 × 16 × 24 cm), and *Human,* 2010 (Ibizan hound) from *Untilled,* 2012. Installation view: *Pierre Huyghe,* Centre Pompidou, Paris (September 25, 2013–January 6, 2014). Courtesy of Marian Goodman Gallery, New York, and Esther Schipper Gallery, Berlin. Photograph by Philippe Migeat, Centre Pompidou, Paris.

its limits insofar as it prevents not only philosophy but the humanities and social sciences from assessing and understanding some of the major developments in recent history, including globalization, technological growth and expansion, environmental deterioration, as well the reiterated exclusion of certain categories of being from the realm of existence. "In the face of the looming ecological catastrophe, and the increasing infiltration of technology into the everyday world (including our own bodies)," argue the authors of *The Speculative Turn,* the guidebook in this field of study, "it is not clear that the anti-realist position is equipped to face up to these developments."[16] *Pierre Huyghe* is a speculative exhibition in that specific sense: its ecosystem is one that provides mind-independent autonomy to the show. The components of the retrospective are selected (a selection that includes spreading videos and performances as well as many organic components susceptible to interacting with the other components of the ecosystem). The exhibition is thereon largely left to itself: it is of course framed by the rules of the institution but transformations are always at play, resulting from the interactions of the components of the exhibition.

Speculatively speaking, the interactions between its components—interactions

I claim to be facilitated by the spreadability of video—intensify the exhibition. That spreadability shows the exhibition to be a situation or an ecosystem composed of intensive properties. I will be using the term *intensive* in its Deleuzian formulation, but I will mostly rely on Manuel De Landa's explanation of it. The intensive properties of an organism or ecosystem cannot be defined without referring to "multiplicity," one of the central concepts of Deleuze's realism (one that assumes the autonomy of material entities from the human mind). *Multiplicity* is the very term by which Deleuze discards the entities sustaining naïve realism, including the perception that "the world is composed of fully formed objects whose identity is guaranteed by their possession of an *essence,* a core set of properties that defines what these objects are."[17] The intensive (a term taken from thermodynamics but extended by Deleuze to other fields) partakes of multiplicity insofar as it defines processes of individuation as occurring not only progressively but also dynamically, through processes of divergent differentiation. The intensive can be contrasted but not opposed to the extensive.

Let us return to the Pompidou exhibition to explain that distinction. The retrospective is made of observable extensive properties, that is, of areas and volumes, as well as lengths between entities. It is metric space. These are inherently divisible: if we were to divide the space into two equal halves, we would end up with two volumes. The intensive properties of a system are properties, such as temperature or pressure, that cannot be so easily observed or divided, that cannot be divided without changing that system in kind—as De Landa explains, "If we take a volume of water at 90 degrees of temperature, for instance, and break it up into two equal parts, we do not end up with two volumes at 45 degrees each, but with two volumes at the original temperature."[18] It is notable that most entities in the Pompidou exhibition cannot be easily divided in equal parts because of their permeable, spreading, moving, sometimes climate-sensitive boundaries. The exhibition promotes these properties: this is where its vitality lies. Huyghe's description of the Pompidou exhibition supports that view. In an interview with Julia Michalska, he states:

> I want to make the works porous so that they can corrupt one another. This could be through sound, light, something biological, the movement of an animal. . . . it's undetermined, uncontrollable. . . . Vitality means the intensity of being alive. I'm interested in how to quantify the different variations of being alive . . . how to intensify the presence of things. I look at how things change, are transformed, or metabolize. The word might not be perfectly appropriate and I might change it. But I am trying to find a word to say "something that is alive." I mean the intensity of life within one entity. . . . I want to see a transformation. Even death is a transformation. It is the end for one entity, but it means food and minerals for something else. This never stops.[19]

Notice how Huyghe defines the act of intensification as a random activity of corruption of one work on another and how he equates vitality with the intensity of "being alive," which in turn is equated with the potential of being transformed. His approach to intensity is fundamentally Deleuzian insofar as it refers to the behavior of components that interact and become different as they interact. The artistic challenge mapped out in the interview is one of enabling intensities, which are paradoxically contingent and unperceivable. Deleuze's most important theses regarding the intensive recognize this paradox. They are twofold: (1) the intensive generates the extensive (the metric space organisms inhabit emerges from a nonmetric continuum through a flow of broken symmetries), and (2) once individuation is reached, the intensive properties that conditioned the individuation process disappear or are concealed beneath the extensive properties of the finalized individual.[20] Deleuze's philosophical project is to overcome the "objective illusion" generated by that concealment, to make the intensive properties manifest. The video intensification of the exhibition space—the video-facilitated manifestation of the abstraction of the exhibition's situation—can be seen as a specific speculative-realist redefinition of art as a stable object. It breaks with correlationism by favoring and allowing the components of the exhibition to influence and affect each other.

A CLOSER LOOK INTO THE POMPIDOU RETROSPECTIVE

Now let us look at the exhibition more attentively. Let us see how video spreads and how it spreads the space to abstract it. The show is installed in the remains of the previous Mike Kelley retrospective, with some alterations, which were kept to a minimum.[21] Some partition walls were cut to receive other works, such as *L'Expédition Scintillante, Acte 3: Untitled (Black Ice Stage;* 2002) (fig. 12.1), so that the corner of the ice rink may expand into another room—here again, a spreading aesthetics. The video *This is not a Time for Dreaming* (2004/2009) was projected behind a partition wall. And the exhibition integrated a section of the exterior courtyard to extend the exhibition space, enclosing it with a transparent wall to protect a microclimate for the bees of *Untilled*'s beehive and the climate modification device made of snow transforming itself into rain and fog of *L'Expédition Scintillante, Acte 1: Untitled (Weather Score;* 2002). An archaeological hole in one of the walls (*Timekeeper,* 1999) showed different layers of plaster and paint from previous exhibitions.

The idea of an ecosystem serves as a template for the juxtaposition of the works. The exhibition begins with an opening procedure, *Name Announcer* (2011), which not only introduces but also exposes the visitors one by one to the other beings in the gallery. The fact that they are named and exposed highlights another fact: visitors are not given any specific function; they are recognized more as individuals than as spectators. Huyghe says, "In that space there are other people, and this is important for me. When you are announced you are exposed—and not so much in an interactive way. You are not requested to do something. You are asked your name and that is all. You don't need to play or behave."[22] That announcement is crucial insofar as it disrupts the spectator-art correlationism: viewers are exposed *to* art and not art exposed *for* viewers.

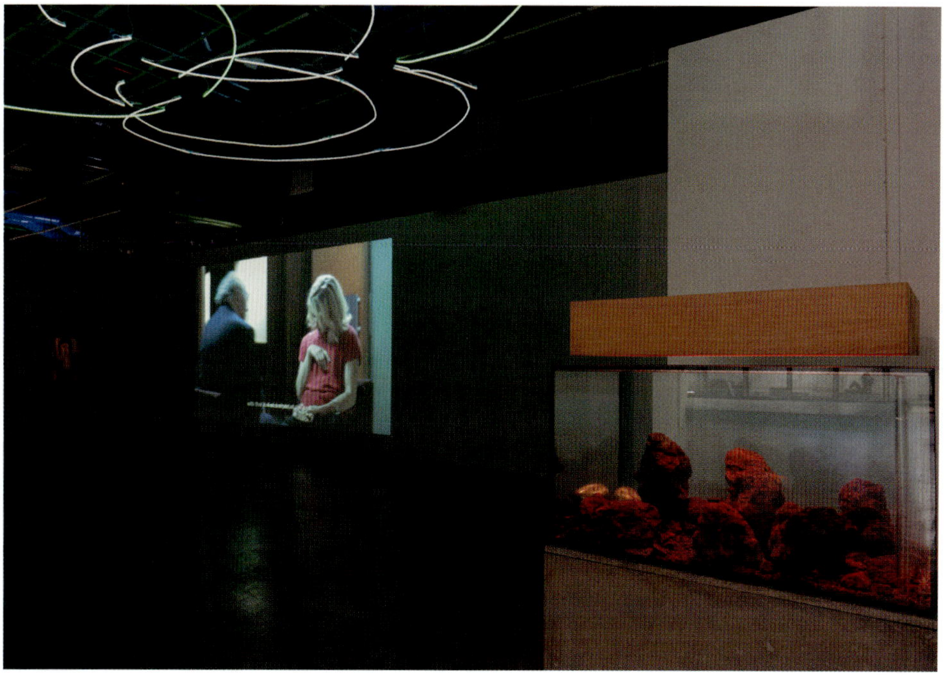

FIGURE 12.4
Pierre Huyghe, *De Hory Modigliani,* 2007 (oil on canvas); *The Host and the Cloud,* 2010 (HD video, color, sound; 121 minutes, 30 seconds); *RSI, au bout du réel,* 2006 (neon); and *Zoodram 4,* 2011 (live marine ecosystem, resin mask after Constantin Brancusi's *Sleeping Muse* [1910]). Installation view: *Pierre Huyghe,* Centre Pompidou, Paris (September 25, 2013–January 6, 2014). Courtesy of Marian Goodman Gallery, New York and Esther Schipper Gallery, Berlin. Photograph by Philippe Migeat, Centre Pompidou, Paris.

The video works (comprising film/videos, 16mm/35mm films transferred to digital beta, and digital beta works) include *Blanche-Neige Lucie* (1997), *Two Minutes Out of Time* (2000), *One Million Kingdoms* (2001), *Streamside Day* (2003), *This is not a Time for Dreaming* (2004/2009), *A Journey That Wasn't* (2005), *Forest of Lines* (2008), *The Host and the Cloud* (2010), and *A Way in Untilled* (2012). Most of the other works in the show are related to performance—human performances, documents of performances and events, traces of performances or simply animal life—including spectators playing a videogame (*Atari Light,* 1999) (figs. 12.1 and 12.2); the skater skating in *L'Expédition Scintillante, Acte 3: Untitled [Black Ice Stage],* 2002) (fig. 12.1); the LED-masked walker (*Player,* 2010) (fig. 12.3); the walker wearing an animal head (*La Toison d'Or,* 1993) (fig. 12.2); the fuchsia-legged Ibizan hound named *Human* from *Untilled* (2012) (fig. 12.3); the bees of the beehive covering the head of *Untilled*'s reclining nude (*Untilled [Liegender Frauenakt],* 2012); invertebrates evolving in the *Zoodram 2* (2010) aquarium; the hermit crab's adoption of a reproduction of Brancusi's *Muse endormie* (1910) as a shelter in *Zoodram 4* (2011) (fig. 12.4); live corner spiders (*C.C. Spider,* 2011); live ants and spiders circulating freely, creating lines from nest to nest located in small holes in the walls (*Umwelt,* 2011); a real fake Modigliani (*De Hory Modigliani,* 2007) (fig. 12.4); posters of *Casting* (1995), *Or* (1995), *L'Écrivain public* (1995), *One Year Celebration* (2003–2006), and *Stars* (2008); a sanded wall exposing a layer of green paint remaining from the presentation of Guy De Cointet's *Tell Me* during the 2013 edition of the Nouveau Festival, evoking Monet's last *Nymphéas,* whose green and white powder had fallen and was spread on the floor by walking visitors (*Shore,* 2013).

The works populating *Pierre Huyghe* compose the metric (extensively defined) space of the exhibition. Yet they emerge from a nonmetric continuum that is not directly perceivable. That continuum unfolds when works start to interact with each other and are transformed in these interrelations. The works were selected and placed to enable the nondissimulation of the intensive properties of the exhibition as a whole. The spreadability of video is pivotal to that intensification (as well as the exhibition layout, which favors the easy circulation of sound and images). Sound tracks are continuously overlapping, combining, and contaminating each other. The display of the works offers visitors numerous occasions to hold in their field of vision a multiplicity of coexisting images perceptually impacting each other because of the movement of the moving images. Looking at *The Host and the Cloud* necessarily leads to the inclusion—within the viewer's visual field—of the fake Modigliani painting hanging close by: the proximity of the two pieces creates a porosity between real and fiction, modern and contemporary muses; it turns the Modigliani female sitter into a character of *The Host and the Cloud.* The viewing of *A Journey That Wasn't*—a documentary/science-fiction video on Huyghe's expedition to the Antarctic in search of an albino creature—is aurally and visually conditioned by the sound of Erik Satie's *Gymnopédies 3* and *4* and the pulsing lights and fog emanating from *L'Expédition Scintillante, Acte 2: Untitled (Light Box)* (2002) installed in the same room. *A Journey,* in turn, imaginatively transports the universe of the light box into the icy continent.

When visitors play *Atari Light*—a video game with joysticks and halogen lamps inserted in a large (960 × 960 cm) overhead grid—the lamps light up in the grid, square by square, creating a flickering effect that spreads over the works installed nearby, a spread that intensifies the spectacle dimension of the golden tap shoes on a scuffed pedestal from *Singing in the Rain* (1996) and the free time declaration of the plant and poster from *Le Procès du temps libre* (1999). During the show, *RSI, un bout de réel* (2006) (fig. 12.4), a neon structure fixed to the ceiling—a 7 × 7 m Borromean knot, created from an unfinished drawing by Jacques Lacan representing the interdependency of the real, the symbolic, and the imaginary—shines at 10 percent of its intensity, but when it appears in the *The Host and the Cloud* just below, it illuminates the whole exhibition. Around November, the soundtrack of the buzzing bees from *A Way in Untilled* was programmed to pollinize for a few seconds all the speakers in the room. This meant that, at any time afterward, listeners in the gallery experiencing a work could suddenly be exposed to the buzz—a contamination that changes, for a while at least, both the materiality and the contemplation of that work. The *Player* walker, whose face is covered with a LED mask in the shape of an open book, regularly circulates in the room, although his or her presence (like that of all the performers) is never guaranteed or pre-announced. Video—more precisely the video screen turned into a mask—is thus spreading in space through a walking human figure. The oscillating identity of the player—she or he is simultaneously a visitor, a viewer, a science fiction reader, and a wanderer, someone whose seeing is augmented by the screen or perhaps partially blinded by it—continuously raises questions about the spectator's perceptual activity: What is it to perceive in a world of screens? What and how do we see through our screens, which are now literally part of our bodies? Do we have a better view of the unperceived? Do we have a better sense of the intensive properties of our surroundings? Has the world become more abstract?

The point of my argument is that the release of intensities does abstract the space insofar as intensities are the properties of the nonmetric space from which the metric space of the exhibition emerges, stabilizes, and restabilizes. This abstraction is not directly perceived, but the viewers experience its interactions, and they will perceive—are exposed to—some of the traces of intensification. Intensification has occurred and is still occurring; it might continue to occur in the future. The spreadability of video has activated that abstraction. Visitors might not directly perceive intensive properties as they emerge, but they become witnesses to their occurrences. When referring to the assemblage of his work in the Pompidou retrospective, Huyghe has used different terms to qualify its dynamic nature, from *cohabitation* to *heterogeneity* to *encounter* and *reorganization,* as well as *mutual corruption.* "I like the idea that things can cohabitate, but maintain their heterogeneity," said Huyghe. "They can be separated or reorganized. How do they relate or not relate? I am interested in this question, and in questioning the conditions of encounter."[23] This variation is eloquent insofar as the works in the retrospective do not all necessarily relate to and affect each other. Perceptually experienced interactions do not necessarily alter the viewer's perception of the works. And some organic components (bees and ants, for instance) die—a fate that shows how some cohabitations are better for survival than others.

However, this being said, the spreadability of video *was* activated to intensify the environment. Video became an object of influence more than a transmitter of sounds and images: it was explored as a means to trigger interrelations that could modify the visitor's perception of the works assembled in the retrospective. In 2011, Huyghe produced a work entitled *Influenced.* Although not part of the Pompidou retrospective, its modus operandi sustained the spreadability function of video reinforced in the show. It consisted of a person present in a gallery space carrying a flu virus. This person—a gallery attendant and not someone acting as an attendant—was chosen either because she or he already had the flu or had accepted to be injected with the virus through a flu shot. Visitors could find a checklist describing the situation and decide to stay or not to stay in the space. But they—like anyone circulating in any public space—had nevertheless been exposed to an infectious organism. They were under influence despite themselves. Such are intensive properties: they influence the becoming other of things as they individuate. Influence also structured the 2010 *The Host and the Cloud* event held in the abandoned Musée national des arts et traditions populaires in Paris on three celebration days (Halloween, Valentine's Day, and May Day). The video made from that event was one of the strongest presences of the Pompidou exhibition, in terms of both size (the projection was the largest of the show) and sound (the Kate Bush song, part of its sound track, could be heard throughout the gallery). Huyghe asked fifteen actors to take up the position of the museum's personnel and participate in sessions of magic, hypnosis, exorcism, psychodrama, and sleeping-pill ingestions, which would affect the actors' states of consciousness. Fifty people were invited to witness these live experiments.[24] In *Influenced* and *The Host and the Cloud,* abstraction—the manifestation of the intensive properties of a situation—was primarily activated by (influenced and influencing) humans circulating in space. In the Pompidou exhibition, it was the spreadability of a nonhuman thing—video—that became one of the central influencing factors enabling the abstraction of space—that is, its intensification.

NOTES

1. The show was held at the Centre Pompidou in Paris from September 25, 2013, to January 6, 2014. Emma Lavigne curated the show, with the assistance of Florencia Chernajovsky.

2. Henry Jenkins, Sam Ford, and Joshua Green, *Spreadable Media: Creating Value and Meaning in a Networked Culture* (New York: New York University Press, 2013), 1–3.

3. Lucian Krukowski, "Abstraction," in *Encyclopedia of Aesthetics,* ed. Michael Kelly (London: Oxford University Press, 1998), www.oxfordreference.com.proxy1.library.mcgill.ca/view/10.1093/acref/9780195113075.001.0001/acref-9780195113075-e-0003?rskey=jq5fAK&result=3.

4. Philippe Dubois, "La question vidéo face au cinéma: Déplacements esthétiques," in *Cinéma et dernières technologies,* ed. Frank Beau, Philippe Dubois, and Gérard Blanc (Paris: INA; Brussels: De Boeck Université, 1998); and *La Question vidéo: entre cinéma et art contemporain* (Crisnée, Belgium: Yellow Now, 2011), 77 and 99.

5. David Joselit, *After Art* (Princeton and Oxford: Princeton University Press, 2013), 2.

6. Joselit, *After Art,* xv.

7. Nam June Paik, "L'arche de Nam June," *art press* 47 (April 1981), 7–9. My translation.

8. Centre Pompidou, Direction des publics, Service de l'information des publics et de la médiation, *"Pierre Huyghe,* 25 September 2013–6 January 2014," press information, www.centrepompidou.fr/media/imp/M5050/CPV/ba/d5/M5050-CPV-25145cad-29bb-4565-bad5-e68d7f5be6ec.pdf.

9. Christine Van Assche, *"The Third Memory,"* Point of View: Extrait du catalogue *Collection art contemporain—La collection du Centre Pompidou, Musée national d'art moderne,* sous la direction de Sophie Duplaix, Paris, Centre Pompidou, 2007. Centre Pompidou virtuel, www.centrepompidou.fr/cpv/ressource.action?param.id=FR_R-1425bb6a5c5ffddcc2ffb89cf4bea055&param.idSource=FR_O-fd7d0bcefd1bc7879ee8ad0d82e17d. My translation.

10. Pierre Huyghe, quoted in Sky Goodden, "Pierre Huyghe Explains His Buzzy *Documenta 13* Installation and Why His Work Is Not Performance Art," *Artinfo Canada,* August, 30 2012, www.blouinartinfo.com/news/story/822127/pierre-huyghe-explains-his-buzzy-documenta-13-installation-and-why-his-work-is-not-performance-art/page/0/2.

11. Emma Lavigne, interview by the author at the Centre Pompidou, Paris, June 25, 2014.

12. Giorgio Agamben, *What Is an Apparatus? And Other Essays,* trans. David Kishik and Stefan Padetella (Stanford, CA: Stanford University Press, 2007), 14.

13. Agamben, *What Is an Apparatus?* 24 and 28.

14. Levi Bryant, Nick Srnicek, and Graham Harmanin, "Towards a Speculative Philosophy," in *The Speculative Turn: Continental Materialism and Realism,* ed. Bryant, Srnicek, and Harmanin (Melbourne: re.press, 2011).

15. Quentin Meillassoux, *After Finitude: An Essay on the Necessity of Contingency,* trans. Ray Brassier (New York: Continuum, 2008), 5.

16. Bryant, Srnicek, and Harmanin, "Towards a Speculative Philosophy," 3.

17. Manuel De Landa, *Intensive Science and Virtual Philosophy* (New York and London: Bloomsbury, 2013 [2002]), xiii.

18. De Landa, *Intensive Science,* 18.

19. Julia Michalska, "Pierre Huyghe Creates a Buzz in Paris," *The Art Newspaper,* September 23, 2013, www.theartnewspaper.com/articles/Pierre-Huyghe-creates-a-buzz-in-Paris/30305, 249 .

20. De Landa, *Intensive Science,* 62.

21. Nicolas Fourgeaud and Tristan Trémeau, "Pierre Huyghe et Philippe Parreno: l'institution enchantée," *art press,* April 2004, www.artpress.com/article/04/03/2014/-pierre-huyghe-et-philippe-parreno-linstitution-enchantee/29403#sthash.fz8afggv.dpuf, 410.

22. Pierre Huyghe, quoted in Chiara Zampetti, "Live Art: Q + A with Pierre Huyghe," *Art in America,* September 13, 2011, www.artinamericamagazine.com/news-features/interviews/pierre-huyghe-esther-schipper/.

23. Huyghe, quoted in Zampetti, "Live Art."

24. Rirkrit Tiravanija, "Pierre Huyghe," *Interview Magazine,* February 10, 2011, www.interviewmagazine.com/art/pierre-huyghe/#_.

13

SPECTRAL PROJECTIONS

Color, Race, and Abstraction in the Moving Image

Maria-Christina Villaseñor

Abstract ab'strakt,'ab,strakt/

1. existing in thought or as an idea but not having a physical or concrete existence.

The world as we perceive it is one teeming with beings, landscapes, and objects in all shapes, sizes, and colors. It is upon the latter, color, that we make critically important determinations about the essential nature of these characters and settings and their place in our world. Yet the scientific definition of color—as a perception or sensation—differs substantially from what is commonly thought of as color: a physical attribute or quality that an object possesses. Color is not an internal, immutable aspect of an object. Rather, it is a subjectively experienced, perceptual phenomenon.

So too, the definition of the term *race* varies widely in what is scientifically, sociologically, and commonly understood, and like color, it leans more toward the a posteriori construct than to the a priori quality. Henry Louis Gates commented, "Race, as a meaningful criterion within the biological sciences, has long been recognized to be a fiction."[1] Yet we regularly interpret the world around us, and are interpreted, through "race," as if its biological and scientific underpinnings were sound, its usage was objective and ahistorical, its shifting semantics were "fixed."

Color and race—such commonplace, commonly aligned terms. Yet their meanings are so difficult to define, let alone agree upon, to give concrete form or clear demarcation. Although both terms fit squarely in the definition of the word *abstract* above, what I wish to examine in this essay is how the terms square with the definition of *abstract* as it relates to art, and most specifically, to abstraction in video art. Especially if, seemingly, the two terms are inextricably entwined in the history of the moving image, all the more reason to examine their resistant positions and vexing entanglements in the practice of video art and abstraction.

Video art by birthright holds a debt to its forebears—the moving image histories of cinema and television. It thus shares a technological history in which the development, selection, and introduction of color reproductive technologies into what was formerly a black-and-white medium was based on a fundamental criteria: that of producing "pleasing flesh tones."[2] As scholar Brian Winston relates in his historical examination, *Technologies of Seeing*, "Essentially, the research agenda for color film (and more latterly color television) was dominated by the need to reproduce Caucasian skin tones," so preference was accorded to film stock that could offer "a whiter shade of white," reproducing profilmic white skin tones significantly lighter than in actuality.[3] Similarly, in the late 1970s WGBH and the 3M Corporation produced "a special television signal, to be recorded on videotape" based on the reproduction of white skin tone so as to offer as a grading gauge to rate optimal stocks of videotape.[4]

Thus to even begin to discuss color and abstraction in moving image making is to de facto begin with an "impure" palette of ideology where one might suppose that only the "purest" of formal concerns—color—lie. Notions of purity in abstraction abound in art history, whether categorized as a quest for "pure" expression, the "pure" culmination of progressive modernist enterprise, or in defining complete nonobjectiveness as the sine qua non of "pure" abstraction. The four artists and works examined in this essay grapple with issues of abstraction and representation, all touching upon issues of color and race in the process, wittingly or unwittingly, relating a story of colonialism that despite best efforts, will not stay politely hidden under notions of pure Abstraction. Their formal purity "polluted," the works here are neither strictly abstract nor wholly absent of representational elements or cues. Rather, they evince a complex, lively grappling with form, function, history, narrative satisfaction or frustration, aesthetic repulsion and delight—what Kobena Mercer has termed "discrepant abstraction" in other artistic media,[5] and perhaps they realize their own uniquely discrepant, disjunctive form of abstraction via moving image media. The works that follow underscore discrepancies and suspensions of belief in confronting issues of color, race, and abstraction, showing us the richness of the spectrum and the arbitrariness of imposed boundaries.

PAUL PFEIFFER: ABSTRACTING FORM, REFERENCING COLOR

> A special relationship exists between black bodies and spectacle. It's almost as though the spectacle could not exist without them. Think of the colonial condition. Frantz Fanon writes about the former child of the colony who goes to the metropolis and finds himself on the subway and has the distinct feeling that he is outside himself, that he is watching

himself. Whenever he lights a cigarette, he sees himself do it. This hovering sense of alienation, being outside and not centered in your own body, is a very strange thing.

PAUL PFEIFFER

Paul Pfeiffer's single-channel video *Home Movie/Four Locations for a Home Movie* (2012) (fig. 13.1) initially appears as a romp of sorts: disjointed documentation, as home movies tend to be, of an outing undertaken by a group of white adults and black children, the era seemingly the early 1970s.[6] (Pfeiffer began with found 8mm film footage, which he then digitized, subtly altered, and edited, presenting the result as an eight-minute loop on a video monitor.) The first shot is that of a VW Bug, the front passenger door open, out of which emerges a young black boy; a single helium-filled blue balloon pops out, quickly followed by a number of differently colored balloons, and finally by three black children and two white women. In the next scene, highway signage suggests the group is headed to the zoo, but when they are shown arriving there, a hand-lettered sign posted at the entrance awaits them, stating that no balloons are allowed. Further reinforcing the unease, there follows a close-up shot of an official-looking, unspecified "No Admittance" sign.

The group is then seen heading back to the VW, proceeding to the Science and Technology Museum, a seemingly more hospitable place. Its spherical planetarium structure visually shares a felicitous relationship to the band of balloons, as does a miniature version of the planetarium in and around which the children play. In the midst of this romping, a blue balloon, untethered, seemingly frolics about with the children among the area's gardens and fountain. The blue balloon appears unmoored, just as the video is unmoored of clear narrative legibility. Pfeiffer appears to have digitally excised the figure holding the balloon in the original footage, because only a slightly ghosted, pixelated abstraction appears beneath the hovering helium balloon.

Subsequent scenes show the children and balloons at play in the adjoining grounds. Various shots suggest some narrative or symbolic significance, but without any seeming subsequent import—an untethered white balloon floats up to the sky, as unanchored helium balloons typically do; a band of motorcyclists arrives but then drives off. Also, various animals appear on the grounds to join the children: a white dog with black spots appears on the scene, followed by a black goat with white spots. The adults and children pet the animals and feed them, while simultaneous snacks are prepared for the children and eaten. A blonde child, a gray dog, and a white man also appear in various shots of these scenes. Finally the full group is seen, the children and adults waving to the camera, the unknown camera operator focused down on them from a high-angled view, and the loop begins anew.

We are left with the mystery of the hovering blue balloon, the somewhat disjointed story, situation, or lack of clear development, but with a very clear sense of our own reliance on simplistic classifications: color—whether of balloons or people—to try and

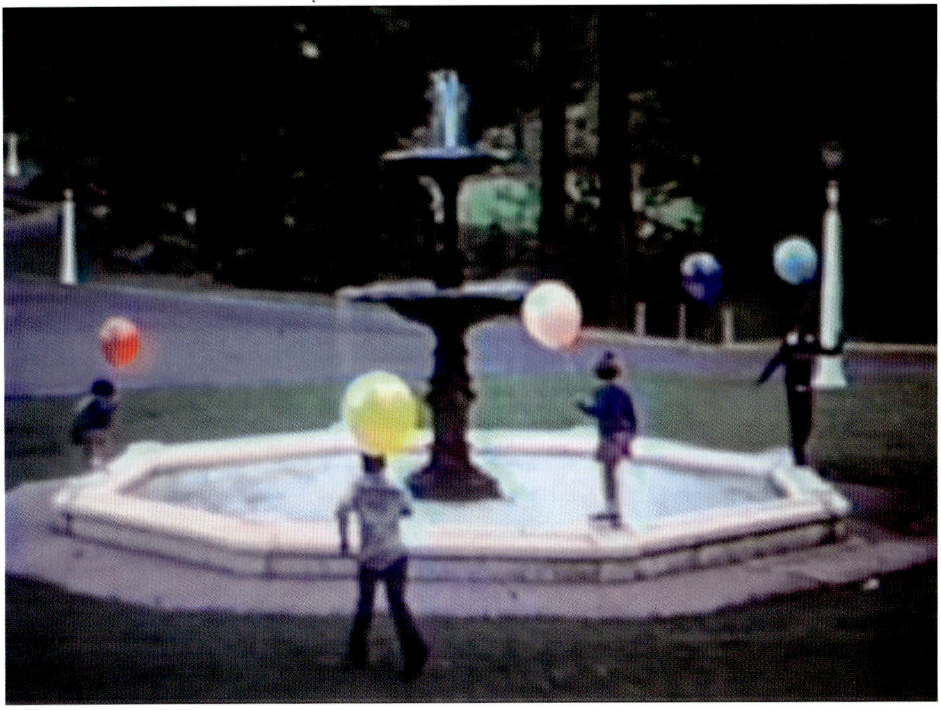

FIGURE 13.1
Paul Pfeiffer, *Home Movie / Four Locations for a Home Movie*, 2012. Produced in collaboration with Aaron Levi. 8mm film transferred to digital video / suite of four Cibachrome prints; 8 minutes, 30 seconds, looped. Courtesy of the artist and Thomas Dane Gallery, London.

make sense or keep track of the proceedings, to piece together context and meaning and create equivalencies from our most rudimentary graspings of color, race, and meaning. We begin to assign meanings to shades of skin, to hues of pelt, to colored globes. The viewing of the captives of the zoo is denied, but who is truly on view and captive in this outing? Is the zoo a stand-in for subjectivity, and the science museum one for objectivity? Is the latter a haven, or just a different stage to play out our questionable practices of "objective" classification?

Equally, Pfeiffer's blue balloon, unmoored but tenaciously present, seems a doppelganger for the Red Balloon in the iconic, eponymously titled French children's film by Albert Lamorisse in which a young boy is befriended by an anthropomorphized red balloon. However, in the French film, balloons—that is, colors and spheres—ultimately have the last word, winning the power to transport a young blond boy from his isolation and persecution by a gang of young children. Globes in vivid colors deliver the boy from his earthly troubles, transporting him across the rooftops of Paris to embark upon a fantastical celestial voyage. In Pfeiffer's video, the blue balloon hovers just so, present but without agency, its holder absent: invisibility equals lack of agency. The blue balloon doesn't overstep its reach and dance and dodge like the Red Balloon, but dutifully hovers, and while no backup arrives neither does any obvious menace appear. Any narrative logic, like the balloon, is untethered. It isn't until the very final scene of the video, which is brief and rapidly returns to the beginning of the loop, that intently focused viewers may notice that one additional black child is now visible in the scene, his presence by absence unremarked the entire time.

Thus the abstracting strategies in Pfeiffer's case have to do with erasure as well as unclear narratives. But these are, after all, home movies, no? Documents without clear narrative structures? And yet the situation seems contrived: the white adults and black children, the signs that seem to serve as intertitles to the film's action. The zoo-goers denied entry, the black child erased, the resistance to linear narrative and narrative closure—unlike the gleeful ending of *The Red Balloon,* colors and shapes do not save the boy, or the day, or signal a clear narrative function or satisfying endpoint. As Pfeiffer himself has said, "People get very uncomfortable with mystery, or with not knowing. The tendency is to immediately cover it up."[7] But Pfeiffer's erasure, his mystery, remains just that, not pentimento hovering beneath a corrected error, but the thing itself.

CORY ARCANGEL: OPEN SOURCE READINGS ON COLOR(S)

I guess I'm a tinkerer, you know?

CORY ARCANGEL

Cory Arcangel considers himself a tinkerer; he chooses tinkering of a technological and mechanical sort, whereas his artwork and participatory/shared apps as art allow others to tinker in the fields of meaning, representation, and reception.[8] Beginning as a video projection and later morphing into a free app for Mac platform computers, the application *Colors* will play QuickTime movies one horizontal line of pixels at a time. It is offered both as a readily executable application and as a source code, thus allowing intrepid coders to further modify the program and riff on the app to create their own apps. Like the controversial move Turner Movie Classics made in the 1980s to "colorize" classic films originally shot and released in black-and-white, Arcangel's *Colors* (2005) (fig. 13.2) seemingly takes a Hollywood movie and transforms it into pulsing lines of pure, abstract color, but with one notable difference: the lines are generated from the digital material of the films themselves. One could argue that a radical transformation has already occurred when something shot and released on celluloid film has been digitized, but this too, is part of the reflective experience of Arcangel's *Colors.*

Taking as his starting point the 1988 Hollywood film *Colors* directed by Dennis Hopper, Arcangel allows one to have a focused experience that perfectly suits his formal investigation of film, digital technologies, and color. In the process, he deconstructs and reconstructs a work that is iconic in popular cultural history, with Ice T's musical title

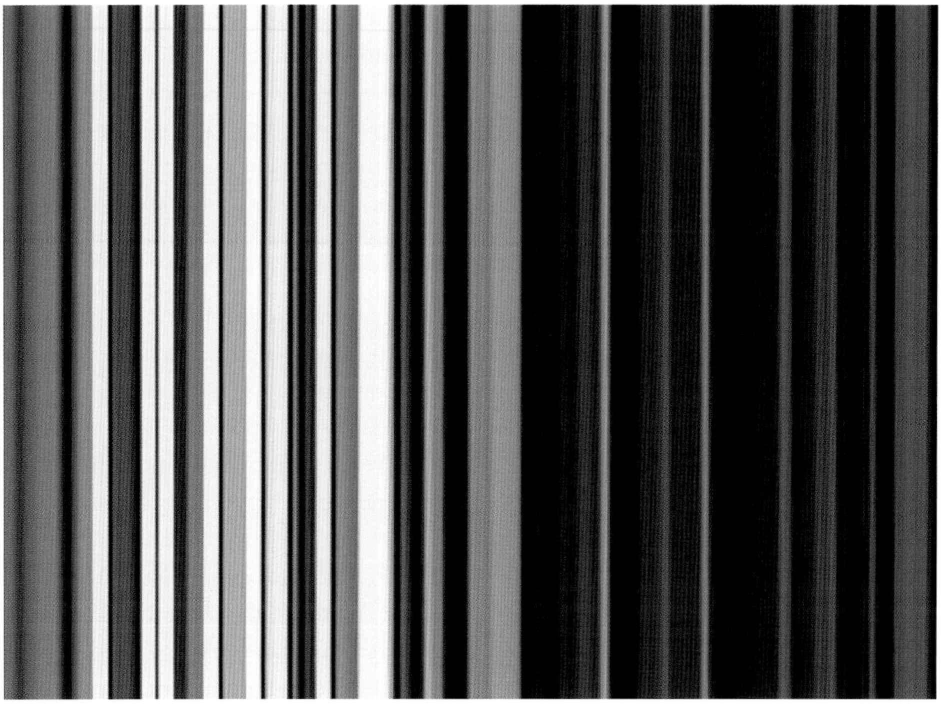

FIGURE 13.2
Cory Arcangel, *Colors* (still), 2006. Single-channel video, artist software, computer; 33 days. © Cory Arcangel, Image courtesy of the artist.

track "Colors" and the film's then-timely exploration of the dueling Bloods and Crips gangs of East Los Angeles, who purportedly made the donning of their gangs' respective red or blue colors a matter of life or death. Because Arcangel's *Colors* operates continuously, its feature-length structure and sound track intact, it offers the opportunity to read the work differently: to exalt, decry, or deplore its narrative aspects, to feel deeply the rhythm of its editing style, to remark on dialogue, or notice the repetition of mass media trope—of how often gunfire erupts in pixelated bursts of fiery red squares, of how resilient the trope of the dark bad guy remains. Vertical lines of color move, create similarly hued masses, and break apart, shift tones and intensities as camera movement, blocking, and movement within the scene, lighting choices, edits, and transitions become wonderfully, if nonrepresentationally, apparent.

In the original film, Hopper, noted for his painting and photography as well as his work as an actor and director, worked with director of photography Haskell Wexler, a storied cinematographer who also directed the influential film reflecting on the power of the media, *Medium Cool*. They crafted a film that draws out the significance of people of color struggling to make a mark on the world, if only through the rough means available to them—clothing colors, graffiti, tattoos, gang hand signs. The original film equally depicts the much more ethnically, and ethically, muddled world of the police force and the people they patrol in a diverse urban environment, although the easy tropes of cinema and the world abound—the cops in blue versus the rival sheriffs in green, the blue and red of the dueling gangs, the recurring blue lights of helicopters searching for the bad guys ensconced in the black of night. Hopper's narrative structure also suggests the stubborn resilience of codes of color, stereotypes, tropes when the true reality is much more complex, and yet these easy patterns are repeated over and over again. In Arcangel's version of *Colors,* this message is additionally underscored. One is both awash in sensory, nonobjective perceptual experience and following a narrative sound track—one foot in and one foot out, as it were, absorbing the narrative flow, yet all the while aware of the structures that go into creating the narrative of the film and the larger narrative of our culture. When a main character is fatally shot, one thinks of Jean-Luc Godard's words "It's not blood; it's red."[9] Yet here the adage can be both "It's not blood; it's red" *and* "It is blood; it's red." Colors operate metaphorically but skin color is index to a reality that is not so readily mutable.

Arcangel's work in *Colors* can be seen as Structural film for a digital age. However, unlike the Structuralists with their "pure" emphasis on form, the narrative is far from peripheral here: there is still a conventional narrative framework that encompasses the work through its sound track and "intactness" as a feature-length film, unedited or unmodified except for its visually abstracted presentation. Hopper's original film operates in an infinity loop of types and tropes that recur continually; only their colors change. So too does Arcangel's modification, but in our digital culture—in which colors are experienced less "in the flesh" than in pixelated representations on the screens of our ever-present smartphones, computers, and multiple digital devices—which loops will persist or be broken remains to be seen.

RICO GATSON: THE PROMISE OF LIGHT

The light in California is very specific.

RICO GATSON

Rico Gatson's video projection *The Promise of Light* (2013) (fig. 13.3) offers a work that reflects a contemporary vogue for stylized color abstractions but nonetheless refuses to function as decorative moving wallpaper as the work shifts, morphs, and gradually reveals itself as a moving palimpsest of history and meaning.[10] In the single-channel projection, glowing orbs of brightly colored lights set against a dark background initially lure the viewer: their saturated color and intensity arise from a deep black void recalling spotlights or theatrical lights at night, heralding mounting excitement and a promise of what's to come, their kaleidoscopic composition and slow morphing equally entrancing. Eventually, these abstracted, candy-colored shapes give way to darker layers from which historical photographic images faintly emerge, as one struggles with perception and reception to

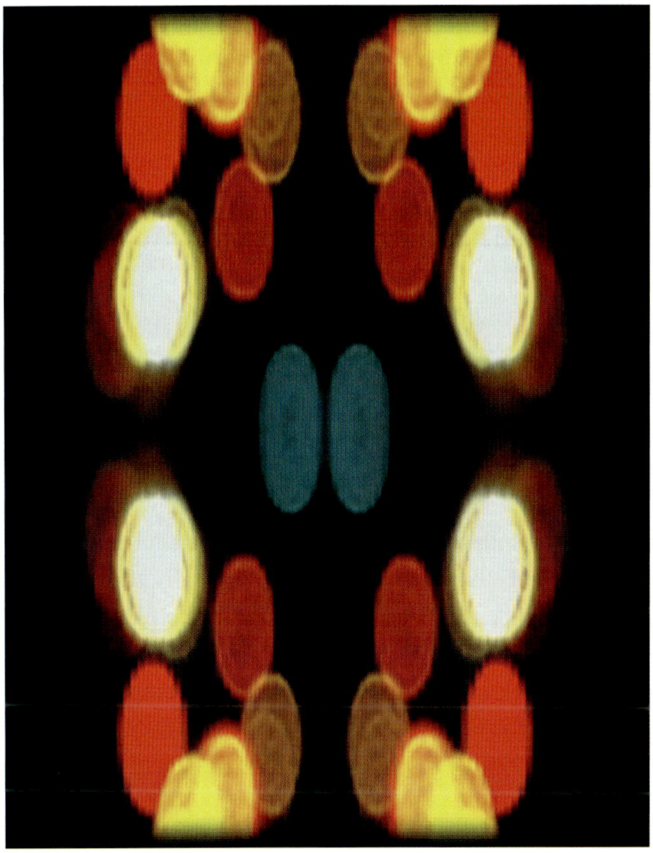

FIGURE 13.3
Rico Gatson, *The Promise of Light,* 2013.
Single-channel video projection; 6 minutes.
Courtesy of Rico Gatson.

decipher their locale, context, and meaning. Gatson has cited his own personal history as a point of departure, literally and figuratively, for inspiring *The Promise of Light,* the impetus coming in part from his reading of Isabel Wilkerson's book *The Warmth of Other Suns,* which examines African Americans' migration out of the South, beginning with World War I and ending in the early 1970s, roughly the time when Gatson's family undertook their own journey westward from Georgia to Southern California.[11]

The video operates in seemingly kaleidoscopic fashion: patterns and geometric shapes of color and light at times originate, diverge, and reconverge in the center of four quadrants that make up the screen and mirror each other. Colored orbs—intense circles of amber, red, yellow and white ringed with saturated hues of yellow and red—emanate from a dark background, moving and multiplying until the darkness lifts and we gradually discern a faint photographic image, seemingly archival, of a large group of black men, seated, all with their torsos bare. Glowing lights continue to refract and mutate above the photographic layer until once again we see only abstract geometric shapes against a dark background. Afterimages play games with the viewer's perception: what seem abstracted patterns, blurred edges of bright lights and shapes mutating, gathering into formation, subtly mirror and give rise to the composition of the photograph to be revealed, which the viewer finally begins to discern, in horror, as figures in a lynching scene.

Next, darkness gives way to a screen fully immersed in amber hues, its shapes formed from shades of color emanating from a horizon and enveloping the spectator in swaths of pure color. Gradually the fields of color form into triangulated shapes, slowly giving way to circular forms of color amidst which we catch a glimpse of another photographic image of individuals and skeletal forms. An amber light emanates orthogonally; shapes coalesce from the fuzzier to the more precise; hard edges and colors intensify and entice. Fields of ambers, ochres, yellows, and reds crystallize as colored circles until as they divide, biomorphically, from the central darkness another historical photograph is revealed of three black men, again with torsos bare, their poses suggesting a fierce dignity in the face of unwilling submission.

In the final passage of *The Promise of Light,* the geometric shapes move about with a sense of urgency underscored by the sound track's faster tempo, the whiteness of the light shapes suggesting a sort of light at the end of the tunnel. Gradually, the darkness gives way to stippled light and darkness, which reveals itself to be a photograph of a field of cotton with fieldworkers in its midst. The screen then bathes us in fields of reds, ambers, oranges, and yellows, like the perceptual color fields one experiences when shutting one's eyes fully and tightly. There is no going forward toward the light without looking back, as much as we may wish to avoid it. The present, and the future, are always colored by the past.

Equally, the audio track suggests movement, a journey of endless transitions—that of a train, with rhythmic clatters and sounds of rushing air, its brakes slowly reducing their pitch and halting. Alternately the sounds can at times be interpreted as the low roar of planes overhead or the rush of cars on the highway. The sounds diminish and increase in volume as the video unfolds, until the sound seems to consolidate and intensify, embodying the form of a low wail, a warning siren, an emergency air horn, an emergency alert. Regardless of its original source, it is plaintive, insistent, and persistent, until the cycle begins anew.

Are the afterimages burned into our retina rogue perceptual tricks, such as floaters or complementary colors appearing as afterimages, colored auras that arise with the worst of migraines—or perhaps the worst migraine of all, induced by history and memory, activated by the factual, resisting erasure, an iris in or fade to black, to use cinematic terms, on history?

Gatson's video debuted in his 2013 one-person exhibition at the Ronald Feldman Gallery in New York, which also featured a number of Gatson's sculptural works, paintings, photographs, including imagery abstracted from aerial photos of the fires blazing during the Watts Riots of 1965, and wall pieces in which an intensely hued yellow background is visible in louvered slices through black slats suggesting Venetian blinds. In various ways, Gatson is commenting directly on the light in California, his subjective experience of it, and, equally, an art-historically significant, collective experience of it. He is actively engaging and taking as his principal "subject" formal properties of light and color, yet also working with them in a way that is ultimately and inextricably intertwined with his own personal history as an African American and how that reflects on the experience of a larger group. With the intense perceptual sensations of color and light the viewer experiences during *The Promise of Light,* a relation can been seen to the work of the Light and Space artists of California, who ironically began working and receiving attention during the same period that Gatson's family migrated to California—artists such as James Turrell and Robert Irwin and abstract painters such as Diebenkorn, whose works offer ethereal, abstract explorations of light, space, and perception. However, Gatson's experience of California's oft-cited soft, cerulean light may also be a differently colored one, inflected with imagery of the past, as the historical photographs of a history replete with prejudice may attest. But also of a more recent past, of California where the flashing lights from police cars patrolling race wars, the fiery glow of the Watts Riots' conflagration, and iconography of burning crosses change the atmospheric cast and offer a shift in perception. An idealized light, just as an idealized, "pure" abstraction is not to be in *The Promise of the Light.*

ARIEL JACKSON: CHILD'S PLAY

> So like, how do we protect our colors without having to give them to somebody else to protect?
>
> CONFUSERELLA IN ARIEL JACKSON'S *HERE'S HOPING (AKA THE BLUES)*

Ariel Jackson is, at the time of this writing, a talented emerging artist, just beginning to establish her artistic career on the edges of figuration and abstraction, fiction and documentary, animation and live action.[12] An "outsider" to the New York art world, she hails from Louisiana, a part of the country where the lines between fantasy and reality and race and ethnicity are paradoxically more fluid *and* more fixed than almost anywhere else in the United States. Her nascent body of work reflects these paradoxes and differences through stylistic and formal means as well as, on occasion, through the persona of Confuserella, a character who underscores the artist's theme of the struggles between young African American women coming of age and the media's projections of how they should act and appear.

In the video installation *Here's Hoping (AKA The Blues)* (fig. 13.4), Jackson returns to her persona of Confuserella, an incarnation of a young black woman who dons a long blonde wig and dresses in a figure-conscious style. (In an earlier video, a man suggests she assume this get-up, and she appears juxtaposed against hip-hop-style videos, self-consciously gyrating in way that shows her clear discomfort with the persona she adopts.) Confuserella addresses her viewers and begins to relate how her troubles began

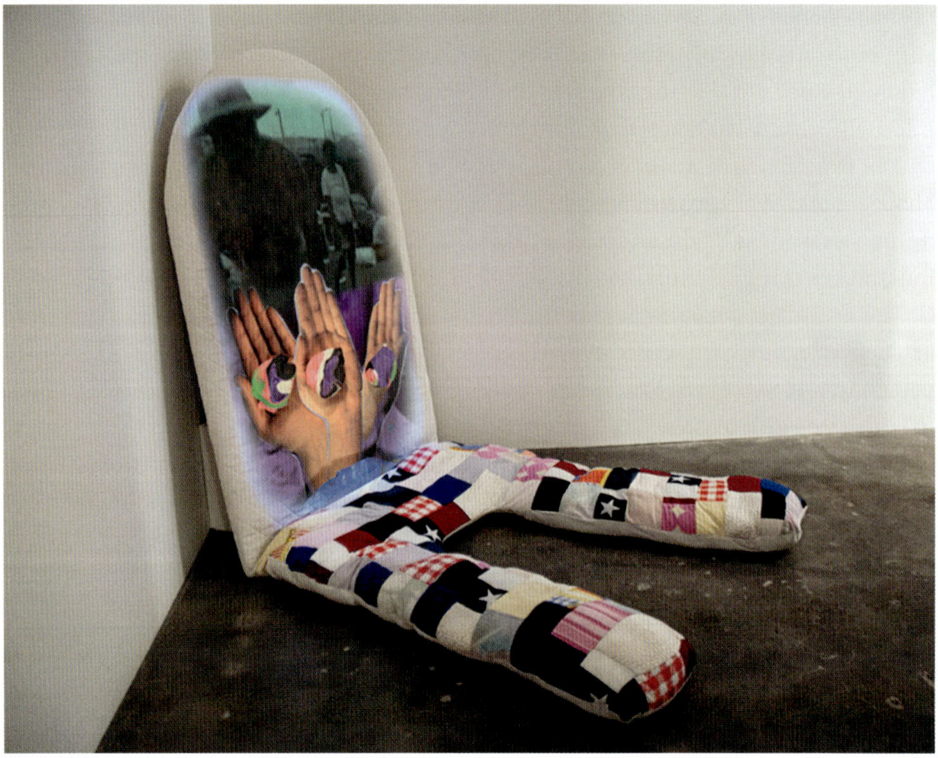

FIGURE 13.4
Ariel Jackson, *Here's Hoping (AKA The Blues)*, 2013. Installation, video, stop-motion animation, greenscreen; 7 minutes, 30 seconds. Courtesy of the artist.

when the "blues" began to take over the "reds and yellows" and then didn't know how to quit. The story line about these color wars is staged via stop-motion claymation, in which sun, earth, and water are depicted through crude clay modelling. The allusion seems clear as the clay shapes are depicted against a backdrop of images that appear to be taken from Hurricane Katrina footage. The "blues" stand in for an unrelenting tide of water that breaks through and wreaks destruction, the terrible real-life outcome we know all too well.

Or is it that we think we do, but we can never fully give concrete form to the trauma nor a concrete, fixed name to the depth and extent of its impact, nor can we fully localize where all the blame and also the hope may lie? Further, the presentation of *Here's Hoping (AKA The Blues)* as a single-channel video projected onto sculptural objects suggests the cosmic smashing into the domestic sphere—with sculptural elements that can be read as a mattress pad and ironing board and a home-quilted pillow for reclining or as a spaceship being fired off, a twenty-first-century Surrealistic assemblage that is all too real in the form of Katrina and yet beyond full comprehension in its devastating mix of the celestially unknowable "force majeur" and the earthbound criminal, intentional neglect of classes of people. Confuserella is clearly struggling psychologically in her accounting of what occurred and can only assign colors—blues, reds, and yellows—as stand-ins. Whereas their referents were clearly, iconographically, water, sun, and earth, now the colored clay shapes lose their distinct, representational forms and the "blues" begin to overwhelm the other "colors"—that seemingly now represent the diversity of inhabitants in the region—breaking them apart and subsuming them into one amorphous, muddled mass. Representation cannot hold. Kobena Mercer's *Discrepant Abstraction* once again applies: "What also comes to light from a 'discrepant' perspective are the various ways in which abstract art conversely addresses historical experiences of colonial trauma . . . that are strictly speaking 'unrepresentable' when they overwhelm their witnesses and survivors."[13]

Jackson, who studied at the Cooper Union School of Art in New York, which aptly bestowed upon her the school's Robert Breer Film Award, is obviously well-schooled in the history and practice of experimental film and animation. Like Breer, she irreverently combines abstract and representational imagery, interlacing photographically based footage and sculptural forms created for the camera. Yet she neither dispenses with nor ahistorically repeats such methods and materials of abstract filmmaking. Rather she attempts to mold such means to her own artistic realities, truths, and questions, trusting that there is no such thing as "fixed," in truth or in form, and that one can only rely on the questions.

CONCLUSION: LIVING COLOR: POST-ABSTRACT, POST-MEDIA, POST-IDENTITY?

To examine the works discussed in this essay is to raise questions rather than fix conclusions. Has art history grown beyond formal dogma—that is, notions of formal "purity" or exclusivity of medium? Have we left behind an era of identity politics, when artists were pushed to "act as ambassadors of their identities" as Paul Pfeiffer has phrased it, and if so, are designations such as "post-Black" (into which Rico Gatson has been grouped) truly meaningful?[14] If irrespective of intent, an artist such as Cory Arcangel creates an app as art that allows us to choose to read a work as a racial touchstone and yet by investigating its formal properties, transforms it, making it more true to itself in the process, perhaps the answer is yes. If Rico Gatson is able to grapple with the formal properties of color, light, and sound, all the while causing us to question our own visual acuity and capacity to absorb history, perhaps the answer is yes. If Ariel Jackson is able to compress experimental cinematic practices, historical footage, racial tension, and dramatic irony into a primal, multihued lump of clay and create a poignant new vision out of it, perhaps the answer is yes. If Paul Pfeiffer conjures childhood wonder and alienation at alternate turns and shows that clear classifications, linear narratives, and logical anchors are anything but, perhaps the answer is yes. Theirs is not a world of the "pure" yes, the "pure" abstraction, the "pure" form. Forms, categories, and colors are muddled and give rise to new permutations. There are no true boundaries on the spectrum.

NOTES

Epigraph: *Oxford English Dictionary,* s.v. "abstract," www.oxforddictionaries.com/definition/english/abstract.

1. Henry Louis Gates, "Writing 'Race' and the Difference It Makes," *Critical Inquiry* 12, no. 1 (Autumn 1985), 4; the full quote: "Race, as a meaningful criterion within the biological sciences, has long been recognized to be a fiction. When we speak of 'the white race' or 'the black race,' 'the Jewish race' or 'the Aryan race,' we speak in biological misnomers and, more generally, in metaphors. Nevertheless, our conversations are replete with usages of race which have their sources in the dubious pseudoscience of the eighteenth and nineteenth centuries."

2. Cinematographer Joseph Valentine, "Make-up and Set Painting Aid New Film," *American Cinematographer,* 1939, cited in Richard Dyer, *White* (London and New York: Routledge, 1997), 93. See also Eirik Frisvold Hanssen, "The Functions of Colour," lecture, Stockholm University, 1999, www.academia.edu/292978/The_Functions_of_Colour.

3. Brian Winston, *Technologies of Seeing: Photography, Cinematography and Television* (London: British Film Institute, 1996), 39.

4. Dyer, *White,* 94.

5. Kobena Mercer, *Discrepant Abstraction* (London: Institute of International Visual Arts; Cambridge, MA: MIT Press, 2006).

6. **Section epigraph:** Jennifer González, "Paul Pfeiffer," *BOMB Magazine* 83 (Spring 2003), http://bombmagazine.org/article/2543/paul-pfeiffer.

7. "Paul Pfeiffer and John Baldessari in Conversation," in *Paul Pfeiffer,* ed. Dominic Molon and Jane Farver, exhibition catalogue (Chicago: Museum of Contemporary Art; Cambridge, MA: MIT List Visual Arts Center, 2003), 35.

8. **Section epigraph:** Cory Arcangel, audio commentary discussing *Colors* on Moma.org, www.moma.org/explore/multimedia/audios/34/809.

9. Godard's quip has alternately been cited as a line from his 1967 film *Weekend* or as his response ("Not blood, red") to the remark "There is a good deal of blood in *Pierrot [le Fou]."* Jean-Luc Godard, "Parlons de Pierrot," interview by Jean-Louis Comolli, Michel Delahaye, Jean-André Fieschi, and Gérard Guégan, *Cahiers du Cinéma,* October 1965. For an English translation of the interview, see "Let's Talk about Pierrot," in *Godard on Godard,* ed. Jean Narboni and Tom Milne (New York: Viking Press, 1972), 217.

10. **Section epigraph:** Rico Gatson, *Rico Gatson:* The Promise of Light *at Ronald Feldman Fine Arts,* 2013, http://youtu.be/bkoow6vjJZo.

11. Isabel Wilkerson, *The Warmth of Other Suns: The Epic Story of America's Great Migration* (New York: Random House, 2010).

12. **Section epigraph:** Ariel Jackson, Confuserella's monologue, *Here's Hoping (AKA The Blues),* 2013.

13. Mercer, *Discrepant Abstraction,* 20.

14. "Paul Pfeiffer and John Baldessari in Conversation," 33.

14

GO WITH THE (UNREGULATED) FLOW

Fluidity, Abjection, and Abstraction

Trinie Dalton and Stanya Kahn

TD: At first I thought we should start with Kristeva because she gives a literal translation of abjection in terms of fluids, but when we were talking about projection and dreams, I was reminded of how we both translate the projection in a dream into a visual or narrative aspect, not literally but in a sensory or tonal or mood way. Projection is tied to abjection in terms of interior to exterior, right?

SK: Yeah, that makes sense to me. The kind of consciousness and action and psychic material that happens in dreams is in between kinds of consciousness, similar to the ways that Kristeva talks about the abject being neither subject nor object.[1] I'm really compelled by that. It's a radical space, a slippery space, and I also like how she almost anthropomorphizes this notion of the abject, where it becomes a wily creature that is both rebellious and persistent, uncanny and unnamable.

TD: Right. That's subject matter in both of our work. Even though we're not literally translating dreams.

SK: Right. Although sometimes I do.

TD: Do you?

SK: A lot of the drawings I've made in the past two years come from dreams. I had a dream where I was crossing a bridge over a bright green river and on the bank were two Sasquatches having sex. One of them was going down on the other one.

TD: Nice!

SK: They were roaring with pleasure. I couldn't tell their genders—there was just orange, shaggy hair, huge limbs. And in the dream I yelled from the bridge, "Hey, Yeti!" and tried to take their picture with my cell phone. *(Both laughing.)* Talk about the uncanny abject and not being able to capture it, right? We want to snap it, we want to Instagram it, we want to post it! But you can't snap a photo of the abject; it doesn't work. Or it's abject to try? Anyway so I made a few drawings of it (fig. 14.1).

TD: That's your snapshot!

SK: Yeah. Sometimes material in the videos comes directly from dreams too. Images, sometimes texts. Going further into ideas about abjection—this is perfect. *(Laughs.)* I had this dream in which I was trying to kill a rat; I was stabbing it with a screwdriver and every time I stabbed it, the rat would critique me: "Really? Don't you know where my heart is? Nope, that's not it." I recently used that in a new video I'm working on. Everyone in the piece is a medical professional. These two women break into an empty luxury apartment building to do a surgery on a fellow medical professional who's been injured . . .

TD: It's clean in there. Already disinfected.

SK: Exactly. They find a bottle of expensive mescal to clean his stomach and knock him out. And of course they start drinking it too. After the surgery they're all lounging on this huge white couch in a living room with massive panoramic views and I prompt one of the women to tell the rat dream. And she tells the rat dream as if it's her own, adding, "The rat goes, 'I thought you were a doctor. Don't you know where my heart is?'" *(Laughing.)* And the other one says, out of the blue, "I have this recurring dream every night about fighting a giant beaver with a fork." *(Laughs.)* It was an excellent surprise.

TD: Perfect. *(Laughing.)*

SK: The guy they've just operated on is nodding in and out while the ladies eat a birthday cake they found there, so they've all got icing on their faces and blood. *(Laughing.)*

TD: Whoa, quadruple abject!

SK: Yeah. And throughout the film I prompt people to share their knowledge, and it turns out that he is into animal symbolism. So the rat-dream lady turns to him and asks, "What do beavers symbolize?" *(Laughing.)* And he goes *(slurring)*, "Why would you want to kill something that builds things?" *(Laughing.)*

TD: Wow! Awesome response. He's bringing fertility back into it too.

SK: He's in a state of rupture; his whole abdomen has been cut open and operated on without anesthetic by these two people who were strangers to him. Which was a pretty abject scene itself. He is in some version of repair but it's

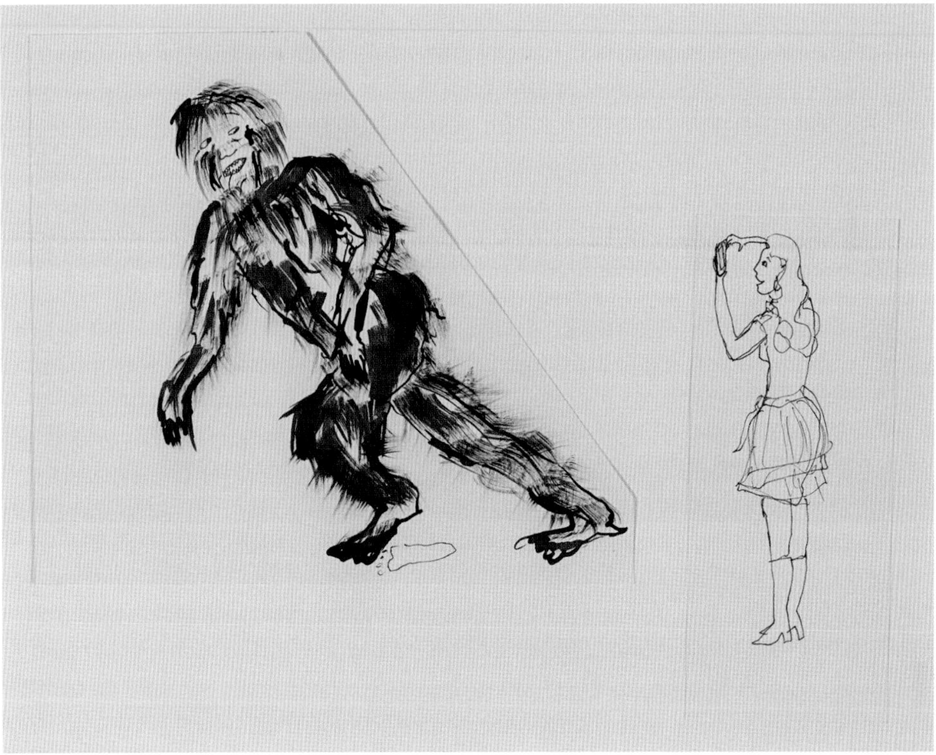

FIGURE 14.1
Stanya Kahn, *Hey Yeti 2*, 2013. Ink on paper, 14 × 17 inches. Courtesy of the artist and Susanne Vielmetter Los Angeles Projects. Photographer, Robert Wedemeyer.

not clear if he'll survive, which recurs in my work. I like to hear what could be said on that kind of precipice of obsolescence, before you go. And it introduces the possibility of a corpse entering the picture. Which Kristeva has a lot to say about (fig. 14.2).

TD: That's perfect because thinking about animals as totemic ties into abjection manifested in the monstrous. My initial understanding of Kristeva was surrounding this monster that signified the in-between state—and how that is like narrativity or an idea or concept being translated into the visual. That's like a rough, jagged definition of totemism. Visual art is like that. What you were describing has so much narrativity in it, and the abjection happens in multiple ways.

SK: I don't immediately identify my work with more traditional notions of abjection in art. I had to consider it consciously for this conversation. So I thought about narrative as the way in, ways in which you can take story, whether it's in

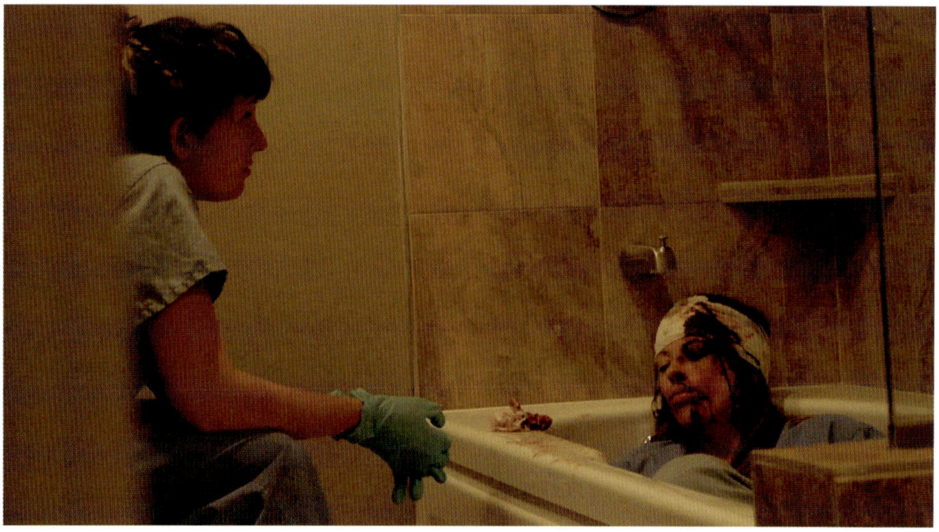

FIGURE 14.2
Stanya Kahn, *Don't Go Back To Sleep,* 2014. HD video with sound; 74 minutes. Courtesy of the artist and Susanne Vielmetter Los Angeles Projects.

the fictional sense, or the Grand Narrative, or Histories, social stories, and you can pack as much of that information as you can into one image, or symbol—as in this totemic form you refer to, which so many cultures do, as a way to speak, a way to open up the language. In my drawings and also in the videos, everything has to carry some load of meaning, but also there might be an image or sound that doesn't particularly tell a discreet or legible story or offer a piece of information. It might just perform, on a visceral, energetic, or symbolic level. I also wonder if it's abject to maul the traditional story by combining the scripted with the improvised. It's what I do; I don't work in traditional story space; I don't make a beginning, middle, and end.

TD: I don't either. It's not an accurate reflection of life, which is the Surrealist's perspective. And that perspective actually derives from wanting to be realistic.

SK: I admire the people who can do it and I think that you can contain a lot of wildness inside a traditional arc, but it's just not my approach and not something I'm good at. After a recent lecture, a student asked me, "Can you talk about how you deal with time?"

TD: That's hard—yeah, and good.

SK: It's a good question. If we're thinking about in-between spaces and the ways in which subject space and object space function—we try to make them function in a logical way, but if you're in an abject in-between, where you have a wild, undefinable thing that carries its own energy and is rejecting the norm and refusing to fit in, I think, well, that's in fact how time itself is in a sense. So I was trying to explain to her that maybe I'm thinking more in synchronic time than diachronic time.

TD: Me too.

SK: So in video, which is pure time, there's no materiality really, except of course for all the bodies and locations and places involved in the making, but once that materiality is gone and I'm editing, that is where I play with time and can create time and timing, and that's where I am trying to make a synchronic experience.

TD: Me too.

SK: And sometimes I loop back in time and forward and sideways and sometimes offer the illusion of very little time passing at all. I still love the pleasure of narrative and I try to leave threads of it for a viewer to grasp, but they won't be handles that will lead to one specific place.

SK: I'm sorry, the dog chewing his ass is so distracting. Stop. Stop.

TD: Poor Charlie.

SK: What would Kristeva say? "The dog chews its hind end, endlessly in its anxiety"?

TD: Yeah. *(Laughs.)*

SK: But what I was going to say is in that process, the maker is offering certain details but not others to stimulate the viewer to imagine and make meaning. I'm thinking about how much agency can I invite on the part of the viewer. I'm interested in the body of the viewer being activated and energized. This notion of the abject reminds me of ideas about what a revolutionary is.

TD: There is a politic behind the work. Open-endedness is the politic: you're inviting the viewer into the experience, and for me that's more like Roland Barthes's "Death of the Author."

SK: Sometimes it means making something that causes a disturbance or a disorientation and moments of feeling lost or alienated in, hopefully, a Brechtian sense. When viewers say, "No! That's impossible. What are you doing? This doesn't make any sense at all!" they reconnect with themselves as a person with agency. There's something about traumatizing the viewer that is important to talk about when we think about abjection though. It has to be productive. The pat term is "shock value," which I'm not interested in at all.

TD: Sure.

SK: I was listening to the radio this morning and they were playing a recording of Elaine Brown reading a letter [Black Panther] Ericka Huggins wrote when she was in prison and her husband had just been killed. Her letter was clear and angry and impassioned, an articulate call to rise up against fascism and capitalism and patriarchy. She was able to so clearly tie that into the larger scale of loss that is ongoing. She was talking about health care and access to resources and institutionalized racism. I'm thinking about this ability to translate personal trauma into and always related to the larger social and cultural traumas. When someone says, "Oh, your work is scary" or "Your work is disgusting," I have to pause and think maybe that's because I've been in close proximity to trauma, confronting and processing it. I do think one's proximity to distress affects the syntax of one's work. For me, there's an early imprint of language and abruption. Being raised around revolutionaries, not just thinkers (them too) but people who were armed and getting arrested and cops were breaking into our houses and people were dying and getting shot—it was heavy. And there was a rhetoric around revolution and change that was constant. "This is what is righteous. This is what we are fighting for, this is the goal." And then you grow up out of that and realize some of those movements failed and part of your association with the actions is the rhetoric, the language of it. You reflect and you internalize an understanding that something is not totally effective in the language and actions, maybe in language itself. It can let you down. Some of us gravitated toward poetics, to images, gestures, sounds, the body, punk rock to play with the power of communicating.

TD: I want my work to be more like a mirror or a device in which people can make their own changes within themselves. That's a more revolutionary position because it produces a myriad of experiences instead of all one collective experience, which is a problem with the rhetoric of revolutionary dialogue, you know?

SK: Yes.

TD: What you were saying about your characters in the new film and art sounds almost related to the ritualistic. In traditional ritual, there would be a clown, a character who, through comedy—and Brecht made me think of this—elicits self-reflection. Mirroring devices in the work allow comedy to become abject, and that's what can actually promote real change in the art or reading experience. The grotesquerie is not about shock value but rather about creating a clowning space or mimicry that can be disgusting, but the trauma is mediated by humor or moments of uncertainty or that uncanniness that you were talking about. Those are all methods to abstract the narrative. And in that, maybe abstraction and abjection are pretty close.

SK: They're very close, and this idea of fluidity, and not literally, but then also yes, because like you said, there is Kristeva and the actual fluids. She talks about blood and pus and her own personal disgust with the skin of milk. She talks about it touching the lips, and how her organs quiver and her groin churns and she has all these gross-out sensations throughout the body as the milk

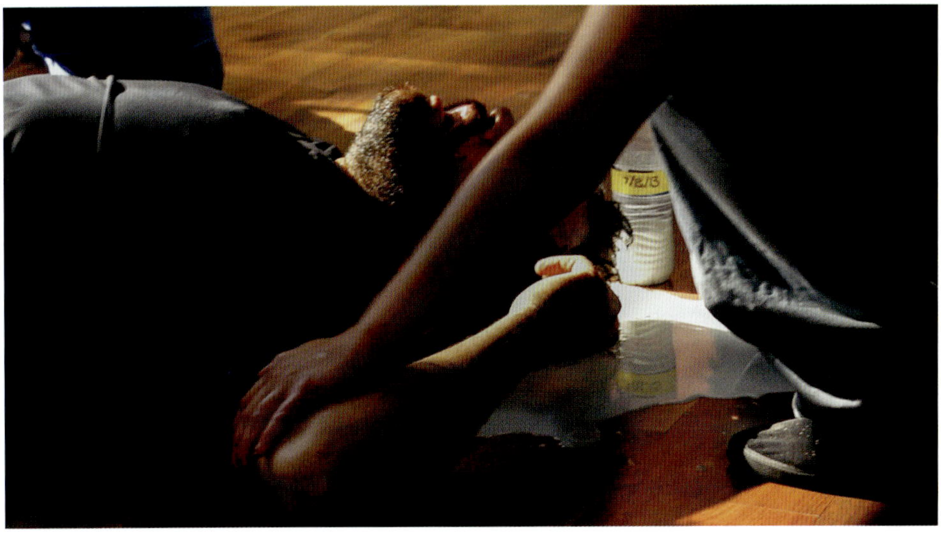

FIGURE 14.3
Stanya Kahn, *Don't Go Back To Sleep*, 2014. HD video with sound; 74 minutes. Courtesy of the artist and Susanne Vielmetter Los Angeles Projects.

touches her lips. Coincidentally, milk and blood are featured heavily in my new film we've been discussing (fig. 14.3).

TD: Oh, that's right, there is milk in there.

SK: And there's improvisation, the ultimate flow of the unknown, and I use it to build types of narrative. And abstraction and abjection really come together in this process I think. Kristeva's definition of the abject includes something that disturbs identity or disturbs systems and order, right? The abject cannot be ordered or systematized, so I thought the practice of improvisation in relationship to the more conventional modes that civilized life is striving for, like control, foresight, planning, mapping, contracts, agreements. All those things are useful, but to improvise is to threaten that system a bit. I've been practicing improvisation for twenty years. It's not just like, "Oh, I'm just making shit up right now." It is, but that comes from a practice of building and developing sensory techniques for tapping into stored information, shaping it as it comes out. There's no such thing as being entirely thorough. We can't do it.

TD: Flow is an abject action then, right? It abstracts structures of communication, the way information is conveyed. Bataille's idea of formlessness echoes what you're talking about. It's not a free-for-all. This kind of flow is triggering wild surrealism or subconsciousness through shape and control—using techniques and systems. Formlessness is a system.

SK: Right, and working with film or video, you actually are fully committing to a system in the end. In the end there's a closure. It's not a live performance or experience that can change every time. It will have an end and be rendered and mastered and output. I really like that dialectic of trying to source from uncontrolled spaces and states of being, to braid those with preconceived strands, into something that becomes a system—which the viewer then brings meaning to as well. My texts aren't cohered by one trajectory of story, and I shoot in small chunks with editing in between. I don't know thoroughly what's going to happen in each shooting scenario or in the piece as a whole. But I have visions, plans, and convictions. Plus impulses.

TD: Oh, I didn't know you were editing in progress.

SK: Yeah. Always. The work is alive as it's going. I'm never executing a preconceived screenplay. And this flow is inevitably in the editing process too. I get to respond in the moment to how one thing sits against another. Not to say that it's all just pure intuitive reactionary making. It's also thinking; it becomes another kind of writing. All of those stages of process become flow that is in some ways unregulated in relationship to convention.

TD: Yeah, because there's no overall arc. Gordon Lish, in literary theory, coined this term *consecution*. One's not thinking of the overall story content but rather, editing each sentence as you go to direct you to the next.

SK: That makes sense. But for me, there's a meta, a larger aggregate form hovering. While the fractured ways of working are about being more in the moment, they offer views into a possible bigger picture. They reflect me back outward as well. I think that's related to my broader interest as an artist and person: if there is no immediacy and lived experience inside a particular code or set of meanings that a person's making in the world, then it's not grounded in anything for me. So whether we're talking about revolution or having a politic or process, the involvement of being present in a moment necessitates the body and its information being involved; that's always the grounding point. I let that show me what the bigger picture might be. Because I do want a bigger picture. It just might not look like a traditional big picture.

TD: I associate these mirroring elements with abstract film and video: the history of experimental psychedelic film—Oskar Fischinger, Jordan Belson, Bruce Connor, Harry Smith, Ira Cohen, their contemporary lineage . . . symbolic imagery that triggers archetypes. What you're saying about tapping into something larger feels related but different. They used symbolic imagery consciously—Harry Smith's alchemical imagery, for example.

SK: Harry Smith is a great example of that process, incorporating micro and macro into constructed meaning. I joked to someone last week that I may have just made an hour-and-a-half-long trailer. *(Laughter.)* I've got so much montage in this film and I wondered, what does that mean? I like to wonder if I can come up with some new structure that doesn't have a name. Something that combines so many unknowns. For example, I'm editing this long-form video using short-form techniques. What kind of experience is possible for the viewer in an extended experience of short-form techniques?

TD: New meaning gets made, and that's abstraction, the history of abstract language. It's funny that it's referred to as a language, but when I was at Yale doing visits last week, the painters I was visiting were saying, "Oh, this is in the language of abstraction." And I was like, "Oh, really?" But I guess it's a symbolic language, right? The symbols conjure up emotion or a sensibility or a read—

SK: That you can't control.

TD: Yeah.

SK: And that's the exciting part: you can't name it in relationship to the eye, to the self. I love when Kristeva says that the person faced with the abject is literally beside herself like another self. I read it to mean that you become partially disembodied. Sitting next to a corpse, you are shocked into facing your own end, and you can't name the abject thing; you can't pin down the response feelings. So you literally split. Maybe that relates to my willingness to throw props, words, images, actions, sounds into the works that are not easily metabolized by story or the traditional process. Which is counter to the convention that says you shouldn't include anything in your film that doesn't drive it forward, right?

TD: Right.

SK: I have a ton of things that could literally just slow it down to almost a standstill. *(Laughs.)* Sometimes I'm thinking, "Well, what if we just stop right here and open up another can of worms?"

TD: Yeah, exactly!

SK: But like with sex, it sets up this assumption, like the Grand Narrative—this expectation that there's a main thing that's coming, the main thing is *going* to happen. And to apply that kind of notion to the filmic, to the pleasures in filmic time and space—well, what are some of those tropes? It's like montage: "Ooh yeah, we love it when you make it seem like time is passing really fast and we get a bunch of information quickly so we can move to the next thing on our journey toward the *main* thing! Yeah! I'm gonna finally get the thing!"

TD: It's like a heroic quest. The picaresque.

SK: I have no heroic quest, except all of these little small quests and all the information that you need about the piece happens maybe seventeen times throughout it in different ways, cumulatively. And that's why I thought, "What if it's like a big long trailer?" What if we just do "foreplay" and never do It, then what are we doing? Some extended connecting that doesn't need a goal.

TD: It doesn't.

SK: It is what it is. Now of course, my work does have a goal. And trailers really work as selling agents, positioning the viewer as consumer. And that's the opposite of what I'm doing. On a larger level too, if you turn the project inside out: I invited nonactors who didn't know each other to be the people in this recent film [*Don't Go Back to Sleep* (2014)] (figs. 14.2 and 14.3). I put them into scenarios in which they had to speak as themselves but in contrived situations. They offer information and are in effect also creating the story as we go.

TD: In psychedelics, I learned to take the pressure off the destination. That's how I would define the word *psychedelic*. The pressure is off the productivity of an end result.

SK: "Let's not go anywhere. Let's just stay right here on the couch." *(Said in a spacey voice with laughing.)*

TD: That was a good lesson that came from trying those things.

SK: And if you bring material from the place where you had no control—your subconscious—into your conscious, controlled waking space as a maker and handle it like a material, you're making a thing you couldn't have made without the two spaces.

TD: I think that's what monsters are though: You give that feeling a face and some fur and some fangs. To rework the aesthetics comedically, or to make a new aesthetic.

SK: And those things actually become necessary if you think about it from a feminist perspective.

TD: Yeah.

SK: We have to have other material to work with as women, other than what's there or what's given or what's expected—otherwise uh-oh, right? We have to pull from *every* place. As a girl child in this culture, you grow accustomed to being resourceful because you learn so quickly, so young, that not only will you not have access to that which men and boys seem to have but also you won't be heard. Not only will your body be invaded, your language might seem garbled. You think you're speaking really clearly but it's not understood or it's not heard or you're told it's of no importance and you go, "Oh well, that didn't work." It starts early on, this gleaning. I really like Donna Haraway's idea of monstrous women, creatures constructed from multiple and various parts.[2]

TD: I do too.

SK: She embraces the cyborg, saying the idea of "woman" has been so reconstructed and overdetermined we are not whole or complete and never were. Instead of despairing in this postmodern, Frankensteinian position, Haraway embraces the monstrous power.

TD: Yeah, I think that's how montage really works here, as a structural form.

SK: In *A Thousand Plateaus,* Deleuze and Guattari talk about the ways an activity can reach a "pitch of intensity,"[3] that a compilation of actions and interactions can seem to be leading toward a climax but there's no climax or dissipation, just a level of intensity that can be reached. I don't think intensity here has to mean freneticism. And they describe how this sustaining intensity can make a sort of imprint that can then be used in other activities, creating a network of intensities, connected by roots—rhizomes. Brian Massumi, who translated that book, talks about the body and affect in his own work, and I related so much to his thinking in terms of how I use improvisation, responding in the moment. He addresses the walking-is-controlled-falling idea as a way to talk about potential for reflection and volition in the moment of falling and catching oneself.[4] I like that as a metaphor for being out of control and having a moment to reflect or to catch oneself from falling completely out of control. Maybe in the moment of catching you reflect unconsciously and consciously simultaneously.

TD: That's when involuntary actions kick in?

SK: Exactly.

TD: We still have survival instincts, but they can be pretty hard to trigger. You're finding methods to do that?

SK: I'm trying to put people and myself in situations in which an automatic response is inevitable. Not only is it full of affective energy, but the process offers up new information that I couldn't have preconceived.

TD: Do you think technique-wise that's why you've been moving towards using different kinds of cameras?

SK: Yeah, exploring the relationship between doing and looking, action and regarding. How framing and point of view can bring the body of the performer, maker, and viewer into closer proximity to instigate flows of both empathy and productive alienation. Some of this is happening in the longer film *Don't Go Back to Sleep,* but more explicitly in the as-yet-unfinished *Stand in the Stream* (fig. 14.4). The title comes from a Brecht-Weill lyric: *(singing)* "Don't try to hold on to the wave that's breaking against your foot. / So long as you stand in the stream / fresh waves will always keep breaking against it."

TD: Cool.

SK: There are multiple lenses, screens, and windows in that piece. In *Speed and Politics* Paul Virilio talks about windows in cinema, that the original screen was a window.[5] And our eyes have developed retinal responses to viewing through windows and of course to frame rates. In *Stand in the Stream* I'm recording a lot of screens, live webcam interactions, etcetera, and in many ways this piece is much more about being a watcher, regarding—

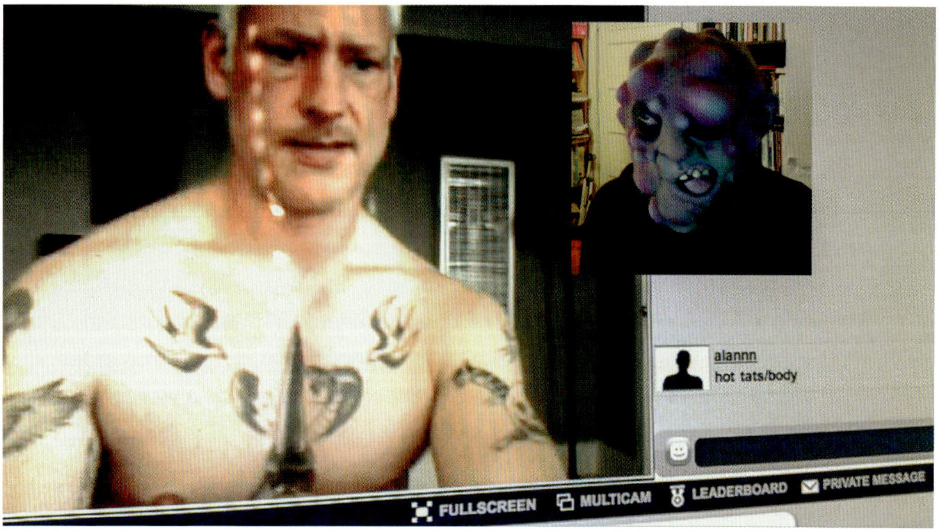

FIGURE 14.4
Stanya Kahn, *Stand in the Stream,* work in progress. HD video with sound. Courtesy of the artist.

TD: Laura Mulvey!

SK: Yes! And Mulvey and Kristeva seem to meet in the ways they talk about objecthood and in watching. Laura Mulvey talks a lot about the woman in traditional cinema as the object of desire who doesn't have language or land.[6] She is there for us to look at. It's the male figure who has mastery over the frame and also the physical space. He has terrain that's his, and he can name it and he can speak. In my work I speak and I command the language, and I have terrain. I'm moving through landscapes and multiple locations. I never thought about it consciously, and when Harry and I were working together, we didn't talk about Laura Mulvey, but when I reread Mulvey I think, "Oh yeah, I went and got some land and some language." Then I also obscured my body so I couldn't exactly be desired in a recognizable fashion. Like co-opting the space of the male lead to try on his brawn, his power. I'm more interested in that than in repeating tropes of the straight, hot, femme protagonist. I'm bored with that. What if that weird sort of nongendered protagonist could also generate its own hotness. And Mulvey points out that while the lead has land and voice, he doesn't always have information. She points out how in Hitchcock, the audience knows what's coming before the characters do (fig. 14.5).

TD: That's what I like about Dario Argento.

SK: Yeah, but it's the opposite in my work. I always withhold the information, the source of danger.

TD: You often don't show the source of the trauma or what happened to the protagonist.

SK: Yeah. I really like when Kristeva says, "The abject is the thing that can't be assimilated." She invokes the corpse. I'm bringing the corpse in. In *Don't Go Back to Sleep* three people die, and their dead bodies are present; they're in the room. The unassimilable, the impossible, a radical presence. I hope I'm wielding the corpse not to scare the viewers or to make them sad, but to bring in the presence of this figurative limit. Maybe the constant presence of the limit reminds us that we have to take action to survive. Does that make sense?

TD: That makes perfect sense, and it's such a natural progression for your work to go there. There's a multidirectional finality to it, like the labyrinth with different roots of intensity. A finality implied in the corpse on first glance, but then it's subverted because once you cut the corpse open, there are even more operations in your new film. It's not about shock or disgust, and the grotesque is just one small facet of it. Recently I watched Brakhage's *Pittsburg Trilogy*—you know, the third one with all the autopsies? It's really intense but so abstracted and beautiful. So much red, and I love how he abstracts figuration. The autopsies become color and shape, materials.

SK: Yeah, cadavers! And also I'm thinking about this obsession with the undead and the zombie state. It's really big again, which is funny. The cadaver is still clomping around. *(Laughter.)* Talk about abject in your face! "Face it! I'm here! I'm here to make you face it!" But the zombie itself can't actually incorporate its own limit. It's really hard to kill a zombie. "Why aren't you dead? Why are you still walking around?" So much unfinished business. One night I was watching *Omega Man* with Mike Kelley; he'd never seen it despite his having a huge collection of zombie movies, so I brought it over. And he said, "See, the zombies are the counter culture; the zombies are the hipsters! Because you can never truly be hip—the system will coopt it—so they're forever caught in between." He talked through the whole movie, which was cracking me up. And it was an incredible stream of erudite observations, quick and on point. He was the most astute viewer I've ever watched movies with, ever.

TD: That's huge. We could probably talk for a really long time about that.

SK: Yeah. Talk about unfinished business and a tremendous loss. Talk about being "beside oneself" with grief. Unspeakable.

(PAUSE.)

SK: *(Continuing.)* In *Omega Man,* the zombies are like a radical political cult: they're fighting the power but they're also being corrupted by their own power. And like Mike was insinuating, you can't quite form a rhetoric that doesn't become reified in a stuck totalitarian rhetoric. In other words, how can you establish a system of liberation? It's sort of oxymoronic. We are in constant

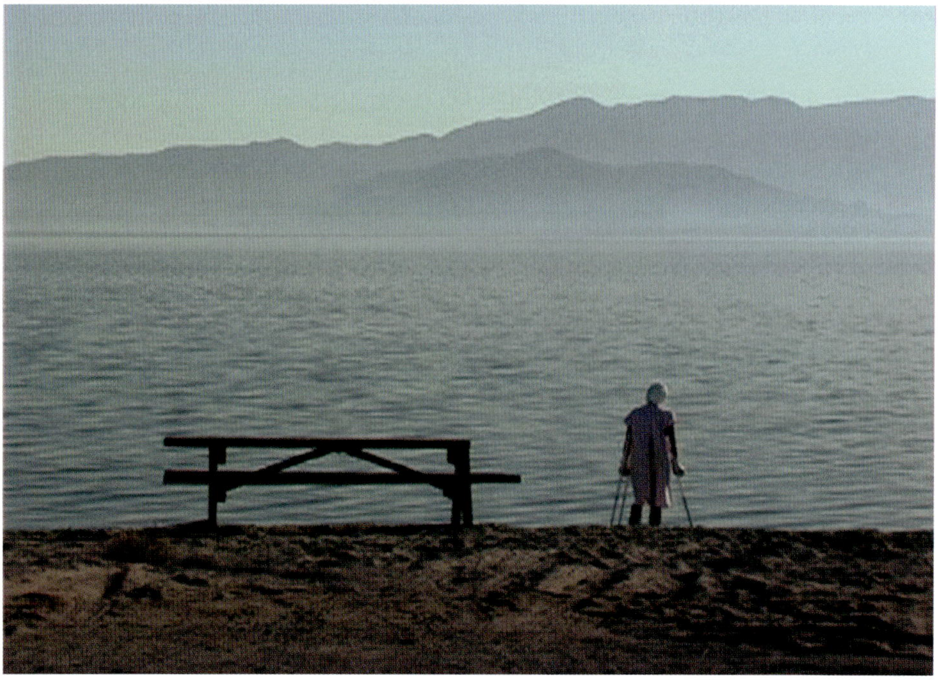

FIGURE 14.5
Stanya Kahn, *It's Cool, I'm Good,* 2010. SD video with 5.1 surround sound; 35 minutes, 20 seconds. Courtesy of the artist and Susanne Vielmetter Los Angeles Projects.

pursuit to articulate a correct position, knowing that there are too many elements, too many locations in which power plays out problematically in our world to make an all-encompassing, defined stance about which way to go. So I've sort of chosen this path to play with rhetoric. I think that's another reason why the corpse shows up so much.

TD: I always thought you were reversing the Mulvey thing about the observer and the observed. Reversing the idea of the gaze, taking charge of the gaze. Giving the volition to the person in front of the camera. And giving voice to the person behind the camera.

SK: The motivated camera. That was something that Harry and I talked a lot about in those earlier works: to acknowledge the agency and gaze that the camera carries. I really like the way that Mulvey talks about visual pleasure in narrative cinema, bringing it back to the Lacanian mirror stage: the baby needing to look at itself in the mirror, and the image in the mirror appearing to be more adept and able-bodied than the baby experiences its own body to be. It's this early experience of projection. And cinema also affords this pleasure to the viewer by projecting on these able-bodied, hot, powerful people on the screen.

TD: Right, vicarious experience. That's why one can come out of a film viewing feeling super-aroused.

SK: Yeah. And Mulvey talks about the image of a woman in cinema as not only the object of desire, but she also represents possible castration because she doesn't have a penis.

TD: I love that. I mean the idea, not castration . . .

SK: *(Laughs.)* So, according to Mulvey, the male has two avenues of escape from this castration anxiety: Fetishistic scopophilia—to build up the physical beauty of the object to the point where it's just totally satisfying in and of itself as an object, fetishized. Or—and this is what is interesting about narrative—to punish that guilty object, so we hurt the female over and over again. She's guilty of possibly castrating us, so we're going to punish her. We know that one—yawn. Regarding the more sadistic, punishing option, Mulvey makes this interesting point about narrative: "This sadistic side fits in well with narrative. Sadism demands a story, depends on making something happen, forcing a change in another person, a battle of will and strength, victory/defeat, all occurring in a linear time, with a beginning and an end."[7]

TD: That's totally what *doesn't* interest me about those types of sexual dynamics. Those power struggles are didactic. Are these the only two options? There's a dualism in that, yet there's a lot of possibility out there. Do you know Barbara Creed's *The Monstrous Feminine?*[8] It riffs on the Mulvey. There's a great chapter about vagina dentata in movies like *Alien* with Sigourney Weaver. Creed discusses a new mode in cinema that offered the woman protagonist a different heroic, co-opting the heroic role outside of sexualization.

SK: The movie *Teeth!* directed by Lichtenstein's grandson, weird. Pasolini, John Waters, Lizzie Borden, Yvonne Rainier, Trinh T. Minh-ha—there have been so many filmmakers who offer alternatives. Too many to list here, which is good. But because cinema is so powerful and we're all suckled on it from a young age, I think that one of the consequences of patriarchy is that we've internalized those dynamics. And now people with their webcams are gazing at themselves while they're making a video of it. There's a whole generation of people growing up watching themselves on screen. I'm curious about the potentials and pitfalls of this.

TD: Oh, like the Basic Bitch boy on YouTube! I clicked on him yesterday. That kid is cute.

SK: Amazing. Adorable. These kids, they become hosts, announcers. There's maybe some power in that. Then there's "hauling" videos in which cute girls display their recent purchases: a crazy weird combo of subjects/objects showing objects/commodities.

TD: It's more than narcissism, for sure.

SK: It is more. I'm divided. There are some artists who are using the webcam eye. I think there's still a problematic with the girl framing herself, gazing at herself to be gazed at again. Does it change the dynamic? I want a change. It's another round of questioning that arose with women using their bodies in early performance art, but now an entirely different historical context. If the pretty girl is still so easily commodifiable, we have to think about to whom and how it's being framed and sold. I made a drawing of a lady zombie and she's missing a boob and she's talking on the phone about how her boob came off in this guy's hand, saying, "He said, 'I like it when you fall apart baby. It makes me feel like I can take care of you.'"

TD: The roles returning to their original—

SK: How horrifying for a woman in our culture, right? That someone squeezes your tit and it comes off? *(Laughs.)*

TD: It's like castration anxiety in reverse.

SK: Abjection relates to the objectification of women, commodities, market, and popular forms of culture and what's considered inside and outside. Counter cultures function to transgress, to question the norm. As the status quo continues to co-opt scary or radical things and then make them palatable for mass consumption, people have to keep finding ways to step outside. Film/video is not market friendly: it's not object based; people have to spend time with it. Maybe experiments in time-based media are innately abject because they exist in an in-between state. They're not objects or pictures or even objects in the sense of the traditional container of the cinema.

TD: This parallels literature too. In narrative, people want linearity because it produces legibility.

SK: I'm OK with existing both as a person and an artist outside of whatever the center is, and if that means always being more a part of an experimental, smaller community of makers, that's OK.

TD: It's cool, you know, it's fine.

NOTES

1. Julia Kristeva, *Powers of Horror: An Essay on Abjection* (New York: Columbia University Press, 1982).

2. Donna Haraway, *Simians, Cyborgs and Women: A Reinvention of Nature* (New York: Routledge, 1990).

3. Brian Massumi, translator's foreword, in Gilles Deleuze and Feliz Guattari, *A Thousand Plateaus* (Minneapolis: University of Minnesota Press, 1978), xiv.

4. Brian Massumi, "Navigating Movements," interview, in *Hope: New Philosophies for Change*, ed. Mary Zournazi (New York: Routledge / London: Lawrence and Wishart / Sydney: Pluto Press, 2002–2003), 210–42.

5. Paul Virilio, *Speed and Politics* (Los Angeles: Semiotext(e), 2006). See also Paul Virilio, "Speed-Space," interview with Chris Dercon, trans. D. Miller, *Impulse* 12, no. 4 (1986): 35–39.

6. Laura Mulvey, "Visual Pleasure and Narrative Cinema," *Screen* 16, no. 3 (Autumn 1975): 6–18.

7. Laura Mulvey, "Visual Pleasure and Narrative Cinema," 14.

8. Barbara Creed, *The Monstrous-Feminine: Film, Feminism, Psychoanalysis* (New York: Routledge, 1993).

15

SINE QUA SON

Considering the Sine Wave Tone in Electronic Art

Philip Brophy

In the long gone nights of broadcast television, the transmitted signal would be terminated around midnight. The home television set would keep receiving, tuned in as it was to the chosen channel's frequency, but the broadcasting station needed to notify the home audience that its shows were over for the night. An announcement might be made; a title or graphics card would be positioned in front of the studio camera; maybe a short collage of scenery culled from the local community would be played. But ultimately, things had to end. So when all the goodbyes were over, the medium itself declared it was going to sleep. A test-pattern chart would fill the screen, accompanied by a softly numbing, high-pitched whine.

Nowadays, the television shutdown is a historical figure, an audiovisual icon of how television declared its status as a medium by emptying itself of any message. The reason for using the tone was simple: the 10 kHz sine wave tone was used for calibrating audio transmission and sound recording. Technicians would feed the signal into VU meters to check that the audio signal flow was stable, continual, and at a prescribed level. What the home audience saw and heard way back then was how the medium was technologically defined through the act of monitoring. When the test pattern's dense lines, checkerboards and crosshair rings were sharp, and when the VU meters held steady at 0 dB, the medium was primed. This is how things went from the '50s well into the '70s (fig. 15.1).

But since then, variants of the uninterrupted sine wave tone have taken on multifarious meanings. In April 2012, NHK television news in Tokyo documented the makeshift memorials conducted across East Japan, commemorating one month to the minute

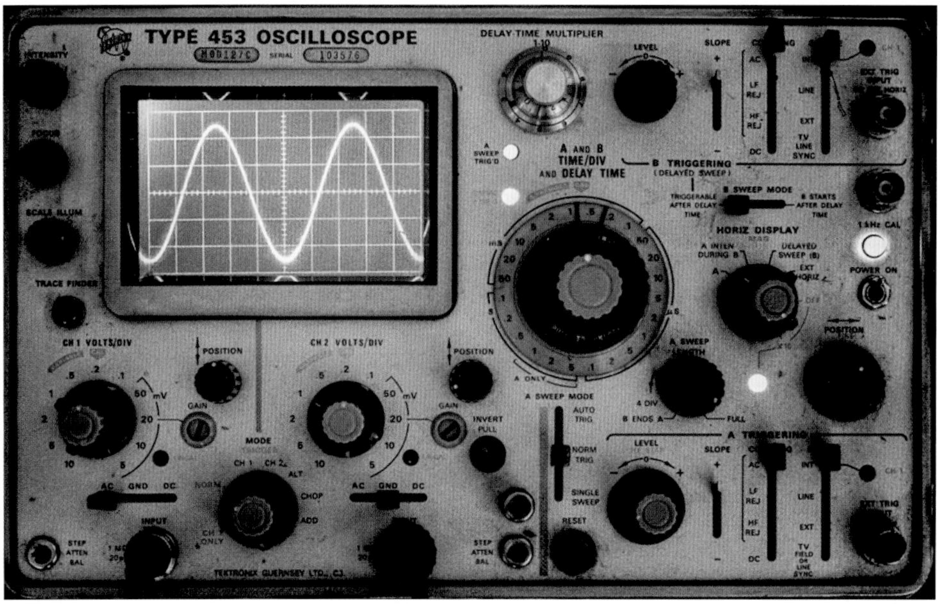

FIGURE 15.1
Stan Hua, *1950s oscilloscope showing a sine wave,* 2006. Digital photograph. Courtesy of Stan Hua via flickr / public domain.

since the Great East Tohoku Earthquake and Tsunami at 2:46 P.M. on March 11. For nearly two full minutes, only a fixed-pitch droning siren was audible—like an old air-raid siren but higher in pitch; more resonant and full-bodied than a single pure sine wave tone, yet reminiscent of its sonic reduction. Groups large and small encircled small clearings; couples and solitary figures huddled in the midst of unfathomable debris. The scenography was always the same: it resembled a million abstract sculptural installations mulched into a flattened forest of gray muddied mess. These fixed-tripod shots of unbearable stillness were captured from various locations along the ravished coastline, whose myriad small ports and seaside fishing and farming communities were decimated by the tsunami's twelve-hour inland surge. Superimposed titles named each location. Everyone stood head bowed in one direction. No one moved or spoke. And each location had the same siren blaring—amazingly holding a unified precise pitch.

Over sixty years after television commenced in Japan at the tail end of the American Occupation, the broadcasting of a sustained tone with neither music, dialogue, or atmosphere communicates a very different kind of "nothingness." The post–3/11 televisual memorial melds the electronic with the acoustic, portraying sites of remembrance while recording the live "performance" of amplified electronically mediated sound. It's a new audiovisual moment but also an old one. Temple bells in Japan do not mark clock or even social time as do European church bells but instead create a moment wherein

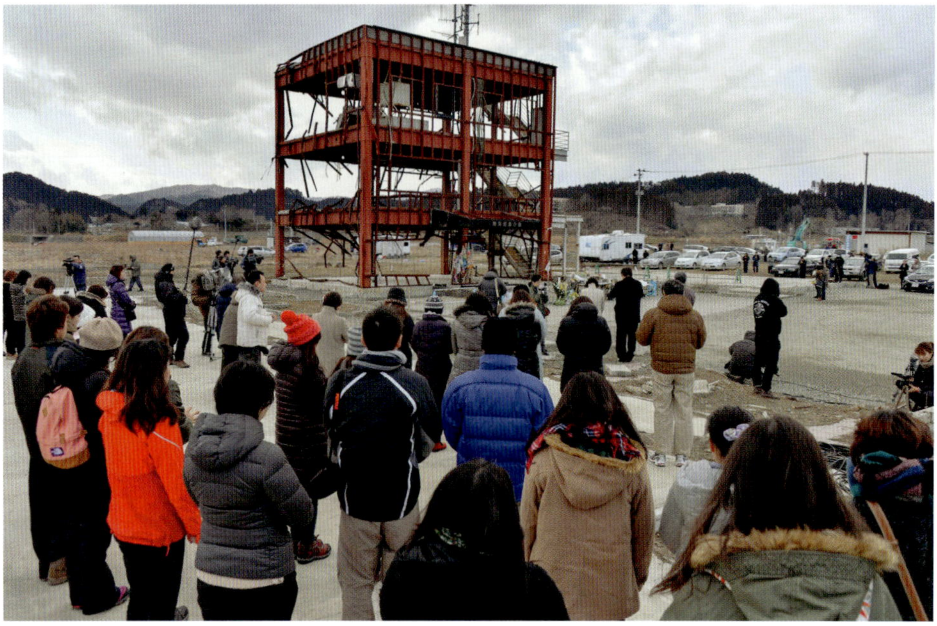

FIGURE 15.2
On the third anniversary of the Great East Japan Earthquake, people pray for the victims of the tsunami at the former Disaster Prevention Center in Minamisanriku, Miyagi, Japan, March 11, 2011. Digital photograph, *Asahi Shimbun* (Japan Commemorates 3rd Anniversary of Great East Japan Earthquake). Courtesy of Getty Images.

personal time and space is interrupted to mark a shift from event (the "experience" of the sound) to contemplation (the "consciousness" enabled by the sound). The intention is to empty the mind to facilitate consciousness, by abruptly halting all other noise and interference that psychoacoustically batters the social mind day in, day out.

Sirens in Japan thus build upon this type of "consciousness marking" while providing an act of intrusion. Japan's air raid sirens share a history between national military applications and local prefectural operations—from the wailing that signaled the fire bombings of WWII to the notification of approaching storms, tidal waves, and tsunamis. The televised memorials of 3/11 (which would continue to be broadcast each month for a whole year, and now appear at least annually) are part of this aural continuum (fig. 15.2). For the oldest generation, these contemporary extended tones emitted into the public sphere could recall the Great Kanto Earthquake of 1923. For the next generation, the Allied Forces' firebombings of WWII. For a current generation, those sirens mostly symbolize acknowledgment of the over 18,000 people who died or were never found following the creeping tsunami as it flooded whole districts within hours. Most importantly, *image* is not the carrier of information here. All representational imagery was rendered abstract by the tsunami (effectively, the land was rendered unrecogniz-

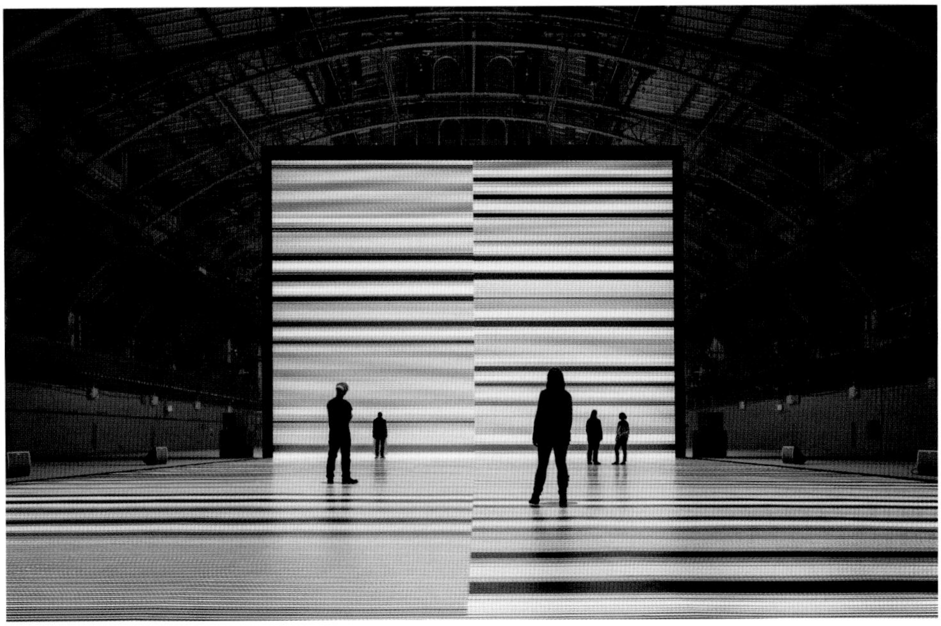

FIGURE 15.3
Ryoji Ikeda, *test pattern [enhanced version]*, 2011. Audiovisual installation; variable length. © Ryoji Ikeda. Photograph © James Ewing, courtesy of Park Avenue Armory and Forma.

able). Rather, *sound* embodies all that was lost and destroyed, all that is no longer present and now invisible.

While people across Japan stood silently to observe the deep density of nothingness augured by the tsunami, similarly large crowds gathered in disconnected pockets within the cavernous Park Avenue Armory in New York in June that same year. They stood still, squatted, laid prone, wandered slowly, spun deliriously; fixated by massive wall and floor projections of brilliant black-and-white stripes that ceaselessly changed thickness and vertically scrolled in a dizzying display of abstract lenticular illusion. Accompanying this: an orchestrated onslaught or what sounds like a billion sine wave tones of frequencies and pulsations hyper-low and hyper-high, but all fiercely declaring an aesthetic of nothingness by virtue of their impressive antimusicality and ascetic aural characteristics. This is Ryoji Ikeda's *test pattern [enhanced version]* (2011) (fig. 15.3), part of an ongoing series of installations commenced in 2008). Ikeda's audiovisual installations over the last decade have set the benchmark for how impressive screen-based video art can be when extrapolated to realize a digital actuality from what was previously only an analog potentiality.

Yet a simple way of describing Ikeda's undeniably stunning work is as an echo of the "end point transmission" of television's originating broadcast format, which utilized the test-pattern graphic with the sine wave test tone. Indeed, many people perceive Ikeda's voluminous iterations of black-and-white stroboscopic glitch-and-wave hi-def projected onslaughts as a postmodern summation of Video Art's medium-specific ontology. They accordingly presume that the works' calculated impression of all the televisions in the world playing within a single spatiotemporal screen zone is a super-logical outcome of Video Art's teleological desire to define itself through synesthetic synchrony. On the one hand, it makes sense: if so much Video Art is about defining itself as medium, form, and even material, any "meta," "hyper," or "super" presentation of the medium will appear to be a crescendo of self-reflexive metonymy. On the other hand, such a simplistic exponential upward curve through history portrays Video Art as yet another heroic endeavor that inevitably results in the most grandiose displays at the expense of any grandiloquent criticality. So before teasing out precisely what is entailed in the shift from analog potential to digital actualization—which will be uncovered as a type of abstraction of audiovision itself—it will be productive to trace the rhizomatic morphology of how the sine wave tone developed to occupy both the "density of nothing" announced by Japan's 3/11 sirens, and the "infinity horizon" heralded by Ikeda's data-saturated screens.

· · ·

From sirens to tones to waves to pulses, the sine wave has sailed, danced, wafted, and skirted across two parallel histories: one entailing applications and procedures in technological broadcast and reproduction, the other covering explorations and modifications in modernist art and production. The latter is wholly dependent on the former, yet the origins of sirens lie in musical instrument applications. Late-eighteenth-century sirens commence as pneumatic tubes with stopcocks incorporated into pipe organ design. Indeed, a siren is essentially an organ with one note, engaged in being either on or off and incapable of controlled modulation or expressivity. While organs of pipe and reed variety are an early pre-Industrial construction of how the musical can be rendered machinic—sustaining pure tone for inhuman durations without discernible breathing or cycling—the siren is an uncannily prescient device that effects an audible "demusicalization" by sounding like an organ while absenting the musician from its sounding. Twentieth-century music explored a small universe of demusicalized strategies and unmusical notions, and it is not surprising that an early work like Edgar Varèse's *Ionisation* (1929–1931) incorporates a hand-cranked siren as a scored instrument.

As the siren was progressively realized to be a contra-musical, unhuman device, its dissonant, noisy, interrupting blasts of sound perfectly matched its intended function during wars and catastrophes. Unlike bells, sirens have no clear connection to the Church's mobilization of its congregation. Bells could equally signal approaching danger, the commencement of mass, and the celebration of a wedding. Sirens just meant danger. The imperative of its voice characterizes noise not as a specific type of sound (for sirens don't actually "sound noisy') but as a violent disruption of normal everyday enterprise, so that everyone pays attention and seeks the reason for a siren's announcement. The siren never says anything specific, except that a situation has developed where one needs to be informed of something specific. It signals threat without stating its source or reason.

At the start of the twentieth century, when electronic sound was first being discovered, explored, and categorized to service audible demonstrations of mathematical phenomena, the notion—and advent—of a pure, nonmusical, uninterruptible tone enabled two phenomenal observations. To the scientific ear, the strangely inhuman purity of the sine wave tone was consonant with the mathematical "beauty" of the sinusoid mathematical curve (the sweeping and swooping repeated pattern that graphically describes a precise and repeatable oscillation). It was as though such clarity of unfiltered tone was the music of mathematical spheres, not organic worldly ones. To the musical ear, the sine wave tone sparked a consciousness of how sound could exist beyond or at least divorced of human instigation. Its infinitely pregnant sustain psychoacoustically demonstrated how sound (and hence, music) could be generated for musical effect despite it bearing no musical means. While Luigi Russolo's infamous *intonarumori* WWI-era noisemaking boxes were brutish and naïve wooden toys designed to shout their status as noise in a sociological sense, post-WWII electronic music exploited noise in a cosmological sense by employing predesigned apparati from acoustic and electrical engineering to expand one's musical consciousness. The peculiar anacoustic immaterial qualities of frequency oscillators, tone generators, electronic filters, and envelope shapers grant electronic music its oft-cited "otherworldly" character—which considered more carefully indicates electronic music's propensity to absent human presence in the means of its production.

But the truly distinctive feature of the sine wave tone (arguably the sonic DNA in formulating electronic music) is not its sound per se. Counter to just about any other sound in the world, the sine wave tone is the sonic realization of a graphical visual display. It requires no imagined synesthetic corollary because its sonority is the outcome of its visuality, and its visuality is the outcome of its mathematical determination. For example, the sound of a flute, a seagull, or a baby laughing result from the pre-existence of their physical manifestation. Conversely, the sounding of a sine wave tone results from a mathematical computation; being a visualized theorem, its sound is not dependent on the physical, acoustical world. Thus considered, the sine wave tone's graphing is the prime means of bringing it into existence and defining its character. This constitutes the unique ontology of the sine wave tone, which further accounts for how readily it was incorporated into the metalinguistic medium-defining interests of the electronic arts.

Some comments on the procedural operations of electronic music can clarify this. Analog electronic music is also known as reductive synthesis. This is because the means of arriving at a sine wave tone was through filtering, so that all harmonics and overtones would be removed from a tone generator. The first phase of sound generation in synthesis is "white noise," which is the simultaneous generation of all frequencies within a broad range (something akin to slamming one's arms across a piano keyboard to produce a dense tonal cluster). The arrival at a set frequency oscillation from the "white noise" spectrum is akin to a prism filtering out white light to specify a color. Thus, all consequent operations in analog synthesis entail modes of reducing, parsing, filtering, and distilling an aspect of sound from a cluster of sonic attributes. For the electronic music composer of the postwar ethos, these operations (tagged "realizations') constituted a modernist variant on the orchestral composer who made creative decisions and intuitively deduced aesthetic outcomes to express artistic intentions. But more than being a McLuhanesque media-savvy take on romantic aspirations, electronic music's grappling with the undertow of unfiltered noise effected a paradoxical inhuman purity. Qualified by mathematical theorem, the sine wave tone fostered a sono-musical self-referentiality that facilitated abstract/nonmusical explorations of composed sound. Twisting the Latin, we could say that the sine wave tone became *sine qua son:* sound with only itself.

These historical factors that shaped early experiments in electronic synthesis and the developing artistry of electronic music contribute to a peculiar yet overlooked semiotics of the sine wave tone. Its inhuman purity, unworldly presence, anacoustic nature, unmusical status, and modernist appeal aggregate a "nothingness," or emptying of content. Its consequent aura implies it to be bereft of signification, communication, and connotation—short of announcing unqualified urgency through an imperative act of social interruption. Crucially, the repertoire of modernist-attuned acts of sonic art concur in treating the sine wave tone this way. Hence, Ikeda's *test pattern* series induces a strangely passive-aggressive sensation of voluminously and impressively declaring nothing, while blaring audio and blasting black-and-white patterns and shapes. As "contemporary" as Ikeda's work is often heralded, it fundamentally echoes John Cage's similarly passive-aggressive para-Zen retort to premodern art sensibilities by declaring in his 1949 essay-cum-performance *Nothing:* "I have nothing to say and I am saying it."

· · ·

Nam June Paik's *Homage à John Cage* (1959) is a sound collage typical of 1950s *musique concrète:* a single-channel monophonic audio collage comprising abrupt contrasts in tone, volume, and character, whereby each successive sound attacks each preceding sound by instantaneously replacing one with the next. It's a brutish Cubist style, here privileging rupture above all else. Paik's piece mostly comprises pre-existing sound sources (records, tape recordings of radio, and maybe even television broadcasts), played at correct and incorrect speeds and directions (the standard X-Y axis of musique concrète's shuttling between too-fast and too-slow, forwards and backwards). While the sourcing and transforming of "concrete" or real-world sounds had been declared a modernist sonic practice by Pierre Schaffer and Pierre Henry a decade earlier, a Cagean aura is foregrounded in Paik's piece, possibly through chance-calculated determinations of the fragments' length as well refuting their referential content. Regardless, the resulting semiotic effect of his audio collage suggests an interdimensional encounter with broadcast audio (radio, TV, vinyl, magnetic tape). Paik's professed core interests lay with the medium of television and how its audiovisuality was pertinent to the electronic era. Consequently, he was a key figure in Video Art who acknowledged the a priori visuality of sound in the electronic realm. *Homage à John Cage* is in one sense an essay on the sound of television as broadcast media, constructing an "imaginary soundtrack" (à la Cage's *Imaginary Landscapes,* 1939–1952) to the random and dissolute changing or "flicking" of channels on a television receiver. The "end transmission" test tone is notably among these audio fragments.

But in another sense, *Homage à John Cage* sounds remarkably like Japanese *kaiju eiga* (monster movie) sci-fi soundtracks from the same period (for example, Ishiro Honda's *Rodan,* 1956; *Chikyu Boeigun* aka *The Mysterians,* 1957; Teruo Ishii's *Kotetsu no Kyojin* serial, released as the films *Atomic Rulers* and *Attack from Space,* both 1957). At the opposite end of the high-art spectrum, these film soundtracks pursued similar techniques with identical electronic componentry to furnish narrative and psychological effects for their own wild, interdimensional scenarios. Unlike their high-art cousins, they channeled the inhuman and immaterial aspects of electronic audio into representational projections of people, aliens, and monsters co-inhabiting a perceivably physical world. This is something the purer abstract endeavors of electronic art never considered (preferring, as they often did, to "say nothing"), presuming that such a context for their work would belittle its greater pursuits. Maybe this is the case ideologically, but not so sonically and semiotically. When "weird" tones signal alien presence, and processed acoustics suggest worldly transformation, such aural effects aptly "sonorize," or audibly visualize, the limits and threshold of humanist representation. More so, the history of electronic audiovisuality of the modernist epoch (leading up to digital applications, to be discussed shortly) is as much defined as it is constrained by an avoidance of semiotic and psychological potentiality in how supposedly inhuman and immaterial sounds might express something succinctly and directly to an open-minded listener.

Karlheinz Stockhausen's *Telemusik* (1966) draws equally upon the legacy of John Cage's philosophical ruminations of sound's immanence in the social, acoustic, and electronic realms and the dedicated research into the industrial, acoustical, and electronic streams of engineering. In this sense, it conforms with how electronic art merges artistic and technological trajectories into a "dual lane" practice. While the bulk of Stockhausen's projects are sited within the WDR Electronic Music Studio of Cologne, *Telemusik* resulted from a commission by NHK in Tokyo to commemorate the fiftieth anniversary of the radio broadcasting station. Not dissimilar to Paik's notion of how sound is encoded and broadcast, *Telemusik* is an essay on similar processes, here influenced by Stockhausen's impressions of Japan. The piece is divided into thirty-two sections, each marked by the strike of a traditional Japanese instrument employed in temple ceremonies (wooden clappers and gourds, metallic cup bells, and larger gongs).

In a modernist electronic comment on traditional acoustic phenomena, Stockhausen's tape-edited markers replicate the acoustic function of bells and other instruments, as cited earlier. It's a clear example of how modernist invention depends on premodern convention. More so, it exemplifies how much modernist self-reflexive, medium-defining electronic art of the twentieth century ends up almost chasing its own ontological tail: in attempting to shape a modern medium, it relied on premodern phenomena.

The content between each of these markers in *Telemusik* is ostensibly a passage of recorded music—much of it from Japan (gagaku traditional court music, Kabuki and Noh theatre music, and various temple ceremonies) but also passages of traditional and folk musics from India, Brazil, Vietnam, China, Hungary, and Africa. Each section of music is manipulated by processing it through electronic devices—mostly ring modulators and parametric filters—so that much of it sounds like streaked clouds of sound randomly caught on a shortwave radio receiver (the means at the time of receiving international radio broadcasts). The semiotic consequence is that the medium feels more present than the message. In Stockhausen's mind, the *tele-* in *Telemusik* symbolizes the nature of radiophonic and televisual broadcast and transmission by bringing the distant closer, as per the Greek etymological meaning of *tele*. Technically, Stockhausen chose passages of "world music" laden with upper or high frequencies. His processing of these sounds induced overtones—a third deeper tone coming from the joining of two higher tones, similar to how one will hear a deeper tone directly in one's ear when subjected to the loud ringing of multiple bells. While *radio* broadcast references *medium* (the electromagnetic radiation of audio in the radio frequency range), *television* broadcast references *space* (the distance between broadcaster and receiver when transmitting audio and vision). Stockhausen's *Telemusik* signposts the complex ways in which the televisual apparatus determined outcomes in electronic music. As we shall see, audiovisuality in electronic art—that is, how sound references its image and how images seek out sonic equivalency—withholds both these ideological origins and the opportunity for transcending them. Specifically, sine wave tones have continued past *Telemusik* into contemporary manifestations of creative and social production, thereby complexifying orthodox modernist ways of ascribing their effects and intentions.

· · ·

Decades after *Telemusik,* Yoshihide Otomo's *Cathode* and *Modulation* (both 1999, and each comprising two numbered iterations) were released on CD (*Cathode,* 1999). The liner notes mention that *Cathode #1* uses "analog techniques from the '50s and '60s." Not surprisingly, it's highly reminiscent of *Telemusik* in tone, gesture, form, and aura, affording the composition a referential base. The title *Cathode* of course points to cathode ray tube (CRT) technology, which was the basis of television monitor design from the mid-'50s until plasma and liquid crystal display (LCD) flat screens were introduced in the mid-'90s. *Modulation* likely refers to many of the processes and effects already discussed here, from ring-modulation distortion to signal modulation for creating aural overtones as well as broadcasting signals. Parsing the modern from the postmodern in these compositions by Otomo is a tricky task. On the one hand, they virtually fetishize a bygone era of tape decks and oscillator dials. The austere events in *Cathode #1* seem to mimic the academic studiousness of Stockhausen and others, while *Cathode #2* is dedicated to Toru Takemitsu—who during the '50s was an originating member of the Jikken Kobo electronic studio in Tokyo, a composer commissioned by NHK, and a colleague of John Cage. On the other hand, *Cathode #1* and *#2* are "image impressions" of the historical experimental milieu as much as they are contemporary sonic explorations, thereby affirming the insistent capacity for the sine wave tone and its related operations to reference modernist history.

Modulation #1 pushes this further and accentuates the contemporaneity of its production more than an evocation of its ancestry. Scored for guitar, *shō,* sampled sine waves, and "silent synthesizer," the piece clashes nylon-string guitar with biting sheets and searing shafts of extremely high, fixed-pitch sine waves interlaced with the *shō*'s piercing reed harmonics. The piece's oppressive yet mannered layering of sinusoidal sonorities pushes *Telemusik*'s privileging of the upper frequency range into a new psychoacoustic dimension. Stockhausen's experience of frequency tones in the analog realm of the '50s and '60s predates the advent of digital synthesis waveform construction and modulation in the '80s and '90s. Thirty-three years after *Telemusik,* Otomo worked with musicians like Sachiko M (sine wave sampling) and Toshimaru Nakamura (no-input mixing desk), sharing a studied evaluation of the "unwanted" frequency range common to the digital domain. These stratospheric frequencies (10kHz and above) simulate a variety of electronic "artefacture" which characterizes much of the domestic and public acoustic realm: the tinnitus whine of television monitors, computer displays, hard drives, air conditioners, fluorescent lighting; the clean yet rupturing beeps and tones of ECG machines, microwave ovens, smoke detector alarms, ATM keypads, cell phones. If Stockhausen sought to bring those distant chimes closer to the listener's aural consciousness, Otomo and his colleagues accept those sounds as now alarmingly proximate. Following modernist rhetoric, works like *Modulation #1* and *#2* push this rampant yet distinctive electro-acoustic ecology into a field for creative musical endeavor predicated on nothingness. Sachiko's sine wave tones generated from sampling "nothing" into her sampler, and Nakamura's squealing feedback produced from sending "nothing" into his mixing desk are clearly part of the continuum of nothingness invoked by the sine wave tone.

Otomo, Sachiko, and Nakamura at this time were also part of a loose movement of Japanese musicians called *Onkyokei* (transliterally, "sound, noise, or echo" plus "group or system"). They individually and collectively investigated the improvisational and compositional virtues of registering this sonic field, specializing in manipulating, performing, and responding to the sonic minutiae rendered apparent by new definitions of "signal" and "noise" in the digital realm (wherein computers, CDs, and MP3s had become ubiquitous means of encoding and disseminating audio). Viewed through a Japanese prism (although most Japanese artists refute any anthropological impulse in their work), *Onkyokei* does resonate with the sculptural art notions of *Mono-ha,* a loose, late-'60s grouping of Japanese artists who explored the "thingness" of objects and environments through acts of voiding artistic identity in order to attune perceptual consciousness to the innate presence, aura, and materiality of the "things" they dealt with (dirt, rock, sand, paper, paint, fiber, etc.). *Onkyokei* could be viewed as an immaterial version of *Mono-ha,* in that the former's "materials" result from the electronic (analog and digital) means of generating and conveying sounds in a way that foregrounds their sonic essence over any artistic rationale of their presence.

Yet that immateriality is sonic: it therefore can be audited as having a unique type of materiality. It would help here to fully explain the aforementioned idea of "artefacture." "Digital artefacts" are the audible aspects of data corruption or signal distortion that occur when audio is digitized by transforming an analog signal into a digital waveform. While the late-'80s advent of laser disc and consequent compact disc technology heralded the notion of diminished signal-to-noise ratio and the supposed disappearance of "surface noise" (such as the hiss of tapes and the crackle of vinyl), it unintentionally gave rise to heightened aural consciousness, wherein minute details of imperfection in digital signal encoding gave rise to "digital artefacts." These range from "glitches" caused by CDs skipping over dirt particles caught on a CD surface to the "lo-res" downsampling of a full-frequency signal, which generates strange, high-pitched modulations of the original signal. Experimental musicians of various persuasions fixated on these new sensory characteristics (and continue to do so today) and exaggerated their effect and presence by finding means to corrupt, distort, and interfere with correct digital processing procedures. For example, by looping digital samples into millisecond lengths, filamental data strips of extremely high-pitched tones are abstracted and sound surprisingly similar to the upper range of analog sine wave tones. The methods of Sachiko and Nakamura exemplify this, producing a type of ultra-high ringing, which once acknowledged can be aurally discerned in many everyday audio manifestations. Collectively, the experimental attraction to such a newly created noise field simultaneously comments on contemporary electro-acoustic ecology, while subverting nominal recording protocol to ponder expanded acts of hearing.

. . .

But as dry and serious as *Onkyokei* often sounds, one wonders about the submerged or even repressed role of theatrical gesture in its purported disavowal of everything but "sound itself." While modern art discourses invariably chronicle all experimental strategies in the electronic arts via the same forward momentum that positions Ikeda's *test pattern* as the desired progeny of early radical and revolutionary audiovisuality, there might be other ways of considering the reductive applications of sine wave tones. To undertake this, channels outside of high art need to be acknowledged.

Kraftwerk's *Radio-Activity* (1975) album was the group's first clear declaration of a contentiously theatrical conservatism in an era when excessiveness and debauchery typified the bulk of rock theatrics. Dressed like German industrialists from the Cold War era, the band members presented themselves as if trapped in a time warp, nonchalantly continuing to compose and perform devoid of any camp or kitsch undercurrents that could qualify their demeanor. *Radio-Activity* subtextually celebrates the discovery of radium and its impact on electronic engineering to instigate radio wave transmission. Of course, a darker edge is connoted by reading the album's title as the state of becoming "radioactive" after exposure to high levels of radium. From sitting too close for too long to the cathode ray tube television to being too close for too long to radioactive terrains, "radioactivity" has perfectly described the most lasting impact of scientific research upon human life following the atomic bomb blasts on Hiroshima and Nagasaki at the close of WWII.

In the McLuhan sense, Kraftwerk were deliberately being "cool" with such a "hot" topic. Indeed, their perversely restrained music forged a highly romantic ideal of emptying humanism in the act of composing music. Their imagery in album covers, promotional photos, and live performances intensified this, picturing them at this stage as nerdy scientists diligently researching rather than artists angsting over their expressive yearning. As children of Stockhausen, they openly toyed with the quasi-scientific contributions to the electronic arts, thereby being the first artists to implicate the pretentiousness of postwar experimentalism dedicated to valiantly "defining the medium." For Kraftwerk, the medium needed no definition: it is what it is. The song "Radio-Activity" is a theatrical paean to the medium's glowing appeal—and is that not what most electronic art does to its chosen media? With Geiger pulses, phased blocks of white noise, ring-modulated oscillator sweeps, short blips of Morse code (all sound effects quite dated by 1975), the song drolly merges broadcast transmissions (radio activity) with radium infection (radioactivity). It's a perverse collapse of medium into message.

In July 2012, Kraftwerk performed the song in Tokyo for the No Nukes 2012 concert—an antinuclear event campaigning for the decommissioning of nuclear reactors across Japan, following the meltdown at TEPCO's No.1 nuclear reactor plant in Fukushima after the 3/11 tsunami destroyed electrical control of the fuel rods' cooling facilities. Kraftwerk intoned the song in Japanese with revised lyrics. Instead of "Radio-activity—is in the air for you and me; Radio-activity—discovered by Madame Curie," they supplanted an imperative: "Radio-activity is also in Japan—in the air and in the water; Radio activity—stop it now." Video footage of the concert captures the Japanese audience responding wildly, first to the opening Geiger-counter clicks, then the phonetically stretched syllables of the title, then the commencement of the Morse code, and finally to the vocoded roll call of disaster sites: "Chernobyl. Harrisburg. Sellafield. Fukushima." Like the sirens emitting a static fixed tone during the 3/11 memorials, Kraftwerk's amended rendition of *Radio-Activity* exposes the deafening content that has been muted in modernist art applications of the sine wave tone and its associated electronica as "pure," "contentless," or "nothing" in both sonic and existential senses.

Between the original release of *Radio-Activity* and its No Nukes 2012 version, Ryoji Ikeda composed a series of electronic tone pieces collectively titled *Channel X* (1985–1995, collected on the CD *1000 fragments* in 1995). Opening with an actual test tone, the suite is comprised of small sketches made from just about all the sounds discussed here from *Homage à John Cage, Telemusik,* and *Radio-Activity.* As such, it invokes the same problematics as Otomo's *Cathode #1* and *#2* by sounding severely innovative while engaged in stark appropriation of dated electronic tropes. More like Kraftwerk and less like Otomo, Ikeda's *Channel X* is purposefully mannered like a roboticized mannequin performing "serious electronic music." A curious theatricality thus reverberates within the music's arch blips and melodramatic noise-bursts, as if the intention is to naturalize the electro-acoustic ecology in acceptance of how humans now inhabit the digital realm.

. . .

But maybe there is a reason for this particular sensation in the music's fawned sterility. Ikeda contributed part or whole scores to three of the spectacular multimedia audio-visual performances of the Kyoto-based group Dumb Type: *OR* (1997), *Memorandum* (1999), and *Voyages* (2002). His work in each instance extrapolated the styles, textures, and forms Ikeda had developed in his solo audio work across this time frame: *Channels, 5 zones* (1994–95), *headphonics* (1995–96), *+/–* (1996), *time and space,* and *0°C* (both 1998), and *matrix* (2000). Since the early '90s, Dumb Type developed an open embrace of all mediarized effects in the staging of their expanded narratives, matrixed audiovisuality, and integration of live performance. The resulting deconstructed postmodern realms referenced the technological taxonomies of advertising more than the high-art legacies of theatre and dance. Ikeda's attenuation to the precise energies and life-force of the "artless" artefacts of broadcast transmission and signal processing forged an aesthetic that perfectly merged with Dumb Type's perspective on unromantic, non-European, antihierarchical theatre textuality.

However as Ikeda's solo audiovisual projects have gathered international momentum since 2000, his work seems to have become mute on this particular interpolation of his work within Dumb Type's oeuvre. Instead, his accompanying statements on how immateriality is aligned with the infinite universe of mathematical data in ways beyond human tabulation position his work as a phenomenal immersion in abstractions of time, space, and form. A missing link lies in an early Dumb Type production before Ikeda joined the group: *S/N* (1994) (fig. 15.4). The last show conceived and directed by founding director Teiji Furuhashi, it openly dealt with his being afflicted with HIV/AIDS. Unlike earlier Dumb Type "cool media" productions, *S/N* combined the group's groundbreaking utilization of electronic media in theatrical space with "hot media" didacticism by addressing sociopolitical issues of HIV/AIDS diagnosis, reception, and management. A key feature of the audio to the production was its embrace of hospital monitoring sound effects: ECG bleeps, MRI drones, fluorescent ringing—all treated like a matrix of sinusoidal tones, white noise sheets, and subharmonic rumbles.

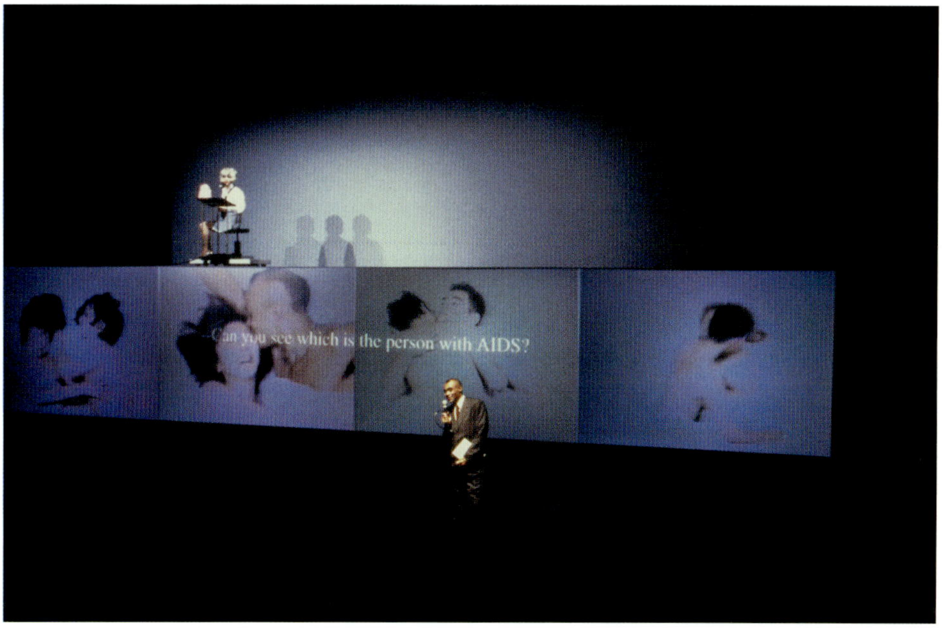

FIGURE 15.4
Dumb Type, *S/N*, 1994. Multimedia performance; variable length. Soundtrack CD composed by Teiji Furuhasi and Toru Yamanaka; 56 minutes, 41 seconds. Copyright Dumb Type.

Perceived within the "hot" content of *S/N*'s tragic narrative, the unremitting "inhumanness" of these sounds inevitably bears psychological resonance. *S/N*'s soundscape deftly "sonorizes" human life and transforms it into audibly monitored data (heart rates, blood pressure, lung rhythms, neural pulsations). The show's expanded multimedia, nonnarrative format conveyed transdimensional sensations of being alive yet on the brink of dying—amazingly, through the intensity of its abstraction more than anything representational or literal. Devoid of traditional theatrical linguistics born of script, direction, and acting, the Dumb Type performers rendered themselves as data signifying this threshold of life. *S/N* stages a liminal world energized by stroboscopic light flashes, blasts of low-end noise, performers running against the flow of a conveyor belt, dancers falling backwards into black voids, operating theatre beds ferried across the choreographed space, multiple screens of scrolling data, projected graphics of formidable complexity. And never far from its horizon: the sine wave tone; the ultimate audiovisual statement of the human/inhuman, live/dead, content/medium axis. The show notably climaxes with the sustained, high-pitched tone of the ECG.

But like all of Dumb Type's work, the power of the sine wave tone's effective figure lies in its fertility and multiplicity within the electronic lexicon. It presents neither a statement about abstraction nor an alignment with modernist experimentalism: it fundamentally grapples with the ongoing semiotic consequences of speaking textually through mediarized conventions. Where so much electronic art still produced today relies on models and theories of a truly outmoded sense of radicalism, subversion, and extremism—as if any bleep made instantly aligns one with everything from Futurist noise to Cagean silence—*S/N*'s sine wave tone oppositely intensifies the point at which representation becomes abstraction, and language becomes effect. It has everything to say, but it's not saying it: it's *sounding* it. The scene is reminiscent of the closing to Sidney Lumet's film *Fail Safe* (1964), when the U.S. president promises to drop two nuclear warheads on Manhattan following the accidental launch of an irreversible nuclear attack on Moscow. By phone, the president informs his staff in Russia: "I'm told that what we'll hear at this end is a high shrill sound. That will be (your) phone melting from the heat of the fireball." When the bombs are about to hit ground zero at the Empire State Building, a countdown montage of ten cine-stills of "everyday life in the city" are shown, each accompanied by a harsh burst of distorted white noise. The screen goes black; the credits roll; the roar of a crowd is cross-faded with the searing noise of a jet engine. Slowly, a sine wave tone obliterates everything. *Fail-Safe* has no score, but a surfeit of musique concrète, electronic processing, and the raw sound of telecommunications. On the surface it sounds like it could have been assembled by Cage, Paik, or Stockhausen. Or even Kraftwerk, Ikeda, or Otomo. Orthodox art-historical analysis may scoff at this folding of sixty years of electronic experimentation. But *S/N* activates an aural consciousness wherein multiple trajectories converge, suggesting how similarities between diverse applications of the sine wave tone strengthen rather than dilute their collective effects and meanings.

Ikeda's *test pattern* is certainly a triumph unimaginable in the nascent epoch of the electronic arts. Its *Gesamtkunstwerk* intensity has captivated a wide audience demographic, nurtured by the marketing nous compulsorily employed for major international art spectacles. Its dizzying maths, its overloaded data, and its razor-sharp asceticism have had a rapturous effect on visitors who otherwise might not give a historical Video Art piece more than a glance. But while the registering of Ikeda's immersive experience seems tied to accepting its artful "meaningless form," it is largely dependent on the viewer/auditor being conditioned to find "meaningful content" in art and culture. Similar to the triggering function of the Pavlovian bell, the sine wave tone—by virtue of its unacknowledged semiotic accrual over half a century—continues to thrill audiences with the liberation from the language-laden mechanisms that guide and control everyday exchange. Yet one wonders if any consciousness is attained in this theatricalized act of listening to nothing. Blips, clicks, glitches, and tones allow one to pretend that one is nothing—but this amounts to just another narcissistic experience that confirms one's malleable identity. Listened to more carefully as signifiers, carriers, and modulators of how medium/message binaries are illusions, one can experience that one is potentially no more than a blip, click, glitch, or tone.

MEDIOGRAPHY

Abramovic, Marina.

2012 *The Artist is Present*. HDCAM, color; 106 min.

Acconci, Vito.

1971 *Centers*. Video, black and white, sound; 22:50 min.

Alonso, Marcos, Günter Geiger, Sergi Jordà, and Martin Kaltenbrunner (Music Technology Group).

2003 *reacTable*. Electronic musical instrument.

Anderson, Thomas.

2002 *Punch-Drunk Love*. 35mm film; 95 min.

Antonellis, Anthony.

2011 *http://www.dfffoo.com*. Internet art.

Arcangel, Cory.

2006 *Colors*. Single-channel video, artist software, computer; 33 days. (See figure 13.2.)

Atlas, Charles.

2003 *Instant Fame*. Installation and real-time video performance.

Atlas, Charles, and Mika Tajima.

2012 *Today Is Not a Dress Rehearsal* (edited versions of Today Is Not a Dress Rehearsal [2009]). Digital video, color, sound.

Atlas, Charles, Mika Tajima, and New Humans.

2011 *The Pedestrians*. Multimedia performance installation. (See figure 11.2.)

Baij, Jeff.

2013 *The Mind's Eye and the Sequel to the Mind's Eye*. Video, continuous loop; 2:18 min.

Bailey, Jeremy.

2012 *The Future of Creativity*. Live software performance; 15:58 min.

Baily, Richard.

2002 Image Savant Studio, digital visual effects for Steven Soderbergh's film *Solaris*. 35mm film, color, sound; 99 min.

Bass, Saul, and John Whitney, Sr.

1958 Opening credits for Alfred Hitchcock's film *Vertigo*. 35mm film, color, sound; 128 min.

Battey, Bret.

2007 *Luna Series 1: Mercurius*. Digital video, color, sound; 6 min.

BBC.

1967 *Horizon: Will Art Last?* BBC television series.

Beck, Stephen.

1973–76 *Video Weavings*. Video, color, sound; 28 min.

1972–73 *Illuminated Music 2*. Video, color, sound; 14 min.

1974 *Cycles*. 16mm film, color, sound; 10:12 min. In collaboration with Jordan Belson. Music by Stephen Beck.

2011 *NOOR (Light) Part 1 of a Trilogy*. HD digital video, color, sound; 7 min. Music composed and performed by Rony Barret (Lebanon) with the Boulder Philharmonic Symphony.

Becker, Lutz.

1967 *Horizon*. 16mm film, color, sound; 3 min. (See figure 1.4.)

Belson, Jordan.

1961 *Allures*. 16mm film, color, sound; 7 min. Music by Jordan Belson and Henry Jacobs.

1964 *Re-entry*. 16mm film, color, sound; 6 min.

1967 *Samadhi*. 16mm film, color, sound; 6 min.

1972 *Chakra*. 16mm film, color, sound; 6 min.

1983 Special effects sequences in Philip Kaufman's film *The Right Stuff*. 35mm film; 192 min.

Benglis, Lynda.

1973 *Now*. Videotape, color, sound; 11:45 min.

1973 *Female Sensibility*. Videotape, color, sound; 13:05 min.

Blake, Jeremy.

2000 *Liquid Villa*. Digital animation with audio; 7:30 min., continuous. (See figure 8.1.)

2001 *Station to Station 1–5*. Digital animation with audio; 16 min., each continuous.

2002 *Winchester*. Digital animation with audio; 18 min., continuous.

Björk [Gudmunsdóttir], with Mathias Augustyniak and Michael Amzalag of M/M Paris, Sjón, Scott Snibbe, Sarah Stocker and Mark Danks of Kodama Studios, Touch Press, Max Weisel of Relative Wave, Nikki Deben, Stephen Malinowski, and John F. Simon, Jr.

2011 *Biophilia*. Interactive digital application for tablet devices.

Brakhage, Stan.

1958 *Anticipation of the Night*. 16mm film, color, silent; 40 min.

1961–64 *Dog Star Man*. 16mm film, color, silent; 75 min.

1963 *Mothlight*. 16mm film, color, silent; 3 min.

1971 *The Pittsburgh Trilogy* (also referred to as *The Pittsburgh Documents)*, released as separate films:

eyes. 16mm film, color, silent; 35 min.

Deus Ex. 16mm film, color, silent; 33 min.

The Act of Seeing with one's own eyes. 16mm film, color, silent; 32 min.

1987 *Dante Quartet*. 35mm film, color, silent; 6 min.

1990 *The Glaze of Cathexis* (part of *Three Hand-Painted Films)*. 16mm film, color, silent; 3 min.

Breer, Robert.

1968 *69*. 16mm film, color, sound; 5 min.

Bute, Mary Ellen.

1952 *Abstronic*. 35mm film, color, sound; 7 min. Music: Aaron Copland, *Hoe Down*, and Don Gillis, *Ranch House Party*.

Cage, John.

1939–52 *Imaginary Landscapes 1–5*. Composition manuscripts.

1949 *Lecture on Nothing*. Performance.

Cillari, Sonia.

2006–7 *Se mi sei vicino* (If you are close to me). Interactive installation, EFS Responsive Environment. http://youtu.be/idNRiQCLzlQ.

Cocteau, Jean.

1930 *The Blood of a Poet*. 35mm film, black and white; 50 min.

Ćosić, Vuk, and Luka Frelih.

1998 *ASCII history for the blind*. Internet art.

1998 *Deep ASCII*. Internet art, video and online, silent; 55 min. (See figure 9.1.)

1998 *Psycho*. Internet art.

2008 *Battleship Potemkin*. Internet art.

Coy, Chris, and Jon Rafman.

2014 *Unexpressed Resentment: A Possible Beginning*. HD video, color, sound; 4:35 min. Audio by Daniel Lopatin (Oneohtrix Point Never).

Davies, Charlotte.

1995 *Osmose*. Three-dimensional immersive environment.

1998 *Ephémère*. Three-dimensional immersive environment.

Walt Disney Productions.

1961–69 *Walt Disney's Wonderful World of Color*. Television series.

Douglas, A. S.

1952 Noughts and Crosses. Computer game.

Draves, Scott.

2005–6 *Dreams in High Fidelity*. Digital video, color; variable lengths.

2014 *Generation 245*. Custom software, Internet-wide collective intelligence, "Electric Sheep," 111 GB, 1080p; thirty-two–screen digital video installation; variable lengths. Studio 99, Microsoft Research Headquarters, Redmond, WA, January 2014. (See figure 6.5.)

Dumb Type.

1994 *S/N*. Multimedia performance; variable length. Sound track CD composed by Teiji Furuhasi and Toru Yamanaka, 56:41 min.; released 1995. (See figure 15.4.)

1997 *[OR].* Multimedia concert, installation, performance; variable length. Sound track CD composed by Ryoji Ikeda and Toru Yamanaka, 70:35 min.; released 1998.

1999 *Memorandum.* Multimedia performance; variable length. Sound track CD composed by Ryoji Ikeda and Toru Yamanaka, 61:43 min.; released 2000.

2002 *Voyages.* Multimedia performance; variable length.

Eames, Charles, and Ray Eames.

1959 *Glimpses of the USA.* Multiple-screen film installation; 12 min.

Fischinger, Oskar.

c. 1926 *Raumlichtmusik* and *Raumlichtkunst.* Multimedia performances with 35mm black and white and tinted film; variable lengths. Accompanied by live music. 2012 reconstruction of *Raumlichtkunst* by Center for Visual Music: HD three-screen installation, color; variable loops. (See figure 6.4.)

c. 1926–27 *Spirals.* 35mm film, black and white, silent; 2 min.

1931 *Studie nr. 8.* 35mm film, black and white, sound; 5 min.

c. 1932 *Ornament Sound* experiments. 35mm film, black and white, sound; several versions with different lengths.

1934 *Muratti Greift Ein (Muratti Gets in the Act).* 35mm film, Gasparcolor, sound; 3 min. Cigarette commercial.

1936–43 *Allegretto.* 35mm film, color, sound; 2.5 min. (See figure 6.1.)

1937 *An Optical Poem.* 35mm film, Technicolor, sound; 7 min.

1942 *Radio Dynamics.* 35mm film, color, silent; 4 min.

1947 *Motion Painting no. 1.* 35mm film, color, sound; 11 min.

Fleming, Victor.

1939 *The Wizard of Oz.* 35mm film, black and white and color, sound; 101 min.

Furukawa, Kiyoshi, with Wolfgang Münch and Masaki Fujihata.

1998–99 *Small Fish.* Interactive audiovisual installation/CD-ROM.

Gatson, Rico.

2013 *The Promise of Light.* Single-channel video projection; 6 min. (See figure 13.3.)

Gehr, Ernie.

1970 *History.* 16mm film, color, silent; 14 min.

Gillette, Frank, and Ira Schneider.

1969 *Wipe Cycle.* Nine-channel video installation, black and white.

Godard, Jean-Luc.

1965 *Pierrot le Fou.* 35mm film, color, sound; 110 min.

1967 *Weekend.* 35mm film, color, sound; 104 min.

1968 *Sympathy for the Devil.* 35mm film, Eastman Color, mono sound; 100 min.

Godard, Jean-Luc, and Anne-Marie Miéville.

1998 *The Old Place.* Video, color, stereo sound; 49 min.

Gordon, Douglas.

1993 *24 Hour Psycho.* Video installation; 1,440 min. (24 hours).

Gottlieb, Carl.

1981 *Caveman.* 35mm film, color, sound; 91 min.

Graham, Dan.

1974 *Time Delay Room.* Closed-circuit video installation.

Hatoum, Mona.

1988 *Measures of Distance*. Video projection, color, sound; 15:30 min. (See figure 4.4.)

Hieronymi, Andrew.

2005 *Move*. Interactive installation. (See figure 10.1.)

Higinbotham, William.

1958 Tennis for Two. Computer game.

Hiller, Susan.

1983–84 *Belshazzar's Feast, the Writing on Your Wall*. Video installation; 21:52 min. (See figure 4.3.)

Hitchcock, Alfred.

1958 *Vertigo*. 35mm film, color, sound; 128 min.

Holt, Nancy, and Richard Serra.

1974 *Boomerang*. Videotape, color, sound; 10:26 min.

Honda, Ishirō.

1956 *Rodan*. 35mm film, color, sound; 74 min.

1957 *Chikyû Bôeigun (The Mysterians)*. 35mm film, color, sound; 86 min.

Hopper, Dennis.

1988 *Colors*. 35mm film, color, sound; 120 min.

Huyghe, Pierre.

1993/1999 *La Toison d'Or*. Constructed live situation / performance documented via Polaroids. (See figure 12.2.)

1997 *Blanche-Neige Lucie*. Super 16mm transferred to 35mm, color, sound; 4 min.

1998 *L'Ellipse*. Triple video projection, Super 16 mm film transferred to Beta digital, color, sound; 13 min.

1999 *Atari Light*. Computer game program, interface, two joysticks, halogen lamps, ceiling construction; approx. 60 × 960 × 960 cm ((60⅝ × 378 × 378 in.). (See figures 12.1 and 12.2.)

1999 *The Third Memory*. Two-channel video projection, with sound, 9:32 min.; single-channel video with sound, 22:30 min.; and thirteen inkjet prints, variable dimensions.

2000 *Two Minutes Out of Time*. Animated film, color, sound; 4 min.

2001 *One Million Kingdoms*. Animated film; 6 min.

2002 *L'Expédition Scintillante, Acte 1: Untitled (Weather Score)*. Snow, rain, fog, programmed precipitation.

2002 *L'Expédition Scintillante, Acte 2: Untitled (Light Box)*. Light and smoke system, sound; 200 × 190 × 155 cm (78¾ × 74¹³⁄₁₆ × 61 in.). Music: Erik Satie, *Gymnopédies 3* and *4* (1888), conducted by Claude Debussy.

2002 *L'Expédition Scintillante, Acte 3: Untitled (Black Ice Stage)*. Black ice rink, female skater, program; 35 × 1024 × 774 cm (13¾ × 403⅛ × 304¾ in.). Music: Brian Eno, *Music for Airports # 4* (1978). (See figure 12.1.)

2003 *Streamside Day*. 16mm film and digital video transferred to digi-beta, color, sound; 26 min.

2004/2009 *This is not a Time for Dreaming*. Video transferred from 16mm film, color, sound; variable dimensions; 24 min. Music by Xenankis, Varèse, and Trenet.

2005 *A Journey That Wasn't.* Super 16 mm film and HD video transferred to HD video, color, sound; 21:41 min.

2008 *Forest of Lines.* Event: July 2008, Sydney Opera. Film: HD video, color, sound; 7:32 min.

2010 *The Host and the Cloud.* HD video, color, sound; 121:30 min. (See figure 12.4.)

2010 *Player.* LED, brass, hand controller, mask; 15 × 16 × 24 cm (5 15/16 × 6 5/16 × 9 7/16 in.). (See figure 12.3.)

2011 *Influenced.* Person in the exhibition space infected with the flu.

2011 *Name Announcer.* Performance.

2011 *Zoodram 4.* Live marine ecosystem, resin mask after *The Sleeping Muse* by Constantin Brancusi (1910). (See figure 12.4.)

2012 *A Way in Untilled.* Film: HD video, color, sound; 14 min.

Ikeda, Ryoji.

1985–95 *Channel X.* Audio; 11:08 min. Collected on the CD *1000 fragments;* released 1996.

1994–95 *5 zones.* Audio; 29:49 min. Collected on the CD *1000 fragments;* released 1995.

1995–96 *headphonics.* Audio; 10:39 min. Collected on the CD +/–; released 1996.

1996 +/–. Audio; 51:48 min. Collected on the CD +/–; released 1996.

1998 *Time and Space.* Audio; 33:04 min. Double mini-CD; released 1998.

1998 *0°C.* Audio; 36.19 min. CD; released 2000.

2001 *Matrix.* Audio; 87:54 min. Double CD; released 2000.

2011 *test pattern (enhanced version).* Audiovisual installation; variable length. (See figure 15.3.)

Ishii, Teruo.

1957 *Kotetsu no Kyojin* serial released as

Attack from Space. 35mm film, color, sound; 76 min.

Atomic Rulers. 35mm film, color, sound; 83 min.

Iwai, Toshio.

1992–94 *Music Insects.* Audiovisual installation.

1995 *Piano as Image Media.* Interactive installation.

2005 *Electroplankton.* Interactive single-player music video game.

Iwai, Toshio, with Yamaha.

2005 *TENORI-ON.* Audiovisual instrument.

Jackson, Ariel.

2013 *Here's Hoping (AKA The Blues).* Installation, single-channel video projection, stop-motion animation, greenscreen; 7:30 min. (See figure 13.4.)

JODI (Joan Heemskerk and Dirk Paesmans).

2002–10 *%Location.* Internet art. http://wwwwwwwww.jodi.org/.

2002–10 *MY%Desktop.* Internet art. http://mydesktop.jodi.org/.

Jonas, Joan.

1970 *Mirror Check.* Videotape, black and white, sound; 1:03 min.

1972 *Vertical Roll.* Videotape, black and white, sound; 19:38 min.

1973–99 *Organic Honey's Vertical Roll.* Videotape, black and white, sound, performance; 15 min. (See figure 4.1.)

Kahn, Stanya.

2010 *It's Cool, I'm Good.* SD video, 5.1 surround sound; 35:20 min. (See figure 14.5.)

2014 *Don't Go Back To Sleep.* HD video, sound; 74 min. (See figures 14.2 and 14.3.)

work in progress *Stand in the Stream.* HD video, sound. (See figure 14.4.)

Kirby, Lynn Marie.

2004 *Jacaranda Tree Chalon Road Exposure: Brazilian Export, from Refracted Case Histories.* Film to digital transfer; 4:30 min. (See figure 7.1.)

2004 *St. Ignatius Church Exposure: Lenten Light Conversions* (from the *Latent Light Excavations Series,* 2003–7). Film and digital video, silent; 6 min.

Kogler, Peter, and Franz Pomassl.

1999 *Cave.* Immersive interactive environment. Computer animation in cooperation with Ars Electronica Future-lab. Sound by Franz Pomassl. (See figure 10.3.)

Kosuth, Joseph.

1969 *The Second Investigation.* Television broadcast. (See figure 3.1.)

Kraftwerk.

1975 *Radio-Activity.* LP; 37 min.

Krueger, Myron.

1969 *Videoplace.* Interactive video projection system.

1971 *Psychic Space.* Interactive environment.

1971 *Maze.* Application designed for *Psychic Space.*

Kubrick, Stanley.

1968 *2001: A Space Odyssey.* 35mm film, color, sound; 160 min.

Lamorisse, Albert.

1956 *The Red Balloon (Le Ballon rouge).* Film, color, sound; 34 min.

László, Alexander.

c. 1925–26 *Farblichtmusik (Color-Light-Music).* Multimedia concerts, some performed in 1926 with Oskar Fischinger.

Léger, Fernand (with Dudley Murphy and Man Ray).

1924 *Ballet Mécanique,.* 35mm film, black and white, sound; 12 min. Original soundtrack by George Antheil.

Levin, Golan.

1999–2000 *Audiovisual Environment Suite* (including *Yellowtail*). Interactive software.

Levin, Golan, and Zachary Lieberman.

2004 *Manual Input Workstation.* Interactive installation.

Levin, Golan, and Scott Snibbe.

1997 *Escargogolator.* Interactive drawing software.

LIA.

2009 *PhiLIA 01.* iPhone application.

2012 *Sumo5.* iPhone/iPad application. (See figure 10.5.)

Lichtenstein, Mitchell.

2007 *Teeth.* Film, color, sound; 88 min.

Lodge, Bernard, Ben Palmer, Hugh Sheppard, and Norman Taylor.

1963 *Dr. Who* original title sequence. BBC. Music written by Ron Grainer and performed by the BBC Radiophonic Workshop. (See figure 1.3.)

Lohanthony.

n.d. YouTube Channel. https://www.youtube.com/user/lohanthony.

Ludy, Sara.

2014 *Dream House*. HD video, color, sound; 10:04 min.

Luining, Peter.

2004 *http://www.ffffoo.com*. Internet art.

Lumet, Sidney.

1964 *Fail Safe*. 35mm film, color, sound; 112 min.

1975 *Dog Day Afternoon*. 35mm film, color, sound; 125 min.

Lye, Len.

1935 *A Colour Box*. 35mm film, Dufaycolor, sound; 4 min.

1957, revised 1979 *Free Radicals*. 16mm film, black and white, sound; 5 min.

1979 *Particles in Space*. 16mm film, black and white, sound; 4 min.

Malick, Terrence.

2011 *Tree of Life*. 35mm film, color, sound; 139 min.

Marclay, Christian.

2010 *The Clock*. Single-channel digital video, stereo sound; 24 hrs.

McLaren, Norman.

1949 *Begone Dull Care*. 35mm film, color, sound; 7:48 min.

1952 *Neighbors*. 16mm film, color, sound; 8 min.

1969 *Spheres*. 35mm film, color, sound; 7:21 min.

1971 *Synchromy*. 35mm film, color, sound; 7:27 min.

McPhcc, Christina.

2010 *MEAT OIL JOY PAINT: A tribute to Carolee Schneemann*. HD video, color, sound; 2:53 min.

2011–12 *Bird of Paradise* (expanded remix based on *Bird of Paradise in Slow Time* [single channel; 120 min.]). HD video, three channel, color, silent; 10 min., looped.

McPhee, Christina, and Pamela Z.

2013–14 *Carbon Song Cycle (A Work for Chamber Ensemble and Expanded Cinema)*. Multimedia; variable dimensions according to architecture; 45 min.

Menkman, Rosa.

2010–11 *The Collapse of PAL*. Video, color, sound; 30 min. (A rendered version of a live audiovisual performance first performed on national Danish television, Copenhagen.) (See figure 9.3.)

Mills, Lorna.

2013 *Garden Variety* (series). Internet art: three animated GIF collages from the blog post of 12–20–2013, 10:10 A.M. http://www.digitalmediatree.com/sallymckay/LornaMillsImageDump/pageback/60891/. (See figure 9.4.)

Murata, Takeshi.

2005 *Monster Movie*. Digital video, color, sound; 3:55 min. (See figure 7.3.)

2013 *Shiboogi*. Digital video, color, silent; 8:18 min. (See figure 7.4.)

Napier, Mark.

2001 *Feed*. Online artwork. http://www.potatoland.org

Nauman, Bruce.

1970 *Live-Taped Corridor*. Wallboard, video camera, two video monitors, videotape player, and videotape; variable dimensions (approximately ceiling height × 975.4 × 50.8 cm [384 × 20 in.]).

2001 *MAPPING THE STUDIO II with color shift, flip, flop & flip/flop (Fat Chance John Cage)*. Seven video projections, fourteen speakers, fifteen chairs, seven scripts, forty-two channels of video, NTSC, color, stereo sound; 5 hrs., 45 min.

New Humans.

2007 *Disassociate*. Installation and multimedia performance featuring Vito Acconci, José León Cerrillo, Howie Chen, Philippe Decrauzat, C. Spencer Yeh, and Mika Tajima.

Otomo, Yoshihide.

1999 *Cathode*. Includes tracks *Cathode #1, #2; Modulation #1, #2*. Electronic music. CD.

Paik, Nam June.

1959 *Homage à John* Cage, *Music for Tape Recorder and Piano*. Action; approx. 10 min.

1963 *Exposition of Music*. Exhibition: four "prepared" pianos, mechanical sound objects, several record and tape installations, twelve modified TV sets, and the head of a freshly slaughtered ox.

1963–66 *Participation TV*. Interactive television sculpture.

1963/1989 *TV Clock*. Twenty-four fixed-image color television monitors mounted on twenty-four pedestals, color and black and white, silent; installation dimensions variable, height approx. 76". (See figure 3.2 [left].)

1965 *Magnet TV*. Seventeen-inch black-and-white television set with magnet; 28⅜ × 19¼ × 24 ½ in. (72.1 × 48.9 × 62.2 cm) overall.

1966 *Variations on Johnny Carson vs. Charlotte Moorman*. Video, black and white, sound; 15 min.

1969 *Electronic Opera #1*. Videotape, color, sound; 4:45 min.

1975 *Nam June Paik: Edited for Television*. Video, color, sound; 29:24 min. Camera / Supervising Engineer: John J. Godfrey. Produced by the TV Lab at WNET / Thirteen (VTR series).

Pearlstein, Alix.

2007–8 *Two Women 2*. Two-channel HD video, color, sound; two alternating takes: 6:47 min. and 4 min. (10:47 min. total).

2008 *After the Fall*. Four-channel HD video, color, sound; two alternating takes: 10:14 min. and 10:34 min. (20:48 min. total).

2008 *Goldrush*. HD video, color, sound; 3:5 min.

2012 *The Drawing Lesson*. Single-channel HD video, color, sound; 7:13 min. (See figure 11.4.)

2012 *Moves in the Field*. Single-channel HD video, color, sound; 20 min. (See figures 11.3 and 11.4.)

2013 *The Dark Pavement*. HD video, color, sound; 6:50 min.

Pfeiffer, Paul.

2012 *Home Movie / Four Locations for a Home Movie*. 8mm film transferred to digital video / suite of four Cibachrome prints; 8:30 min., looped. Produced in collaboration with Aaron Levi. (See figure 13.1.)

2003 *Morning after the Deluge.* 8mm film transferred to digital video loop; projection dimensions: 144" × 192"; 20 min. (See figure 1.1.)

Richter, Hans.

c. 1921–25 *Rhythmus 21.* 35mm film, black and white, silent; 3:22 min.

Richter, Hans, with John Cage, Alexander Calder, Marcel Duchamp, Max Ernst, Fernand Léger, and Man Ray.

1947 *Dreams That Money Can Buy.* 16mm film, color, sound; 80 min.

Robbins, Al.

1980 *Anticata/Strophe.* Video installation with twelve monitors, cameras, color, sound.

Rosler, Martha.

1975 *Semiotics of the Kitchen.* Videotape, black and white, sound; 6:09 min.

1977 *The East Is Red, The West Is Bending.* Videotape; 19:57 min.

1977 *Losing: A Conversation with the Parents.* Videotape; 18:39 min.

1977 *Vital Statistics of a Citizen Simply Obtained.* Videotape; 39:20 min.

1978 *Domination and the Everyday.* Videotape, color, sound; 32:07 min. (See figure 4.2.)

Rozendaal, Rafaël.

2012 *Into Time .us.* Website, http://www.intotime.us/.

Russolo, Luigi.

1914 *intonarumori.* Acoustic device.

Ruttmann, Walter.

1921 *Lichtspiel: Opus I.* 35mm film, black and white and tinted, silent; original version 13 min. Originally accompanied by live music.

Sacks, Steven.

2005 *softwareARTspace.* Software art.

Sagal, Boris.

1971 *Omega Man.* 35mm film, color, sound; 98 min.

Sandin, Dan.

1973 *Five-minute Romp through the IP.* Videotape, black and white, color, mono sound; 6:34 min.

Satie, Erik.

1888 *Gymnopédies 3* and *4*. Piano compositions. *Gymnopédie 3:* 2:29 min. *Gymnopédie 4:* 2:34 min.

Schwartz, Lillian.

1970 *Pixillation.* Computer-generated video images, color; 4 min.

Scott, Ridley.

1979 *Alien.* 35mm film, color, sound; 117 min.

1982 *Blade Runner.* 35mm film, color, sound; 116 min.

Serra, Richard, with Carlotta Fay Schoolman.

1973 *Television Delivers People.* Videotape, color, sound; 5:55 min.

Sharits, Paul.

1968 *T,O,U,C,H,I,N,G,.* 16mm film, color, sound; 12 min.

1974 *Color Sound Frames.* 16mm film, color, sound; 26:30 min.

1975 *Specimen.* 16mm film, color, sound; variable length (composes the first section of *Analytical Studies III: Color Frame Passages,* 1973–74 [22 min.] and the first section of

Analytical Studies IV: Blank Color Frames, 1975–76 [15 min.] as well as generating the content for *Color Sound Frames [Winding],* 1974 [22 min.]). (See figure 5.3.)

1979 *Episodic Generation.* 16mm film, color, sound; 30 min.

1982 *3rd Degree.* 16mm film, color, sound; 24 min.

Simpson, Lorna.

2002 *31.* Thirty-one-channel video installation, video transferred to DVD, color, sound; 20 min. (See figure 4.5.)

Smalley, Travess.

2011 *Primordial Trance Puddle.* HD video; loop.

2011 *Third Trance.* HD video. loop.

Smith, Harry.

1946–49 *Early Abstractions: Films 1–3.* 16mm film, color, originally silent; approx. 8 min.

Smithson Robert.

1970 *Spiral Jetty.* 16mm film, color, sound; 35 min.

Snibbe, Scott.

1989–94 *Motion Sketch.* Interactive application.

1989–96 *Motion Phone.* iPad/iPhone app.

1997 *Bubble Harp.* Interactive art, iPad/iPhone app.

1998 *Boundary Functions.* Interactive installation. (See figure 10.2.)

1998 *Gravilux.* Interactive art, iPad/iPhone app.

Solanki, Sneha.

2012 *Analogue Is Not Digital.* Archive and curatorial project marking the end of analog television. A program of sound works by NTSC & PAL, Jason Sloan, James Hutchinson, Mar Shro, and Janek Schaefer and *Telemancy* by Sneha Solanki, a new commission for basic.fm, was aired September 12–26, 2012, on basic.fm.

Sorensen, Vibeke.

1988 *NLoops.* Video, color, sound; 7 min.

2013 *Illuminations.* Digital, real-time interactive installation: twelve-screen, twelve-projector, color, sound. Music by Vibeke Sorensen.

Stadnik, George.

2006 *Flame.* Digital video, color, silent; 49 min.

Steinkamp, Jennifer.

1995 *SWELL.* Computer-generated projection and installation, color.

Stockhausen, Karlheinz.

1966 *Telemusik.* Electronic composition.

Sturtevant, Elaine.

1967 *Dreams Money Can Buy.* Film (originally 16mm) installation consisting of *Duchamp nu descendant un escalier* and *Roto-relief.*

Sutherland, Ivan.

1963 Sketchpad. Computer program.

Tajima, Mika/New Humans with Charles Atlas.

2009 *Today Is Not a Dress Rehearsal.* Multimedia performance installation. (See figure 11.1.)

Thater, Diana.

2003 *Dark Matter.* Video installation: two flat screen monitors, two DVD players, two DVDs and Lee filters; variable dimensions; loop. (See figure 5.2.)

Thomson & Craighead (Jon Thomson and Alison Craighead).

2002 *Short films about flying.* Networked installation; variable length.

2004 *Template Cinema, Somewhere in Sweden.* Internet art; variable length. (See figure 9.2.)

2008 *Flat Earth.* Desktop documentary; 7 min.

2010 *The Time Machine in alphabetical order.* Video.

Truffaut, Francois.

1966 *Fahrenheit 451.* 35mm film, Technicolor, mono sound; 112 min.

Turrell, James.

1966 *Afrum-Proto.* Tungsten projection.

1974 *Wedgework.* Fluorescent light intallation.

2013 *Breathing Light.* LED installation.

Utterback, Camille.

2001–present *External Measures Series* (including *Untitled 5* [2004] and *Untitled 6* [2005]). Interactive installation. (See figure 10.4.)

VanDerBeek, Stan, in collaboration with Joan Brigham.

1979 *Steam Screens.* Film installation / performance, color.

Varèse, Edgar.

1929–31 *Ionisation.* Musical composition.

Vasulka, Woody, and Steina Vasulka.

1974 *Noisefields.* Video, color, sound; 12:05 min.

Viola, Bill.

1973 *Information.* Video, color, sound; 30 min.

1979 *Chott-el-Djerid (A Portrait in Light and Heat).* Video, color, sound; 28 min.

Vostell, Wolf.

1958 *Theater Is in the Street.* Installation, video.

1959 *TV-dé-coll/age no. 1* ("Ereignisse für Millionen, Partitur" [Events for Millions, Score]). Installation.

1963 *6 TV-Dé-collage.* Six-channel video (VHS and DVD, black and white, sound; 96 min.) shown on six TV monitors; six office cabinets, a telephone, six photographs (black and white), an exhibition, and six seedbeds with watercress. (See figure 3.2 [right].)

Warhol, Andy.

1964 *Empire.* 16mm film transferred to video, black and white, silent; 484 min. (8 hrs., 5 min).

Wenders, Wim.

1977 *The American Friend.* 35mm film, Eastman Color, mono sound; 125 min. (2 hrs., 5 min.).

West, Jennifer.

2004–5 *Marinated Film—the Roll of 16mm That I Had in the Fridge for Over 10 Years.* 16mm film; 9:20 min.

2007 *Nirvana Alchemy Film (16mm black & white film soaked in lithium mineral hot springs, pennyroyal tea, doused in mud, sopped in bleach, cherry antacid and laxatives—jumping by Finn West & Jwest)*. 16mm film, color, silent; 3 min.

2007 *Regressive Squirty Sauce Film (16mm film leader squirted and dripped with chocolate sauce ketchup, mayonnaise & apple juice)*. 16mm film leader transferred to digital video, color, silent; 3:44 min.

2008 *Jam Licking & Sledgehammered Film (70mm film leader covered in strawberry jam, grape jelly and orange marmalade—licked by Jim Shaw, Marnie Weber, Mariah Csepanyi, Bill Parks, Alex Johns, Karen Liebowitz, Roxana Eslameih, Chaney Trotter & JWest—a filmic restaging of moments from Allan Kaprow's "Household")*. 70mm film leader transferred to digital video, color, silent; 3:17 min.

2009 *Lavender Mist Film/Pollock Film 1 (70mm film leader rubbed with Jimson Weed Trumpet flowers, spraypainted, dipped and splattered with nail polish, sprayed with lavender mist air freshener*). 70mm film transferred to digital video, color, silent; 46 seconds, looped. (See figure 7.2.)

2009 *Skate the Sky Film (35mm film print of clouds in the sky covered with ink, Ho-Hos, and Melon—taped to Tate Turbine Hall ramp and skateboarded over using ollie, kick flip, pop shove-it, acid drop, melon grab, crooked grind, bunny hop, tic tacs, sex change, disco flip—skateboarding performed live for Long Weekend by Thomas Lock, Louis Henderson, Charlotte Brennan, Dion Penman, Sam Griffin, Jak Tonge, Evin Goode and Quantin Paris—clouds in the sky shot by Peter West)*. 35mm film print plus DVD projection (transferred from 35mm film); 4:54 min., looped.

2013 *Salt Crystals Spiral Jetty Dead Sea Five Year Film (70mm film negative floated in the Dead Sea and given a healing clay bath in extreme heat in 2008 - stuffed in a suitcase, placed in studio buckets, covered in clay and salt for five years - dragged along the salt encrusted rocks of the Spiral Jetty and thrown in the pink waters in 2013 in below 10 degree weather - Dead Sea floating and mud baths by Mark Titchner, Karen Russo and Jwest - Spiral Jetty dragging and rolling by Aaron Moulton, Ignacio Uriarte and Jwest - DIY telecine frame by frame of salt covered film by Chris Hanke)*. 70mm film negative transferred to high-definition; 54 seconds.

2013 *Spiral of Time Documentary Film (16mm negative strobe-light double and triple exposed - painted with brine shrimp - dripped, splattered and sprayed with salted liquids: balsamic and red wine vinegar, lemon and lime juice, temporary flourescent hair dyes - photos from friends Mark Titchner, Karen Russo, Aaron Moulton and Ignacio Uriarte and some google maps- texts by Jwest and Chris Markers' Sans Soleil script -shot by Peter West, strobed by Jwest, hands by Ariel West, telecine by Tom Sartori)*. 16mm film negative transferred to HD; 9:01 min. (See figure 1.2.)

Wexler, Haskell.

1969 *Medium Cool*. 35mm film, color, sound; 110 min.

Whitney, James.

1957 *Yantra*. 16mm film, color, sound; 8 min. Music by Henk Badings.

1963–66 *Lapis*. 16mm, color, sound; 9 min. Music by Ravi Shankar

Whitney, John, Sr.

1961 *Catalog*. 16mm film, color, sound; 7 min.

1968 *Permutations.* 16mm film, color, sound; 8 min.

1971 *Matrix I.* 16mm film, color, sound; 6 min.

1971 *Matrix II.* 16mm film, color, sound; 6 min.

1972 *Matrix III.* 16mm film, color, sound; 11 min.

1975 *Arabesque.* 16mm film, color, sound; 7 min.

Wilfred, Thomas.

1941 *Vertical Sequence II, Opus 137.* Sculptured light instrument (lumia) composition, silent; 2 days, 12 hrs., 59 min.

Yalkut, Jud.

1966 *Turn, Turn, Turn.* 16mm film, color, sound; 10 min. Music by USCO.

BIBLIOGRAPHY

Agamben, Giorgio. *What Is an Apparatus? And Other Essays*. Translated by David Kishik and Stefan Padetella. Stanford, CA: Stanford University Press, 2009.

American Federation of the Arts. *A History of the American Avant-Garde Cinema*. New York: The American Federation of the Arts, 1976.

Ammann, Jean-Christophe, and Marianne Eigenheer, eds. *Terza, Quarta, Quinta, Sesta & Settima Investigazione* (1968–1971). Lucerne: Kunstmuseum Luzern, 1973.

Antin, David. "Video Art: The Distinctive Features of the Medium." In *Video Art: An Anthology*. Edited by Ira Schneider and Beryl Korot. New York: Harcourt Brace Jovanovich, 1976.

Arcangel, Cory. Cory Arcangel's Official Portfolio Website and Portal. www.coryarcangel.com.

Atlas, Charles, Suzanne Hudson, and Mika Tajima. "1000 Words: Charles Atlas and Mika Tajima Talk about *The Pedestrians*, 2011." *Artforum*, May 2011, 259.

Auping, Michael, and Bruce Nauman. "1,000 Words: Bruce Nauman Talks about Mapping the Studio." *Artforum*, March 2002, 121.

Auslander, Philip. "Liveness, Mediatization, and Intermedial Performance." *Degrés: Revue de synthèse à orientation sémiologique*, Spring 2000, 1.

Batchelor, David. *Chromophobia*. London: Reaktion, 2000.

Baumgärtel, Tilman. *Net.art 2.0: Neue Materialien zur Netzkunst* (New Materials towards Net Art). Nuremberg: Verlag für Moderne Kunst, 2001.

Bazin, Andre, and Hugh Gray. "The Ontology of the Photographic Image." *Film Quarterly* 13, no. 4 (1960): 4–9.

Bellis, Mary. "Color Television History." About.com Inventors. http://inventors.about.com/library/inventors/blcolortelevision.htm.

Benson, Timothy O., Hans Richter, and Doris Berger. *Hans Richter: Encounters.* Los Angeles: Los Angeles County Museum of Art, 2013.

Benson-Allott, Caetlin. "Going Gaga for Glitch: Digital Failure @nd Feminist Spectacle in Twenty-First Century Music Video." In *The Oxford Handbook of Sound and Image in Digital Media.* Edited by Carol Vernallis, Amy Herzog, and John Richardson New York: Oxford University Press, 2013.

Bernstein, Charles. "Disfiguring Abstraction." *Critical Inquiry* 39, no. 3 (Spring 2013): 486–97. www.jstor.org/stable/10.1086/670042.

Birnbaum, Daniel. "Subliminal Messages: Daniel Birnbaum on Jean-François Lyotard's 'The Sublime and the Avant-Garde' (1984)." *Artforum* 51 (September 2012).

Blake, Jeremy. "In Conversation: John Baldessari and Jeremy Blake." *Artforum* 42 (March 2004): 160–65.

Blais, Joline, and Jon Ippolito. *At the Edge of Art.* London: Thames & Hudson, 2006.

Bloemheuvel, Marente, and Eija-Liisa Ahtila. *Cinéma Cinéma: Contemporary Art and the Cinematic Experience.* Rotterdam: NAi Publishers, 1999.

Blom, Ina. "The Autobiography of Video: Outline for a Revisionist Account of Early Video Art." *Critical Inquiry* 39, no. 2 (January 2013): 276–95.

Bosma, Josephine. "The ASCII Art Ensemble." Heise Online. July 9, 1998. www.heise.de/tp/artikel/2/2458/1.html.

———. *Netitudes—Let's Talk Net Art.* Rotterdam: NAi Publishers; Amsterdam: Institute of Network Cultures, 2011.

———. "Online Video Art." Panel at Video Vortex #6, Amsterdam, March 11 2011. Culture Vortex, RAAK, Institute of Network Cultures. 2011. http://networkcultures.org/videovortex/past-events/6amsterdam/.

Brakhage, Stan. *Metaphors on Vision.* Edited by P. Adams Sitney. Book design by George Maciunas. New York: Film Culture, 1963. Available from Internet Archive, https://archive.org/details/metaphorsonvisio00brak.

Brown, William, and Meetali Kutty. "Datamoshing and the Emergence of Digital Complexity from Digital Chaos." *Convergence* 18, no. 2 (2012): 165–76.

Bryant, Levi R., Nick Srnicek, and Graham Harman. *The Speculative Turn: Continental Materialism and Realism.* Melbourne: re.press, 2011.

Buchan, Suzanne, Betti-Sue Hertz, and Lev Manovich. *Animated Painting.* San Diego: San Diego Museum of Art, 2007.

Budak, Adam, and Peter Pakesch, eds. *Diana Thater: Gorillagorillagorilla.* Cologne: König, 2009.

Bulajić, Viktorija Vesna. *Database Aesthetics: Art in the Age of Information Overflow.* Minneapolis: University of Minnesota Press, 2007.

Caldwell, John Thornton. *Televisuality: Style, Crisis, and Authority in American Television.* New Brunswick, NJ: Rutgers University Press, 1995.

Campany, David, ed. *The Cinematic.* Documents of Contemporary Art. London: Whitechapel and Cambridge, MA: MIT Press, 2007.

Cantsin, Monty, and Benjamin Berg. "Mash Smarter Not Harder: An Interview with Benjamin Berg." Furtherfield. May 12, 2013. http://furtherfield.org/features/mash-smarter-not-harder-interview-benjamin-berg.

Cappellazzo, Amy. *Making Time: Considering Time as a Material in Contemporary Video and Film*. Lake Worth, FL: Palm Beach Institute of Contemporary Art, 2000.

Cardiff, Janet, Brian Knep, Liz Phillips, Daniel Rozin, Scott Snibbe, Camille Utterback, George Fifield, Joseph D. Ketner, and Judith Donath. *Act/react: Interactive Installation Art*. Milwaukee: Milwaukee Art Museum, 2008.

Center for Visual Music. "About the [Visual Music] Films: Films/videos in *Visual Music* exhibition, MOCA LA and Hirshhorn, 2005." www.centerforvisualmusic.org/VMFilms.htm.

Centre Pompidou, Direction des publics, Service de l'information des publics et de la médiation."*Pierre Huyghe*, 25 September 2013–6 January 2014." Exhibition brochure. 2013. www.centrepompidou.fr/media/imp/M5050/CPV/ba/d5/M5050-CPV-25145cad-29bb-4565-bad5-e68d7f5be6ec.pdf.

Chun, Wendy Hui Kyong. *Programmed Visions: Software and Memory*. Cambridge, MA: MIT Press, 2011.

Coehlo, René, and Dorine Mignot, eds. *The Luminous Image: An Exhibition of Video Installations by 22 Artists*. Catalogue. Amsterdam: Stedelijk Museum, 1984.

Comer, Stuart, Anthony Elms, and Michelle Grabner. *Whitney Biennial 2014*. Catalogue. New York: Whitney Museum of American Art, 2014.

Costello, Diarmuid. "On the Very Idea of a 'Specific' Medium: Michael Fried and Stanley Cavell on Painting and Photography as Arts." *Critical Inquiry* 34 (Winter 2008): 274–312.

Crary, Jonathan. *24/7: Late Capitalism and the Ends of Sleep*. New York: Verso Books, 2013.

Creed, Barbara. *The Monstrous-Feminine: Film, Feminism, Psychoanalysis*. New York: Routledge, 1993.

Crimp, Douglas. *Joan Jonas: Scripts and Descriptions 1968–1982*. Berkeley: University Art Museum, University of California, 1983.

Crone, Bridget, Nina Danino, Jaspar Joseph-Lester, RUBEDO, and Maxa Zoller. "Round Table Discussion: The Affects of the Abstract Image in Film and Video Art." *MIRAJ, Moving Image Review & Art Journal* 1, no. 1 (January 23, 2012): 79–87. www.ingentaconnect.com/content/intellect/miraj/2012/00000001/00000001/art00008.

Daniels, Dieter. "Television—Art or Anti-Art? Conflict and Cooperation between the Avant garde and the Mass Media in the 1960s and 1970s." In "Overview of Media Art. Mass-Media." Media Art Net. www.medienkunstnetz.de/themes/overview_of_media_art/massmedia/1/.

Decker, Edith. *Paik: Video*. Cologne: DuMont, 1988.

De Landa, Manuel. *Intensive Science and Virtual Philosophy*. London: Continuum, 2002.

Dickerman, Leah, and Matthew Affron. *Inventing Abstraction, 1910–1925: How a Radical Idea Changed Modern Art*. New York: Museum of Modern Art, 2012.

Dinkla, Söke. "Narration." In "Overview of Media Art." Media Art Net. 2004. www.medienkunstnetz.de/themes/overview_of_media_art/narration/scroll/.

Doherty, Claire, ed. *Situation*. Documents of Contemporary Art. London: Whitechapel and Cambridge, MA: MIT Press, 2009.

Dolar, Mladen. *A Voice and Nothing More*. Cambridge, MA: MIT Press, 2006.

Donovan, Tristan. *Replay: The History of Video Games*. East Sussex, U.K.: Yellow Ant, 2010.

Douglas, Stan, and Christopher Eamon. *Art of Projection*. Ostfildern, Germany: Hatje Cantz, 2009.

Dubois, Philippe. *La Question vidéo: Entre cinéma et art contemporain.* Crisnée, Belgium: Yellow Now, 2011.

———. "La Question vidéo face au cinéma: Déplacements esthétiques." In *Cinéma et dernières technologies.* Edited by Frank Beau and Gerard Blanc. Paris: INA; Brussels: De Boeck Université, 1998.

Dunn, David, ed. *Eigenwelt der Apparatewelt: Pioneers of Electronic Art.* Linz, Austria: Ars Electronica, 1992.

Dyer, Richard. *White.* London: Routledge, 1997.

Fang, Irving E. *Television News.* New York: Hastings House, 1972.

Farrow, Clare, Ad Reinhardt, Joseph Kosuth, and Félix González-Torres. *A. Reinhardt, J. Kosuth, F. González-Torres: Symptoms of Interference, Conditions of Possibility.* London: VCH Publishers, 1994.

Fischinger, Oskar. Research site. www.centerforvisualmusic.org/Fischinger.

Flaxman, Gregory. "Transcendental Aesthetics: Deleuze's Philosophy of Space." In *Deleuze and Space.* Edited by Ian Buchanan and Gregg Lambert. Edinburgh: Edinburgh University Press, 2005.

Freud, Sigmund. "On Narcissism: An Introduction." In *The Standard Edition of the Complete Psychological Works of Sigmund Freud.* London: Hogarth Press, 1953.

Friedan, Betty. *The Feminine Mystique.* New York: Norton, 1963.

Frieling, Rudolf. *The Art of Participation: 1950 to Now.* San Francisco: San Francisco Museum of Modern Art, 2008.

Frieling, Rudolf, and Dieter Daniels. *Media Art Net: 1 Survey of Media Art* (Medien Kunst Netz : 1 Medienkunst im Überblick). Vienna: Springer, 2003.

Furlong, Lucinda. "Notes Toward a History of Image Processed Video: Eric Siegel, Stephen Beck, Dan Sandin, Steve Rutt, Bill and Louise Etra," *Afterimage* 11, nos. 1 and 2 (Summer 1983): 35–38. http://vasulka.org/archive/4–30c/AfterImageSum83%281006%29.pdf.

———. "Notes Toward a History of Image Processed Video: Steina and Woody Vasulka," *Afterimage* 11, no. 5 (December 1983): 12–17. www.vasulka.org/archive/4–30c/AfterImage Dec83%285001%29.pdf.

Galbraith, Stuart. *Monsters Are Attacking Tokyo! The Incredible World of Japanese Fantasy Films.* Venice, CA: Feral House, 1998.

Gates, Henry Louis. "Writing 'Race' and the Difference It Makes." *Critical Inquiry* 12, no. 1 (Autumn 1985): 4.

Gilbert-Rolfe, Jeremy. *Beauty and the Contemporary Sublime.* New York: Allworth Press, 1999.

———. "Cabbages, Raspberries and Video's Thin Brightness: Painting in the Age of Artificial Intelligence." *Art and Design* 48 (May-June 1996): 14–23.

Gilbert-Rolfe, Jeremy, and Rebecca Norton. "Awkward × 2: What We Think We're Doing." Lecture at the Art Institute of Chicago, October 25, 2011.

Gonzalez, Jennifer. "Paul Pfeiffer." *BOMB Magazine* 83. Spring 2003. bombmagazine.org/article/2543/paul-pfeiffer.

Goodden, Sky. "The Newest New Media: Lorna Mills on the Evolving Niche of GIF Art." *Artinfo.* October 19, 2013. www.blouinartinfo.com/news/story/973600/the-newest-new-media-lorna-mills-on-the-evolving-niche-of-gif.

———. "Pierre Huyghe Explains His Buzzy *Documenta 13* Installation and Why His Work Is Not Performance Art." *Artinfo Canada*. August 30, 2012. www.blouinartinfo.com/news/story/822127/pierre-huyghe-explains-his-buzzy-documenta-13-installation-and-why-his-work-is-not-performance-art/page/0/2.

Grau, Oliver. ed. *MediaArtHistories*. Cambridge, MA: MIT Press, 2007.

Green, Charles. *The Third Hand: Collaboration in Art from Conceptualism to Postmodernism*, Minneapolis: University of Minnesota Press, 2001.

Greene, Rachel. *Internet Art*. London: Thames & Hudson, 2004.

Grice, Malcolm Le. *Experimental Cinema in the Digital Age*. London: BFI, 2001.

Gschwandtner, Sabrina. "Between Film and Video—the Intermedia Art of Jud Yalkut: An Interview with Jud Yalkut" in Video: Vintage and Current. *Millenium Film Journal*, no. 42 (Fall 2004).

Haeusler, M. Hank, Martin Tomitsch, Gernot Tscherteu, and Ben Van Berkel. *New Media Facades: A Global Survey*. Stuttgart: avedition, 2013.

Hainley, Bruce. "Erase and Rewind: Elaine Sturtevant." *Frieze* 53 (June–August 2000). www.frieze.com/issue/article/erase_and_rewind/.

Hanhardt, John G. "The American Independent Cinema 1958–1964." In *Blam! The Explosion of Pop, Minimalism, and Performance 1958–1964*. Exhibition catalogue. New York: Whitney Museum of American Art, in association with W. W. Norton, 1984.

———. *Ernie Gehr: September 27–October 9, 1983*. With artist's statement by Ernie Gehr. The New American Filmmaker Series: Exhibitions of Independent Film and Video 9. New York: Whitney Museum of American Art, 1983.

———, ed. *Nam June Paik*. Catalogue. New York: Whitney Museum of American Art, in association with W. W. Norton, 1982.

———. *Paul Sharits: April 17–May 13, 1983*. With artist's statement by Paul Sharits. The New American Filmmaker Series: Exhibitions of Independent Film and Video 16. New York: Whitney Museum of American Art, 1984.

Hanssen, Eirik Frisvold. "The Functions of Colour." Lecture. Stockholm University, 1999. www.academia.edu/292978/The_Functions_of_Colour.

Haraway, Donna. *Simians, Cyborgs and Women: A Reinvention of Nature*. New York: Routledge, 1990.

Hardy, Phil. *Science Fiction*. New York: Morrow, 1984.

Harmanci, Reyhan. "For Digital Artists, Apps Provide New Palette." *New York Times*. August 19, 2010. www.nytimes.com/2010/08/20/us/20bciart.html?_r=0.

Heath, Stephen. "Representing Television." In *Logics of Television: Essays in Cultural Criticism*. Edited by Patricia Mellencamp. Bloomington: Indiana University Press, 1990.

Henderson, Brian. "Toward a Non-bourgeois Camera Style." *Film Quarterly*, Winter 1970–1971, 10.

Higgins, Hannah. *Fluxus Experience*. Berkeley: University of California Press, 2002.

Hill, Gary. "And the Right Hand Did Not Know What the Left Hand Is Doing." In *Illuminating Video: An Essential Guide to Video Art*. Edited by Sally Jo Fifer and Doug Hall. New York: Aperture, in association with the Bay Area Video Coalition, 1990.

Hiller, Susan, and Alexandra M. Kokoli. *The Provisional Texture of Reality: Selected Talks and Texts, 1977–2007*. Zurich: JRP/Ringier, 2008.

Hiller, Susan, and James Lingwood. *Susan Hiller: Recall: Selected Works 1969–2004*. Gateshead, U.K.: Baltic, 2004.

Höltgen, Stefan, Johannes Maibaum, and Mathias Rech. "Tennisspielen mit Physik." *Retro Magazin* 24 (2012): 32–37.

Holdsworth, A. "Televisual Memory." *Screen* 51, no. 2 (2010): 129–42. doi:10.1093/screen/hjq007.

Howard, John N. "OSA's First Four Presidents." *Optics & Photonics News*, February 2009, 12–13. www.opnmagazine-digital.com/opn/200902/?pg=14#pg14.

Howe, David J., and Stephen James Walker. *The Television Companion: The Unofficial and Unauthorised Guide to "Doctor Who."* Tolworth, Surrey: Telos, 2003.

Iles, Chrissie. "Images between Images: Lorna Simpson's Post-Narrative Cinema." In *Lorna Simpson*. Edited by Kellie Jones, Thelma Golden, and Lorna Simpson. London: Phaidon, 2002.

———. *Into the Light: The Projected Image in American Art, 1964–1977*. New York: Whitney Museum of American Art, 2001.

Iwai, Toshio. "Piano—as Image Media." *Leonardo* 34, no. 3 (2001), 183.

———. "A Short History of the Works." Doors of Perception. Updated 1993. http://museum.doorsofperception.com/doors1/transcripts/iwai/iwai.html.

Iwata, Satoru. "2. A Question of Realism." In "Iwata Asks: Wii Sports." Nintendo of Europe. www.nintendo.co.uk/Iwata-Asks/Iwata-Asks-Wii/Iwata-Asks-Wii-Sports/2-A-Question-of-Realism/2-A-Question-of-Realism-217824.html.

Jakobson, Roman. "Visual and Auditory Signs." In *Selected Writings*. Vol. 2, *Word and Language*, 334–37. Hawthorne, NY: Mouton, 1972.

Jefferson, Thomas, Andrew A. Lipscomb, and Albert Ellery Bergh. *The Writings of Thomas Jefferson . . . Published in Their Entirety for the First Time*. Vol. 10. Washington, DC: Issued under the Auspices of the Thomas Jefferson Memorial Association of the United States, 1903.

Jenkins, Henry, Sam Ford, and Joshua Green. *Spreadable Media: Creating Value and Meaning in a Networked Culture*. New York: New York University Press, 2013.

Jones, Amelia. *Self/image: Technology, Representation, and the Contemporary Subject*. London: Routledge, 2006.

Jordà, Sergi, Günter Geiger, Marcos Alonso, and Martin Kaltenbrunner. *The reacTable: Exploring the Synergy between Live Music Performance and Tabletop Tangible Interfaces*. Music Technology Group, Pompeu Fabra University, Barcelona. http://mtg.upf.edu/files/publications/reactable_tei2007.pdf.

Joselit, David. *After Art*. Princeton, NJ: Princeton University Press, 2013.

———. *Feedback: Television against Democracy*. Cambridge, MA: MIT Press, 2007.

Joseph, Branden W. "Chance, Indeterminacy, Multiplicity." In *The Anarchy of Silence: John Cage and Experimental Art*. Edited by John Cage and Julia Robinson. Barcelona: Museu d'Art Contemporani de Barcelona, 2009.

Kane, Carolyn L. *Chromatic Algorithms: Synthetic Color, Computer Art, and Aesthetics after Code*. Chicago: University of Chicago Press, 2014.

———. "Digital Art and Experimental Color Systems at Bell Laboratories, 1965–1984:

Restoring Interdisciplinary Innovations to Media History." *Leonardo* 43, no. 1 (February 1, 2010): 365–66.

Keefer, Cindy. "*'Raumlichtmusik'*—Early 20th Century Abstract Cinema Immersive Environments." *Leonardo Electronic Almanac,* Creative Data special issue, 16, no. 6–7 (October 2009). http://www.leonardo.info/LEA/CreativeData/CD_Keefer.pdf.

Keefer, Cindy, and Jaap Guldemond, eds. *Oskar Fischinger 1900–1967: Experiments in Cinematic Abstraction.* Amsterdam: EYE Film Institute; Los Angeles: Center for Visual Music, 2013.

Klütsch, Christoph. *Computergraphik: Ästhetische Experimente zwischen Zwei Kulturen: Die Anfänge der Computerkunst in den 1960er Jahren.* Vienna: Springer, 2007.

Kosuth, Joseph. *Art after Philosophy and After: Collected Writings, 1966–1990.* Cambridge, MA: MIT Press, 1991.

———. "Meaning and Responsibility." *Art and Design Magazine* 9, no. 1 (January 1994): 71.

Kosuth, Joseph, and Fiona Biggiero. *Joseph Kosuth: "The language of equilibrium": Venice Biennale 52. International Art Exhibition* (Joseph Kosuth: *Il linguaggio dell'equilibrio:* Biennale di Venezia 52. Esposizione Internazionale d'Arte). Milan: Electa, 2009.

Kosuth, Joseph, Henri Loyrette, Marie-Laure Bernadac, John C. Welchman, and Jacinto Lageira. *Joseph Kosuth: "ni apparence ni illusion"* (neither appearance nor illusion). Paris: Musée du Louvre, 2010.

Krauss, Rosalind. "Video: The Aesthetics of Narcissism." *October* no. 1 (Spring 1976): 50. doi:10.2307/778507.

Krauss, Rosalind, Annette Michelson, George Baker, Yves-Alain Bois, Benjamin H. D. Buchloh, Leah Dickerman, Devin Fore, et al. "Abstraction: A Special Issue." *October* no. 143 (Winter 2013).

Kristeva, Julia. *Powers of Horror: An Essay on Abjection.* New York: Columbia University Press, 1982.

Krueger, Myron W. *Artificial Reality II.* Reading, MA: Addison-Wesley, 1991.

Krukowski, Lucian. "Abstraction." In *Encyclopedia of Aesthetics.* Edited by Michael Kelly. New York: Oxford University Press, 1998.

Kwastek, Katja. *Aesthetics of Interaction in Digital Art.* Cambridge, MA. MIT Press, 2013.

———. "Immersed in Reflection? The Aesthetic Experience of Interactive Media Art." In *Immersion: Historical and Current Perspectives on a Key Term in Art and Media Studies.* Edited by Burcu Dogramaci and Fabienne Liptay. Amsterdam/New York: Rodopi, 2015.

Kwon, Miwon. *One Place after Another: Site-Specific Art and Locational Identity.* Cambridge, MA: MIT Press, 2002.

Landauer, Susan, JoAnne Northrup, Ann M. Wolfe, and Lindsey M. Wylie. *Selections: The San Jose Museum of Art Permanent Collection.* San Jose, CA: San Jose Museum of Art, 2004.

Latimer, Quinn. "The Film Looks Like a Licked Sunset: A Conversation with Jennifer West,." East of Borneo. March 03, 2011. www.eastofborneo.org/articles/the-film-looks-like-a-lickedsunset-a-conversation-with-jennifer-west.

Le Grice, Malcolm. *Experimental Cinema in the Digital Age.* London: BFI, 2001.

Levin, Golan. "Painterly Interfaces for Audiovisual Performances." MS thesis, MIT Media Laboratory, 2000. www.flong.com/storage/pdf/articles/thesis300.pdf.

Lind, Maria, ed., *Abstraction*. Documents of Contemporary Art. London: Whitechapel and Cambridge, MA: MIT Press, 2013.
London, Barbara, ed., *Bill Viola*. Exhibition catalogue. New York: Museum of Modern Art, 1987.
Lord, Susan, and Janine Marchessault. *Fluid Screens, Expanded Cinema*. Toronto: University of Toronto Press, 2007.
Lovink, Geert. *Dark Fiber: Tracking Critical Internet Culture*. Electronic Culture: History, Theory, Practice. Cambridge, MA: MIT Press, 2002.
Lovink, Geert, and Rachel Somers Miles, eds. *Video Vortex Reader II: Moving Images beyond YouTube*, Amsterdam: Institute of Network Cultures, 2011.
Lovink, Geert, and Sabine Niederer, eds. *Video Vortex Reader: Responses to YouTube*, Amsterdam: Institute of Network Cultures, 2008.
Lundsten, Lars. "Modal Ontology of Television: How to Create Social Objects." *American Journal of Economics and Sociology*, April 1999.
Lyotard, Jean-François. *"Les Immatériaux." Art & Text* 17 (1985): 47–57.
———. *The Postmodern Condition: A Report on Knowledge*. Minneapolis: University of Minnesota Press, 1984.
———. "Presenting the Unpresentable: The Sublime." *Artforum* 20, no. 8 (April 1982): 64–69.
———. "The Sublime and the Avant-Garde." *Artforum* 22, no. 8 (April 1984): 36–43.
Ma, Ming-Yuen S., and Erika Suderburg. *Resolutions 3: Global Networks of Video*. Minneapolis: University of Minnesota Press, 2012.
Maloney, Patricia. "Interview with Mika Tajima." *Art Practical*, August 2, 2012. www.artpractical.com/column/interview_with_mika_tajima/.
Manovich, Lev. "Abstraction and Complexity." In *MediaArtHistories*. Edited by Oliver Grau. Cambridge, MA: MIT Press, 2007.
———. *The Language of New Media*. Cambridge, MA: MIT Press, 2002.
Massumi, Brian. "Navigating Movements." Interview. In *Hope: New Philosophies for Change*. Edited by Mary Zournazi, 210–42. New York: Routledge, 2003.
———, trans. Translator's foreword. In *A Thousand Plateaus: Capitalism and Schizophrenia*. By Gilles Deleuze and Félix Guattari. Minneapolis: University of Minnesota Press, 1987.
McLuhan, Marshall. *Understanding Media: The Extensions of Man*. New York: McGraw-Hill, 1964.
McPherson, Tara. "U.S. Operating Systems at Mid Century: The Intertwining of Race and UNIX." In *Race after the Internet*. Edited by Lisa Nakamura and Peter Chow-White. New York: Routledge, 2012.
Meaney, Evan. "On Glitching." *INCITE Journal of Experimental Media* 2, 2010. www.incite-online.net/meaney2a.html.
Mehring, Christine. "Television Art's Abstract Starts: Europe circa 1944–1969." *October*, July 2008, 29–64.
Meigh-Andrews, Chris. *A History of Video Art: The Development of Form and Function*. Oxford: Berg, 2006.
Meillassoux, Quentin. *After Finitude: An Essay on the Necessity of Contingency*. Translated by Ray Brassier. New York: Continuum, 2008.

Menkman, Rosa. "Glitch Studies Manifesto." In *Vortex Video Reader II: Moving Images Beyond YouTube*. Edited by Geert Lovink and Rachel Somers Miles. Amsterdam: Institute of Network Cultures, 2011.

Mercer, Kobena. *Discrepant Abstraction*. London: Institute of International Visual Arts; Cambridge, MA: MIT Press, 2006.

Michalska, Julia. "Pierre Huyghe Creates a Buzz in Paris." *The Art Newspaper*, September 23, 2013. www.theartnewspaper.com/articles/Pierre-Huyghe-creates-a-buzz-in-Paris/30305.

Molon, Dominic, and Jane Farver, eds. *Paul Pfeiffer*. Chicago: Museum of Contemporary Art; Cambridge, MA: MIT List Visual Arts Center, 2003.

Moradi, Iman, Ant Scott, Joe Gilmore, and Christopher Murphy, eds. *Glitch: Designing Imperfection*. New York: Mark Batty Publisher, 2009.

Moritz, William. "Abstract Film and Color Music." In *The Spiritual in Art: Abstract Painting 1890–1985*. Edited by Maurice Tuchman et al. New York: Abbeville Press, 1986.

Motherwell, Robert. "Abstract Painting and Sculpture in America." In *What Abstract Art Means to Me: Statements*, Vol. 18. Edited by George L. K. Morris. New York: Museum of Modern Art, 1951.

Muller, Lizzie, and Caitlin Jones. "Interview with David Rokeby." *Very Nervous System:* Documentary Collection. Daniel Langlois Foundation. 2009. www.fondation-langlois.org/html/e/page.php?NumPage=2187.

Mulvey, Laura. "Visual Pleasure and Narrative Cinema." *Screen* 16, no. 3, 1975: 6–18.

Murata, Takeshi. "3-D Landscapes of Melting Color." The Creators Project. Intel and VICE Media. http://thecreatorsproject.vice.com/creators/takeshi-murata.

O'Grady, Gerald, and Bruce Charles Posner. *Articulated Light: The Emergence of Abstract Film in America*. Cambridge, MA: Harvard Film Archive, 2001.

Paik, Nam June. "About the Exposition of Music." *Decollage* 3 (1962).

———. "L'arche de Nam June." *Art Press*, no. 47 (April 1981): 7–9.

Paik, Nam June, Jon Ippolito, and John G. Hanhardt. *Nam June Paik: Global Groove*. New York: Guggenheim Museum, 2004.

Paul, Christiane. *Digital Art*. New York: Thames & Hudson, 2003.

"Paul Pfeiffer and John Baldessari in Conversation." In *Paul Pfeiffer*. Edited by Dominic Molon and Jane Farver. Exhibition catalogue. Chicago: Museum of Contemporary Art; Cambridge, MA: MIT List Visual Arts Center, 2003.

Pfaffenbichler, Norbert, and Sandro Droschl. *Abstraction Now*. Graz: Edition Camera Austria, 2004.

Pilson, John. "Alix Pearlstein." *BOMB Magazine*, Winter 2012–2013, 133. http://bombmagazine.org/article/6926/alix-pearlstein

Platou, Per. Foreword. In *Glitch: Designing Imperfection*, by Iman Moradi. New York: Mark Batty Publisher, 2009.

Podesta, Patti, ed. *Resolution: A Critique of Video Art—Exhibition, Symposium and Publication*. Los Angeles: Los Angeles Contemporary Exhibitions, 1986.

Price, Brian. "Color, the Formless, and Cinematic Eros." *Framework: Journal of Cinema and Media* 47, no. 1 (Spring 2006): 22–35.

Ragona, Melissa. "From Bell Labs to Best Buy: Takeshi Murata and Jacob Ciocci in Conversation with *PREDRIVE: After Technology* Curator Melissa Ragona." *Rhizome,* November 26, 2008. http://rhizome.org/editorial/2008/nov/26/from-bell-labs-to-best-buy/.

Rees, A. L. *Expanded Cinema: Art, Performance, Film.* London: Tate Gallery Publications, 2011.

Renov, Michael, and Erika Suderburg, eds. *Resolutions: Contemporary Video Practices.* Minneapolis: University of Minnesota Press, 1996.

Richmond, Susan. "The Ins and Outs of Female Sensibility: A 1973 Video by Lynda Benglis." *Camera Obscura: Feminism, Culture, and Media Studies* 23, no. 3 69 (2008): 91–92. doi:10.1215/02705346-2008-008.

———. *Lynda Benglis: Beyond Process.* London: I. B. Tauris, 2013.

Robbins, Al. *"Anticata/Strophe"* (October 3–19, 1980). Program note. New American Filmmakers Series. New York: Whitney Museum of American Art, 1980.

Roget, Peter Mark, Barnas Sears, and George S. Blanchard. Preface. In *Thesaurus of English Words and Phrases; So Classified and Arranged as to Facilitate the Expression of Ideas and Assist in Literary Composition.* Boston: Gould and Lincoln, 1855.

Ross, Christine. *The Past Is the Present; It's the Future Too: The Temporal Turn in Contemporary Art.* London: Bloomsbury Academic, 2012.

———. "The Temporalities of Video: Extendedness Revisited." *Art Journal,* Fall 2006, 83.

Russell, Legacy. "Digital Dualism and the Glitch Feminism Manifesto." *Cyborgology,* December 10, 2012. http://thesocietypages.org/cyborgology/2012/12/10/digital-dualism-and-the-glitch-feminism-manifesto/.

Salen, Katie, and Eric Zimmerman. *Rules of Play: Game Design Fundamentals.* Cambridge, MA: MIT Press, 2003.

Salter, Chris. *Entangled: Technology and the Transformation of Performance.* Cambridge, MA: MIT Press, 2010.

Schapiro, Meyer. *Modern Art, 19th and 20th Centuries.* New York: G. Braziller, 1978.

Schreuder, Catrien, Noud Heerkens, and Jane Bemont. *Pixels and Places: Video Art in Public Space.* Rotterdam: NAi Publishers, 2010.

Searle, John R. *The Construction of Social Reality.* New York: Free Press, 1995.

———. *Speech Acts: An Essay into the Philosophy of Language.* Cambridge: Cambridge University Press, 1969.

Sharits, Paul. "Statement Regarding Multiple Screen / Sound 'Locational' Film Environments—Installation." *Film Culture* 65–66 (1978): 79–80.

Shaw, Jeffrey, and Peter Weibel. *Future Cinema: The Cinematic Imaginary after Film.* Cambridge, MA: MIT Press, 2003.

Shiff, Richard. "The Undecidable." Lecture, Biannual Conference, "40 Years of Unexplained Change: Art, History, Subjectivity since 1973," Art Center College of Design, Pasadena, CA, November 10, 2013.

Sicinski, Michael. "The Bay Area as Cinematic Space in Twenty-five Stops or Less." In *Radical Light: Alternative Film & Video in the San Francisco Bay Area, 1945–2000.* Edited by Steve Anker, Kathy Geritz, and Steve Seid, 272. Berkeley: University of California Press, 2010.

Silverman, Kaja. *The Acoustic Mirror: The Female Voice in Psychoanalysis and Cinema.* Bloomington: Indiana University Press, 1988.

Singer, Marilyn. ed. *A History of the American Avant-Garde Cinema: A Film Exhibition.* New York: American Federation of Arts, 1976.

Sitney, P. Adams. "The Idea of Abstraction." In *Film Culture: An Anthology*, 22. London: Secker & Warburg, 1971.

———. *Visionary Film: The American Avant-Garde.* New York: Oxford University Press, 1974.

Smithson, Robert. *Robert Smithson: The Collected Writings.* Edited by Jack D. Flam. Berkeley: University of California Press, 1996.

Snibbe, Scott. "Scott Snibbe, Interactive Artist—Part 1, CNN, the Next List." Vimeo. December 18, 2011. vimeo.com/39725809.

Snibbe, Scott Sona, and Golan Levin. "Interactive Dynamic Abstraction." In *Proceedings of the First International Symposium on Non-photorealistic Animation and Rendering*, Annecy, France, June 5–7, 2000. New York: ACMm 2000, www.snibbe.com/download/publications/academic/2000Dynamic_NPAR.pdf.

Snibbe, Scott, and Fiona Whiton. *Visceral Cinema: Chien.* Los Angeles: TELIC, 2005.

Spielmann, Yvonne. *Video: The Reflexive Medium*, English ed. Cambridge, MA: MIT Press, 2008.

Spigel, Lynn. *Make Room for TV: Television and the Family Ideal in Postwar America.* Chicago: University of Chicago Press, 1992.

Spivak, Gayatri Chakravorty. *An Aesthetic Education in the Era of Globalization.* Cambridge, MA: Harvard University Press, 2012.

———. "Echo." *New Literary History* 24, no. 1 (1993): 17. doi:10.2307/469267.

Stedelijk Museum. *The Luminous Image.* Catalogue. Amsterdam: Stedelijk Museum, 1984.

Steyerl, Hito. *The Wretched of the Screen.* Berlin: Sternberg Press, 2012.

Sutherland, Ivan Edward. *Sketchpad: A Man-Machine Graphical Communication System.* New York: Garland, 1980.

Tekinbaş, Katie Salen, and Eric Zimmerman. *Rules of Play: Game Design Fundamentals.* Cambridge, MA: MIT Press, 2003.

Tiravanija, Rirkrit. "Pierre Huyghe." *Interview Magazine.* February 10, 2011. www.interviewmagazine.com/art/pierre-huyghe/#_.

Totaro, Donato. "Wavelength Revisited." *Hors Champ* 6, no. 11 (February 4, 2011). http://offscreen.com/view/wavelength.

Tyler, Parker. "Dragtime and Drugtime; or, Film à la Warhol." *Evergreen Review*, April 1967.

Valdez, Sarah. "Substance Abuse: The Films of Jennifer West." *Art on Paper*, May–June 2008, 2.

Van Assche, Christine. *"The Third Memory."* Point of View: Extrait du catalogue *Collection art contemporain—La collection du Centre Pompidou, Musée national d'art moderne*, sous la direction de Sophie Duplaix, Paris, Centre Pompidou, 2007. Centre Pompidou virtuel. www.centrepompidou.fr/cpv/ressource.action?param.id=FR_R-1425bb6a5c5ffddcc2ffb89cf4bea055&param.idSource=FR_O-fd7d0bcefd1bc7879ee8ad0d82e17d.

van den Boomen, Marianne, Ann-Sophie Lehmann, Sybilles Lammes, and Joost Raessens, eds. *Digital Material: Tracing New Media in Everyday Life and Technology.* Amsterdam: Amsterdam University Press, 2009.

Varnedoe, Kirk. *Pictures of Nothing: Abstract Art since Pollock.* Princeton, NJ: Princeton University Press, 2006.

Vasulka, Woody, and Peter Weibel. *Buffalo Heads: Media Study, Media Practice, Media Pioneers, 1973–1990.* Karlsruhe, Germany: ZKM/Center for Art and Media Karlsruhe, 2008.

Virilio, Paul. *Speed and Politics*. Los Angeles: Semiotext(e), 2006.
———. "Speed-Space." Interview with Chris Dercon. Translated by D. Miller. *Impulse* 12, no. 4 (1986): 35–39.
Viskovatoff, Alex. "Searle, Rationality, and Social Reality: Extensions and Criticisms—John Searle." *American Journal of Economics and Sociology*, January 2003.
Vostell, Wolf. *"Television Décollage" & "Morning Glory": 2 Pieces by Wolf Vostell*. New York: 3rd Rail Gallery, 1963.
Wagner, Anne Middleton. *A House Divided: American Art since 1955*. Berkeley: University of California Press, 2012.
———. "Performance, Video and the Rhetoric of Presence." *October*, no. 91 (Winter 2000): 59–80.
Weibel, Peter, and Timothy Druckrey. *Net Condition: Art and Global Media*. Graz, Austria: Steirischer Herbst, 2001.
Welchman, John C. "A Crab in the Tree." In *"An Interpretation of This Title": Nietzsche, Darwin, and the Paradox of Content*, Vol. 1; *"Waiting For: Texts for Nothing": Samuel Beckett, in Play*, Vol. 2, by Joseph Kosuth, 10–15. South Yarra, Victoria, Australia: Macmillan, 2012.
———. "Histories and Subjects in Contingency." In *Joseph Kosuth: "ni apparence ni illusion" = neither appearance nor illusion*, by Joseph Kosuth and Marie-Laure Bernadac. Ghent: MER Paperkunsthalle; Paris: Musée du Louvre, 2010.
West, Jennifer. "500 Words." Artforum.com. May 15, 2009. http://artforum.com/words/id%3D22838%2C.
———. *"Warm Bodies in a Room: A Derive/Drift through 80 Films."* LAXART Facebook post. November 16, 2013. https://www.facebook.com/LAXARTLosAngeles/posts/10151988272527645.
White, Anthony G. "TV or Not TV: Lucio Fontana's 'Luminous Images in Movement.'" *Grey Room* 34 (Winter 2009): 6–27.
Whitney, John, and James Whitney. "Audio Visual Music." In *The Avant-Garde Film: A Reader of Theory and Criticism*. Edited by P. Adams Sitney, 83–86. New York: New York University Press, 1978.
Whitney Museum of American Art. *Ernie Gehr*. Program Note No. 9. The New American Filmmakers Series. New York: Whitney Museum of American Art, 1983.
———. *Paul Sharits*. Program Note No. 16. The New American Filmmakers Series. New York: Whitney Museum of American Art, 1984.
Wiebel, Peter, Woody Vasulka, Steina Vasulka, and David Dunn. *Eigenwelt Der Apparatewelt: Pioneers of Electronic Art*. Santa Fe, NM: Vasulkas, 1992.
Wilkerson, Isabel. *The Warmth of Other Suns: The Epic Story of America's Great Migration*. New York: Random House, 2010.
Williams, Raymond. *Television: Technology and Cultural Form*. New York: Schocken Books, 1975.
Winston, Brian. *Media, Technology and Society: A History from the Telegraph to the Internet*. London: Routledge, 1998.
Winston, Brian. *Technologies of Seeing: Photography, Cinematography and Television*. London: BFI, 1996. 39.
Young, Paul, and Paul Duncan. *Art Cinema*. Cologne: Taschen, 2009.

Youngblood, Gene. *Expanded Cinema*. New York: Dutton, 1970.
Zampetti, Chiara. "Live Art: Q+A with Pierre Huyghe." *Art in America,* September 13, 2011. www.artinamericamagazine.com/news-features/interviews/pierre-huyghe-esther-schipper/.
Zinman, Gregory. Handmade Cinema—A Guide to the People, Practices and Themes of Artisinal Moving Image Production. Web portal. 2012. www.handmadecinema.com/.

ILLUSTRATIONS

CONTRIBUTORS

TILMAN BAUMGÄRTEL is assistant professor of Film and Media Studies in the College of Mass Communication at the University of the Philippines in Diliman, Manila. Baumgärtel contributes to *Telepolis, Die Zeit, die tageszeitung,* and *Spiegel-Online* among other publications.

PHILIP BROPHY is an Australian musician, composer, sound designer, filmmaker, writer, graphic designer, educator, and academic. Brophy has been published in journals such as *Virgin Press, Art & Text,* and *Fast Forward.* He has taught at the Philip Institute of Technology and the Royal Melbourne Institute of Technology.

MICHAEL CONNOR is the editor and curator of Rhizome at the New Museum. Connor's work focuses on artists' responses to cinema and new technologies. Solo and collaborative projects he has curated include *Liquid Crystal Palace,* Honor Fraser, Los Angeles; *JODI: Street Digital,* Museum of the Moving Image, New York; *Wild Sky,* Edith-Russ Haus, Oldenburg, Germany; *Screen Worlds,* Australian Centre for the Moving Image, Melbourne; *Essential Cinema* at the Toronto Film Festival; and *The New Normal* touring exhibition. Connor previously worked as curator at Foundation for Art and Creative Technology, Liverpool, and head of exhibitions at BFI Southbank, London.

SARAH COOK earned her PhD at the University of Sunderland and is a curator, writer, and cofounder of CRUMB, the online resource for curators of new media art (www.crumbweb.org). Cook has curated and co-curated international exhibitions of contemporary art and new-media art. She is co-author (with Beryl Graham) of *Rethinking Curating: Art after New Media* (MIT Press, 2010) and co-editor (with Sara Diamond) of *Euphoria and Dystopia: The*

Banff New Media Institute Dialogues (Banff Centre Press, 2011). She is currently a Dundee Fellow at Duncan of Jordanstone College of Art and Design.

TRINIE DALTON is author of six books that move between fiction, the visual arts, and critical writing. She also writes texts for artists' monographs: new releases including David Altmejd (Damiani), Laura Owens (Rizzoli), two for Dorothy Iannone (Siglio and Berlinische Galerie/ Kerber Verlag), and Anna Sew Hoy (Oslo Editions); past contributions include those to catalogues for the 2008 Whitney Biennial, New York Minute (JRP | Ringier), and Vitamin 3D (Phaidon). She is faculty director of the MFA in Writing and Publishing at Vermont College of Fine Arts, as well as core faculty in Fiction in VCFA's low-residency writing program. Dalton has also taught at Art Center College of Design, University of Southern California, School of Visual Arts, Columbia University, Bard College, New York University, and Pratt Institute.

CHARLOTTE FROST is an academic and broadcaster focusing on art's relationship with technology. A specialist in the impact of Internet tools on art history and criticism, she has researched the history of digital and new-media art, the hidden technicity of art-historical discourse, emergent art-critical practices and broadcast technologies, and the digital future of art books. She earned her doctorate in film and visual media in the School of History of Art at Birkbeck College, University of London.

JEREMY GILBERT-ROLFE is a painter who also writes about art and related topics both on his own and with Rebecca Norton, as part of their collaborative Awkward × 2. Gilbert-Rolfe's publications include *Immanence and Contradiction* (1985), *Beyond Piety* (1995), *Frank Gehry: The City and Music* (2000), and *Beauty and the Contemporary Sublime* (2000). Recent essays include a short piece on Ad Reinhardt for the *Brooklyn Rail* and an essay for the Michael Goldberg retrospective's catalog (Jacksonville MoCA). Recipient of one of the first NEA Fellowships in Art Criticism (1974) and the College Art Association's Frank Jewett Mather Award for Art Criticism (1997), he teaches in the Graduate Art Program at Art Center College of Design.

JOHANNA GOSSE is an art historian specializing in experimental film and media and postwar American art. She received her PhD in the History of Art from Bryn Mawr College, with a dissertation on the films of San Francisco–based artist Bruce Conner. Gosse has curated and helped organize numerous film programs and exhibitions, taught courses on art and film history, and has published essays in *Radical History Review, The Journal of Black Mountain College Studies,* and exhibition catalogues.

JOHN G. HANHARDT works as consulting senior curator of Film and Media Arts at the Smithsonian American Art Museum after having served as senior curator of Film and Media Arts at the Solomon R. Guggenheim Museum and curator and head of the Film and Video Department at the Whitney Museum of American Art. Hanhardt is also responsible for establishing the film department and the film study collection at the Walker Art Center in Minneapolis. He is the foremost expert in Nam June Paik's work, established the Nam June Paik Archive at the Smithsonian, and was the organizing curator for two landmark exhibitions of Paik's work.

CAITLIN JONES is the executive director of the Western Front Society in Vancouver, British

Columbia. Prior to this appointment she had a combined curatorial and conservation position at the Solomon R. Guggenheim Museum and was the director of programming at the Bryce Wolkowitz Gallery in New York. A key member of the Variable Media Network, Jones has also been responsible for developing important tools and policy for the preservation of electronic and ephemeral artworks. She has been a contributor to Rhizome, and her other writings have appeared in a wide range of exhibition catalogues, periodicals, and other international publications.

STANYA KAHN is an interdisciplinary artist working primarily in video with a practice that includes sound design, drawing, writing, and performance. In a long-term investigation of how rhetoric gains and loses power, Kahn's projects often situate language in the foreground of works that are dialectically driven by the demands of the body. Kahn is a 2012 Guggenheim Fellow in Film/Video. Her solo and collaborative works have shown in the Whitney Biennial (2008); the California Biennial (2010); MoMA, New York; MOCA, Los Angeles; The Getty Center, Los Angeles; the Hammer Museum, Los Angeles; the Sundance Film Festival, Utah; Migrating Forms Film Festival, New York; the Center for Art and Media, Karlsruhe; PS1 Museum of Contemporary Art, New York; Susanne Vielmetter Los Angeles Projects; and Elizabeth Dee Gallery, New York, among others.

CINDY KEEFER is an archivist and curator and the director of the Center for Visual Music archive in Los Angeles. Keefer curates and presents film and media programs and exhibitions at museums, cultural centers, symposia, and archives worldwide, in addition to restoring dozens of short abstract films by Oskar Fischinger, Jordan Belson, the Whitneys, John Cage, and many others. She lectures, publishes, curates, and teaches on visual music and abstract film worldwide; she restored and curated the Fischinger *Raumlichtkunst* three-screen museum installation; and she is the editor of a new monograph, *Oskar Fischinger (1900–1967): Experiments in Cinematic Abstraction*. She is currently writing a book on Jordan Belson and the Vortex Concerts (1957–59).

KATJA KWASTEK is professor of modern and contemporary art at the VU University Amsterdam, with a research focus on media aesthetics. Previously, she taught at Ludwig-Maximilians University (Munich), Rhode Island School of Design (Providence), LBI Media. Art.Research (Linz), and Humboldt University (Berlin). Her publications include "Ohne Schnur—Art and Wireless Communication" (*Revolver*, 2004) and *Aesthetics of Interaction in Digital Art* (MIT Press, 2013).

KATE MONDLOCH is associate professor of Contemporary Art at the University of Oregon and the author of *Screens: Viewing Media Installation Art* (University of Minnesota Press, 2010). She has been published in a variety of journals, including *Art Journal*, *Feminist Media Studies*, *Leonardo*, and *Vectors* and has been awarded research fellowships from the American Council of Learned Societies (ACLS), the University of California Humanities Research Institute, and the Oregon Humanities Center. She currently serves on the editorial board of *Art Journal*.

CHRISTINE ROSS is a professor and the James McGill Chair in Contemporary Art History in the Department of Art History and Communication Studies at McGill University. Her books include *The Past Is the Present; It's the Future Too: The Temporal Turn in Contemporary*

Art (Continuum, 2012); *The Aesthetics of Disengagement: Contemporary Art and Depression* (University of Minnesota Press, 2006); and *Images de surface: l'art vidéo reconsidéré* (Éditions Artextes, 1996). She has co-edited (with Olivier Asselin and Johanne Lamoureux) *Precarious Visualities: New Perspectives on Identification in Contemporary Art and Visual Culture* (McGill-Queen's University Press, 2008). She is currently co-editing a book entitled *The Participatory Condition* for University of Minnesota Press. First laureate of the Artexte Award for Research in Contemporary Art (2012), she is the cofounder of the Department of Art History and Communication Studies at McGill University.

LUMI TAN is associate curator at The Kitchen, New York, and has previously held curatorial positions at the FRAC Nord-Pas de Calais, France, and P.S.1 Contemporary Art Center. She is associate editor of *The Exhibitionist: Journal of Exhibition-Making* and a contributor to *Artforum.com, Frieze,* and *T: The "New York Times" Style Magazine.*

MARIA-CHRISTINA VILLASEÑOR is a media maker, writer, and curator. Her works *The Momentary Enemy* and *El Puente* have been screened nationally and internationally at venues including the Brooklyn Museum, the Bangkok Experimental Film Festival, the Los Angeles Asian Pacific Film Festival, and the Williamsburg Film Festival. As a former assistant curator of Film and Media Arts at the Solomon R. Guggenheim Museum, she also curated for the Guggenheim Museums in Berlin and Bilbao, has guest-curated media programs for Creative Time and Exit Art, and has organized and toured film programs internationally to venues including the Havana International Film Festival, the Museo de Bellas Artes Buenos Aires, and the Prague Febio Fest.

JOHN C. WELCHMAN works in modern and contemporary art history and critical theory, has published extensively in the world of art historical discourse, and is a professor in the Visual Arts Department at the University of California, San Diego. Currently Welchman is finalizing two books on the relation between art, film, and the representation of faces—*The Celluloid Face* and *Faces and Powers*—and a monograph on the career to date of Mike Kelley (Taschen).

SIONA WILSON is associate professor of Art History at the College of Staten Island and the Graduate Center, the City University of New York. She is author of *Art Labor, Sex Politics: Feminist Effects in 1970s British Art and Performance* (Minnesota, 2015). Her research interests are grounded in issues of sexual difference and the intersection of art and politics in postwar and contemporary art. She has published on photography, sound practices, experimental film and video, and performance art, and is contributing editor for *Art Review.*

GREGORY ZINMAN is an assistant professor in the School of Literature, Media, and Communication at the Georgia Institute of Technology. His writing on film and media has been published in the *New Yorker, American Art, Film History, A New History of German Cinema, Animation Journal, Millennium Film Journal,* and *Special Effects: New Histories, Theories, Contexts.* He is currently finishing his first book, *Handmade: The Moving Image in the Artisanal Mode,* and is co-editing, with John Hanhardt and Edith Decker-Phillips, *Nam June Paik: Selected Writings,* forthcoming from the MIT Press.

INDEX

Page numbers in italic refer to figures.